THE COLD WAR AGAINST LABOR

VOLUME TWO

An anthology edited by
Ann Fagan Ginger and
David Christiano

STUDIES IN LAW AND SOCIAL CHANGE NO. 3
♦ ♦
Meiklejohn Civil Liberties Institute
P.O. Box 673, Berkeley, CA 94701

© 1987 by Meiklejohn Civil Liberties Institute

All rights reserved.
No part of this book may be reproduced in any form, by photostat, microfilm, xerography, or any other means, or incorporated into any information retrieval system, electronic or mechanical, without the written permission of the copyright owner.

Address all inquiries to:
Meiklejohn Civil Liberties Institute
Post Office Box 673
Berkeley, CA 94701
(415) 848-0599

Library of Congress Cataloging-in-Publication Data
The Cold war against labor.

(Meiklejohn Civil Liberties Institute studies in law and social change; no. 3)
Includes index.
1. Trade-unions—United States—History—20th century. 2. Trade-unions—Law and legislation—United States—History—20th Century. 3. Labor laws and legislation—United States—History—20th century. I. Ginger, Ann Fagan, 1925– . II. Christiano, David, 1948– . III. Meiklejohn Civil Liberties Institute. IV. Series.
HD6508.C62 1987 331.88'0973 87-18510
ISBN 0-913876-19-4 (set)
ISBN 0-913876-20-8 (pkb.:set)

Cover photograph by George Tames, courtesy of The New York Times Pictures.

Page 468:	Photograph from *The ILWU Dispatcher*.
Page 481:	Cartoon by Fred Ellis.
Page 501:	Drawing by William Gropper.
Page 519:	Drawing by Bits Hayden.
Page 565:	Lithograph by Victor Arnautoff.
Page 586:	Woodcut by Angel Bracho and Celia Calderon.
Page 590:	Painting by Edward Biberman.
Page 600:	Photographs from *Salt of the Earth*.
Page 637:	Drawing by Pele de Lappe.
Page 654:	Woodcut by Louise Gilbert.
Page 709:	Cartoon from Civil Rights Congress.
Page 790:	Drawing by Charles White.
Page 808:	Photograph by Jim Kottra.
Page 825:	Photograph by Harvey Richards.
Page 855:	Cartoon by Peggy Lipschutz.
Page 876:	Drawing by Irving Fromer.

Design by Zipporah Collins.
Typesetting by Another Point, Inc., Oakland, CA.
Printing and binding by the Banta Company.

Printed in the United States of America.

◆◆ CONTENTS ◆◆

VOLUME ONE
◆◆◆◆◆◆◆◆◆◆◆◆◆◆◆◆◆◆◆◆◆◆◆◆◆

PART ONE ◆ WHERE DO WE STAND TODAY?   1

1	We Promise You Nothing But a Good Fight	2
2	From Strike to Decertification Fight: The Danly Machine Story	15
3	Destroying Fifty Years of Labor Law	20
4	Not Enough Angry Young Men	36
5	The Changing Situation of Workers and Their Unions	39
6	Burial of Old Beth	50
7	Fighting for Jobs Outside the War Machine	53
8	Testifying for Comparable Worth	69
9	Representing Everyday People	82
10	Anti-Union Push on All Fronts	86
11	The Need for Labor Unity	89
12	Labor Needs a Labor Party	98
13	Our Work Is Cut Out for Us	102

PART TWO ◆ THE SHINING MOMENT AFTER WORLD WAR II   109

14	The Army Set My Foot on the Path of Labor	110
15	The Black Community Prepares for Postwar Political Action	117
16	The U.S. Makes Peace and Full Employment into Law	119

iii

17	A Worker Returns from the War	125
18	A CIO Staffer Works and Dreams	132
19	Teaching Workers at the California Labor School	137
20	The Union Was Like a Family	152
21	Operation Dixie	164
22	United Public Workers: A Real Union Organizes	172
23	The CIO Joins the International Labor Movement	187
24	U.S. Labor Emerges from the War	200
25	U.S. Capital Emerges from the War	214

PART THREE ♦ THE ATTACKS BEGIN — 233

26	The Attorney General Denounces a Plot	234
27	The CIO Holds Its 1946 Convention	236
28	Big Business and Government Unleash Taft-Hartley	243
29	The Attorney General's Subversive List	250
30	What To Do About the Taft-Hartley Act	258
31	This Is Fighting Taft-Hartley?	261
32	Challenging Taft-Hartley in the Courts	264
33	NLRB Attacks on Unions	266
34	Unionists Build the Progressive Party	268
35	Congressional Committees Call Labor Witnesses	279
36	The Real Marshall Plan	283
37	The CIO Expels One Million Workers	297
38	The Supreme Court Speaks	306
39	Super Profits Required Red-baiting	314
40	"Recovery" Requires Cold War	317

PART FOUR ♦ WORKERS FIGHT BACK FOR THEIR RIGHTS — 323

41	The First Bitter Fruits of Taft-Hartley	324
42	Cold War Battles Inside the UAW	326
43	Ford Local 600	342

44	UE Local 735 Confronts a Hanging Judge	346
45	National UE: Corporate Target for Extinction	374
46	The Heritage of Architects, Engineers, Chemists and Technicians (FAECT-CIO)	378
47	CIO Unions Attack CIO Office Workers	385
48	United Public Workers: The Conscience of the Capitol	389
49	NLRB and Taft-Hartley Attacks on Unions and Leaders	399
50	Taft-Hartley and the International Fur and Leather Workers Union	404
51	A Union President Takes His Stand	419
52	Destroying the California CIO Council	430
53	NMU Expulsions and Coast Guard Screening	438

VOLUME TWO

54	Red Scare in Paradise: ILWU in Hawaii ♦♦ Edward Long ♦ Edward Beechert ♦♦ ♦ Boxes: Lou Goldblatt ♦ ILWU Pamphlet ♦	447
55	Teachers on Trial ♦♦ Mildred Schoenberger ♦ Teachers Union of Philadelphia ♦♦ ♦ Box: New York Post ♦	472
56	One Los Angeles Teacher's Story: Frances Eisenberg ♦♦ The Editors ♦♦	491
57	More Congressional Investigating Committees ♦♦ The Editors ♦ James F. Wood ♦♦ ♦ Box: Frank Wilkinson ♦	496
58	Academic Fallout ♦♦ Ann Fagan Ginger ♦♦	504
59	The Fatal Score ♦♦ Alvah Bessie ♦ The Editors ♦♦ ♦ Box: Barbara Sherwood ♦	509

PART FIVE ♦ COLD WAR AGAINST COMMUNITIES — 513

60	In the City Was a Garden ♦♦ Henry Kraus ♦♦	514

61	**Canceling Workers' Insurance Policies** ♦♦ Albert E. Kahn ♦♦	523
62	**A Community Medical Center for Workers** ♦♦ Stephen H. Fritchman ♦♦	528
63	**Trumpet Player: 52nd Street** ♦♦ Langston Hughes ♦♦	533
64	**AWOL** ♦♦ George Bratt ♦♦	535
65	**A Boy and His Gun** ♦♦ Patrick E. Gorman ♦♦	537
66	**The Climate of Terror** ♦♦ Eve Merriam ♦♦	539
67	**Fighting Jim Crow in the Nation's Capital: Mary Church Terrell** ♦♦ Marvin Caplan ♦♦	544
68	**Defending Foreign Born Workers** ♦♦ Fred Rinaldo ♦♦	553
69	**Justice Attacks Workers' Schools and Clubs** ♦♦ The Editors ♦♦ ♦ Box: "Man's Right to Knowledge: The Case of the Jefferson School" ♦	561
70	**Our Battle in the Southland** ♦♦ Rev. C. Tyndell Vivian ♦♦	567
71	**Attacking Dr. DuBois and Peace Information** ♦♦ The Editors ♦♦ ♦ Box: W.E.B. DuBois ♦	573
72	**The Don Juans of the F.B.I.** ♦♦ Meridel LeSueur ♦♦	577
73	**The Rosenberg-Sobell Case: Ultimate Weapon of the Cold War** ♦♦ Helen L. Sobell ♦♦	583

PART SIX ♦ FIGHTING FROM BORDER TO BORDER — 591

74	**Mine, Mill, and Smelter Workers: The Salt of the Earth** ♦♦ The Editors ♦ Frank Arnold ♦ Virginia Derr Chambers ♦ Clinton E. Jencks ♦ Morris Wright ♦♦ ♦ Box: Harvey Matusow ♦	592
75	**Effects of Union McCarthyism on Black Workers** ♦♦ Philip Foner ♦♦ ♦ Boxes: The Editors ♦ Irving Fromer ♦	615

76	**National Negro Labor Council**	627
	♦♦ Mindy Thompson Fullilove ♦ Charles H. Wright ♦ William Hood ♦♦	
	♦ Boxes: NLC Yearbook ♦ House Committee on Un-American Activities ♦	
77	**Two Historic Conferences for Women's Rights**	643
	♦♦ Mindy Thompson Fullilove ♦ Vivian McGuckin Raineri ♦♦	
78	**Red, White and Black in Southern Labor**	648
	♦♦ Anne Braden ♦♦	
79	**Focus on Memphis: Union Hall to City Hall**	661
	♦♦ Michael Honey ♦♦	
80	**The CIO and AFL Merge in 1955**	667
	♦♦ The Editors ♦♦	
81	**United States vs. Marie Reed**	671
	♦♦ Vivian McGuckin Raineri ♦♦	
	♦ Box: Jack G. Day ♦	
82	**Subversive Activities Control Board Attacks**	679
	♦♦ The Editors ♦♦	
83	**Steelworkers in Buffalo: A Personal Perspective**	681
	♦♦ Joseph Cantor ♦ Frank Wilkinson ♦♦	
	♦ Box: Victor Rabinowitz ♦	
84	**ILWU Communist Slays the Son of Taft-Hartley**	707
	♦♦ The Editors ♦♦	
85	**Expelled Teamster Fighting for Democracy**	712
	♦♦ Jack Weintraub ♦♦	
86	**A Plumber Gets Curious About Exporting McCarthyism**	723
	♦♦ Fred Hirsch ♦ Virginia Muir ♦♦	

PART SEVEN ♦ **WHERE WE DO WE GO FROM HERE**   769

87	**ILGWU Organizer Murdered: Why?**	770
	♦♦ The Editors ♦♦	
88	**Organizing Federal Workers**	772
	♦♦ Vivian McGuckin Raineri ♦♦	
89	**Organizing Teamsters in the 1980s**	780
	♦♦ Ron Teninty ♦♦	
90	**Affirmative Action**	787
	♦♦ Leonard McNeil ♦ William J. Brennan, Jr. ♦♦	

91	**United Farm Workers Use the Boycott** ♦♦ Suzanne Meehan ♦♦	800
92	**Is There Life After the Mill Closes Down?** ♦♦ The Editors ♦ "Franco" Curtis ♦♦	805
93	**Pressman's Blues** ♦♦ Jim Ginger ♦♦	809
94	**Women and Unions: Today and Tomorrow** ♦♦ Carolyn J. Jacobson ♦ The Editors ♦♦ ♦ Boxes: NY/CLU Child Care Committee ♦ Women for Racial and Economic Equality ♦	813
95	**The Need for Peace Is Revitalizing U.S. Labor** ♦♦ Benjamin Riskin ♦ The Editors ♦♦	823
96	**Proposing a Rational Economic Plan to the Legislature** ♦♦ Oregon AFL-CIO Employment & Economy Committee ♦♦	835
97	**Legislation Promoting Full Employment** ♦♦ Charles Hayes ♦♦	839
98	**The Spirit of the 1985 AFL-CIO Convention** ♦♦ The Editors ♦♦	847
99	**New Tactics for Labor** ♦♦ Norman Roth ♦ Ellen Green ♦ Plant Closures Project ♦ Nicolaus Mills ♦ Lance Compa ♦♦	850
100	**Proposals for Action** ♦♦ William Winpisinger ♦ AFL-CIO Committee on the Evolution of Work ♦ The Editors ♦ Leonard McNeil ♦ Ron Teninty ♦ Charles Hayes ♦♦ ♦ Boxes: Oregon AFL-CIO Employment and Economy Committee ♦ Joyce Miller ♦ Amy Newell ♦	866
Honor Roll		880
Index		884

54 ♦♦ RED SCARE IN PARADISE: ILWU IN HAWAII

JOHN WAYNE TO THE RESCUE?

♦♦ Edward Long ♦♦

Moving from academia to the world of politics, Edward Long is now a Congressional aide in Washington, D.C.
  Adapted from "The Red Scare in Paradise: Anti-Communism in Hawaii," unpublished paper by Edward Robert Long (1981).

In a 1951 film, John Wayne plays a special agent of the House Un-American Activities Committee (HUAC), who goes to Hawaii to stop a Soviet plot to take over the prize U.S. territory. The Communists in "Big Jim McClain" were amoral and godless people, capable of using any means—including murder—to carry out subversion. Ex-Communists atoned for their past sins against humanity by drowning their guilt in alcohol, and one, by working as a nurse in a leper colony. But Wayne and Hollywood saved Hawaii—and the entire United States—by single-handedly fighting the Hawaiian Communist Party, just as it was about to wage a longshore strike to paralyze the islands.

Hollywood's script for Wayne stands in sharp contrast to the actual 6-month strike waged by the International Longshoremen's and Warehousemen's Union (ILWU) in 1949. The union called the strike—one of a series of strikes in Hawaii after World War II—to put an end to the 42 cents per hour wage differential that separated longshoremen on the Islands from their brothers on the West Coast.

Pitted against the union were the Big Five corporations: Alexander and Baldwin, Tho. H. Davies, C. Brewer, Castle and Cooke, and American Factors. They owned most of Hawaii's sugar and pineapple plantations, as well as its major shipping companies and most other related businesses on the islands. Since the United States annexed Hawaii in 1898, the Big Five dominated not only the Territory's economy but its government as well. And, through intimidation, racism, and anti-union legislation, the Big Five kept workers in virtual peonage, until years of struggle on the part of native Hawaiian and Japanese dockworkers to organize a union for themselves paid off with the formation of longshore locals in Hilo and Honolulu in 1935.

THE 1934 GENERAL STRIKE IN SAN FRANCISCO

Union organizers in Hawaii were inspired by the success of the 1934 general strike along the entire West Coast. Maritime workers waged an historic struggle for recognition of seafaring unions, abolition of company-controlled hiring halls for seamen, and control of hiring halls by longshoremen. Shipowners in San Francisco rejected these demands and called in the police, with their tear gas and billy clubs, to scare the strikers into submission. As the struggle stretched into months, class lines sharpened: shipowners, police and the National Guard on one side, dockworkers and seamen on the other.

The San Francisco strike led to the Battle of Rincon Hill, where strikers fought the police to a standoff on a small dirt hill near the Embarcadero. That battle, led by Harry Bridges, then a little-known seaman from Australia, was only part of an all-out war raging along the San Francisco waterfront. It had tragic consequences—100 men were wounded, and two were left to die. The deaths at the hands of the police sparked the entire San Francisco labor community to call a three-day general strike, with the support of the AFL Central Labor Council.

Face to face with this overwhelming expression of workers' solidarity, the shipowners conceded to the maritime workers' demands: union recognition, and new hiring halls jointly operated by management and the International Longshoremen's Association (ILA).

WORLD WAR II BRINGS MARTIAL LAW TO HAWAII

♦♦ Edward Beechert ♦♦

Professor Beechert is an historian at the University of Hawaii. He participated in some of the events he recorded in this selection.

Adapted from "The Communist Party and the Labor Movement in Hawaii" (unpublished paper presented at Southwest Labor Studies Conference, California State University, Dominguez Hills, April 24, 1979).

The Japanese government's air attack on the Hawaiian port of Pearl Harbor on December 7, 1941, and U.S. entry into World War II sharply altered labor-management relations on the Hawaiian Islands. The federal government in Washington immediately imposed martial law on Hawaii because of its strategic importance. The military prevailed until April 1944. During this time, the military governmor took over the responsibilities of the territorial governor. He denied workers the right to change jobs and froze their wages. Military courts replaced civilian courts. Officials of the Big Five quickly staffed important positions in the wartime government, and enthusiastically supported military rule.

Plantation management worked closely with military authorities as Civil Defense officers and members of the Selective Service Boards, as well as assuming military authority for carrying out their normal peacetime activities. This was particularly the case on the waterfront. Plantation employees joined the regular longshore crews to help handle the increased military shipping. But the employers kept them on the lower wage plantation payrolls while pocketing the higher longshore wages paid by the government for their work.

The ILWU warmly endorsed the national CIO "Win the War" stance. Even before Phil Murray's demand for a no-strike pledge from CIO unions, Harry Bridges instructed the Hawaiian locals that the war effort demanded full cooperation.

The regional director of the ILWU in Hawaii reported in early 1942 that the Hawaiian locals would rally behind this pledge.

With the outbreak of war, Bridges proposed setting up a wartime hiring hall to dispatch longshoremen to the war zones of the Pacific as needed. Ships sailing to Pacific islands were often forced to lie at anchor while inexperienced soldiers grappled with the unfamiliar problem of unloading ships. Bridges wanted to improve the turn-around time of the ships as a crucial contribution to the war effort. For undisclosed reasons, the government in Washington and Hawaii failed to react to the plan.

War presented difficult problems for Hawaii's Japanese population. Most were second- and third-generation Americans, who remained largely segregated. Employers discriminated against them. The school system provided little beyond elementary education to their children. They were herded into vocationally-oriented high schools, when they were available. The English standard schools leading to college were not for them. The attitude of the military and the business community was overtly hostile. On Kauai, the ILWU Director reported: "The Civilian Defense people on Kauai, largely supervisory personnel from Kauai Terminals, ignored as far as possible the union members who offered their services, and in all cases made discrimination against the union men perfectly plain. Being of Japanese extraction, whether citizens or not, and having been strikers in a Japanese strike, they were not only made to feel suspect, but were in fact suspected, and in many cases openly so."

Ichiro Izuka of Kauai, who had joined the ILWU and the CP with such enthusiasm, soon fell afoul of this draconian military system. Assigned like others to military work, Izuka participated with enthusiasm, in the spirit of the wartime pledge. He also continued to distribute literature. In April, the police seized Izuka and two other men and brought them before the Civilian Defense Hearing Board. Other than a peremptory order to "lock 'em up", the chairman of the Board had nothing to say. They kept Izuka in solitary confinement for one week and then brought him back before the board, which consisted of three plantation managers and an Army officer. The board accused Izuka of distributing leaflets, advocating a strike, and promoting slowdown on defense projects.

He protested that he was committed to the ILWU-CIO's "no-strike, no-slowdown" policy.

After some further questioning, Izuka was held in jail from April 11 until August 12, 1942. When they released him, the authorities banished him from waterfront and defense work. This effectively ended his active participation in the ILWU, although he continued to work for the union as secretary-treasurer. These war years embittered Izuka forever.

ILWU ON THE RISE

♦♦ Edward Long ♦♦

In less than a year of military rule, union membership on the islands dropped from 10,000 to 4,000. But after the relaxation of wartime controls in 1943, the ILWU renewed its prewar organizing drive among workers on the docks and plantations. Lou Goldblatt, international secretary-treasurer of the ILWU, spearheaded the drive, convinced that the ILWU should drive full steam ahead on this organizational program: "The other problems of labor unity, etc., will be a lot easier in solution once we have built a powerful ILWU base in the islands. Particular attention should be directed toward organization of sugar refineries, warehouses and transport groups connected with them." The ILWU executive board took its first step by appointing Jack Hall as ILWU Regional Director for Hawaii.

The union drive to organize sugar and pineapple plantations built on experiences in forming its two longshore locals. It was fueled by worker anger at martial law restrictions that prevented them from changing jobs and froze their wages. Charles Fujimoto explained that "Higher wage standards were introduced by unionized workers who came here from the mainland in large numbers to work in defense-related industries at mainland union wage standards. Many Hawaii workers in the defense industries and others benefitted from the higher wage standards, but sugar and pineapple workers did not. With the job freeze, wage freeze, and the growing differential between plantation [w]ages and others, there was mounting dissatisfaction among sugar and pineapple workers with substandard wages and living conditions. So, when some active union longshoremen started organizing sugar workers, there was instant success. Pineapple workers soon followed."

In 1944 the NLRB decided that the Wagner Act applied to over half of the islands' plantation workers. Thousands of workers, disgruntled with the wartime controls, joined the ILWU. The Japanese were counted among the union's strongest supporters, deeply impressed by the ILWU's condemnation of the wartime internment of 110,000 Japanese-Americans on the mainland.

The ILWU at this point set up a 6-week institute at the California Labor School in San Francisco for workers from Hawaii. The School staff was asked to stress one point in all classes: that racism had destroyed every struggle in the Islands for 400 years. Isobel Cerney, head of the School's English Department, reports that this lesson was taught and received with equal enthusiasm.

The ILWU began to assert itself as a force in electoral politics on the islands. In 1944 it participated with several other major CIO unions in Hawaii to form a political Action Committee (PAC), which began registering voters and sponsoring pro-labor candidates. The PAC was an immediate success, electing 16 representatives (out of a total of 31) and eight senators to the territorial legislature. A year later, this pro-labor coalition helped enact the Hawaii Employment Relations Act, which gave plantation workers the same rights to collective bargaining as industrial workers on the mainland. The union's victories paid off in political appointments as well. In 1945, Territorial Governor Ingram Stainback appointed Jack Hall to a post on the Honolulu Police Commission.

By 1946, ILWU membership in Hawaii had increased to 33,000. The union not only posed a formidable political challenge to the Big Five but had under contract all longshoremen in the Territory and almost all sugar and pineapple workers. Both sides tested their strength that year. The ILWU demanded a 40 cents an hour wage increase, a 40-hour week, and a union shop for workers on the sugar plantations.

The employers stubbornly refused to accept the demands, and resorted to one of their often used strike-breaking tactics. They dispatched 6,000 workers from the Philippines to act as scabs. The ILWU heard about this effort in time to hide two organizers on one of the ships transporting the strike-breakers to the islands. With the aid of the ship's Filipino stewards who belonged to the CIO Maritime Union, the two signed up all of the Filipinos into the ILWU before the ship docked in Hawaii.

The strike lasted 78 days. In the end, the employers flatly refused to grant the ILWU a closed shop. But they did agree to a 20 cents an hour wage increase, and an end to the system of plantations paying workers wages plus perquisites such as housing, water, wood, electricity, and kerosene. (The companies had counted perquisites as part of labor costs and bloated their value for tax purposes while acting as if perquisites were given as generosity.) The workers' unity prevented the companies from trying evictions this time.

Workers asserted their political power as well. In the closing days of the strike, the CIO-PAC elected 35 labor-endorsed candidates, and, for the first time since annexation, Republicans lacked a majority in both houses of the legislature.

In the spring of 1947, Governor Stainback, a Roosevelt appointee, set out on an anti-Communist crusade serving the interests of both the Big Five and the national Democratic Party. In April at an Army Day Commencement, Stainback made his first public address on Communism, warning that Hawaii, too, was not "free from the danger of a Cold War." He spoke in the same fervid tones on the Fourth of July, and on Labor Day he denounced Communists in Hawaii's labor movement at an AFL rally, targetting the ILWU.

A TURNCOAT'S "TRUTH"

♦♦ Edward Beechert ♦♦

Veteran longshore organizer Ichiro Izuka provided ample grist for Stainback's anti-Communist campaign with the release of a pamphlet in November, 1947. Entitled "The Truth About Communism," the pamphlet bore Izuka's name as author, but in fact was jointly authored and edited with Paul Beam, a Honolulu advertising agency executive, and Arnold Wills, then Hawaii Regional Representative of the NLRB. With the financial backing of one of the Big Five corporations, Izuka published 10,000 copies of the pamphlet for distribution. Izuka detailed the history of the Communist Party in Hawaii and charged that a number of ILWU leaders, including Jack Hall, were Communists.

What turned Izuka against his former union and former Party?

The breaking point, according to his pamphlet, was the union decision in 1946 to endorse the Republican candidate for Delegate to Congress, rather than the Democratic candidate. Joseph Farrington, publisher of the Honolulu *Star Bulletin*, won the endorsement largely as a result of his firm stand on the issue of statehood for Hawaii. The Democratic candidate, along with the Governor of the Territory, firmly opposed statehood.

The endorsement and its aftermath provide a good example of the tendency to attribute events to Cold War conspiracy. Actions taken by unions accused of Communist "domination" were assumed to be the result of "plotting." But labor eagerly pursued the goal of statehood as a way to reduce the power of the Big Five. Farrington won by a narrow vote. It is impossible to pinpoint the influences leading to victory in elections as close as this one. Izuka, however, had no difficulty with the matter: "[The Democrat] lost because a conspiratorial Communist Party deceived the workers of Hawaii, who did not know they were Communists, into following their leadership in simple trust."

After drifting away from the waterfront work after the war, Izuka worked first at an army base and then for the Teamsters. His change, he said, stemmed from a desire to "get away from further FBI investigation." The former longshore organizer became involved in a Teamster effort to raid the pineapple cannery in Honolulu, led by a dissident ILWU leader who was dismissed from the union. Izuka claimed that his livelihood was being threatened by the Communist Party, saying: "For this reason, I had no other alternative but to expose the Communist Party of Hawaii."

Governor Stainback fired another round in the Red Scare barrage on Armistice Day, 1947, when he vowed to conduct a crusade to eliminate Communism from the Territory. The speech centered around what the Governor called a plot to seize control of the Territory in a pamphlet entitled, "What We Must Do." According to the Governor, military intelligence delivered this document to him in March, 1947. Prior to this, he asserted he had had no knowledge of Communist activity in the Territory. "What We Must Do" was a memo John Reinecke had written in 1935, while he was teaching at Honokaa, to reflect his thoughts on conditions in rural Hawaii. He analyzed Hawaii's plantations and what would be needed to change the grim reality of that system as the New Deal got under way.

The plan opens with the suggestion that "The great, ultimate aim of all activity must be the organization of workers in the sugar cane and pineapple industries into militant industrial unions, whose aim shall be the domination of those industries." The "plan" proceeds to discuss briefly the program of organizing in "lesser industries," urging that organization aim at breaking down racial wage scales. "An intensive campaign of propaganda" will be necessary to bring the working class to the necessary level of consciousness. "Radical labor must stand uncompromisingly against all forms of racial and interracial discrimination."

In sections dealing with youth, religion, and civil rights, the program is very much in line with federal civil rights legislation passed in the 1960s, as, for example, "taking the Christian religion out of the public schools." One point in the plan was guaranteed to anger the media: "Arouse the public to the danger of the 'sugar coated' press." Perhaps Governor Stainback was angered by the concluding thought of the short document:

Organize a radical political party aiming to drive the Democrats and Republicans together and so expose their identity. Even one member in the Legislature would give the workers of Hawaii a better chance for publicity and power than they have at present.

When the Governor released the 13-year-old document, it created an enormous stir. School officials quickly started a move to dismiss Reinecke and his wife from their positions as teachers. In the uproar, who recalled that Reinecke was not a member of the Communist Party and literally not acquainted with any Communists in 1935?

The major ideas of the document, "What We Must Do," had in fact become reality by 1947. In the Red scare climate, it probably seemed to many that a "plot" had succeeded, but Reinecke himself could not have predicted in 1935 that an industrial-type union would begin organizing in Hawaii by 1937. The Congress of Industrial Organizations itself was only formed in 1935! In fact, most of the pamphlet's ideas were not particularly radical or unusual. But how could he make this clear at the dismissal hearing?

On November 25, 1947, the Superintendent of Public Instruction suspended the husband-and-wife teaching team, and set a hearing for December 18 on 11 charges. All revolved around their alleged "membership in a secret organization"— the Communist Party—in violation of an old statute outlawing such groups.

IN THE REINECKES' DEFENSE

♦♦ Edward Long ♦♦

Reinecke publicly responded to the charges against him and his wife in the November 29, 1947 edition of the *Honolulu Advertiser:*

In our hearings before the Commissioners of Public Instruction, we are prepared to prove both our good reputation as teachers and also our active devotion to the ideals of democracy. Mrs. Reinecke and I have never made any secret of our political views. We are ready to state them in public for the edification of the attorney general as in the past we have always been willing to state them in private conversations and letters to the local newspapers.

Through our civic activities since 1927, we have constantly upheld the fundamentals of American democracy—political, economic, and racial. It is just because we have worked openly for our beliefs and perhaps more actively than most well-minded citizens, that we have incurred enmity and have been singled out to bear the first blows of a purge that is political in purpose.

Although we are called undemocratic, no single instance of undemocratic conduct is stated. Nor can any be found.

The Commissioner of Public Instruction finally opened the hearings in October, 1948. School officials brought in "expert" witnesses to testify about "international communism", and to read Marxist texts into the record. The only evidence they offered to connect Reinecke with any such activity was his "What We Must Do," and a letter written to the author of a Communist Party pamphlet to correct its errors on Hawaii. No instance of misconduct during their long teaching tenure was produced at the trial.

The attorney general handled this problem in a unique manner. He said, "The teaching of doctrines opposed to those of American democracy by teachers as skilled as the Reineckes could not be expected to be open and apparent and evident to all. On the contrary, their teaching would be clever and difficult to detect."

A long parade of witnesses from the community testified eloquently about the Reineckes and their devotion to teaching and to their students; others testified strongly to their high level of competence. Most important, 75 citizens, including representatives from the CIO-PAC and the ILWU, organized the Hawaii Civil Liberties Committee (HCLC) to rally support for the

Reineckes. During the late 1940s and 1950s, the HCLC courageously fought against other cases of political repression on the islands, including the HUAC investigations of 1950 and the Smith Act trials of 1953.

Public sentiment for the Reineckes did not count. After a month of hearings, the Commissioners ruled that John Reinecke was "not possessed of the ideals of democracy" based on a finding of membership in the Communist Party, and revoked his life tenure teaching certificate. They found that Aiko Reinecke was also a member, but were not satisfied "she did not possess the ideals of democracy." They rescinded her teaching contract, but allowed her to retain her teaching certificate. This ended 20 years of teaching for Aiko and 17 years for John Reinecke.

FIGHTING INTERNAL UNION SPLITS

♦♦Edward Beechert♦♦

During 1947-1948, the ILWU successfully resisted an effort by one of its prominent members from the island of Hawaii to form a new "non-Communist" union. Amos Ignacio, a union officer and a member of the Territorial Legislature in 1944 and 1946, announced his resignation from the ILWU and his intention to lead an independent union on December 14, 1947.

The reaction of ILWU leadership was swift. They determined to put the issue to the membership and ask them to vote in a referendum as to their wishes. It was a bold, dramatic move, perhaps unique in modern labor history.

Hall was confident that the rank-and-file could reach a mature judgment on one of the most emotional, confusing issues in American labor, and would not bolt the ILWU. He helped schedule a Unity Conference to air the issues to the sugar workers on January 3, 1948, in Hilo. He said, "From all reports, Ignacio's abortive revolt is folding quite rapidly. Our Filipino leadership has really been hitting the ball in the field and the results are good." Hall also shed some light on the series of anti-Communist moves:

We have received definite information from guys who were involved that this break was planned as long ago as three months. They intended to pull the move coincident with negotiations or with a strike and remain on the job. The Izuka pamphlet was tied in but was not to come out until that time. The pamphlet jumped the gun in part because the Governor was on the spot in Washington. In view of this, and the development of our consolidation program and the day's pay drive, Ignacio had to move ahead of schedule.

The three-day Unity Conference opened with a full assault on the charges. Ignacio refused to attend unless Bridges, Goldblatt, and Hall were barred from attending, but Izuka made a wandering, confused lecture on world communism. In the discussion period, it was clear that the rank-and-file distrusted him.

Long accustomed to red-baiting on the West Coast, the union leadership made it clear that the ILWU made its own policy and ran its own affairs: "We will not be controlled by any outside political groups, by anybody from the outside. The ILWU will govern its own affairs, and no political party, no racial group, no religious group shall govern the affairs of this union. The union will be run by its members."

The outcome of the conference was clear and decisive. The referendum on the Big Island (Hawaii) was 5,560 to remain with the ILWU and 125 against. The home unit of Ignacio, Pepeekeo Sugar Company, turned down the Union of Hawaiian Workers by a vote of 357 to 2. Results were similar on other islands. The Conference, in addition to voting for the referendum, also urged that the union leaders not sign the Taft-Hartley affidavits, attacked the American Legion, and endorsed statehood for Hawaii.

The Ignacio affair had a lasting effect on the ILWU. The overwhelming majority of workers remained with the union and expressed confidence in the leadership, but it was clear that the union's unit leadership structure and education program needed considerable strengthening. It also needed better internal communication to make union policy objectives clear. Ignacio's action was less effective than in 1946, but it did detract from the ongoing work of the union. While the Hilo Unity Conference was taking place, preliminary negotiations on the reopening of several contracts had to be started.

Considerable effort went into building the union mechanism the following year. A special business agent was assigned to the Hamakua Coast of the island of Hawaii, the area in which Ignacio's strength seemed greatest. By careful attention to grievance handling, particularly those arising from the poor camp housing, the union demonstrated its basic purpose—representing workers: "[T]he reason they were accusing us of being reds or something else is that we were raising these grievances that they [employers] were trying to avoid and to deny.... Actually they were on the defensive and they were using this red label to disrupt our work."

The ILWU, even while the attack was underway, was busy with sugar and pineapple contract negotiations. Longshore negotiations were to receive special emphasis in 1948. The union was determined to end the colonial wage differential of Hawaiian longshoremen by establishing parity with the Coast. The differential in pay was then 42 cents. "As part of the program of the ILWU to keep moving and to keep fighting and to stay close to the membership," Goldblatt said, "we were prepared to close that gap by as little as a penny a year until finally it was abolished. Longshoremen working the same shifts, same type of cargo, for the same companies belonged to the same union and yet this enormous differential."

During the Hilo Unity Conference, president Bridges was in Honolulu to open pineapple negotiations. The task of strengthening the union organization and conducting negotiations in three industries presented formidable problems. The longshore negotiations quickly bogged down and it became apparent that a strike would be necessary. The union concluded the employers assumed the union was not strong enough to withstand a long strike and would accept a modest offer. Thus, it became a critical test for the union.

Strike!

The longshore strike began in April 1949. The Big Five immediately launched a virulent campaign against the union. The Honolulu *Advertiser* featured the strike as a Communist plot to "Sovietize" Hawaii. They ran a daily editorial on page one. These usually took the form of a letter to or from "Joe Stalin" with "instructions" and "reports" on the progress of the plan to "overthrow" the economy. They were written in the best comic book fashion. Community organizations were formed to oppose the strike. One such organization, We The Women, counter-picketed the longshoremen, carrying brooms. Ladies of high fashion marched around for some time with their unfamiliar tools "to clean out unwanted labor agitators."

The issues in the strike were complex and the situation created by the strike compounded the difficulties. Hawaii relied on food shipped in from the States. What would the people eat if ships were not unloaded? Public alarm reached a high level and was aggravated by the propaganda campaign. Businesses were reported to be failing. Despite assurances and offers by the union to unload food supplies, anxiety remained high.

PRESSURE FROM THE MAINLAND

♦♦ Edward Long ♦♦

The union membership overwhelmingly rejected the employers' 12 cents offer, despite pressure from President Truman, Stainback, and members of the territorial delegation to Congress. Employers appealed to the mainland, and particularly to the Truman administration, for assistance. The publisher of one of Hawaii's major newspapers placed a two-page ad in the *New York Times* on June 23:

> ... Like most American citizens, we are NOT in a position to prove this strike is Communist-directed. But we do know that every move in the whole picture for fifteen years tallies exactly with the Communist manuals and their teachings—without any exceptions. We do know that every Communist list, as issued by the House Un-American Activities Committee of the House of Representatives, contains as listed Communists the names of men who are crucifying Hawaii.

By the middle of summer, the Hawaiian economy was virtually paralyzed. Few goods entered or left the islands: shelves in stores were empty; and 30,000 islanders were out of work. In August, the Governor pushed a measure through the territorial legislature which gave him the power to seize and operate the docks. Immediately, the government took over the major shipping companies, and ships were loaded by scab labor and took off for mainland ports.

But longshoremen from coast to coast and around the world refused to handle the cargo.

THE UNION WAS THERE LIKE GLUE

If you keep going back to the membership and maintaining the closest possible ties with them—you just got to be there like glue—then, at a certain point, not only can the red-baiting attacks be absorbed, they can be turned back against the red-baiters themselves.

It became an hilarious thing in some situations to see *our* members in effect taking the red-baiting issue and turning it against the people who were attacking them. As when these women were picketing the union headquarters to clean out the union and so forth, the "broom brigade," they called it. You'd have Longshoremen there who'd find some Hallowe'en masks, and one of them would be walking along with a sign saying

AREN'T WE DEVILS?

And just have themselves nothing but fun with it.

The main subject of discussion in the morning was whether everybody had gotten their checks from Moscow.

♦♦Lou Goldblatt

With the government now operating the docks, the ILWU feared that Stainback might call on President Truman to invoke the Taft-Hartley Act. To diffuse this pressure, and possibly to secure a fair deal from the administration, Hall asked Jack Burns to go to Washington. Burns was a prominent Island Democrat the ILWU had supported in an unsuccessful bid for territorial delegate in 1948. He believed that the strike was over a "fundamental economic issue"—the 42 cent wage differential. But, as he recalled in an interview in 1964: "The Big Five called it a political strike. They called it Communist. What else *could* they do? Their position was completely untenable."

When Burns arrived in Washington, he discovered that the federal government had already been persuaded by the Big Five and congressional conservatives to force the ILWU to end the strike. At first, most government officials refused to see him, thinking he was an emissary of the Communists. But Burns, a Catholic, soon befriended Father McGowan of the National Catholic Welfare Conference, who got Burns appointments with fellow Catholics Phil Murray and Maurice Tobin, Secretary of Labor.

Burns first appealed to the CIO, informing the CIO officials that the longshore strike was simply a dispute over wages, with anti-Communism an anti-union tactic deployed by the Big Five. The Island Democrat convinced Harry Reid, assistant to the Secretary-Treasurer of the CIO, that the strike was simply a long overdue struggle for longshoremen's economic demands.

Reid suggested that Burns contact Alex Campbell in the Justice Department and Frank Tavenner, chief counsel of the House Un-American Activities Committee. According to Reid, HUAC was planning to hold hearings in Hawaii on the Communist issue; and, under pressure from the Big Five, the Justice Department intended to push for an immediate trial of Bridges on the West Coast.

In May, 1949, the government had charged that Bridges lied about not being a Communist Party member when he applied for citizenship in 1945. When Burns told Campbell about the history of the Big Five and of 50 years of Republican rule in Hawaii, the Justice Department adviser admitted that the Bridges trial had in fact been arranged to prejudice the strike, and agreed to delay it until late November.

Burns repeated his story to Tavenner, who called off a HUAC hearing for several months after securing from the Island Democrat a statement that Communists did have influence in the ILWU.

Burns next met with Tobin, Truman's Secretary of Labor. Tobin began the meeting by demanding that Burns admit that Bridges and the ILWU leadership in Hawaii and on the West Coast were Communists.

Burns countered by detailing the history of interlocking directorships among several Hawaiian shipping companies and of the virtually unchecked power the Big Five held on the islands, convincing Tobin, who agreed to drop a Taft-Hartley injunction against the ILWU. Burns also persuaded Tobin to call on Hawaiian employers to arbitrate with the union.

Faced with Tobin's proposal, the failure of Stainback's dock seizure bill, and the solidarity of the longshoremen, the Big Five agreed to arbitration, and in October, accepted a federal mediator's offer of a 21 cent increase for Hawaiian dockworkers.

This was a major victory for the union! Resisting pressure from Stainback, Truman, and the Big Five, the ILWU strengthened its position on the waterfront and in the entire Hawaiian economy.

TAFT-HARTLEY IN HAWAII

By the end of 1949, it was clear that the fight of Unions to knock out the Taft-Hartley law by refusal to comply was lost. The vast majority of Unions throughout the country had buckled under the pressure and had complied and their officials had signed the non-Communist affidavits required to permit the Union to use the NLRB election machinery. For the ILWU there was little value in refusing to comply after the fight to knock out the law was lost. So, at the turn of the year, the Island ILWU officials signed the non-Communist affidavits.

Jack Hall as an appointed Regional Director was not legally required to sign. However, since it was clear to everyone that the only purpose of the affidavits was to put union officials on the spot, Jack climbed on the spot with the rest of the elected officials and signed the first ILWU non-Communist affidavit.

The affidavit, certifying that the signing official was not a member of the Communist Party, laid the individual open to framed charges of perjury. It put the finger on every official. It was a gross violation of personal freedom. It solved nothing as far as stopping attacks on the Union were concerned but it laid the way open for the union participating on the ballot in NLRB certification elections.

♦♦ILWU Pamphlet, 1952

HUAC IN HAWAII

♦♦Edward Beechert♦♦

The House Committee on Un-American Activities came to Hawaii in April 1950 to hold hearings. Excitement ran high because the U.S. House of Representatives had just passed a Hawaii statehood bill. A Constitutional Convention to draft a constitution for Hawaii had been called. People felt HUAC's arrival could influence the chance of a statehood bill passing the Senate.

The hearings had a very definite anti-labor flavor. The chief witnesses were the now familiar Ichiro Izuka and several others, including Bert Nakano and Jack Kawano. Nakano was one of the prime movers of the organizing efforts on the Big Island. Kawano, as head of the Honolulu longshore unit, had been prominent in organizing since 1937. Nakano identified himself as a Communist and added a few names to the growing list. Beyond explaining how he got his "card," he had little to say about specific party activity.

No one produced evidence of specific Communist policy or program. Izuka, for example, could do little more than recite the ILWU endorsement of Farrington as an example of Communist domination of the workers. Nakano had no examples of Communist activity to offer, other than his own recruitment. Kawano merely testified that he was not a Communist.

The press and employers held to the position that strikes, unions, labor political action, etc., were "caused" by the presence of Communists in the labor movement.

Bridges pointed out to the Hawaiian leadership that the strategy of the employers now was to convert the ILWU into company unions: "Here in Hawaii employers use the line—'We like unions, just get rid of the Communists and Harry.'"

The Committee summoned Jack Hall to a hearing on April 13. Beyond giving his name and address, Hall refused to testify, citing the Fifth Amendment. In a press statement, after his appearance, Hall noted that he had already filed a non-Communist affidavit in compliance with the Taft-Hartley Act.

HUAC called 26 ILWU members. A total of 39 witnesses refused to testify and were dubbed the "Reluctant Thirty-Nine."

Chairman Walters promised to bring contempt citations against the "Reluctant Thirty-Nine," asserting that the Fifth Amendment did not protect witnesses before Congress. Walters cited the case of the Hollywood Ten as proof of the Supreme Court attitude. He overlooked the fact that the Ten had relied solely on the First Amendment. This was precisely the reason for the legal advice offered in Honolulu, to rely on the additional protection of the Fifth Amendment.

One of the "Thirty-Nine" was ILWU member Frank Silva, who had been elected to the state Constitutional Convention. When the Convention convened, someone made a motion to expel Silva on charges vaguely similar to those used against the Reineckes—"contumacious conduct." The maker of the motion observed that Silva "cannot serve both the ILWU and the Convention. He has made his choice." On the same occasion, the chairman of the Constitutional Convention observed that "Mr. Silva is a most unfortunate young man. In his devotion to labor he has allowed himself to become tainted." No one raised any question about the numerous Convention delegates from corporations, or their affiliations.

What was the impact of this hearing on the strength of the ILWU?

With Bridges' conviction in San Francisco at the same time and the International in the midst of a CIO expulsion trial, the leadership was concerned about the effects on the membership.

If Hall were also convicted it would be minimal, but would require, nonetheless, considerable attention. He planned to have a thorough airing of the issue at the upcoming annual conference of the Hawaii locals. The first two items on the agenda were a report on the CIO expulsion trial and a report on the House Un-American Activities Committee. Following the meeting, the leadership of all units toured the Territory, explaining the results of the Conference and the conclusions of all delegates.

The impact of the hearing on the union is difficult to assess. The need to address the issue of red-baiting certainly detracted from ongoing union needs and development. The time and energy of the officers and staff was certainly diverted from more productive tasks. No long-lasting or obvious damage, however, resulted from the hearings.

The issue of communism and the Communist Party proved to be more of an issue in Hawaiian politics than in the labor movement. This became evident at the Democratic Party's annual convention, which convened shortly after the hearings closed. The convention divided between the conservative Stainback faction and the more liberal group around Jack Burns. Sixteen delegates to the convention were members of the "Reluctant 39." When the convention defeated a motion to expel the 16, the conservative faction walked out. Burns was elected chairman of the Party.

More trouble loomed ahead. Shortly after Congress dismissed the contempt citations against the "Reluctant Thirty-Nine," HUAC held another hearing, this time in Washington, D.C. The featured witness was former Local 137 president, Jack Kawano. In 50 pages of testimony, Kawano tried to give a detailed picture of a union run by the Communist Party rather than its elected officers. He described many meetings, largely by naming people present, but few were clearly meetings of the Communist Party. In most cases, people were present whom he said were not members of the Party.

Speaking of the meetings before 1941, he said: "During those days their [CP] policy to me was not too clear, except I had the feeling they were mainly interested in helping labor unions get organized, and they were doing their best to assist people to form unions.... Maybe they were concentrating more in educating people, because when these outsiders came to our meetings, the subjects they brought up were not too interesting.... They wanted us to do a lot of reading, and things like that."

The leadership again decided to take the HUAC issue directly to the membership. They assigned teams of elected officers to visit each ILWU unit to explain and discuss the issue with the membership. Meanwhile, union business continued unabated. Various committees carried forward negotiations in each of the major industries. There were simply too many rank-and-file elected delegates to these ILWU committees for anyone to accept charges of dictation by any outside group or individual.

There were still serious economic grievances in Hawaii's semi-colonial economy. And long-standing racial prejudices and segregation still marked Hawaiian society. They were as important to the members as the eocnomic issues. Workers clearly viewed the union as the instrument to overcome these problems. Elections to committees or as delegates, participation in education programs and sports activities—all these activities made the union too open and too accessible to the rank-and-file to fit the descriptions given by Izuka and Kawano in their testimony.

Still, the union was hurt by the constant barrage of accusations. Confidence was shaken, but not lost. Unit leadership positions were often difficult to fill. After the Ignacio affair, the union assigned a special representative to the Hamakua coast of the Big Island to rebuild the units there. By skillful handling of grievances and painstaking work, he encouraged and coaxed people to stand for unit office and to carry on the unit work. It was in the handling of housing grievances and defending workers threatened with loss of employment that the union built its following, rather than working in conspiratorial "cells," described by the "friendly" witnesses as largely made up of non-union members.

Smith Act Charges

The HUAC hearings did not destroy the ILWU. Bigger ammunition was required, and a bigger target.

In August, 1951, newspaper headlines screamed that ILWU head Jack Hall had been arrested under the Smith Act, along with six others often named by Izuka and Kawano. Hall was the only ILWU official, but others were associated, directly or indirectly, with the labor movement. Eileen Fujimoto was employed in the Union office; her husband, Charles Fujimoto, had announced in October, 1948, that he was chairman of the Hawaii Communist Party. Koji Ariyoshi was editor of the labor-supported newspaper, *The Honolulu Record*; John Reinecke was already a victim of the witchhunt; Jack Kimoto was a newspaper writer; and James Freeman a construction worker.

The charges were similar to those in other Smith Act trials: "conspiracy to advocate and teach the violent overthrow of the U.S. government." The indictment also listed 11 overt acts that ranged from Fujimoto's announcement of his chairmanship of the Communist Party to Jack Hall's visit to San Francisco for an unspecified purpose.

Union members saw the indictment as a clear attack on the union and an attempt to strip away its leadership, on the heels of Kawano's testimony. Once again the union was forced to mobilize its resources and prepare to meet the attack, organizing a legal staff, a newsletter, and a news commentator from the mainland to deal with the coming trial.

The ILWU hit hard at the essentially anti-labor nature of the trial and the threat the proceedings held for others. Harriet Bouslog, of the union firm of Bouslog, King and Symonds, made this clear in a Labor Day speech, later published as a pamphlet. She warned that, "If this campaign of the government to silence all opposition succeeds first among persons labelled 'communist,' it will then move to militant trade union leaders, judges, and others."

But Hawaiian labor and the left had a few tricks up its sleeve, learned in the bitter struggles to build the ILWU. When two FBI agents contacted ILWU education director David Thompson, and discussed the possibility of Hall "cooperating," Thompson expressed some interest. After they left, Thompson set up a tape recorder and hidden microphone for the next two meetings with the agents. During the course of these meetings,

468 ♦ Part Four ♦♦ Workers Fight Back for Their Rights

♦♦LISTENING IN ON THE FBI♦♦

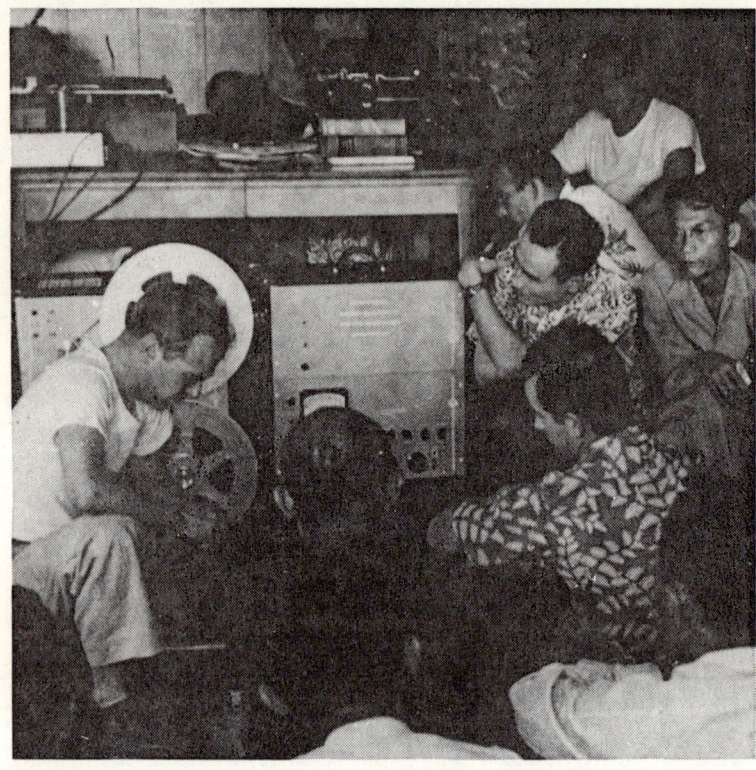

ILWU education director David Thompson set up hidden microphones to tape FBI agents attempting to pressure ILWU leaders to "cooperate" in their witch hunt. Union members listened with interest.

♦♦ Credit: *The ILWU Dispatcher.*

the agents offered to remove Hall from the trial of the other six, in return for his "cooperation" in removing the Hawaii ILWU from the international union. If he cooperated, the agents promised to "see if it couldn't be straightened out whereby it would be six instead of seven."

Thompson pointed out that the agents must know that Hall had already signed a non-Communist oath under the Taft-Hartley Act.

The agents answered with questions as to whether such an oath could be believed.

Thompson wondered, in that case, why Hall had not been indicted for perjury, rather than for travelling to San Francisco?

On this issue, one of the agents replied, "Now we've come to you with a question that has arisen in our minds, is Jack Hall still a member of this conspiracy. We tend ourselves to want to believe 'no'; you seem to think 'no.' What can we offer ... ?" As an inducement to cooperate, the agents pointed out the benefits to be derived: "If he'd get rid of that, he thereby gets rid of 90 percent of the things they've been trying to get on him, the wedge they've had on him all this time."

The implication of their remarks was that the local ILWU would be well rid of the International. They further confirmed this when they indicated that they did not really believe that the Communist Party in Hawaii posed any serious threat.

Jack Hall and the Union gave the agents their answer on the ILWU radio news program a few days later. They played selected portions of the tape recordings to the Island audience. And immediately the union formed defense committees for the Territory and began to collect the funds necessary for a legal defense.

TRIAL OF THE HAWAII SEVEN

♦♦ **Edward Long** ♦♦

The Smith Act trial of the Hawaii Seven was held in October 1952, to coincide with hearings of a Senate subcommittee on a bill to grant statehood to Hawaii. Since the 1930s, the Big Five and old-guard Republicans had resisted statehood, which would enfranchise all persons in Hawaii and seriously threaten the conservatives' political hegemony on the islands.

Congressional conservatives also opposed annexing a state with a large Asian population, but they preferred not to argue on racial grounds. It was neater to claim that Hawaii was in the grip of Harry Bridges and the Communists.

To prove that as members of the Communist Party the seven conspired to teach and advocate subversion, the prosecution built its case around the testimony of ex-Communists from the mainland, who had no knowledge of Communist activities in Hawaii, and the writings of Communist leaders and Marxist theoreticians. Citing the texts of Lenin, Stalin, Marx and Engels, government attorneys contended that these writings advocated subversion and that the defendants subscribed to such theories.

To support its case, the government called to the stand its first witness, Paul Crouch, a professional ex-Communist from the mainland, who testified as to the subversive nature and goals of Communism. Ichiro Izuka and Jack Kawano also testified against the Hawaii Seven, repeating the stories about the Hawaiian Communist Party and Communist influence in the ILWU, which they had told earlier to HUAC. Based on their allegations, in July 1953, a jury convicted the seven, and a federal judge sentenced six of the accused to five years' imprisonment and a $5000 fine; Eileen Fujimoto, the only woman among the Seven, received three years and $2000.

The Seven appealed their convictions. But the appeals court was not ready to think about the question while the same issue was before the U.S. Supreme Court in the case of the California CP leaders.

That case dragged on until June 1957, by which time the Korean War was over, and so was Joe McCarthy. The Warren Court looked at the charges in the California *Yates* case; they looked at the law, and they reversed the convictions. They held that, under the Smith Act, advocacy, to be criminal, must urge people "to do something, now or in the future, rather than merely to believe in something." The statute, according to the Court, outlawed "advocacy of action," not merely "advocacy in the realm of ideas."

Based on *Yates*, in January 1958, Judge Chambers of the Ninth Circuit Court of Appeals set aside the Hawaii convictions: "One may as well recognize that the *Yates* decision, leaves the Smith Act, as to any further prosecution under it, a virtual shambles."

By the 1950s, the ILWU rivaled the Big Five as an economic

and political force on the islands, although the union could not prevent runaway plantations and jobs. The union had won for Hawaiian longshoremen wages and working conditions equal to those on the West Coast, and secured for plantation employees wages undreamed of by farm workers on the mainland. Politically, during the 1950s and 1960s, the ILWU pushed the legislature to adopt some of the most progressive social welfare legislation of any state in the union: Hawaii doubled appropriations for general-welfare assistance, raised unemployment benefits and the state's minimum wage, and extended the islands' unemployment compensation law to cover agricultural workers.

The ILWU gave the Hawaiian people of color a voice in the islands' political and economic life, leading to racial harmony on the islands. Never again could the Big Five control the Hawaiian economy and preserve their power by encouraging racial divisions among the workers, over half of whom were Chinese and Japanese.

The ILWU succeeded where all other Island unions failed, because it organized all workers on the docks and plantations, regardless of race and type of work, and because it faced down Red-baiting in every form. The planters could not persuade the islands' workers that a Communist-dominated ILWU threatened Hawaii's security. They had suffered through decades of exploitation before their union won higher wages and improved working conditions.

To them, "union" meant "ILWU."

55 ◆◆ TEACHERS ON TRIAL

◆◆ Mildred Schoenberger ◆◆

Mildred Schoenberger taught commercial subjects and mathematics in New York high schools and at Herbert H. Lehman College, the Bronx Branch of Hunter College. She is now an active member of Women for Peace in Berkeley.

Material is from the author's own experiences as an active member of the Teachers Union from 1931 until it dissolved, and from Celia Zitron, The New York City Teachers Union: 1916-1964 *(Humanities Press 1968), which describes the Union's rich history from its founding in 1916.*

In December, 1948, two days before the Christmas holidays, two inquisitors traveled by train and ferry to a Staten Island elementary school. A severe snowstorm was raging, but they were sent by New York City School Superintendent William Jansen and they had a job to do. The weather did not deter them.

They summoned Mrs. Minnie Gutride from her first grade classroom with no prior notification. They proceeded to question her about meetings she allegedly attended seven or eight years earlier.

Confronted suddenly by the two interrogators and a recording secretary, Mrs. Gutride requested the right to consult a lawyer.

They immediately threatened to charge her with "conduct unbecoming a teacher."

She left school frightened and shaken.

Minnie Gutride lived alone. Her husband had gone to Spain in the 1930s to defend the fragile new democratic government against Franco fascism. He fought with the Abraham Lincoln Battalion of the International Brigade, and gave his life in that cause. In the ensuing years, Mrs. Gutride had become a staunch member of the New York City Teachers Union, although she taught in an area where the Union was weak.

Now, alone in her home, she went over and over the events of the day. She could see no viable alternatives. Minnie Gutride committed suicide that lonely night in 1948.

When her body was found the next morning, shock waves spread through the public, not only at the questioning of Mrs. Gutride, but at the brutality of the Board's procedure. For its opening gun in a long campaign to destroy the Teachers Union, the Board of Education had chosen a spot where they expected the least resistance.

Postwar Becomes Cold War

Teachers Union members, like people everywhere, had high hopes for better schools in a better society after the end of World War II. Instead, the Cold War followed closely on the heels of peace. Military budgets rose year by year, and civil liberties suffered.

In the summer of 1948, members of New York City Teachers Union struck over wages and working conditions at a private radio-electronics school. The school called in the Hartley Labor Committee to investigate, the Hartley who co-sponsored the Taft-Hartley Act. The Hartley Committee immediately subpoenaed a number of leading Union members, and asked whether they were Communists or knew any Communists in their union. Then the inquisitors read aloud to witnesses the Attorney General's list of "subversive organizations" and asked questions about membership in each of the hundred or more organizations. [*See section 29.*]

Samuel Wallach, former Union president, answered the Hartley Committee:

I have been a teacher for fifteen years—a proud American teacher. I have tried in all those years to inspire my youngsters with deep devotion to the American way of life, our Constitution, and Bill of Rights. From my teaching my pupils developed the feeling that they are living in a country where nobody has the right to ask what are your beliefs, how you worship God, what you read. As a teacher and believer in fundamental principles, it seems to me that it would be a betrayal of everything I have been teaching for me to cooperate with this Committee in an investigation of a man's opinions, his political beliefs, his religion, or his private views.

Mr. Wallach's statement became a rallying cry for academic freedom around the country. Friends and supporters printed it as an advertisement in the *New York Times* on November 12, 1948, and it was endorsed by 5,000 educators, Albert Einstein heading the list.

The next serious blow to the teachers came from within the profession. The National Education Association (NEA), with 900,000 members, reversed its traditional stand for peace and academic freedom. In June, 1949, it issued a report, "American Education and International Tensions," which foretold the continuation of the Cold War into the "adulthood of children now in school." The report accepted this eventuality without question, and said schools must work toward a reorientation of outlook and expectation in order to build the support of the people for the cold war or possible hot wars to come. Programs must be developed that contribute to the nation's needs.

The NEA Report also supported the barring of Communist teachers from the schools but at the same time condemned the "careless, incorrect and unjust use of such words as 'Red' and 'Communist' to attack" those who are not Communists, but merely have views different from those of their accusers. "The whole spirit of free education will be subverted unless teachers are free to think for themselves."

In the prevailing atmosphere of fear, 3,000 delegates to the NEA Convention shouted their approval of this Cold War report. Dissenting delegates confided to friends that they dared not speak or vote their opposition.

Only Rose Russell, Legislative Representative of the Teachers Union, spoke out against the report. She insisted that teachers be judged solely on their professional performance. The delegates heard her; some long remembered what she said, but only a visiting teacher from Norway felt free to congratulate Mrs. Russell publicly on her stand. Later, one delegate told her privately: "The eyes of history are upon us and their verdict will be different. We will be ashamed of what we have done here."

Another blow was struck at the Teachers Union from within the labor movement. The Union had joined the national trade union organizations, first the AF of L, then the CIO, rejecting the idea that "professionals don't need unions." After the 1949

CIO convention stripped away the autonomy of its affiliated unions, a series of expulsion proceedings were instituted against 11 international unions with one million members. Among them was the United Public Workers (successor to the State, County and Municipal Workers), of which the New York Teachers Local 555 was a part. [*See sections 22 and 48.*] This was not the first time the Teachers Union found itself without national labor affiliation.

The Feinberg Law

In late 1949, the New York State Legislature, without hearings and without debate, rushed through the Feinberg Loyalty Law, quickly signed by Governor Tom Dewey. It had been preceded by the Lusk loyalty oath law after World War I and the Rapp-Coudert investigations of teachers just before World War II. The Feinberg Law paved the way for the longest lasting political persecution in the history of public education in the United States, carried on by the New York City Board of Education, the Superintendent of Schools, the city government, the State Legislature and Board of Regents, and a number of Congressional investigating committees.

Against this formidable array, the Teachers Union waged an uncompromising battle for academic and political freedom.

The Feinberg Law made the New York State Board of Regents responsible for "the elimination of 'subversive' persons from the public school system, and for promulgating a list of 'subversive' organizations."

Three legal actions were instituted in 1949 against the Feinberg Law, one by the Teachers Union, one by State Senator Morritt in the name of a group of New York City teachers, and one by the Communist Party. Two lower court judges ruled the law unconstitutional, and some hope returned to the embattled teachers. Then the highest court of the state reversed and the Union took its case to the United States Supreme Court. On January 3, 1952, by a vote of six to three, the Court upheld the constitutionality of the Feinberg Law with Justice William O. Douglas, Hugo Black and Felix Frankfurter in dissent.

Now the Regents planned to carry out the loyalty checks on teachers through a "pyramid of spying." The *New Yorker* of May 10, 1952, commented: "Now if we can just get Feinberg to OK the supervisor, and get the Attorney General to OK Feinberg, we're all set. That is, we're all set provided we can get somebody to OK the Attorney General."

The Board of Regents was empowered to add to the list of proscribed organizations any additional ones it deemed subversive.

Banning the Teachers Union

George A. Timone was known to be associated with the extreme right. There were protests when Mayor O'Dwyer appointed him to the New York City School Board in 1945. On April 6, 1950, Timone presented a resolution to the Board of Education that would ban all official dealings with the Teachers Union. Opposition to this resolution was immediate and overwhelming. Petitions and resolutions poured in from faculties, parent groups, trade unions, Protestant clergymen of all denominations, rabbis, the American Civil Liberties Union, the Public Education Association, and others. Three meetings were held on the issue. The atmosphere crackled with concern, indignation, and anger.

Timone said he offered his resolution in response to public demand, but 128 people asked to be heard at the first hearing, 100 of them strongly opposed to the resolution. Hundreds of teachers picketed the second hearing. Finally, on June 1st, the Board prevented further discussion and passed the resolution.

During the debate, a Timone supporter had charged that the Union kept dragging in "phoney" racial issues. A parent representing the ghetto areas of Bedford-Stuyvesant-Williamsburg responded indignantly:

I don't think the Union has to drag up anything phoney. The issues are already there.... We are glad to have an organization as strong, as well able to speak up for us.... Why doesn't the Board spend its time cleaning up acts of overt bigotry, instead of acting against this organization ... ?

Perhaps this parent had in mind a famous pamphlet issued by the embattled Teachers Union: "Prejudice and Bias in Textbooks Used in the New York City Schools." This pamphlet included many examples: "... Most slaves were happy ... the planter ... was intelligent enough to know that he, like the animal trainer, could get best results through kind treatment. ..." and "Uruguay is a progressive country. Most of the people are white." This textbook exposure created such a sensation that the Board of Education was forced, eventually, to remove eight of the most objectionable texts from its approved list. But this was one step forward amid numerous steps back for education.

Academic Freedom?—the Battle Rages

In 1949, the year of the Feinberg Law in New York, the liberals stampeded at the University of Washington in Seattle. Three professors had been cited for contempt by the Canwell Committee, counterpart of the House Committee on UnAmerican Activities; two had been known for 13 years as Communists. The Faculty Committee on Tenure and Academic Freedom held searching hearings in the case for seven weeks and concluded that those professors had been known through the years as good teachers, distinguished scholars, and men of integrity who should be retained on the faculty. Instead, University President Raymond B. Allen said, "[S]uch teachers are incompetent, intellectually dishonest, and derelict in their duty to find and teach the truth." The Board of Regents fired them.

Professor Sidney Hook, ideological leader of the witch-hunters, approved the dismissals without trial on the basis that "it would be difficult to determine when a teacher was defending a conclusion because he honestly believed it followed from the evidence and when he was carrying out his task as a good soldier in the party cause."

Alexander Meiklejohn, dean of American educators and noted defender of constitutional liberties, supported the thesis that performance in the classroom was the only criterion for judging a teacher. As a result of dismissing the three Communist professors, he said:

The entire faculty is on probation. Every scholar, every teacher is officially notified that if, in his search for truth, he finds the policies of the American Communist Party to be wise, and acts on that belief, he will be dismissed from the University ...

The stage was now set for an accelerated attack. The Board of Education suspended eight teachers on May 3rd, 1950, including Union President Abraham Lederman and Secretary Celia Zitron. The charge: refusal to answer questions about membership in the Communist Party.

The teachers based their refusal on their right under the Fifth Amendment to the U.S. Constitution not to be forced to become witnesses against themselves.

The Board removed the teachers from their classrooms just when they were needed most, as their students were preparing for the Regents Examinations in June, only a month away. The sudden disappearance of their teachers disrupted their classes and upset their studies. In the case of Celia Zitron, there was no substitute qualified to cover her program, which included classes in four foreign languages.

Their fellow teachers reacted in shocked protest to such arbitrary treatment of respected colleagues with whom they had worked for many years.

Alice Citron, another of the suspended eight, had been a prime mover in the Harlem Committee for Better Schools founded in 1935, which had succeeded in getting the first new elementary school built in Harlem since 1900. When she was suspended, 48 of the 55 teachers in her school wrote a strong letter supporting Miss Citron to School Superintendent Jansen. She was known to dig into her own pockets to supply teaching materials that should have been supplied by the Board of Education, or to buy shoes and other personal necessities so her pupils could come to school. No wonder Harlem parents also came to her defense.

New York officialdom made every effort to prevent public airing of the issues in the suspensions. Student leaders invited Celia Zitron to speak to the student body at Queens College; the administration banned the meeting. Five hundred students stood outdoors in the rain to hear her speak off campus. Immediately the administration revoked the charters of the four student organizations that had invited her.

The Teachers Union had no reserves in its treasury. A Freedom Fund Committee was set up to raise money for legal expenses and to bring the campaign of the eight suspended teachers to the public. Union members and friends raised thousands of dollars in contributions, and through theatre parties and bazaars.

A moving letter was received from Dr. Ranuccio Bandinelli, member of the National Italian Academy and university professor for 20 years in Italian and Dutch universities:

... In 1944 I was taken by fascists and kept in jail as hostage.... And I am deeply worried to see the United States, which was once a symbol of freedom, begin a way which leads to a kind of fascism. May I recollect to you that, in 362 A.D., Christian teachers were forbidden to teach ... ? The historian Ammianus, who was not a Christian, wrote that this law was a 'very bad one, and ought to be hidden under perpetual silence.'

And that law did not succeed in stopping the growth of Christianity.

Letters came from all parts of the country to Board of Education President Maximilian Moss. College professors seldom got involved with problems of teachers in the public schools, nor was it common for university faculties to defend members against attack. But the University of California faculty was itself engaged in a struggle against the dismissal of almost 200 of its members for refusing to sign an oath swearing nonadherence to a list of "subversive" organizations. William P. Cartwright, president of the UC Academic Assembly, sent a message urging reinstatement of the eight teachers, "and to insist that teachers be judged on the performance of their classroom duties. Competence in such performance is, and if academic freedom is to survive, must be, the only test for fitness to teach. We, here at the University of California, have experienced the disastrous effects that accompany departure from the criterion of competence. The disruption of scholarly research, the impairment of proper instruction, and a contagion of fear and suspicion—all follow ineluctably once a breach is made in our cherished heritage of academic freedom."

Letters started arriving from abroad, where fascism and repression were well-known: from New South Wales; Madras, India; from Bulgaria, France, Rome, and Vienna; from the National Union of Educational Workers in Queretaro, Mexico; from the teachers' section of the Central Union of Public Workers in Belgium.

Exemplary Teachers on Trial

Against its own by-laws, the Board of Education appointed an outsider as trial examiner in the case of the eight suspended teachers. He was Theodore F. Kiendl, member of one of the country's richest law firms.

The suspended teachers were charged with "conduct unbecoming a teacher," because of their refusal to answer questions. David Friedman was also charged with membership in the Communist Party. He was tried first. The Board's first witnesses against him were Joseph Kornfeder and Louis Budenz, who had emerged as paid informers in trials of Communist Party leaders back in 1949. Their testimony ranged far and wide in time and space to feed the atmosphere of hysteria and to supply sensational headlines to the press. But it never mentioned David Friedman.

Rose Russell, acting as co-counsel, questioned whether Dr. Jansen had any evidence from supervisors or any other source that Mr. Friedman advocated overthrow of the government or uttered any treasonable words.

Dr. Jansen replied: "No."

Professor Thomas Emerson of the Yale Law School was called by the defense as an expert on constitutional liberties and academic freedom. Trial examiner Kiendl ruled that his testimony would be irrelevant since "I do not think academic freedom is here on trial at all." The teachers were accused *only* of refusing to answer Dr. Jansen's questions.

The trials of the other seven teachers followed, with an array of witnesses who presented a picture of teachers of extraordinary ability and devotion, admired and respected by their colleagues and their students. Assistant Corporation Counsel Daniel Scannell reacted to all this by saying: ". . . a true analysis of this situation must make us aware that [their very excellence] increases the danger of having in our schools teachers who belong to such a conspiracy against our democracy."

Shades of the Salem witchcraft trials of the late 17th century! When women were charged with being witches and riding their broomsticks over the town at night, there could not be found one witness who saw them do it. This was deemed proof positive of their witchcraft, since they had the power to make themselves invisible.

During the course of the trial Rose Russell charged that the Corporation Counsel and the Superintendent of Schools had devised a trick for subverting the fair play and tenure provisions of the Education Law, by posing questions which they had no right to ask. They brought no charges, no witnesses, no evidence to be openly heard, tested, or cross-examined. On such a basis, Mr. Kiendl recommended dismissal of the eight teachers on February 8, 1951 for refusal to answer.

The Board used Section 903 of the New York City Charter, which had its origin in the 1932 Seabury investigation of widespread graft and corruption during Mayor Jimmy Walker's administration and was never intended to be used in cases like these. It provided that city employees who refuse to testify concerning affairs of the city on the ground of self-incrimination be removed from their jobs.

In September, 1954, Professor Harry Schlochower of Brook-

♦♦ A TREE GROWS ♦♦

Anti-communism aimed at public school teachers prompted Fred Ellis to draw this political cartoon for the November 18, 1951 issue of the *Daily Worker*.
♦♦ Credit: Fred Ellis.

lyn College refused to answer, was removed, and sued for reinstatement, with the support of the Union. The Union filed a similar suit for 29 other teachers. State courts upheld the dismissals, but there was hope that the U.S. Supreme Court would agree to hear the cases and do justice.

NOT RED, BUT ROTTING

The committee on the New York State capital budget heard dozens of parents complain of rat-infested buildings, crumbling roofs, filthy toilets, whole neighborhoods without schools and no plans for construction. One editorial, commenting on the evacuation of a school where a pillar had collapsed, said: ". . . We wonder whether the elusive peril of naughty ideas is as menacing to our schools as the danger of sudden death in the classroom. Our schoolhouses are not red but they are rotting."

♦♦New York Post, February 28, 1952

Meanwhile, the Teachers Union kept on introducing new projects. Union teachers arranged special events for Negro History Week and provided all kinds of material on Black history and culture. In 1952, the Union began publishing an annual Negro History supplement in the *Teacher News*. Requests for multiple copies of this supplement came from practically every state in the U.S., and from as far away as Sierra Leone. *Teacher News* published other supplements on Puerto Rico Day, Italian American History, the Jewish Centenary, and Pan-American Week.

In 1952, George Timone pushed through the Board a resolution banning the use of school buildings by organizations on the Attorney General's "subversive" list, and included the Union although it had never been listed by the Attorney General. In addition, some hostile principals, on their own, restricted the use of teachers' letter boxes to "recognized" organizations.

Controversy—and Fear

During the Cold War, the word "controversial" took on a new meaning. Teachers who assigned students to give factual presentations of current events, and encourage students to seek information from all sides, to participate in free discussion, and to form independent opinions, became suspect. A department chairman, observing a lesson on control of atomic energy, criticized the teacher for posing this question: "What are the opposing viewpoints (American and Soviet) on the control of atomic energy?" According to the chairman, this question presupposed "that there are opposing viewpoints on the question, each of which is equal in standing and worthy of the same consideration."

An article in "Strengthening Democracy" (organ of the Board of Education, sent regularly to every teacher) presented the officially accepted version of what constituted a controversial issue. Jack Estrin, a Social Studies teacher, in the November-December 1952 issue, cited proposals in the United Nations on reduction of armaments, unconditional prohibition of atomic weapons, and ratification of the Geneva protocol prohibiting germ warfare. "These are not controversial issues," he wrote. "They are propaganda against the minds of free men."

Those who were suspended or forced to resign faced painful dislocations in their lives. Teachers with years of experience faced blacklisting in their profession. Few had other marketable skills, and they had to retrain to make a living. The Teachers Union Freedom Fund did its best to help ease the transition. One teacher worked in a fish store until he finished retraining in a new educational field. Others became carpenters or drove taxis. Some became remedial reading specialists. Some teachers went into ventures which turned out to be more remunerative than teaching had ever been, but not as satisfying.

There was another tragic case. A man was found in the street, dead of a heart attack. He was identified by a letter in his pocket, summoning him for questioning, another victim of the witch-hunt.

Although an appeal was pending on the first eight suspended teachers, Dr. Jansen continued with his inquisition. Hundreds of additional teachers were summoned for questioning. In addition to the stock query on past or present membership in the Communist Party, they were grilled on what books they read, on people they knew, what contributions they made to which causes, whether they belonged to the American Labor Party (ALP), or if they ever signed nominating petitions for Congressman Vito Marcantonio (NY-ALP), or for other minority party candidates.

Many teachers resigned who may not have been in any of the "subversive" organizations listed by the U.S. Attorney General, or designated as such by Dr. Jansen. They feared perjury charges, for there was no quick or certain protection against the lies of paid informers who were hired to say anything the witch hunters wanted. It was the teachers' word against that of the informer, with the chance to win on appeal a distant dream. Many teachers objected in principle to answering questions about their private lives, but they were reluctant to say so on a witness stand. An impressive number did take a public stand, lashing out against the threat to this country's best traditions of freedom of thought.

PHILADELPHIA STORY IN 1955

♦♦ Teachers Union of Philadelphia ♦♦

From The Case Against the School Board, *by the Teachers Union of Philadelphia, 1955.*

You are a teacher. You have been teaching for 23 years in the Philadephia public schools. During that time you taught in the elementary and junior high schools, and now you are teaching in a senior high school. During those 23 years you taught about 4,000 children. You were a popular teacher. Parents often worte letters to you expressing their appreciation for the interest you showed in their children. Over the years, many of your former pupils returned to report on the progress they were making in their careers.

As a teacher you always emphasized the cardinal virtues. You talked about honesty, about fair play, about the golden rule. You talked about the basic values of democratic living. You talked about these things, and you made them a part of classroom life.

You were popular with your colleagues in the school, and you had many personal friends on the faculty. You were always regarded as one of the good teachers in the school, and you often had a practice teacher assigned to your class for apprentice training. When an extra job had to be done, your principal knew he could depend on you to accept the task and perform it well. You coached one of the minor teams; you directed the school play. You helped organize the assemblies, and you helped at the football games. In short, you were an important and an integral member of the teaching staff of your school.

Here you are, then, at the peak of your career and growing into middle age. You started to teach shortly after graduating from a first-rate university, and you have devoted your life to teaching children. You have had a financial struggle, since your salary never was adequate. But in spite of the jobs after school, the summer work, the tension you found in a classroom with 45 children, you gave all that was in you to the career you had chosen. You loved teaching, you were fond of young people.

When you left your classroom with its familiar objects—the map on the wall, your books on the desk, the pair of galoshes in the closet, unmarked test papers in your desk, a half-completed letter to a parent under the blotter—you did not know that this was your last day as a teacher.

Just before dinner, you turn on the radio, and you hear a news announcer inform you that you have been suspended from your job. An hour later, a registered letter arrives from the Superintendent, repeating the information you have just heard.

Thus, in a moment, end a career, your way of life, and your livelihood.

IN THE COURTS: MOSTLY DELAY, SOME VICTORIES

♦♦ Mildred Schoenberger ♦♦

Early in 1955 the U.S. Supreme Court agreed to hear Professor Schlochower's challenge to New York City charter section 903—the "inform or be fired" clause. But at the same time the Court refused to hear the cases of 13 other teachers. The only difference in the cases was some of the language used by the lawyers; the facts were identical. On April 9, 1956, the U.S. Supreme Court ruled that dismissal of Professor Schlochower solely for the use of the Fifth Amendment privilege was unconstitutional. The vote was 5 to 4. In the absence of any inquiry as to his fitness to teach, the Court held that "the summary dismissal of appellant violates due process of law." (350 U.S. 551.)

A clear, if close, victory for one, but it did not help the 13. Then New York Commissioner of Education Allen ruled that teachers could not be discharged for refusing to inform on other teachers because that would be detrimental to proper functioning of the educational system and would destroy the morale of teachers. He dropped charges against five public school teachers and one college professor.

The Board of Higher Education promptly sued to set aside this order.

By January, 1957, the Board of Higher Education had figured out how to dismiss Professor Schlochower legally. They called him to another hearing, this time their own, not the U.S. Senate's. They asked him questions they knew he would refuse to answer, then fired him for "willfully and intentionally" refusing "to make full and fair disclosure of all the facts within his knowledge" and further refusing "to cooperate fully and to answer all proper questions."

At this point, staring at a *Bleak House* of litigation, Schlochower resigned in order to continue his life. But by May of 1959, solidariy and stubbornness began to pay off. The New York Court of Appeals affirmed Commissioner Allen's "no informing" order. In June at a departmental hearing, Hunter College Professor Hughes repeated his 1954 admission of Communist Party membership 1938-1941, repeated his refusal to give names of 11 others in his Communist Party club, said only one was now at Hunter College, and that his case had been "closed". In July, the Board ordered Hughes reinstated with full back pay ($54,000, less earnings since suspension in 1954). In 1960, Hughes won an additional $5,100 as accrued interest on his back salary.

New York City's First Teachers' Strike

Until the Cold War hysteria hit the schools, the Teachers Union had slowly rebuilt its membership back to over 7,000 from the attrition it suffered during the repressive Coudert days of 1940-41. Even in 1950, when McCarthy was riding high, the teachers knew who best served their interests when they voted for the Teachers Union pension candidate, Samuel Greenfield. He garnered 48 percent of the vote and would certainly have won the election in a fairer field. It was the Union's growing influence that the authorities feared.

The McCarthyite investigations conducted by the Congressional committees and the Board of Education drove hundreds of Union members out of the school system. Some were suspended, tried and dismissed. Others retired or resigned because they were unwilling to become informers.

The 12 years following passage of the Timone Resolution in 1950 deprived the Teachers Union of organizational rights and free access to the new teachers who entered the system during that period. They remained uninformed as to the real program, activities and literature of the Teachers Union. Their only source of information was the lurid distortions in the sensational press and the literature of the extreme right-wing teacher groups that had free access to the letter-boxes.

The Teachers' Guild, despite its acquiescence in the Cold War hysteria, was no more successful in organizing. Political respectability was not enough when meaningful programs for solving the deep-seated problems of the schools was the need of the day. In 1960, the Guild and a group of more liberal members of the Secondary School Teachers Association joined forces and organized themselves as the United Federation of Teachers, affiliated with the American Federation of Teachers. This new group threatened the first teachers' strike in the history of New York City. Their demands included better salaries and working conditions and also a referendum on collective bargaining and voluntary dues check-off.

After some fruitless negotiations with the Board of Education and several postponements, the UFT called a one-day work stoppage on November 7, 1960. It produced no immediate concessions on salaries or working conditions, but despite earlier threats to suspend participants, there were no crackdowns. Threats of reprisal roused such a storm of protest from school faculties, the United Federation of Teachers, and the Union that the city's Condon-Wadlin Law prohibiting strikes by public employees was never invoked.

The strike had a profound effect on the teaching staff. Even among those who opposed it and crossed the picket lines, there was universal jubilation at the realization that this most unpopular Board of Education could be defied with impunity. The low esteem in which the Board was held crossed all political lines and was well-deserved. Their reputation had been sullied by whispers of corruption and there had never been a measure before the Board of Estimate, the City Government, or the State Legislature, beneficial to teachers or the schools, that had won the Board's support. The stoppage galvanized the staff into a new sense of unity and they began to look to the United Federation of Teachers for leadership.

In the light of the onslaught against them since 1949, the Union realized it was in no position to win a collective bargaining election at that time. Nevertheless, they supported the principle of collective bargaining before the Board of Education, in *Teacher News*, and in the schools. The referendum was held in June, 1961, and resulted in a three-to-one vote in favor of collective bargaining. The date set for the collective bargaining election was December, 1961. It was a three-way race with the National Education Association, the United Federation of Teachers, and the Teachers Union competing.

The Union petitioned for the lifting of the Timone resolution. The Board did not comply with the request but, according to NLRB rules, they were compelled to allow the Union access to teachers' letterboxes and participation in election discussions. The lifting of restrictions did not occur until October, 1961, which gave the Union only a few weeks to repair the damage of their 12-year isolation. Now a two-pronged whispering campaign got under way. Teachers were told that the Board of Education would not deal with the Teachers Union if they won, or that a vote for the Teachers Union would throw the election to the NEA.

The long and short campaigns against the Union did their work. The United Federation of Teachers won the election by an absolute majority. The Teachers Union vote was disappointingly small.

Militant Teachers Find New Forms

The battered remnants of the Teachers Union did not disband. Although the UFT had grown, it was still a minority organization and still had to prove itself in concrete achievements for the teachers and the children of New York. For Union members, the negative role of the Guild in the academic freedom struggle, their inertia in other professional and social concerns of the school system to which the Teachers Union was dedicated were additional causes for unease and mistrust. Union members were devoted to their organization, the embodiment of all their highest educational and humanist ideals. There were members who wept at the thought of its demise. They feared the negation of all their years of dedicated struggle for progressive educational policies, for integrated staffs, for the removal of racial bias from textbooks, for equality of educational opportunity, for freedom of inquiry, and freedom of expression for both teachers and students.

However, despite the lifting of the Timone resolution in 1962, it was an illusion to suppose that sufficient membership could ever again be recruited in the face of the existence of an elected collective bargaining agent. After months of anguished discussion, the executive board reached the conclusion, and the membership became convinced that "the most effective way for Union members to carry on the fight for better schools from now on is to unite with other union-minded teachers" and to set before them as model and inspiration the unsullied standards and traditions of conscience and courage shown in the 40 years of Teachers Union history.

The Union ended its formal existence in January, 1964, but its work and influence did not cease. In 1967, the U.S. Supreme Court reversed its 1952 decision and declared the Feinberg Law unconstitutional in *Keyishian v. Board of Regents* (385 U.S. 589). The use of the disclaimer oath on job applications had been outlawed in 1964 in a case brought by University of Washington faculty, staff and students, *Baggett v. Bullitt* (377 U.S. 360). In 1968, in *Gardner v. Broderick* (392 U.S. 273), the Court ruled that section 903 of the City Charter was unconstitutional.

Based on these decisions, teachers fired in the 1950s pressed their suits for reinstatement, back pay and pension rights. After prolonged litigation and negotiations, in 1973 the New York City Board of Education reinstated and rehired 33 teachers and 10 more in 1976. Twenty-one years after their unjust, immoral and illegal treatment at its hands, the Board passed a vote of apology unanimously and agreed to grant the teachers their pension rights based on years served before the suspension, plus the years since the 1967 decision. They also made some amends by putting in the teachers' share of the pension contributions for those additional years.

The teachers were finally offered the opportunity to return to the classroom. But victory came too late for the students of New York to learn from the courageous men and women whose teaching they had been denied. The dismissed teachers were all getting on in years and chose to retire.

In April, 1982, the City of New York paid nearly a million

dollars to provide pensions for seven college teachers and lump-sum payments to the estates of three others: Richard Austin, Joseph Bressler, Dudley Strauss, Sarah Reidman Gustafson, Bernard Riess, Oscar Shaftel, Vera Shlakman, Elton Gustafson, Myron Hoch and Murray Young. Comptroller Goldin said, "The settlement terms ... right a terrible injustice inflicted on a group of New York teachers who were exercising their constitutional rights to refuse to testify about personal and political matters."

ONE VICTIM HONORED

One of the teachers dismissed from Brooklyn in 1941 as a result of the witch-hunting work of the Rapp-Coudert Committee was Dr. Alex Novikoff. By 1948 he had rebuilt his career and got an appointment to teach at the University of Vermont. But they wouldn't leave him alone. The Jenner investigating committee asked him questions about political beliefs and associations. He refused to answer and was dismissed in 1953.

In 1954, he was appointed to the Albert Einstein College of Medicine. There he engaged in significant cancer research for which he has received many honors. He was elected to the National Academy of Sciences and received Columbia University's Distinguished Service Award.

On May 21, 1983, the University of Vermont gave him an honorary degree in recognition of his "integrity and courage as a scientist, a faculty member and citizen."

Indeed.

Veteran members of the Teachers Union finally began to enjoy the well-deserved comfort of a secure retirement, and, even more, the supreme satisfaction that comes with complete vindication.

56 •• ONE LOS ANGELES TEACHER'S STORY: FRANCES EISENBERG

♦♦ The Editors ♦♦

A witness before the Joint Fact-Finding Committee on UnAmerican Activities of the California State Senate charged that several teachers in Los Angeles were guilty of "communistic indoctrination" of their students. One of those charged was Mrs. Frances R. Eisenberg of Canoga Park High School.

In October 1946, the Los Angeles Board of Education held four days of hearings on these charges, listening to the testimony of Mrs. Eisenberg, other charged teachers, and some of their students and former students.

The Board then issued its findings:

• The evidence does not support the complaint that these teachers imposed Communistic doctrines upon students in their classes, or that they "slanted" or improperly influenced the policy or articles of the school paper, *The Hunter's Call.* Both teachers emphatically denied sympathy with or approval of Communism.... Concerning the complaint that the teachers "slanted" class discussions of political and controversial issues to the "left" or to their own view, the evidence is conflicting, though a majority of the students or former students testified and made statements favorable to the teachers in this regard....

• As to the complaint that copies of the *Daily Worker* and alleged Communistic periodicals were displayed in the classrooms of these teachers, the testimony is conflicting, and the teachers deny the charge. However, there is sufficient evidence to indicate that periodicals of almost every kind were permitted in the classrooms, and were not limited to the literature approved by the Curriculum Division; and that the *Daily Worker* was on a few occasions present in the classrooms. The testimony presented does not establish that said paper was used for the purpose of indoctrination or was presented by the teachers as subject material for study.

• As to the complaint that Mrs. Eisenberg was a member of the board of the People's Educational Center which the Legislative Committee stated is a Communistic front organization, Mrs. Eisenberg admitted that she was a member of the People's Educational Center, that she was assigned on said board by the president of her teachers' union, Local No. 430, American Federation of Teachers, and that said union is designated in the official literature of said People's Educational Center as an affiliated organization. Mrs. Eisenberg, however, stated that she did not know whether or not the People's Eudcational Center was a Communistic front, that she was not aware of the Communistic affiliations of any member of said board, and that she was not active and attended only a few meetings.

The State Senate (Tenney) Committee took sharp issue with these findings in its 1947 report: "The handling of the Canoga Park affair indicates a serious lack of intelligence and realism in its attempt to cope with the skilled propagandists for Communist totalitarianism.... The case of Mrs. Eisenberg is crystal clear. She is a member of the Local 430 of the *American Federation of Teachers*, a thoroughly Communist dominated trade union.... She is acquainted with and associates with known Communists, such as John Howard Lawson. The Communist books of Carey McWilliams are in the library of the *Canoga Park High School*...."

Mrs. Eisenberg continued teaching and working in AFT until October, 1952. Meanwhile, the California legislature passed the Levering Act, which required public school teachers and professors to answer questions regarding Communist Party membership when subpoenaed, or face charges of dismissal. In September, 1952, the Los Angeles Board of Education adopted regulations to enforce the Levering Act.

On October 28, 1952, Frances Eisenberg was called before the Tenney Committee.

Q: Your name is Frances Eisenberg?

A: That is correct.

. . .

Q: Mrs. Eisenberg, are you acquainted with Jean Wilkinson?

. . .

Q: Mrs. Eisenberg, are you acquainted with Jean Wilkinson?

A: Well, in view of the paper that I just read and the fact that she was subpoenaed here, I feel that I can't reply to that question other than saying that a question of that sort would force me to repudiate my oath to uphold the State Constitution and the Constitution of the United States, which expressly forbid that kind of question, and I feel that I would be compelled, therefore, to give testimony against myself.

Q: Well now, —

Mr. Esterman: Is this a lady who was called today and who did appear before the Committee?

Mr. Combs: Yes.... She is the wife of Frank Wilkinson.

Mr. Combs: Well, do I understand, Mrs. Eisenberg, that your refusal to answer the question is based on the fact that under the Fifth Amendment you feel your answer might tend to subject you to a prosecution?

. . .

The Witness: My position is that no American can be compelled to bear witness against himself.

Senator Burns: Also for the record, counsel and Mrs. Eisenberg, the Chair will rule that the answer is not sufficient and the reasons given are not sufficient, and the Chair will direct you again to answer the question.
(Discussion off the record.)

Senator Burns: Now, I want another stipulation, that each and every question where the reply is in this form, that the ruling of the Chair is that the answer in this form is insufficient and the witness is directed to answer the question.

. . .

Mr. Combs: Now, Mrs. Eisenberg, I show you a letter which purports to be on your stationery and ask you if you will identify it?

. . .

The Witness: The letter is in my handwriting.

Mr. Combs: Did you consult with any persons other than members of your own immediate family about the sending of such a letter to Mr. Holtzendorff?

A: I consulted with my conscience.

. . .

Q: Did anybody ask you to write the letter?

A: No.

Q: Are you a member of the Los Angeles Federation of Teachers?

A: I am an officer and very proud to be a member of that organization.

Q: How long have you been affiliated with it?

A: Well, roughly speaking, about 10 years. It is 17 years old.

Q: Yes. Isn't that the one that Mr. Harold Orr is president of? [Orr had been an unwilling witness before the same Committee.]

A: Yes, he is president.

Q: Is he still the president?

A: Yes, he is still the president. We are very proud of him. He has done a wonderful job.

Q: Did you at one time edit a publication for the union?

A: I now do. I am the editor.

Q: What is the name of that?

A: *The Los Angeles Teacher.*

. . .

Q: . . . Are you familiar with an organization that was known as The Peoples Educational Center in Los Angeles?

A: The same reply.

Q: Is it not a fact that you were a member of the Board of Directors of that institution?

A: The same reply.

Q: Are you a member of the Communist Party of Los Angeles County?

A: The same reply.

Mr. Combs: That is all.

The Los Angeles Board of Education promptly moved to discharge Frances Eisenberg and Paul Orr.

They sued for reinstatement.

In November, 1952, the Levering Act was put on the state ballot and the voters approved it, making it a part of the state constitution.

In 1954, the California courts upheld the Levering Act and the discharges of Eisenberg and Orr.

In 1971, the California Supreme Court issued a favorable ruling on the right to apply for reinstatement of a person dismissed from a government job under a law later declared unconstitutional.

Frances Eisenberg and six other teachers dismissed in the '50s for refusal to answer political questions promptly pursued their remedies in court.

After almost 30 years, they were awarded $200,000 in settlement of their damages and won reinstatement to their teaching jobs.

57 ◆◆ MORE CONGRESSIONAL INVESTIGATING COMMITTEES

◆◆ The Editors ◆◆

In the 1950s, Congressional investigating committees continued to call labor witnesses, and many continued to refuse to answer questions.

In its never-ending attack on the United Electrical Workers Union, the House Committee on UnAmerican Activities called Julius Emspak, Thomas Quinn, Thomas J. Fitzpatrick and Frank Panzino in August 1949. Emspak, General Secretary-Treasurer of UE, was asked [349 US 155, at 177, 178]:

Mr. Tavenner: ... Are you acquainted with Joseph Persily?

Mr. Emspak: Because of my interest in what is going on these days, because of the activities of this committee—

Mr. Moulder: Are you going to answer the question?

Mr. Emspak: Because of hysteria, I think it is my duty to endeavor to protect the rights guaranteed under the Constitution, primarily the First Amendment, supplemented by the Fifth. This committee will corrupt those rights.

Mr. Moulder: Do you think it corrupts you to answer the question?

Mr. Emspak: I certainly do.

Mr. Moulder: Why does it corrupt you?

Mr. Emspak: Your activities are designed to harm the working people of this country. Every action this committee has ever taken has done that. You interfered last summer in the election of a local union at the request of a priest. You know that. You dragged down the prestige of this country.

Mr. Moulder: ... Your statements are preposterous. The purpose of this committee is to expose communism as it exists in this country.... [Y]ou refuse to answer the question?

Mr. Emspak: No. I answered it.

The other witnesses gave similar answers. They were all charged with contempt of Congress. Emspak and Quinn were convicted because they were found not to have claimed their Fifth Amendment privilege to refuse to answer questions when the answers might tend to incriminate them.

ONE WORKER'S FIGHT BACK IN 1952

♦♦ James F. Wood ♦♦
See section 17 for author's note.

I was called into the office at Bechtel, the engineering firm where I worked in San Francisco, and served with a subpoena to appear before the House Un-American Activities Committee. As a result, I was discharged two days later and had about three weeks before my appearance before HUAC.

A few of us had tried to organize a union among the draftsmen and engineers at Bechtel, and I had been working very hard with the Rosenberg-Sobell Committee. Earlier I had worked on the FEPC campaign, and for Henry Wallace and the Progessive Party in 1948. So I wrote a leaflet about my subpoena and my discharge, and how they grew out of my activities. I passed it out to all the employees at Bechtel. Then I had to find a lawyer.

Several people were in the same situation, so we went to the ACLU together.

Two lawyers met with us. They asked the first person some general questions and then concluded by asking if he was currently a member of the Communist Party.

He said no, he had resigned.

They accepted his case and assigned an attorney to represent him. When they came to the next person, they said, "Now what about you?"

He said, "Well, I didn't."

"What do you mean, you didn't?"

One of the lawyers said, "I think he means he didn't resign."

The discussion went on and finally the main lawyer said, "Since you are not free to act on your own, we cannot represent you. We advise you to go elsewhere for a lawyer."

The man who had been subpoenaed said, "That's news to me because I *am* acting on my own." Then he left, and so did I, because I felt they had no business asking that question.

I went to a labor lawyer, Richard Gladstein, who advised me to take the Fifth Amendment as well as the First Amendment, which was my preference.

I did.

After that, I stubbornly insisted on giving Bechtel as a reference when I applied for other jobs, even though they had refused to give me a letter of recommendation. I would be accepted by a firm's engineering office but later dinged by their personnel office, so my only chance of employment was on small, temporary jobs with no prior employment checks.

During the rest of the '50s I was employed about half the time and would have as many as five jobs a year. (I was ultimately rehired at Bechtel in 1972, 20 years after I was fired.)

WATKINS TAKES THE FIRST ONLY

♦♦ The Editors ♦♦

While the appeals of UE's Emspak and Quinn were pending, HUAC called John T. Watkins in April, 1954. He had worked for International Harvester between 1935 and 1942. For 11 years he served as an officer of the Farm Equipment Workers International Union, later merged into UE. In 1953, he joined the United Automobile Workers as a labor organizer. Now he told the Committee: "I am not now nor have I ever been a cardcarrying member of the Communist Party." He explicity contradicted witnesses who said they had recruited him into the Party, although he said that from 1942 to 1947 he cooperated with the Party, made contributions and signed petitions for Communist causes, and attended caucuses at an FE convention at which Communist Party officials were present. He added that on several occasions he opposed their position. "In a special convention held in the summer of 1947 I led the fight for compliance with the Taft-Hartley Act by the FE-CIO International Union. This fight became so bitter that it ended any possibility of future cooperation."

The Watkins testified: "I am not going to plead the Fifth Amendment, but I refuse to answer certain questions that I believe are outside the proper scope of your committee's activities ... nor do I believe that this committee has the right to undertake the public exposure of persons because of their past activities."

He would answer all questions about himself and about people he believed were still members of the Party, but would not answer questions about past members.

Watkins was convicted of contempt of Congress, and appealed.

The next year, 1955, six years after UE leaders Emspak and Quinn testified, the Supreme Court reversed their convictions.

Thereafter, many witnesses refused to answer committee questions based on the Fifth and First Amendments and were not cited for contempt because of the privilege against self incrimination, "a right that was hard-earned by our forefathers," the Court said in *Quinn v. United States*, 349 US 155, at 161 (1955).

The Supreme Court Decides Watkins' Fate

In June, 1957, the Supreme Court considered the conviction of UAW organizer John W. Watkins. The vote was 6-1; Chief Justice Warren wrote the opinion. (It is said, in this connection, that his father had been blacklisted after participating in the Pullman Strike called by the American Railway Union and Eugene V. Debs in 1894.) Now Warren wrote:

> The Bill of Rights is applicable to investigations as to all forms of governmental action. Witnesses cannot be compelled to give evidence against themselves. They cannot be subjected to unreasonable search and seizure. Nor can the First Amendment freedoms of speech, press, religion, or political belief and association be abridged.
>
> ...
>
> Abuses of the investigative process may imperceptibly lead to abridgment of protected freedoms. The mere summoning of a witness and compelling him to testify, against his will, about his beliefs, expressions or associations is a measure of governmental interfer-

ence. And when those forced revelations concern matters that are unorthodox, unpopular, or even hateful to the general public, the reaction in the life of the witness may be disastrous. This effect is even more harsh when it is past beliefs, expressions or associations that are disclosed and judged by current standards rather than those contemporary with the matters exposed.

Nor does the witness alone suffer the consequences. Those who are identified by witnesses and thereby placed in the same glare of publicity are equally subject to public stigma, scorn and obloquy. Beyond that, there is the more subtle and immeasurable effect upon those who tend to adhere to the most orthodox and uncontroversial views and associations in order to avoid a similar fate at some future time. [*354 US 178, at 188, 197-198.*]

After they reversed Watkins' conviction, the Court did not take the next logical step and uphold the right of a witness to refuse to answer questions about political activity based solely on the First Amendment. But the Court did reverse the contempt convictions of several lawyers, performers, teachers, and union members because other rights of theirs had been denied by the committees. They reversed the conviction of a former steelworker from Gary Indiana, who had refused to answer questions before the Committee studying "so-called colonization by the Communist Party in basic industry" in 1958. He and three fellow steelworkers based their refusals on their rights under the First Amendment alone. By 1963 the highest court still was not ready to uphold their right to have political beliefs and to keep them to themselves. But the Court was ready to hold that a worker had a right to make the Committee obey its own rules. Since the Committee said a member of Congress would decide whether to grant a witness a hearing in executive session (without the fanfare of press coverage that could destroy a career), the Committee could not later permit a mere Committee staff person to make that decision. So held the Court majority (5-4) in *Yellin v. United States*, 374 US 109.

This was one of the decisions that encouraged defiance by witnesses and attacks on HUAC and its goals. In several cities from San Francisco and Los Angeles to Honolulu and from Memphis to Buffalo, when HUAC came to town, the progressive movement, including many union members and students, made life uncomfortable for them. Facing massive demonstrations, local politicians not known for their liberal views feared the repercussions of permitting the Un-Americans free rein in their towns. Several times a committee had to leave uncere-

✦✦ ABOLISH HUAC! ✦✦

STILL ALIVE – the "ISM"

ABOLISH HUAC!

Harold Ickes, Secretary of the Interior during the New Deal, said of HUAC: "It has been used to frighten and smear Americans who really believe in the Constitution. It has been used as political blackmail . . . it has terrorized government employees. . . . It is a betrayal of our Bill of Rights." (From *A Quarter Century of Un-Americana, 1938–1963* (New York: Marzani & Munsell, 1963).)

✦✦ Credit: William Gropper. Reprinted with the permission of Sophie Gropper.

moniously before it had called all of the unfriendly witnesses whose lives it was prepared to destroy. [*See descriptions in sections 54, 78 and 83.*]

♦♦♦♦♦♦♦♦♦♦♦♦♦♦♦♦♦♦♦♦♦♦♦♦♦♦
♦   ♦

FORCE AND VIOLINS VS. HUAC

While labor was frequently the peripheral target of the Un-American Activities Committee, in the spring of 1956 in Los Angeles it was the primary target; and as in all HUAC hearings, it was indivisible from the Committee's inherent racism.

The Musicians Union local servicing the entertainment industry was Jim Crow, representing white and Black musicians separately and unequally: the better paid jobs went first to the white unionists, with the Blacks getting only those calls for which no white musician was available. Progressives in both white and Black sections decided to put an end to this discrimination, and petitioned the national American Federation of Muscians to put an end to this practice, with one union for all.

In the midst of this internal union controversy HUAC came to L.A., issuing more than 50 subpoenas to the white unionists who were leading the fight against Jim Crow.

What was the most effective tool the victims could find to defend against the witch-hunt?

Discovering that HUAC had subpoenaed the full complement of a small symphony orchestra, plus two jazz quartets, the subpoenaed musicians arranged a concert on the eve of the hearings, entitled "Force and Violins." Promotional ads were placed in all major newspapers depicting an English horn being searched over by a pair of Sherlock Holmes characters. The concert was a sell-out.

HUAC became the laughing stock in town!

A measure of the breadth of the opposition to HUAC was seen when Dorothy Chandler, wife of the publisher of the conservative *Los Angeles Times* and President of the Los Angeles Philharmonic Orchestra, publicly announced that four of the subpoenaed musicians who were members of Philharmonic would not be removed from their key positions.

Others were not so fortunate, and possibly half of those

subpoenaed were thereafter blacklisted.

Most important: HUAC's mission failed! The following year witnessed the end of Jim Crow in the Musicians Union in Los Angeles. Our Citizens Committee to Preserve American Freedoms, organized in 1952 to defend HUAC subpoenees in L.A., had reason to be proud!

◆◆**Frank Wilkinson,** Executive Director Emeritus, National Committee Against Repressive Legislation

◆◆◆◆◆◆◆◆◆◆◆◆◆◆◆◆◆◆◆◆◆◆◆◆◆◆◆◆◆◆

Finally, the Committee To Abolish HUAC, growing out of Wilkinson's Committee in Los Angeles, became a mighty force from coast to coast. It began carrying on a campaign unique in U.S. history, to convince Congress to kill the monster it had created. [*See the outcome of its work in section 83.*]

58 ⋅⋅ ACADEMIC FALLOUT

♦♦Ann Fagan Ginger♦♦

During the Cold War, the author was a lawyer and wife of Ray Ginger; they divorced in 1957. For 25 years, she has been president of Meiklejohn Civil Liberties Institute and wife of James F. Wood.
© *By Ann Fagan Ginger*

On June 15, 1954, Ray Ginger was Assistant Professor of Research in Business History at the Harvard Business School with a 3-year contract and a best seller, *The Bending Cross: A Biography of Eugene Victor Debs.*

On June 16, 1954, Professor Ginger was forced to submit his resignation to the Harvard Corporation, and flee to New York.

However, the anticipated event that caused his dismissal never came to pass, and after several years, Dr. Ginger made his way back into academia, although never onto the faculty of a top-ranking U.S. university. He went on writing, teaching (and drinking) at the University of Calgary. He died of cirrhosis of the liver during the Christmas season of 1975.

This is one version of his story, paralleled at institutions of higher learning all over the United States.

Ray Ginger (1924-1975)

Narrator   Would Ray have dared live out his years
              If Harvard, when the need appeared,
              Had said: "This University
              Will not demand conformity"?

58 ♦♦ Academic Fallout ♦ 505

Would Ray have quaffed a safer juice
If fabled Harvard had produced,
In '54, from minds with spine,
One sparkling glass of freedom wine?

Instead, Ray found, with neutral myth
That academic monolith
Gave forth the ivied stench of fear.
He caught no scent of courage there.

From Bundy and Kissinger, Galbraith and Conant,
No clarion call against the rodent
That was gnawing the rope of hard-won knowledge
Created from free research at the College.

♦

The Harvard Business School had needed
To balance its staff with a different breed.
They'd picked Ray Ginger, young and eager,
A midwest boy, not rich, but clever;

Eugene V. Debs his thesis choice,
That railroad man with ardent voice
Who raised a union, saw it smashed to hell
And read Karl Marx in his prison cell.

Suddenly Harvard demanded to know—
Today, tonite, before tomorrow—

Harvard Narrator	"Are you now, or have you ever been?" The latest test of mortal sin.
Harvard Narrator	"Are you now or have you ever been?" An oath grown loud into a din Of microphones and TV lights, Of grillings, blacklists, broken rights.

That day Ray's wife, law books in hand,
Was spotted with a "wanted" man
Who drove her home, when she was weary,
With son in tow from a law library.

Ann	(I was writing a brief for that man of math, Professor Struik, M.I.T. The charge was "forceful overthrow," Which meant I'd never get a fee.
	Law books are large, my time was near, I saw no need to stop and ponder. An extenuating circumstance? To whom should I protest, I wonder?)

Harvard	"The driver, 'they' warned us, (there's little time) He's Civil Rights Congress!"
Ray	"That's a crime?"
Harvard	"We're not engaged in search for truth— Sign this new oath!"
Ray	"Don't be uncouth."
Harvard	"We gave you a contract, a chance for fame— Academic freedom."
Ray	"Only in name."
Harvard	"But minds we buy, they should stay bought."
Ray	"That's not the lesson I was taught. From 'yellow dog' to 'loyalty,' An oath's an oath. That's history. When the boss says, 'Sign,' a worker refuses— That's the course a free man chooses."
Harvard	"You vow that you will never sign— So easy, on the dotted line? You're a suspect class!"
Ray	"But who's to say Am I suspect, or is it they? I've other questions at this time: What exactly is our crime? And what's the oath's redeeming value?"
Harvard	"Let's simply change the subject, shall we? This oath is based on a clear, felt need."
Ray	"It's blasphemy against our creed! On whom does it hang the test of truth? And where does it place the burden of proof? The First Amendment states our rights— You can't retract them over night. If free souls slowly find their reason No witches need to burn this season."
Harvard	"Sign this new oath—or leave, we warn, Right now, before the headlines— And we will pay you one check more— Three months until your breadline."
Ann	"You're a prof and I'm a lawyer— There must be some way we can prosper. Let's try the Law School faculty."
Ray	"You think we'll find some sympathy?"

Ann	"Mark DeWolf Howe's the man to see, A prof of proper pedigree— ACLU, AAUP, You need not lack for empathy."
Howe	"What issue's here? Why don't you sign? You've no support, right down the line. And *Harvard* asked; it's not some other, Divulge it, sir, as to your mother."
Ray	"Why stay and wait? Subpoenas sure From one committee, or from four; The state, the feds, both Senate and House— They call the man, and then the spouse. The Fifth Amendment, could I take it?"
Ann	"The precedent's murky—let me check it. Long years ago it saved John Lilburn— Perhaps today it will be your turn."
Ray	"What of the First? That friend to all, That absolute—when did it fall?"
Ann	"With Thomas Paine and Plymouth Rock, 'The Rights of Man'—all out of stock." ("Why didn't you sue," they ask today, "For a 3-year contract clearly broken?" "With a Harvard judge and a Boston jury? We'd be out of court in one quick hurry. Kind Joseph Welsh, McCarthy's foe, Had not yet worked his retribution. And he bemoaned the taint alone, Not loss of right to revolution.")
Narrator	It was late June. Next month he came, A second son, born without pain In Beth Israel Hospital, deep in Manhattan In the charity ward for the misbegotten. The social worker asked the questions. The wife gave answers, full of caution.
Hospital	"But it makes no sense, if he's a teacher— You must have friends, and funds, and future...?"
Ann	(How to explain, how much to tell What happened just before we fell?) "He's unemployed," (blacklisted, too, In this time of the toad when false is true.

| | It's 'fifty-four, please understand,
| | There is a man holds in his hand
| | The lists that fire, the lies that burn—
| | It's Senator Joe McCarthy's turn.)

Narrator   At subway stop two men appear.
FBI   "Are you Ray Ginger? FBI here.
           We want to know, now you have fled,
           Have you lost faith in all that's red?
           Will you name names, with time and date?
           —You'll find we will accommodate."
Ann   So how can you build a family life
           With Law-and-Order creating strife?

◆

Narrator   There is a rule—black letter law—
           That one intends the probable.
           When Harvard demands that somebody flee
           They light his path to obscurity.

           But he wasn't subpoenaed after he left,
           An academic cast adrift.
           So "Ginger, Ray" was not their quarry.
           He took the rap for Harvard.
Prof   "Sorry,
           He made his choice."
Prof   "He's grown quite sour."
Prof   "I hear he's lost his teaching power."
Prof   "His tongue's grown sharp; his pen cuts deep."
Prof   "He mumbles Marxist in his sleep."
Narrator   Finally, with wife number three,
           Ray Ginger fled to Calgary
           With McCarthy's cross still firmly affixed
           He moved backward in time, away from the risk.

           Just two decades the fallout took
           To leave its mark on every book.
           And Harvard's crop, sown cowardly,
           We're reaping now, relentlessly.

           And still the ironies come down—
           You know, Ray died in Boston town.

59 ⋅⋅ THE FATAL SCORE

♦♦ Alvah Bessie ♦♦

Alvah Bessie, a Hollywood playwright, became one of the "Hollywood Ten" who defied the inquisitors. After serving his one year sentence for contempt of Congress, he wrote Men in Battle *and* Bread and a Stone.
This excerpt is from the 1985 Bill of Rights Journal *(National Emergency Civil Liberties Committee), published with permission.*

In addition to permanent exclusion from one's chosen field of employment, social ostracism, divorce, and voluntary exile (a list that numbers many hundreds if not thousands), there have been even greater tragedies that cannot be forgotten. For in the roll call of victims of the proliferating local, state, and national witchhunting committees, there are many who cannot answer. Their premature deaths from "natural" causes and from suicide may be laid directly or indirectly at the doors of these inquisitorial outfits.

Number among them: John Garfield, heart attack preceding his second scheduled appearance before the un-Americans; Harry Dexter White, assistant to the Secretary of the Treasury, heart attack following appearance before the Committee, where he denied Whittaker Chambers' accusations that he had headed an espionage ring; Mady Christians, actress, died following blacklisting, which followed Committee testimony; John Brown, actor, died following blacklisting by all media after decades of performing on the radio; Edwin Rolfe, poet, blacklisted, unemployable, heart attack.

Also, Frances Young, blacklisted actress-wife of blacklisted actor-writer, suicide; Madelyn Dmytryk, former wife of then-blacklisted director, suicide; Philip Loeb, blacklisted actor, suicide; E. Herbert Norman, Canadian ambassador to Egypt, accused by a Senate committee of having been a Communist, suicide; Lawrence Duggan, State Department official, suicide following charges before the un-Americans that he had been a courier for Whittaker Chambers; Abraham Feller, UN general counsel, suicide following appearance before the Senate Internal Security Committee; Raymond Kaplan, Voice of America engingeer, suicide following attack by Senator McCarthy's committee.

Also, Francis O. Matthieson, Harvard professor and renowned critic, suicide following accusation by J.B. Matthews before a Massachusetts legislative committee that he was a Communist-front member; Walter Marvin Smith, Justice Department attorney, suicide after being mentioned as a notary in a transaction involving Alger Hiss; Morton E. Kent, former State Department official, suicide following FBI hounding; John Winant, U.S. ambassador to Britain under FDR, suicide following charges that he had failed to facilitate entry of U.S. troops into Berlin; William K. Sherwood, brilliant young Stanford University research scientist, suicide by poison two days before his scheduled appearance before the un-Americans in San Francisco.

Sherwood's widow, Barbara, attempted to read a statement before the Committee in June of 1957. She was thrown out of the hearing room. This is her statement.

♦♦♦♦♦♦♦♦♦♦♦♦♦♦♦♦♦♦♦♦♦♦♦♦♦♦

MEMBERS OF THE UN-AMERICAN ACTIVITIES COMMITTEE

You have helped kill my husband and make my four children fatherless. That is our personal tragedy.

It is as nothing to the crime you have committed against the children of America and the children of the world.

For when you drove my husband to his death, you destroyed a man of bright promise, a talented fighter in the army of devoted men who are warring against disease.

My husband thought that he had found an important clue to the understanding of cancer and schizophrenia. Perhaps he was mistaken. Only time, and the opportunity to continue his researches, could have supplied the answer.

This opportunity your committee has denied him, and the loss is not only mine.

Throughout his lifetime, my husband had but one goal: to ease the suffering of mankind.

It was this goal that drew him to support the Loyalists in the Spanish Civil War, that inspired his youthful identification with radical causes.

It was this goal that led him, when greater maturity had mellowed and deepened his understanding, to abandon politics completely and devote himself single-mindedly to science.

Is it a crime for a young man in his twenties to dream of a bright new world?

Must the children of our country leave their idealism in the cradle so that their future careers will not be blighted by the Un-American Activities Committee?

And is it fitting, now that he is dead, that you insinuate he was a traitor to his country?

Is not his death enough for you?

Must you also besmirch his honor, now that he is no longer able to answer you?

Members of the Committee, what you have done and what you are doing is an evil thing. Do not persist in it. Go away, go home, bow your heads in prayer and ask forgiveness of your God.

♦♦Barbara Sherwood

RECOGNIZING NECESSITY

♦♦ The Editors ♦♦

One of the paradoxes of the Cold War was the ability of some of its victims to make more money in the new fields to which they were driven by the repression than they had made in the old fields they had chosen out of their early social consciousness. Lessons of analysis, discipline, and group effort learned in the YCL, CP, trade unions, and left-progressive organizations paid off, for some, when they found themselves running family businesses or in other capitalist endeavors.

Later, during the student, Black, and anti-war revolts of the '60s and '70s, some activists learned, for the first time, about the earlier left leanings of their parents, now seemingly happily ensconced in the middle class suburbs.

For the majority, however, the Cold War had no happy ending at the bank.

••PART FIVE••

COLD WAR AGAINST COMMUNITIES

♦♦♦♦♦♦♦♦♦♦♦♦♦♦♦♦♦♦♦♦♦♦♦♦♦♦♦♦♦

Right after World War II, U.S. workers enjoyed a rich community and cultural life. On Saturday night you could take the family to a Hollywood movie, written and acted by progressive union members. You could probably find a place to worship where there would be talk of brotherhood and peace. There were plenty of picket lines to walk, peace petitions to sign, and big parades on Labor Day and May Day.

Veterans could move into public housing projects and attend dances at foreign-language halls, or study at Workers Schools. CIO-PAC worked for candidates who sometimes got elected, while Ladies Auxiliaries worked with the Congress of American Women. Even in small towns, people could subscribe to the Book Find Club and to progressive publications in several languages, could find a liberal teacher and send the kids to a progressive summer camp in the East.

All this had to be destroyed if U.S. labor was to be forced into line. Selections in Part Five describe a few of the people's support systems, and how Big Business and government set out to obliterate them. Having announced a new "Red" enemy abroad, the establishment opened fire at home on the common people, their unions, their culture, and their community.

They faced a strong resistance.

♦♦♦♦♦♦♦♦♦♦♦♦♦♦♦♦♦♦♦♦♦♦♦♦♦♦♦♦♦

60 ⋄⋄ IN THE CITY WAS A GARDEN

⋄⋄Henry Kraus⋄⋄

Once editor of the UAW's newspaper and author of a classic book about the union, The Many and The Few *(Los Angeles: The Plantin Press, 1947), Henry Kraus turned to medical reporting in France during the 1950s and '60s. Today he is working on a history of the UAW-CIO as a MacArthur Fellow.*

This section, adapted from his book, In the City Was A Garden *(New York: Renassance Press, 1951), is reprinted with permission. The names of the characters in this book, a dramatic narrative chronicling events that Kraus and his wife Dorothy experienced, are fictitious.*

To the early settlers at Garden City the name of this San Pedro federal housing project was a source of mockery. The homes were opened while the building rubble was still on the ground. Lawns, flowerbeds and shrubbery eventually gave the project a more obvious title to its florid name. The residents, many of whom played no small part in the process, could and did take a proprietary pride in the exuberant result. Yet it was not this but a different growth that was to characterize the new community more particularly. We at Garden City were drawn together by a commanding impulse: a shared need, a goal in common. We were people with a purpose.

Months before World War II ended people began to anticipate its conclusion and a strange thing took place. Each new success, rather than starting off fireworks of joy, set men to talking worriedly about what-came-next. As work in the shipyards tightened, as Negro and women workers began to be laid off, the lurking insecurities woke to full awareness. V-J Day was only a short respite of joyous effusion....

A large proportion of Garden City breadwinners did not have jobs to return to and unemployment compensation ran out with frightening swiftness. There were no jobs in the harbor but still people stayed on. Families who had long nurtured plans which included a shift of location now suddenly (or not so suddenly) changed their minds. Turnover of rental units during the six months following V-J Day was only slightly above average and thereafter it took a sharp drop.

Mutual Home Ownership Program

It was well known among residents that by the terms of Lanham Act, Garden City (and other federally owned projects) must be declared surplus on termination of hostilities. So, to many of us, mutual home ownership was the logical consequence of four years of living and working in the project, a flowering of the cooperative program into a splendid and permanent form. We made inquiries to the Housing Authority to see how to go about initiating such a program.

Then, one day in January 1946, Garden City residents were stunned by a news item announcing that the federal government was planning to "dispose of" our project and others in a similar category. In our case the Navy was mentioned as being interested. Not a word was said about the occupants or "mutual home ownership."

And suddenly, what the black people had feared for themselves became a reality for all. With the papers full of tales of suicides and other desperate acts of homeless people, the news fell just short of creating panic. A special session of the residents council was convened to consider the emergency. What *could* the residents do: petition, protest? No, there was a better alternative. If the government wanted to sell, we must offer to buy—on a mutual home ownership basis!

There would be no time for preliminaries now. The 600 residents would either have to agree to buy the project or face the likelihood of being evicted. The residents council entered with all vigor into the campaign to popularize the cooperative program. A mass meeting was scheduled and the sudden crisis packed the hall. There were several dozen representatives likewise from other harbor projects which were in the same situation as ourselves. Philip Connelly of the Los Angeles CIO Council gave us a pledge of his support.

The Burke Controversy

There arose at this moment in Los Angeles a clamorous public controversy surrounding the editor of the *Daily People's World*, a leftist West Coast newspaper. Sidney Burke and his family had been living for some months at Rodger Young Village when it was discovered that the editor was not eligible for his apartment. At worst only a clerical error was involved since Burke, a former seaman, had been on the waiting list and should have been assigned to another project when his turn came.

The City Council took vehement note of the matter. The mayor issued a stern edict calling for the immediate eviction of the Burke family. The Housing Authority, operating under its longterm eligibility rules, ordered them transferred to the first opening—at Garden City.

The protests burst into greater fury. The City Council, 11 to 1, demanded that the Burkes be expelled from their new home, threatening "drastic action" for noncompliance. Nicola Giulii, chairman of the Authority, announced a revision of the Authority's "Application for a Dwelling" form to include the following question:

Do you advocate or have you ever advocated, or are you now or have you ever been a member of any organization that advocates the overthrow of the government of the United States by force or violence? If so, give complete details.

There was a deep reluctance on the part of many to become involved in this case. The Burkes were strangers and the wild publicity that had been given them encouraged timidity. The first complaint against this family had been registered with the dreaded House Committee on Un-American Activities, then present in Los Angeles, who turned it over immediately to the newspapers.

The harbor local of the National Maritime Union (CIO) had taken formal notice of the eviction, charging that it had been ordered "in an atmosphere of a witchhunt." The NMU cited Burke's war record: he held service ribbons for both the Atlantic and Pacific and a combat bar for enemy action; and he had served for two-and-a-half years and risen from ordinary seaman to third mate.

When the seamen's appeal to the City Council was read, Libby Burke asked for the floor:

The really dangerous thing here is that if the authorities succeed in shelving the disgraceful housing situation by using smokescreens like this, what will happen to the other things that are so important to the people, like your own mutual ownership program, for example? That's what really counts, and not my husband's political beliefs or the work he does, neither of which is as yet illegal in this country by the way.

Several council members, including myself, spoke in favor of the resolution to revoke the eviction. Edith Cunningham, the mother of two, stressed Mrs. Burke's two young ones: "Are we going to let them put them out on the street?"

The other side was strangely silent throughout. It was only when the chairman was ready to take the vote that Dean Sherman rose. "Communism is not the issue here," he began amazingly. "Some of us may even sympathize very much with Mrs. Burke and her family. But after all it's a choice of one family against 599 families. Because, if we adopt this motion, you can kiss mutual home ownership or anything else you aspire to goodbye."

His argument made a visible effect on its devotees. The decision was 17 to 15 against the resolution. There was a moment of stunned silence; then the Sherman group gave out with a big cheer.

There was a positive feature to the surprise victory of Dean Sherman, which members of the old group promptly seized on. He had indicated a desire to help mutual home ownership. All right! They were prepared if he was to suppress all other differences and concentrate on this one great issue.

Local Elections

Under these auspices, our residents council election campaign began, arousing the general participation of the project in a way that had never before occurred. The insignificance of the posts sought was no criterion. Far more was involved: the ultimates of life's meaning. Both sides felt this sincerely, profoundly. On one side were those who opposed allowing the Burkes to reside in Garden City. On the other, those who sympathized with the Burke family. All the accessories of a bigtime election were present, the accusations of people being "bought off," of candidates changing sides in midstream, of "stoolpigeons" being planted in the other camp.

The Sherman group sent their missionaries out among the black people. Mrs. Voorhees was considered a specialist in this field. Indeed it was unthinkable to this good woman that Negroes—whom she saw as honest, devout, guileless children—would even listen to the "Communists," atheists and anti-Christs that they were. She sought out O.W. Holmes, one of our candidates, and told him how the Communists sought to pit race against race by playing on and exaggerating the grievances of the Negro people.

But Mr. Holmes was a longshoreman and he was amused by Mrs. Voorhees' story: "I don't think the Communists play such an important role, leastwise they're not pulling the wool over anybody's eyes that I can see or making them do things they don't want to do."

"Oh, my! How can you say that, Mr. Holmes, when you know that the government's full of them. And I'm not saying that President Roosevelt is a Communist but his wife surely is. . . ."

"Well, I guess that makes me a Communist too!"

The Sherman group had the further disadvantage of not having placed a single Negro on their slate. We had seven black people out of the 21 on ours.

On the Sunday starting the last week of the campaign, I was making the rounds of some of the "doubtful" people when my wife, Dorothy, called me at a neighbor's. "Have you seen the latest leaflet the Sherman crowd are distributing?" Dorothy's voice vibrated with anger. "It's fantastic. Prints a long list of names of people they say are Communists." Nowhere did the handout actually say that the listed people were Communists. Only that they had "repeatedly supported Communists and the Communist cause," and "repeatedly opposed the anti-Communists."

The first burst of anger at the appearance of the list wilted in most cases to second thoughts of fear and retreat. Several of those named got Sherman's promise to print an "apology," covering them alone, by pledging to disassociate themselves from our group.

Next day Henry Fisher and I went to see a labor lawyer. He examined the leaflet. "It's very doubtful if the leaflet is libelous. First, it seems to have had pretty careful legal screening. And then again, there are conflicting precedents as to whether calling a person a Communist constitutes libel."

♦♦COMMUNISTS IN ACTION♦♦

This drawing appeared in the pamphlet, "The Communist Manifesto in Pictures" published by International Book Store, Inc. in San Francisco in 1948.
♦♦ Credit: Bits Hayden.

"But people may lose their jobs over this," Fisher said.

The lawyer, an old, experienced hand, screwed his face into a grimace. "Of course. That's exactly the kind of stock these characters deal in."

It wasn't until several weeks later that Jim Patterson, a Negro who was on our slate, was fired from his job as guard in the Navy depot on Terminal Island. Patterson was given a few vague words about "unsatisfactory associations" before being terminated. The father of five young boys chose to appeal the decision through regular civil service channels.

Our campaign came to a whimpering end. Half our candidates retired without an answering shot. Under the circumstances it was remarkable that our group won seven of the 21 places on the new committee, including O.W. Holmes and myself.

A strange calm asserted itself at the council meeting at which the new committee was installed. Even those who had been hurt by the leaflet appeared eager to let the matter rest.

FPHA Appraisal

Then Lillian Berger lifted a letter from her file. "I just got this this evening. It came special delivery. From Washington." Suddenly we knew that it was the Federal Public Housing Authority appraisal, so long and impatiently awaited. Finally she read a figure: one million, six-hundred-thousand dollars. It sounded utterly out of reach, and no one seemed prepared to reduce astronomy to arithmetic.

But capable Mrs. Berger had of course taken care of that. Her sharp-chinned face took on an almost beatific look. "That makes two thousand, six hundred and sixty-six dollars and sixty seven cents apiece." She offered it as though on a glittering golden platter. "Actually, it's a good deal less than it cost to build these units under pre-inflation values," she added.

There was a momentary hush, then a sort of group sigh of pleasure, and finally a splash of applause. Forgotten were the obstacles still standing in the way, the experience just gone through which cast its own cloud on what was yet to come.

As Lillian Berger picked up her papers, prepared to surrender her post, her husband came forward. Disregarding the gavel, Berger flayed the "cowards who wouldn't even sign their names but came like thieves in the night to attack people and besmirch their character." He broke off, then turned to his wife, and the two swept magnificently out of the hall.

The dam had been burst. Bob Lamar, off his ship for a couple of days, quoted the United States Constitution and said that no one had the right to monopolize Americanism. Artemiza Ramirez, her voice heavy and her eyes full, told of her opponent saying that the "Reds" in the project ought to be put in concentration camps. "How do they know how many Communists there are here?" Essie Rodney demanded. "I thought we had a secret ballot." Word-chary Buck Despol uttered one of his rare comments: "I been a Democrat all my life." And Edith Cunningham reported that the project manager had told her that quarrels between neighbors that reached the office had hit an all-time high during the campaign.

A motion was made and adopted to reprimand those who had distributed the "Communist" list together with the election committee's official announcement. Dean Sherman said that only one or two people had handed out the two leaflets together. "It certainly was never sanctioned by us."

I had been as eager as anyone for "peace" but this was a little too much!

Mutual Home Ownership Gutted for the Last Time

As it happened, new developments in Washington called desperately for a united front of the tenants. The U.S. House of Representatives had just adopted a measure which if validated by the Senate would finally succeed in tearing the project away from its occupants.

Shortly after President Truman won his surprise victory at the polls in November 1948, Federal Public Housing Authority (FPHA) announced its readiness once more to dispose of the permanent housing projects along mutual ownership lines, with somewhat changed financing. The residents of Garden City were at long last offered the opportunity of purchasing their homes cooperatively.

But it was too late. Membership in the organization had fallen way off. As old residents left the project, new tenants had not been asked to join; money shortage and other obstacles had buried the plan beyond salvage. As the interest of private real estate groups perked up again the remnants of the old council crowd turned to the city as a last resort, urging that it purchase the project and operate it as a low-income rental unit. Negotiations between FPHA and the local Housing Authority had been brought, in the words of an official, "to the point of the actual signing of the transfer documents when, late last year [1950], because of the threatening international situation, a temporary freeze was put on all disposition of housing projects."

Thus did the noble idea of tenant ownership at Garden City, which was to be the seal and pinnacle of five years of cooperative effort, come to an end.

61 ♦♦ CANCELING WORKERS' INSURANCE POLICIES

♦♦ Albert E. Kahn ♦♦

A prolific writer, the late Albert Kahn served as president of the Jewish Peoples Fraternal Order of the IWO during the Cold War.
 This section is adapted from his pamphlet, "The People's Case: The Story of the IWO" (1951).

"The atmosphere in Washington today," wrote Joseph and Stewart Alsop in their column in the *New York Herald-Tribune* on March 17, 1948, "is no longer a postwar atmosphere. It is, to put it bluntly, a pre-war atmosphere." "A pattern of suppression is today evolving at the highest levels of the Federal Government," soberly warned a public statement issued by 22 faculty members of the Yale University Law School.

Such was the atmosphere in which President Truman promulgated his Loyalty Order, and the Attorney General compiled his list of "disloyal organizations" in the country. [*See section 29.*] Among the prgressive organizations included on the initial list on December 4, 1947, was the International Workers Order, founded at a national conference of 200 delegates in March 1930. Incorporated under the insurance law of New York State, the society had "the purpose of providing insurance benefits and advancing the mutual protection, health, cultural, educational and recreational interests and well-being of its members"—workingmen and their families.

Beginning with a membership of some 5,000 Jewish men and women, most former members of the Workmen's Circle, the IWO embarked upon a spirited membership campaign. At its peak, the membership of the IWO numbered 185,000, functioning in 15 national societes, some named after Garibaldi, Cervantes, Douglass-Lincoln, and others after Croatian, Czech, and other nationality groups. The national societies conducted concerts and folk festivals, dramatic performances and pageants, dances, lectures and sports tournaments. An indication of their variety and extensiveness is the cultural program of a single year in the Jewish Peoples Fraternal Order alone: 18 chorus groups, 25 dance groups, 6 dramatic groups, 65 concerts in 61 cities, 131 showings of films, several nationwide lecture tours, publication and distribution of books of prose and poetry.

The phenomenal growth of the IWO was due to the practical, much-needed benefits which Order members derived from an insurance program whose every feature was painstakingly designed to meet the special problems of the working people: policies at rates far below those of commercial insurance firms; the absence of any waiting period for the payment of sick benefits; low-cost medical care for whole families, and no discrimination for "bad risks."

As the only large interracial non-discriminatory fraternal benefit society in the United States, the IWO—in the words of Edward L. Nelson, Executive Secretary of the Douglass-Lincoln Society—"shook the very foundation of the theory that Negroes must be charged more for insurance." From the first, the IWO sought to achieve desperately needed and long overdue legislation providing social security and unemployment insurance for the American people, old age pensions and national health programs, low-cost housing, public works and adequate educational facilities. IWO members zealously fought for the right of labor to organize and bargain collectively for a living wage. IWO branches and lodges rushed food and funds to strikers, set up first-aid medical stations and mobilized public protest against company-instigated violence.

World War and Inquisition

The day after the Japanese attack on Pearl Harbor, the General Executive Board of the IWO met in a special emergency session. In a statement translated into all the languages of the national societies and swiftly distributed among Order lodges throughout the country, the Board pledged: "We unreservedly place our organization, our labors and our lives at the service of this, our homeland." Approximately 10,000 members of the IWO, a large percentage of whom were volunteers, served in the U.S. armed forces. Many were wounded in action; several hundred died on the battlefields of Europe and Asia. On the homefront, in the nation's factories, mines, and mills, IWO members sought by every possible means to give full meaning to Roosevelt's phrase—Arsenal of Democracy. The Order membership itself bought $30,000,000 worth of war bonds and contributed, in addition, more than $10,000,000 to American and Allied war relief agencies and for the rehabilitation of war-torn Europe.

But victory brought inclusion of the IWO on the list of "subversive organizations," which had swift and far-reaching effects.

The Commissioner of Internal Revenue rescinded the tax exempt status of the Order's Relief and Rehabilitation Fund and revoked the Treasury Department's previous ruling that the Order itself was a tax exempt organization. IWO members in Government employ were hounded by federal investigators and, in a number of cases, dismissed from their jobs. Several key figures in the Order were arrested for deportation. In various states, insurance commissions initiated proceedings to revoke the insurance licenses of the organization. At the same time, the 1949 issue of *Dunne's Insurance Report*, the largest policyholders insurance service in the world, had rated IWO insurance as "A plus (Excellent) ... [with] a margin of safety ... greatly above average.... We conclude that the International Workers Order, Inc. of New York is worthy of public confidence and so we recommend it."

The total assets of the IWO at the time of this Dunne Report exceeded $6,000,000! The Order had in force insurance amounting to more than $110,000,000 and had paid out up to that time more than $13,000,000 in benefits.

On February 18, 1949, the Order sued the U.S. Attorney General to enjoin him from continuing to designate the Order as a subversive organization and directing him to remove its name from his list, and to find the Executive Order unconstitutional.

But, over one year later, the IWO remained on the list, and the Superintendent of Insurance for New York filed a petition to liquidate IWO business and dissolve its corporate existence.

Court proceedings commenced on January 29, 1951, challenging the dissolution order. During the first five weeks of the trial, 13 witnesses testified for the prosecution—a sordid array of labor spies, renegade Communists, professional informers, and persons with police records.

The prosecutor granted that as an insurance institution the IWO was in an unquestionably sound financial condition. But he solemnly advised the judge, "The possibility is not to be ignored that in the event of war or threatened war with Russia, the organization would find some means to transfer its assets to that country.... You know, your Honor, we are at war with Russia! ... The losses of Latvia, Lithuania, Estonia, Poland, Hungary, Romania, Bulgaria, East Germany, Czechoslovakia, China, and North Korea are fresh in our minds. The precarious situations in France and Italy are our current concern. ..." While this trial was going on in the state court, across the street in federal court, Judge Irving Kaufman was trying the cases of Julius and Ethel Rosenberg and Morton Sobell for atomic espionage.

A dramatic highlight of the IWO trial came when the defense attorneys called to the witness stand the insurance examiner whose report had precipitated the liquidation proceedings against the Order. Under insistent questioning, he admitted that despite an extensive study of IWO records he had been unable to discover the slightest indication of insurance malpractices or financial unsoundness in the organization.

Two weeks later, the U.S. Supreme Court ruled that the manner of the Attorney General's listing of the IWO in December 1947 as a subversive organization was "arbitrary" and "unconstitutional." The vote was 5-to-3 (341 U.S. 123). Since the liquidation proceedings against the Order had been initiated on the ground of its inclusion on the Attorney General's list, there now seemed sound reason to expect the voiding of the liquidation action.

But on April 5th, 1951 Judge Kaufman sentenced the Rosenbergs to death, and Sobell to 30 years. And on June 4th, the U.S. Supreme Court upheld the convictions of the 11 national leaders of the Communist Party under the Smith Act.

So on June 25, Judge Greenberg sustained the right of the Insurance Department to liquidate the insurance benefit society.

Thereafter, the State of New York confiscated the property of 162,000 Americans, many of whom were unable to obtain new insurance protection, and none of whom could purchase non-discriminatory, low-cost insurance comparable to that provided by the IWO.

62 ◆◆ A COMMUNITY MEDICAL CENTER FOR WORKERS

◆◆Stephen H. Fritchman◆◆

Before, during, and after the Cold War, Stephen Fritchman was pastor of the First Unitarian Church of Los Angeles.

The following is reprinted with permission of Frances Fritchman from Stephen Fritchman's book, Heretic: A Partisan Biography *(Boston: Beacon Press, 1977).*

An invitation by the Community Medical Foundation in Los Angeles to serve as president of its board of trustees at first sounded like the conventional request for a Unitarian minister to add another neighborhood organization to his list of groups calling for some token board meetings and ceremonial appearances. When Ken Hartford, the executive director, invited me in 1951 to make a visit to the center, showed me the cramped quarters, the manifestly inadequate equipment and the hard-pressed staff, I knew this was no pro-forma invitation to be an absentee sponsor who had a "Reverend" before his name. Here was a group busy in precept and practice defying the sacrosanct rubrics of the California Medical Association.

The Community Medical Center, operated by the Foundation, was unique at that time in the State of California. It was established in 1946 to serve middle and low-income individuals and families from the working class areas around its quarters on South Broadway, in Watts and South Central Los Angeles, "the forgotten people of medicine," as their brochure put it.

Dr. Alexander Riskin and a handful of other doctors who had served in World War II believed there existed a critical need for a cooperatively-run clinic to serve a predominantly poor neighborhood with all ethnic groups among the patients. The fundamental concept was that it should be interracial, nonprofit, and doctor-and-patient and union-controlled. The clinic's medical policies were drawn up by the medical staff, but otherwise it was to be governed by a lay foundation working closely with the recipients of the medical care. This proved to be no tranquil or easy accomplishment.

Most Unitarians considered themselves sympathetic with workers but actually did not know them as living, breathing flesh-and-blood people. Truck drivers, garbage collectors, electricians, auto mechanics, furniture workers were people, but not persons one expected to find at the P.T.A. or a church potluck dinner. I had struggled against this genteel exclusiveness of Unitarians for two decades, and knew that the only way I could expect to see workers inside my own church on Eighth Street was to share their acute problems as low-income citizens with plenty of gripes and frustrations. Unless a few of us "of the cloth" could break this isolation, I felt our entire profession would soon be an endangered species and at least irrelevant chaplains to the more affluent sections of the bourgeoisie.

I saw, also, that a clinic in which working people shared responsibility could make a great difference in their own lives—for better health care and for recognition as people usually ignored in the decision-making process.

The California Medical Association and the state government were militantly opposed to such a project. It was an open threat to the medical profession and its highly profitable privileges, both in prestige and the cash nexus. The unions that cooperated with the clinic knew that the experience of enjoying low medical fees and first-rate health care would inevitably educate their members in many other areas also, in the factory and shop, in the schools, in the markets and in their community social agencies. And so it proved to be.

We had some mighty struggles to put our principles into practice where the traveling was uphill all the way. The Center doctors who banded together were very able physicians and surgeons; yet all of them became the target of abuse and slander from many of their colleagues: Drs. Harold Koppelman, Irwin Cole, Leo Bigelman, Milton London, Price Cobbs,

Thomas Perry, Cyril Shepro, Robert Peck. We became close friends. Supporting them in those years of struggle were a group of lay men and women, incorruptible trade-unionists and community workers.

During 1953 and 1954, history was testing the commitment of men and women who, in their words and work, showed a concern far beyond their immediate class loyalties. President Dwight Eisenhower had admonished his listeners at a Dartmouth College Commencement in June of 1953 to beware the book-burners, warning that thought-control was endangering freedom. The president was referring to Joseph McCarthy's demand that books by Communists and fellow-travelers in State Department libraries be removed. One year later, in June 1954, J. Robert Oppenheimer lost his clearance as a consultant to the Atomic Energy Commission, against the advice of many leading scientists. His crime: that his "associations with persons known to be Communists have far extended beyond the tolerable limits of prudence and self-restraint." An investigating panel for the A.E.C. also suggested that he be dismissed for "lacking enthusiasm" for the hydrogen bomb project.

Meanwhile, in the same month, a socialist and democratic government in Guatemala was overthrown and a military fascist junta took power (with intervention by the C.I.A. admitted in 1975), and U.S. Social Security amendments added new categories of beneficiaries, which increased the rolls by ten million people, including farm and domestic workers.

In such times, with such efforts to show a token attitude of liberalism, but to punish any deep involvement in the struggle to change the prevailing system of state power, the men and women, trustees, staff and patients at the Medical Center did their job and did it well. They succeeded in providing first-rate medical care, preventative and curative, on an individual doctor-patient basis, to income groups unable to pay specialists' fees or to qualify for charitable aid. This was long before the timid beginnings of prepaid health care to the poor and aged by state and federal agencies.

Soon after I joined the Foundation the decision was made to move to larger quarters in an old-time mansion on South Lake Street, where major alterations made it a far more desirable location for our program. By this time the clinic had served some 20,000 patients, with a staggering total of 72,000 patient visits with 25 kinds of treatment. Here was an authentic people's center with x-ray technicians, nurses, laboratory specialists, office workers, custodians, doctors and surgeons who were indeed of all nationalities, all creeds, all races. It was a pilot plant of medical humanitarianism in an America that gave scant evidence that it cared about the masses of its citizens. It was a rough task at times, in our board and committee meetings, to have trade-unionist trustees understand some of the basic problems faced by the doctors, the accountants, and the office staff, to reconcile the contradictions between the various groups, inexperienced in commitment to a cooperative venture. We were an island surrounded by a social matrix which advocated doctrines of competition and self-aggrandizement as the appropriate values to be pursued.

In April, 1954, the Community Medical Foundation held a testimonial dinner in my honor, where 800 friends shared an evening of collective celebration of the fact that we could now, eight years since the first clinic opened, speak of our undertaking as "one of the nation's most successful health organizations." So much that a minister does day after day seems tragically intangible, like water that soaks into the ground and is lost; but after that night I was persuaded that the particular oar I pulled at the clinic for four years was not an act of sheer futility. Even a dissenting parson could feel a momentary flame of pentacostal fire hovering over his head.

The Community Medical Center was evidence to me that a truly humane society with none oppressing and none oppressed was a realistic goal for mankind. I decided that I had chosen an exceptionally rewarding vocation, as catalyst or middleman, a dealer in futures for what the Book of Common Prayer called "all sorts and conditions of men."

The 1954 onslaught by state and federal investigators into opinions and politics succeeded in scattering some of the patients who were understandably fearful of having the inquiries reach them, as well as threatening the physicians and staff workers with the very real possibility of jobs being lost and new employment being made even more difficult to find in the prevailing social climate. There was hardly a one of those in our community clinic who did not receive in due time a subpoena to testify regarding their "socialistic" sins before one or another of the state or federal investigative committees.

I am sure other groups will brave the tide in years to come until a rational health and hospitalization plan is achieved by federal legislation. Programs of health care for all citizens have already been achieved in the Soviet Union, Great Britain,

Scandinavia, the People's Republic of China, and many other countries.

It can happen here.

A few long-lived Americans in Los Angeles will some day remember a modest and premature venture on South Lake Street in the days of Senator Burns in Sacramento and Senator Nixon in Washington and know that witch-hunting and welfare-fund impoundment did not forever prevent a subsidized national health program. Chicago, Seattle, and Los Angeles will some day catch up with Toronto, Odessa, and Shanghai. Broken bones will be mended free of charge, in all America, from sea to shining sea.

This pilot project dissolved in 1955. Many factors brought it to a close, primarily a ruling by the State Board of Business and Professional Standards, which made it impossible, for all practical purposes, to conduct a doctor-patient cooperative enterprise. Doctors could have clinics, with diverse specialties represented, but without the innovations that had characterized our center of service to low-income groups.

63 ❖❖ TRUMPET PLAYER: 52nd STREET

❖❖ Langston Hughes ❖❖

This poem by the famous Afro-American writer Langston Hughes appeared in the Winter 1947 issue of Masses & Mainstream.

Masses & Mainstream, *successor to* The Masses *of the 1910s and* New Masses *of the 1930s, was a Marxist literary magazine featuring short stories, poetry, essays, reportage, criticisms, columns, drawings, and political cartoons. The magazine's editors, in addition to publishing the work of leading writers and artists from left and progressive circles, consciously sought out new talent, especially among working people.*

The Negro
With the trumpet at his lips
Has dark moons of weariness
Beneath his eyes
Where the smoldering memory
Of slave ships
Blazed to the crack of whips
About his thighs.

The Negro
With the trumpet at his lips
Has a head of vibrant hair
Tamed down,
Patent-leathered now
Until it gleams
Like jet—
Were jet a crown.

The music
From the trumpet at his lips
Is honey
Mixed with liquid fire.
The rhythm
From the trumpet at his lips
Is ecstasy
Distilled from old desire—

Desire
That is longing for the moon
Where the moonlight's just a spotlight
In his eyes,
Desire
That is longing for the sea
Where the sea's a bar-glass
Sucker size.

The Negro
With the trumpet at his lips
Whose jacket
Has a *fine* one-button roll,
Does not know
Upon what riff the music slips
Its hypodermic needle
In his soul—

But softly
As the tune comes from his throat
Trouble
Mellows to a golden note,
And smoky fog
Of pearl-grey air grows sweet
As dreams come back
To 52nd Street.

64 ⋄⋄ AWOL

⋄⋄ **George Bratt** ⋄⋄

This poem by worker-poet George Bratt appeared in the May, 1951 issue of Masses & Mainstream.

Where are you Karl Tappe, former shaper man for H. Karp &
   Son?
Did you finally call the turn on wishful thinking
and really go back to Chicago?
And was your rendezvous with Karl Tappe, furniture worker
of two decades ago, a success?
Or did you simply fail to snap out of your vacation paycheck
   drunk?

You didn't leave us, your shopmates, much of a forwarding
   address.
Just "Not here" via your old Valencia St. hotel,
and a blank space in our local business agent's report.
Now you are an unsettled memory that stands punctually by
each morning ready to start up the machines.

Although you were witty, loved musical shows and had a
voice to appeal to receptive women,
noon-hour sessions with you were no great cultural treat.
It took job action to get you to vote at the polls,
and the threat of a five-dollar fine to integrate you
with a union meeting.

But that long silent partnership we had with you!
Those grinding, interminable, laborious hours when Tappe,
pencil in hat, was king,
the dust and crap spurting off the shrieking shaper
and haloing you truly as an adorable human being!—
Where now are we to find the clue to *him?*—
In the unsigned door jambs of sundry homes?
Hidden away in the machined drawers of their kitchen cabinets?
In the thousand nameless places where workers have left
the token of their sweat, sacrifice and devotion?

Where are you now, Brother Tappe?
Where are you fellow-worker?

65 ♦♦ A BOY AND HIS GUN

♦♦Patrick E. Gorman♦♦

The late Patrick Gorman, veteran secretary-treasurer of the Amalgamated Butcher Workman-AFL, and a socialist, is said to have written this poem. [Gorman is described in section 50.]

My neighborhood was all run down—
Ramshackled, I would say—
But I lived so long in one old house
I could not move away.
Then rodents came upon the scene
And with them came a dread,
So I bought my youthful son a gun
So he could shoot them dead.

My boy was happy with his gift;
His rodent aim was fine.
He shot to kill, and kill he did.
He got one every time.
But soon I got an awful shock—
A shock that turned me pale.
My boy not only killed a rat—
He killed a nightingale!

The Clock of time proved well to me
He should not have a gun
A weapon with the power to kill
Entrusted to my son.
The years rolled on, my boy grew up
And all my well laid plans
Resulted in a broken heart—
My boy had killed a man!

A jury listened out his trial,
The guilty verdict read.
A prison term was meted out,
My boy just drooped his head.
He shed a tear and so did I—
They led him down a stair
I somehow found a soul in him—
His lips had moved in prayer.

Back to my run down neighborhood I wandered, sad, alone—
The house, ramshackled, welcomed me—
Twas solace, it was home.
I gazed upon a photograph,
I kissed it—twas my son.
I wondered what he might have been
Had I not bought a gun.

66 ◆◆ THE CLIMATE OF TERROR

◆◆Eve Merriam◆◆

Eve Merriam, author of poetry and prose, had this poem published in the November 1950 issue of Masses & Mainstream, *reprinted with the author's permission.*

Can the tree, uprooted from earth, echo any green?
Leaf, whirling in wind, bear fruit upon the air?
This is my native ground.

My husband, my unborn seed, childhood, womantime
Leaf-tangled and liquid with memoried hope,
Hand, heart are here.

Now it is Judgment Day.
American, ashamed, I cannot abdicate.
In the dock I stand.

Once I hated Germans.
All. My voice was cold and hard as a stone.
The last meek clerk filing his pallid papers
Who never saw a gas chamber, never fired a gun,
The mother crooning My baby, my baby is my whole wide world...
Murderers.

Still I would tear out tree from ground
And wait stupidly for April;
Exile hand from arm, breath from body,
Pump my heart into a glass jar—

—Pleading to the Koreans north and south:
Not I who stake your birthright,
Not my commandment "Shoot and then ask questions."
—To the Viet-Namese, the Huks, the human targets everywhere:
These bullets marked made in U.S.A.
I did not order them,
My name is less capitalized than Du Pont.

—To the marshallized millions
By the grace of gold and trumanity
Starving on a mash of gangster films and Coca-Cola:
This meal was not my planning.

—To the women of China, in daylight after blindness,
Blinking at the nightmare boast:
"I dropped the atom bomb and I would do it again."
Understand, I have no access to the White House.

—To the conscience of the world:
I am not the Chase National Bank,
Neither General Motors nor MacArthur.

Do not curse me.
Do not spit upon my head.
I am not the wardrobe-traveled tourist
Modelling this season's dollar;
I am that other America
Standing aside
Good, kind, disliking Jim Crow.

(Blood upon my dress?
Berry stains from a picnic in the sun.

A shadow covers the sun,
A fiery cross...)

So the hand broken off at the arm
Like a deadwood branch;
Maggots picnic on the strump.
So the breath from the body
Gaping, ghostly:
Shall the glass jar live?

America, ashamed, I cannot abdicate.
There is no separation.
There is no separate peace.

Whom shall I blame?
The squirrel, the robin, the cow champing in the grass?
Being human, being American,
I cast a shadow across the sun.

My hand upon the vault,
My touch upon the trigger.

My native land defaced with more than billboards.
The iodine bottle fed to children for milk,
The cesspool drained into a dinner glass
And thirstily crying for more,
Crying Communist, Communist,
And crying for more.
Hostages: teacher, artist, scientist, worker
And more, war more...
The Bull of Birmingham snorts:
"Twenty-four hours for all the Reds to get out of town,"
And his horns are gouging for
Every daughter and son of Sojourner Truth.
In the State capital of Mississippi
Newspaper editor and governor declare a holiday:
Open season for hunting down "civil righters."
Epithet: you dirty Constitution-lover.
On to Union Square, New York, where the mounted police
Add to their chivalry: women and young people first
And allthegoddamjews.
Detectives' heel on a Negro's neck:
"Now will you say Mister?"

Hiding my face hugging my silence,
Into the dock I fall.

Joliot-Curie unbending stands above me.
Nina Popova will not stroke my brow.
From Malaya cutting through the jungle and the foremen's lash,
From the mines of Africa fiercer than diamonds
The jury's eyes melt down my hiding place.
From Neruda's Chile, the copper mine-shaft under the twilight sea
Rises in noonbright judgment;
From the Mexican mountain-top, farmer tilling the purple cliff
Leaps down to vow his verdict;
From the ends of the earth
The unmistaking universal call.

Criminal, your government, your condemnation.
Your country the climate of terror.
Shall you be exempt because
You perspire in the heat?
    Guilty.
Shall you be relieved
By fanning yourself with a kerchief?
    Guilty!
You must stamp out the fire with your own burning hands.
    Guilty

Of only the greatest crime do I plead
Not guilty.

That of despair,
That of the barren stub-end of the world.

Return
Breath to body, flesh to flesh,
Tree to root
And stand my native ground.

Behold, with pain with burning and with ashes
The leaf put forth
And the tiny fisted bud;
I am fruitful at last,
I multiply.

The few, the thousandfold
The strong and the timid (I too am timid)
Stand our native ground.

From the night of the poor we gather,
And in the darkness build
Not waiting for the darkness to lift,
But pushing it back, rolling the morning in

Taking (for we know it is ours to demand)
As the solid ground beneath our feet
Peace

Taken for granted, natural,
Peace indivisible and everywhere, unbroken as sunlight,
A firm foothold

And go on
To taller things.

67 ♦♦ FIGHTING JIM CROW IN THE NATION'S CAPITAL: MARY CHURCH TERRELL

♦♦ **Marvin Caplan** ♦♦

Marvin Caplan served as Publicity Chairman during the campaign to desegregate eating-places in the nation's capital. Today he is chair of Friends of Histadrut, active in Neighbors Incorporated, which works for integrated housing in the capital, and writes for the Washington Post *and other periodicals. And see author note in section 14.*

Excerpted from chapter 44, "The Lost Laws Are Found Again" by Marvin Caplan, from Mary Church Terrell's book A Colored Woman in a White World. *(© 1968 by the National Association of Colored Women's Clubs, Inc., reprinted with permission.)*

In 1948, a private organization, the National Committee on Segregation in the Nation's Capital, published a report on "Segregation in Washington." This excellent survey of the condition of colored people in the capital observed, "Some people say that the time is not ripe for colored people to have equal rights as citizens in the Nation's Capital, and that white people are 'not ready' to give them such rights." But in 1872, during the brief period when all the people in the capital could vote, the popularly elected Assembly of the district passed a law giving Negroes equal rights in restaurants, hotels, barber shops and other places of public accommodation. Stiff penalties were provided for violation.

As late as 1904 this civil rights law was (still) familiar—But around the turn of the century it mysteriously disappeared from the compiled statutes of the district, and it cannot be found in the present codes. Since there is no record of its repeal, some lawyers speculate that it may still be technically in full force and effect.

Their imaginations stirred by the report, a number of lawyers did more than speculate. In May 1949, the Washington chapter of the National Lawyers Guild submitted to the District Corporation Counsel an opinion in which it argued that since the laws had never been rescinded, they were still in force. It asked the District to begin prosecuting anyone who was violating the old statutes. Seven attorneys signed the opinion: Joseph Forer, who did most of the legal research; former Judge of the Municipal Court, James A. Cobb; Daniel Crystal; Margaret A. Haywood; the late Charles H. Houston; J.H. Krug; and Herbert S. Thatcher. The District's Corporation Counsel kept the matter under study.

In the summer of 1949, a number of impatient citizens, colored and white, met and decided the time had come to try to organize the considerable public sentiment that existed in support of the laws. They formed The Coordinating Committee for the Enforcement of the D.C. Anti-Discrimination Laws." And they had the wisdom, a few months after they formed the committee, to elect Mrs. Mary Church Terrell as their chairman.

"In the 1890s a colored person could dine anywhere in Washington," Mrs. Terrell once remarked. This was in a newspaper interview she had in 1944. She went on to say in that deep, compelling voice, which grew more somber, perhaps with the recollection of how bit by bit the rights of citizenship Negroes fought to win after the Civil War were wrested away from them: "I remember stopping at the drug store on the corner of 9th and F streets for service in the late 1890s. The white clerk told me that it was my last service, that the behavior of a loud Negro man there previously had caused them to alter their policy. . . ."

The Quest of the Coordinating Committee of 1949

The Coordinating Committee had no constitution, no by-laws, and no membership dues. Its sole membership requirement was that a person exhibit unrelenting determination and willingness to work for the reinstatement of the lost laws. Its sole purpose was to coordinate the efforts of all the established organizations in the city that wanted to see the old laws enforced again. More than 100 civic, social, and labor groups participated in its campaigns.

The Committee's first step was to attempt to prod the Corporation Counsel into making a decision on the issue raised in the Guild's opinion. It was decided that the quickest way to do this was to present the counsel with a specific instance in which colored persons had been refused service by a local restaurant and ask him to bring suit against the place for violating the laws of 1872 and 1873. Mrs. Terrell was never the person to shrink from a task because of her age or the prospect of public humiliation. She insisted on taking part in the restaurant test.

On Friday, January 27, 1950 she and a small party of friends, including a single white person, entered Thompson's cafeteria in the seven-hundred block of 14th Street, Northwest. The members of the party took their trays and began pushing their way around the counter, past the astonished serving women. But by the time they reached the checkers, the manager appeared and told them it was Thompson's policy not to serve Negroes.

The group immediately withdrew.

The same day their attorneys submitted a complaint to the Corporation Counsel, who could no longer delay reaching a decision. A month later he advised the Commissioners that the laws appeared to be in effect, and the District government agreed to test them.

But legal tests are seldom launched without difficulty. Because of technicalities, it was necessary to return to Thompson's twice more and file two more complaints. Mrs. Terrell led the next two expeditions; the second time her companions included several pastors and Miss Essie Thompson, a member of Local 471, whose headquarters, incidentally, became the Coordinating Committee's meeting hall.

At last the case was on its long exasperating journey through the courts. But to Mrs. Terrell and the Coordinating Committee, this was only the beginning of their work. As the widow of a judge of the Municipal Court, Mrs. Terrell knew that what happens in the streets outside the courthouse frequently affects the decisions reached inside the building. Under her direction the Committee now undertook to gain public support for its position. The task was formidable. For more than 50 years the people of the city that had directed the war against slavery had accustomed themselves to a pattern of segregation as rigid and unquestioned as any in the far South. "The South is in the saddle here," Mrs. Terrell observed in 1944. "I feel it everywhere...."

But in addition to the unorganized opposition of those white and colored citizens who had been schooled to accommodate themselves to segregation, there was the organized strength of the Washington Restaurant Association. As soon as the District government made it clear it would prosecute Thompson's restaurant, the Association sent a letter to its members telling them to continue to discriminate against Negroes and requesting contributions of at least $25 from each of them to create a Defense Fund that the *Afro-American* estimated would amount to $100,000.

Now the real work of the Coordinating Committee began. So many devoted people played important parts in the campaigns that followed, it is difficult to know whom to single out for mention. Yet Mrs. Terrell said if she were ever forced to name the one person upon whose assistance she most depended, she would choose Mrs. Annie Stein, Executive Secretary of the Committee. A statistician by training, Mrs. Stein had come to the Committee after years as a government employee and then as a trade union organizer for the National Women's Trade Union League. To the apartment which she shared with her husband and young son and daughter, members of the Committee often came for mailing parties or to paint picket signs on the dining room table. During some of the fiercer engagements Mrs. Terrell came to meet informally with picket captains and map out new plans, rather after the manner of a general weighing the reports from the battle front.

Developing an Approved List

By sending small interracial parties into downtown restaurants, the Committee discovered several places ready to defy the dictum of the Restaurant Association and serve everyone—in short, to obey the law. As a result, the Committee was able, in June 1950, to issue the first restaurant list—more than 20 places, other than government cafeterias, that did not discriminate. These lists were periodically rechecked and revised. The last one which the Committee put out in 1953 gave the names of more than 60 places. The eager demand for these lists, by white as well as colored persons, was further evidence of how burdensome and unconscionable many people in the capital found segregation. The State Department and several embassies were standing customers for the lists, since they enabled them to direct colored foreign dignitaries to restaurants where they could eat without embarrassment.

It was sometimes possible to add places to the list through direct negotiations with restaurant owners. Here Mrs. Terrell, eloquent by conviction and practiced in argument from her long years in the classroom and on the lecture platform, moved to the fore, leading delegations impressively sprinkled with ministers and attorneys into the business offices. Quite often a single call was enough to convince a restaurant owner or the manager of a dime store lunch counter to try serving the public without regard for color. Even when decisions in the Thompson case went against the District and so, indirectly, against the Committee, only a few places on the list reverted to their old discriminatory policies.

But after many relatively easy successes, the Committee met resistance it could not overcome by negotiation or even threat of boycott. It had set itself the goal of getting all the variety stores on 7th Street, the shopping area with the largest colored trade, to allow colored shoppers the privileges of their refreshment counters. But the Kresge store there planted itself obstinately in the way of this objective. And its manager refused to meet with Committee delegations. Confronted by this impasse, the Committee's situation looked critical. If they lost at Kresge's, places they had already won to their point of view might go back to their old policies, and places they approached in the future would be much harder to deal with.

Target: Kresge's

Against the counsel of a sizable minority that felt the whole idea was undignified and dangerous, it was decided, in the late fall of 1950, to try distributing leaflets at the entrance of the store, urging the public to boycott the place until all customers were treated equally. From the distribution of leaflets it was a logical step to the use of another weapon: picket lines. But the idea of picket lines provoked long and anguished debate at Committee meetings. Most of the members had had no experience with picket lines, and many of them felt such tactics were disreputable. Also, those Committee members who had walked a line for their unions knew that picket line duty is no pleasure and that lines are always difficult to maintain. Many remembered that a line several years earlier, to persuade a drug store in a Negro neighborhood to employ colored salespeople, had proved a heartbreaking failure.

If the whole issue of picketing was a crucial one for the Committee, it was equally so for Mrs. Terrell. It put her leadership to test. She faced, as all reformers must, a terrible question: How long can one be "respectable" and still be effective? By rearing and position, she was inclined against the use of such blunt methods as picketing that carried to the public's mind a suspicion of radical agitation. But she knew from her own experience with the situation that tact and diplomacy were of no use in this case. A public demonstration was the next logical step. And once Mrs. Terrell was convinced of that, considerations of respectability and community position never troubled her again. The long debate was over.

♦♦♦♦♦♦♦♦♦♦♦♦♦♦♦♦♦♦♦♦♦♦♦♦♦♦♦♦♦

Turning a deaf ear to last-minute warnings of the impending race riots and violence that would result, Mary Church Terrell put on her fur coat, wrapped a scarf around her head, and with her cane in one hand and a picket sign in the other, led the first detachment of pickets in a snowstorm.

None of the predictions of disaster came true. Threats and insults were hurled at the marchers by only a small percentage of the whites who went by. The great majority of the people said nothing, and a few persons of both races expressed their sympathy.

After more than six weeks of picketing, Kresge's trade was so seriously affected the store gave in. The pickets were invited to have a cup of coffee at the counter, seated there for the first time in many years.

♦♦♦♦♦♦♦♦♦♦♦♦♦♦♦♦♦♦♦♦♦♦♦♦♦♦♦♦♦

Target: Hecht's

A few blocks up the street from Kresge's is the Hecht Company, one of the largest department stores in Washington. It has a large colored trade, but colored shoppers were not permitted to eat at the lunch counter in the basement. Shortly after Kresge's changed its policy, Hecht's presented the Coordinating Committee with an irresistible excuse to call upon the management. During World Brotherhood Week, in February 1951, the company ran a full page ad featuring a message from Eric Johnston, Economic Stabilization Administrator and General Chairman of Brotherhood Week. Two hands reached across the page and met in a warm clasp. And below it Mr. Johnston called everyone to the work of building "bridges of brotherhood."

But when Mrs. Terrell and a delegation confronted the manager of Hecht's with a copy of the message and asked him if the store meant to act upon Mr. Johnston's advice, they were told that the ad had only been "a gesture." The basement lunch counter would continue to be reserved for white customers only. After several months, the store broke off all negotiations with the Committee.

At once the members of the more than 100 groups supporting the group's work were rallied to a boycott of the store. And when that seemed to have little effect, out came the picket signs. For six months, from a tropical Saturday in July to a slushy Christmas Eve, the Coordinating Committee maintained a line in front of the store's main entrances every Thursday night, Friday noon, and all day Saturday. The marches were enlivened now and then by guest appearances. Once a prominent local boxer took part. Another time, Josephine Baker, the noted singer, joined Mrs. Terrell in a tour of duty. The colored ministers of the city turned out several times and marched around and around in front of the store. Labor unions, notably Local 471, sent trained pickets and donated funds to carry on the struggle.

The climax came the last shopping night before Christmas Eve when a picket line of about 100 people marched in a hailstorm outside the doors. Led by a member dressed as Santa Claus, and carrying picket signs that had begun to swell and run, the cold and dripping pickets marched singing words they had set to the tunes of well-known Christmas carols.

Annie Stein predicted: "They'll put up with us during December when business is good and during the Christmas rush and maybe a week or so after that. But when the January white sales start and we're still out there. . . ." January came and still the management refused to meet with a delegation from the Committee.

Then one weekend, in about the middle of the month, a colored man who worked as a porter in Hecht's tipped off the Committee that the store had decided to change its policy. The following Tuesday a colored Committee member presented herself at the lunch counter. She was now able to buy a sandwich and a cup of coffee from a waitress who seemed to pay no attention to the shade of her skin. Though the daily press, which habitually ignored the Committee's picketing, made no mention of what had happened, the news spread rapidly.

A day or so later, Mrs. Terrell, Mrs. Stein, and three women reporters from the *Afro-American*, the Pitttsburgh *Courier*, and the *Associated Negro Press* had lunch at the basement counter. The store management would not admit it had changed its policy. When reporters for the colored newspapers and the department store trade press inquired, they were informed that the store had never discriminated against colored people.

Target: United States Supreme Court

A few months after a similar triumph at Murphy's variety store, the Committee members were thrown into despair. On January 22, 1953, after a year's deliberation, the U.S. Court of Appeals ruled 5 to 4 that the old laws of 1872 and 1873 were no longer valid. But there was a shred of consolation in knowing that the Supreme Court had still to hear the case.

There was tremendous pressure on the District government to appeal. It came not only from the Coordinating Committee and the groups anxious to be rid of segregation, it came also from the influential groups in the city who wanted home rule. For by questioning the right of Congress to delegate any of its authority over the city's government to a lesser body, the appellate court cast serious doubt on its power to permit the citizens of Washington to govern themselves.

Then, too, what had started as a simple dispute between a few citizens of the District and a restaurant had become a national symbol of the fight against discrimination. Both the Democratic administration of Harry S. Truman and the Republican administration of Dwight D. Eisenhower found it politically expedient and morally right to add their weight to that of the many community groups trying to salvage the old laws. The Department of Justice during the Truman administration filed a "friend of the court" brief in the Court of Appeals. The Republicans submitted one to the Supreme Court.

The case was appealed in a few weeks. The Supreme Court heard it argued in April, and on June 8, before adjourning for the summer, it unanimously reversed the Court of Appeals and ruled that all the vital portions of at least one law were still in effect.

"EAT ANYWHERE!"

the *Afro-American* commanded in a great banner headline. And Mrs. Terrell, who after all had started the whole thing, said: "I will be 90 on the 23rd of September and will die happy that children of my group will not grow up thinking they are inferior because they are deprived of rights which children of other racial groups enjoy."

68 ♦♦ DEFENDING FOREIGN BORN WORKERS

♦♦ Fred Rinaldo ♦♦

Born in New York City, Fred Rinaldo became a screenwriter in Hollywood. Finding himself blacklisted, he became publicist and spokesperson in defense of the foreign born.

Based on material in "Pride of a Nation: A History of the Los Angeles Committee for Protection of the Foreign Born, renamed the Los Angeles Committee for Defense of the Bill of Rights, 1950-1982" by Fred Rinaldo, which provides a useful, short history of U.S. immigration law and political deportations.

In 1950 the Justice Department conducted a nationwide roundup of foreign-born workers and political activists as the McCarran Internal Security Act was put into effect with a vengeance, coinciding with the Smith Act trials of leaders of the U.S. Communist Party in New York. In Los Angeles the terror hit particularly hard. The Mexican-American tradition of struggle for farmworker unions and against poverty in the barrios ran headlong into the Immigration Service (INS) policy of importing "braceros" and deporting "undesirables" at will.

There were midnight roundups, people plucked from their jobs, off the streets, some dumped unceremoniously over the border, others held incommunicado without bail. A few names indicate the diversity of the ethnic groups attacked: Grundahl, Gastelum, Chernin, Martinez, Kim, Jun, Larsen, Kachim, Carlisle, Hyun, Hynes, Ramirez, Salse, Chaunt, Tabeck, Cruz....

The community responded with the formation of the Los Angeles Committee for Protection of Foreign Born. Rose Chernin, an activist in civil rights work, was named Executive Director. The Reverend Walter Mitchell, an Episcopal Bishop in Arizona, was the first honorary chairperson. Soon there were the Mexican Committee, Jugoslav Committee, and Hungarian, Russian, Jewish, and Asian Committees. At its peak 2,000 members of the foreign born community were active, plus an uncounted number of citizen sympathizers. The original directors were Dorothy Marshall, Catholic activist; Mrs. Charlotta Bass, black publisher of the *Los Angeles Sentinel*; Judge Robert W. Kenny, former attorney general of the state of California; and Hon. Judge Stanley Moffatt. Among the sponsors were Rabbi Franklin Cohn, Professor Linus Pauling, and Hollywood screenwriter John Howard Lawson. Shortly afterward the Rev. Stephen Fritchman, newly appointed pastor of the 1st Unitarian Church in Los Angeles, joined Reverend Mitchell. [*See section 62.*]

The Committee took on the Terminal Island Four as its first key case: Harry Carlisle, Miriam Stevenson, David Hyun and Frank Carlson. They were being held without bail, threatened with immediate deportation under the McCarran Act, which also provided for the establishment of concentration camps to hold "subversives" indefinitely without trial. It declared the existence of a "world Communist movement" and provided for supervision and control of "aliens" ordered deported for being subversives.

The situation of the Terminal Island Four was grave under decisions that deportees have almost no constitutional rights because "deportation is not punishment". Yet to send David Hyun, a successful architect, back to his native South Korea, a viciously reactionary dictatorship, would have been to guarantee his torture and eventual murder.

The Committee had to defend the Four, had to secure bail!

The Committee sent out a call for attorneys. Over fifty responded. Under the leadership of Attorney John Porter, the lawyers established defense teams. The attorneys met regularly to exchange experiences and outlined a broad attack on the Immigration Service. But the job seemed insuperable. The Committee had over 150 cases, each one with a different slant. But first, now, immediately, to save the Terminal Island Four! The Committee attacked on a variety of fronts. They established picket lines before the Immigration and Naturalization Service. They distributed leaflets county wide. Delegations sought support from unions and churches and people's organizations. They made weekly visits to the Four, and established a Bail Fund.

After six months of feverish activity, after two unsuccessful trips to the U.S. Supreme Court, the right to administrative bail was established for the Terminal Island Four. When that bail was reduced from some absurd figure to $20,000 apiece (still an absurd figure), the Committee was ready with the cash.

Their trials lay ahead. And other cases were pressing for attention: Rose Kuntz, who came to the U.S. in 1913, was denied citizenship because of her arrest record as an organizer for the ILGWU. And Maria Cruz, in the U.S. since the age of eight, the wife of deportee Jose Cruz—Maria was being pressured by the FBI to turn stool pigeon or face deportation herself.

In those hysterical times some of the deportees were under terrible pressure. Diamond Kim and John Jun were Koreans who edited and published a progressive Korean paper in Los Angeles. The South Korean dictator, Park, had employed terrorists in this country to eliminate all opposition. The Kim-Jun paper was bombed, family members received death threats. It was partly because of this that Diamond Kim and his wife, Fanya, accepted voluntary deportation to North Korea.

But the Los Angeles Committee for Protection of Foreign Born had proved you *could* "fight City Hall". The Terminal Island Four were free.

Denaturalization Under Walter-McCarran

In 1952 Congress passed the Walter-McCarran Act, designed to counter the fight-back of the foreign born. It was an "improvement" on the 1950 McCarran Internal Security Act. The 1952 act provided not only for deportation of "aliens," but for denaturalization of citizens who were foreign born, who could then be deported. The Act required all 3 million non-citizens to be fingerprinted and forced to re-register annually. The Act forced the foreign born to prove their right to remain in this country. It relied on membership in the Attorney General's list of "subversive organizations" as grounds for deportation. There was no statute of limitations protecting someone arrested for deportation 30 years ago. Guilt was by association, i.e., if there were Communists in your organization, you were one unless you could prove you weren't. The Act was so horrendous that President Harry Truman vetoed it. But an hysterical Congress, under full flight from the Bill of Rights because of the impact of the Cold War and McCarthyism, overrode the veto.

Rose Chernin was one of the first citizens to be chosen for denaturalization. She was out on bail, pending appeal of her conviction under the Smith Act. Her denaturalization trial was sensational.

The government had been parading a professional stoolpigeon around the country to testify in Smith Act trials. She had never seen the man in her life, but he testified to having been present with her at many Communist meetings.

During a recess a well known Hollywood performer who had come to the trial noticed the U.S. Attorney pointing out Rose to the witness.

A ploy was quickly arranged. Rose rushed home and changed her dress. She returned to the courtroom and sat discreetly in the back. A woman Rose's size sat next to the Hollywood performer, where Rose had been sitting.

In cross-examination, attorney John Porter asked the witness to pick Rose out from among the spectators in the courtroom.

The witness arose, walked up to the Hollywood personality and pointed to Rose's friend sitting next to her.

John Porter asked her to rise, to give her name.

Consternation!

Would the real Rose Chernin stand up?

Rose did.

Suffice it to say, Rose won her case. And the judge went out of his way to castigate the government for its methods in preparing the case.

♦ ♦
♦ ♦

THE NITTY GRITTY

The Committee staff met every Monday noon at the office. If Monday was Memorial or Labor Day, the staff met anyway in the dingy offices stacked with leaflets, pamphlets, old chairs and tables covered with work in progress.

Deportees who were waiters saw to it that lunch was provided during staff meetings. But the focal point of the occasion was "check-up." When banquet tickets were the subject of the day, each group had to report on its sales. If one group was lagging, its representative might try to get by on generalities.

The Chairperson of the Ticket Committee would glare and press for more details. He (or she) would become sardonic: "Of course it really doesn't matter, we have so much time. . . ."

Suddenly tempers would flare. Charges of bureaucracy, male supremacy, veiled hints of political deviation, would fill the air. Table tops were pounded.

But as suddenly as the storm arose, it would settle and business would go on. The debate resembled a little marketplace haggling more than a confrontation. To an outsider it could be disconcerting, but to the staff it was a welcome break in the monotony of repeated tasks.

♦ ♦
♦ ♦

Defense of Mexican-Americans

The Los Angeles Committee paid special attention to the problems of the Mexican-American, both the undocumented and the U.S. born residents who were soon to coin for themselves the designation "Chicanos."

In April, 1954, President Eisenhower appointed a retired U.S. Army General like himself, as Commissioner of the United States Immigration and Naturalization Service, a post traditionally held by a civilian, and Congress confirmed this appointment. Lieutenant General Joseph M. Swing, known to reputable newsmen as "a professional, long-time Mexican hater," was with General John ("Blackjack") Pershing on the punitive expedition of the U.S. into Mexico in 1916-17. He had been Commanding General of the U.S. Sixth Army in Syngman Rhee's South Korea.

On June 14,—American Flag Day—Attorney General Brownell announced that a militarized campaign, "the Government's biggest offensive against Mexican 'illegals' in history", was about to begin, using the Walter-McCarran Act of 1952. A quota of 40,000 Mexican-Americans was set for the California district by Brownell and General Swing and accepted by local immigration authorities.

At one minute past midnight, on June 17, "Operation Terror" began. Under the Attorney General's personal order and under General Swing's personal command (in the words of Brownell and immigration officials): "Flying squadrons" of U.S. deputies "swept" through the fields, factories and communities "to ferret out ... to capture ... to herd over the border" defenseless Mexican laborers.

The L.A. Committee worked with anyone who would help to protest this outrage, but the climate of terror was pervasive.

Late in July, 1954, Commissioner Swing set the figures deported in the mass roundups at 97,777: 53,374 in the California-Arizona area: 44,303 "caught" in Texas. Another 45,953 "illegal" entrants were listed as returning "voluntarily" to Mexico and 10,917, Swing said, "were seized at roadblocks while attempting to do so." (*Los Angeles Times*, July 30, 1954).

Petitioning the United Nations

The Los Angeles Committee built a special consulting service for undocumented persons in need of advice. It issued a card: *Know Your Rights*, in English and Spanish, briefing persons on their rights under the Constitution to refuse entry into their homes to officers without proper warrants, to refuse to testify without the presence of an attorney, etc. In fact, the Committee was never able to defend all the Mexican nationals that needed help. But of those cases it did handle, it won every single one.

On April 17, 1959, the Committee presented a petition to the United Nations signed by Natalia (Ramirez), attorney, Eliseo Carillo, Dr. Linus Pauling, Hon. Elmer Benson, Reverends William H. Melish and Harry F. Ward. It protested violations of the human rights of Mexicans and Chicanos in the United States, based on the Universal Declaration of Human Rights, adopted by the United Nations in 1948.

What should concern the United Nations is not only this continued violation of its own Universal Declaration of Human Rights by one of it signatories and charter members, the United States of America, but the effect which this state of affairs must have on the friendly and neighborly relations between two of its member nations, the United States and Mexico.

Our consciences, not only as citizens of the United States but as members of the human race, do not allow us to remain silent in the face of all this human suffering. Were we not to speak out, then we ourselves could not be absolved of the moral responsibility for this intolerable situation.

We are mindful of the fact that the United Nations has in the past heard such grievances as, for instance, in the case of the South African Union, when such complaints were laid before it by individual citizens of that country.

We trust that the Human Rights Commission of the United Nations will give us an equally fair hearing in the grave matter we herewith lay before its body. An impartial investigation by the United Nations will, we are convinced, bring to light the facts. On the basis of such an investigation, the United Nations General Assembly could, if it so chose, bring to bear its great moral prestige upon those responsible for the situation so that, in the future, the human rights of more than five million people of Mexican descent who are living permanently or temporarily in the United States will be restored and respected.

The Times, They Were A' Changing

By 1960, out of 56,000 investigations, the government had been able to secure only 1,000 legal deportations and 643 denaturalizations in political cases. However, where there had been a proper legal defense with a mass protest movement behind it, the government's record was minimal. The Los Angeles Committee had yet to lose its first case. Its support was constantly growing.

The Democratic Party put in its 1960 platform:

> We must remove the distinction between native-born and naturalized citizen to assure full protection of our Laws to all. There is no place in the U.S. for second class citizenship. The protection provided by due process, right of appeal and statute of limitations can be extended to non-citizens without hampering the security of our nation.

The subsequent election of John F. Kennedy brought hopes that were quickly dashed. Rep. Walter put forth yet another bill designed to undercut the victims' power to stay in this country with delays and appeals, and to further restrict the freedom of noncitizens. The bill passed Congress and was signed into law by President Kennedy in 1961. One result was that 52 people on "lifetime parole" were forced to appeal their cases to prevent deportation. By 1964, millions of Americans had found voices lost in the McCarthy era through the marches led by the Rev. Martin Luther King, Jr. in Birmingham and Selma. The 1964 Civil Rights Act was passed and the U.S. government abandoned another 27 political alien cases.

The Committee went on the offensive. It dared the government either to bring the last 18 cases to immediate trial (after all, over 15 years had gone by) or drop the charges. Attorney General Brownell had boasted he would deport 10,000 non-citizens and denaturalize another 12,000. But his rhetoric was empty. An era was ending.

In 1965 the Supreme Court ruled that Communist Party members were right when they claimed the right to refuse to register as "subversives," under the constitutional privlige against self-incrimination, and it threw out the registration order against the Veterans of the Abraham Lincoln Brigade, which like the Los Angeles Committee, had managed to survive.

McCarthyism was legally dead and the defense of the foreign born could take new forms.

69 •• JUSTICE ATTACKS WORKERS' SCHOOLS AND CLUBS

♦♦ The Editors ♦♦

The Attorney General began his official attack on progressive workers' organizations with the publication of the Attorney General's list of "subversive organizations" in 1947 under President Truman's Executive Order 9835 [*see list in section 29*]. (The FBI had long been keeping tabs unofficially.) No one who remained a member of any organization listed by the Attorney General could expect to keep a job with the federal government.

Many of the strongest organizations fought back. The Joint Anti-Fascist Refugee Committee of veterans of the Abraham Lincoln Brigade in the Spanish Civil War challenged the Attorney General's list in the courts. So did the International Workers Order [*see section 61*] and the American-Soviet Friendship Society. The Supreme Court heard their pleas in 1951, but the justices could not agree on the unconstitutionality of the list and wrote six rambling opinions. Thereafter other listed (or to-be-listed) organizations fought in the courts, including the National Lawyers Guild, many of whose members were labor lawyers.

These cases were not won. Still, after 1957 the list lost its effectiveness. When challenged, the Attorney General often took names off the list to avoid further litigation. Of course, by then many listed organizations had ceased to exist, and their creative genius remains to be recorded in oral and written histories.

Meanwhile, in 1950, during the Korean war, Congress gave the Attorney General a new weapon against organizations that did not conform to Cold War ideology, the McCarran Internal Security Act. It set up an administrative nightmare that Justice Hugo Black described bluntly: "The plan of the Act is to make it impossible for an organization to continue to function once a registration order is issued against it. To this end, the Act first provides crushing penalties to insure complete compliance with the disclosure requirements of registration. ..." The Act then established penalties for *not* registering under the Act as a "Communist-action" or "Communist-front" organization and for not registering as a member of such an organization. The penalties? "Not more than $10,000 and/or five years *for each day* of failure to register." Justice Black did the mathematical projection: "Thus, for a delay of thirty days in filing required reports, a fine of $300,000 and imprisonment for 150 years could be imposed by a trial judge." (367 US 1, dissenting at 141 (1961).)

After conducting hearings against the Communist Party, the Attorney General turned to attack many of the community organizations that supported union members and their activities, from the much-loved California Labor School and Jefferson School [*described in section 19*] to the American Committee for Protection of the Foreign Born [*see section 68*].

HERBERT BROWNELL vs. THE JEFFERSON SCHOOL

During the administrative hearings against the New York school for workers before the Subversive Activities Control Board in 1953, the government called as one witness Marlene Maclane Kowall, daughter of a movie actor tough-guy. She testifies she was a dancer, a model, a messenger girl, an "editorial assistant" for the magazine *Counter-Attack*, and a paid informer for the FBI. She attended the Jefferson School under instructions from FBI agents, taking a number of courses in two years and submitting regular reports to the FBI. She says she learned that political economy teaches that "if the bosses don't do what you want, punch them in the nose," and dialectical materialism is nothing more nor less than "atheism."

Reading from a test in philosophy which she herself introduced into evidence, the Jefferson School attorney asks:

Q: "What did they teach you about Epicurus?"

A: "It was a matter of indifference to me.... I went only to get what vital information I could [on] ... any connection I could find between the Communist Party and the School."

This "conspiratorial" Jefferson School occupies a nine-story building. It is an adult evening school. Its courses are short and its fees are low. Anyone who wishes can walk off the street and register for one of its more than 75 courses or attend one of its frequent forums. An average of 10,000 students enroll each year.

By 6:30 o'clock every week-day evening the lobby of the Jefferson School fills with students. The Bookshop is crowded. So also is the basement cafeteria.

♦♦"Man's Right to Knowledge:
The Case of the Jefferson School" February 1954

Attacking the Red and the Black

Attacks on the federal level against so-called "Red" organizations spurred attacks at the state level against "Black" organizations, from the traditional NAACP to the newer Congress of Racial Equality (CORE) and the newest Southern Christian Leadership Conference (SCLC) and Student Nonviolent Coordinating Committee (SNCC).

The legal arguments against statutes to curb "subversive Red" organizations and "violent Black" organizations were the same. Wherever the "Blacks" won, it ultimately helped the "Reds," by making clear the ridiculous and undemocratic nature of blanket attacks against all members of any organization that operated in a totally nonviolent manner. In the courts, however, ultimate federal protection of some Black civil rights organizations was not used as precedent for stopping harassment of "Red" peace and civil liberties organizations. It was as if the legal tree had branches that were totally unconnected to the trunk, which is the First Amendment right to associate together for social change.

Louisiana considered the Southern Conference Education

Fund and the National Lawyers Guild unLouisianian for advocating racial and social change. Several Southern states required the NAACP to register as a foreign corporation, and then made it impossible to do so by requiring production of membership lists, which could lead to loss of members' jobs, homes, and lives.

Government Attacks on the California Labor School

The California Labor School [*described by Isobel Cerney in section 19*] became a prime target for government persecution. Attacks came in measured steps, all of them from Washington, not Sacramento or San Francisco.

In 1948 the U.S. Attorney General, without any notice to the School and without any public investigation, announced to the press that he was placing the School on his list of "subversive" organizations.

Then the Treasury Department revoked the tax exemption the School had enjoyed as a non-profit educational institution. This forced the School to pay taxes, and prevented donors from deducting their contributions from income taxes. The Treasury also ruled that the School never had been eligible for tax exemption, and made a demand for back taxes from 1942 to 1948, totaling about $7,000. The School faithfully made all tax payments from 1948 forward, but the federal government attached the School's bank account for the back taxes and endlessly harassed the institution.

In 1954, the Attorney General ordered the School to register as a "communist front" organization under the provisions of the McCarran Internal Security Act of 1950. The School refused, as did all other organizations receiving this order. On March 31, 1955, the U.S. Justice Department filed an action against the California Labor School before the SACB to enforce this order. Attorney General Brownell did not accuse the School of violating any law, but of conducting classes to train Party members and prospective Party members in the programs, objectives, and policies of the Communist Party, and using the School to recruit members into the Party.

The basic charge: "Throughout its existence, the School never knowingly has deviated from the positions taken and advanced by the Communist Party...." Examples? The School and the C.P. both opposed federal and state anti-Communist legislation, Smith Act trials of C.P. leaders, the Taft-Hartley

♦♦DICK McSMEAR♦♦

A storm broke when this color lithograph was hung in the Graphic Arts Workshop exhibit at the 1954 San Francisco Art Festival only to be removed by Festival officials. The censorship backfired: *The Nation* used the artwork on its cover, and the media rushed to interview its subject, then Vice President Richard Nixon.

♦♦ Credit: "Dick McSmear" by Victor Arnautoff was reproduced with the permission of the artist's son, Vasily V. Arnautoff.

Act, and legislative committees investigating Communism. Both supported the Stockholm Peace Appeal, the Chinese People's Republic, and "the Party concept of the status of racial and nationality groups in the United States." (During the SACB hearing of the Communist Party, Assistant District Attorney William A. Paisley explained: "It doesn't matter whether the particular view or policy is held by many people, by some people, or by all the people of the world. The issue is whether the Soviet Union and the Communist Party of the U.S. hold similar views.")

The Attorney General's action spelled the beginning of the end for the California Labor School after six weeks of public hearings in San Francisco before the SACB.

In 1956, San Francisco representatives of the Treasury Department suggested that perhaps a compromise settlement could be worked out to cover the old taxes from 1942 to 1948, first demanded in 1948. Negotiations were conducted over several months, and it was agreed that the case could be settled for $3,000, to be paid by the School at $1,000 down and $50 per month. Letters confirming the agreement were exchanged by the parties.

The School had paid $1,200 when, without warning or explanation, the Treasury Department sent a letter revoking the agreement.

In March 1956, the SACB handed down its decision: the School had been "dominated by Communists." The Labor School tried to raise the money to appeal from this ruling, but could not do so. On May 3, 1957, Holland Roberts announced that the School would close in June for that reason.

A few days later, the IRS grabbed the School and padlocked the door, declaring that their purpose was to forestall a May Day celebration and removal book sale the School had announced for May 5. The books, leftovers from the School bookstore and discards from the School library and saleable for perhaps $50, remained unsold behind the padlocked door. But the May Day meeting took place on schedule in another hall, with hundreds of friends and supporters of the School rallying around and offering their financial and moral support. Books and ideas, teachers and students, and the idea of a California Labor School could not be killed so easily.

The SACB itself was done in by court decisions in 1967 [see section 82].

70 ♦♦ OUR BATTLE IN THE SOUTHLAND

♦♦Rev. C. Tyndell Vivian♦♦

A Board Member of the Southern Conference Educational Fund and Regional Representative of the Southern Christian Leadership Conference, the Rev. Vivian of the Community Church, Chattanooga, Tennessee gave an address on June 6, 1963 before 2,000 New Yorkers at a rally of the Citizens Committee for Constitutional Liberties against the 1950 McCarran "Communist registration" act.

Excerpts of this address follow, from a pamphlet introduced by Miriam Friedlander, who was elected to the New York City Council in the 1980s.

In the South we tell a story about Governor Ross Barnett. It seemed that he died. When he awakened, he was on a golden street. He looked all around him and said to himself, "I made it, I made it, I made it!" Then he started running down that golden street until he came to the Pearly Gates, and he started beating on them, shouting, "Let me in, let me in!"

A little window opened and St. Peter looked out. "Who dat down dere beatin' on dem Pearly Gates?"

There was a great pause and then Barnett said, "Forget it!" (Laughter) (Applause)

I tell you this because I am from the Deep South. In our campaign for freedom we are going to make a lot of people say, "Forget it!" They know we are going to be free and we're not going to stop until freedom comes. (Applause) In the process, we have come to the realization that there can't be freedom for a few of us. There must be freedom for all of us or there will never be freedom for any of us. (Applause)

The McCarran Act is the denial of our freedom as well as yours. It's a grotesque that lurks in the uncleared wasteland of the Southern struggle. We realize that it's a part of the tactics of suppression used by the enemies of reason, free speech and thought.

I was in Birmingham for the two crucial weeks there and I saw the dogs used as a symbol of repression. The dogs were turned loose by "Bull" Connor in Birmingham, and the FBI was turned loose by McCarran in New York. Both may be all right in their place but neither was properly being used in our situation. It is not that we do not see the FBI in the South or that you do not have dogs in the North. But in the North the dogs do nothing, and in the South the FBI does nothing to stop brutality and murder. (Applause)

We have come from the Southland tonight not only to see that animals are not turned on men but to see that men are not turned into animals, that their right to think and act is not denied, their personalities are not destroyed, and their consciences and humanity not trampled on in the name of law and order. (Applause)

When I read the news that seven top Communists had had their cases dropped by the government, what stuck in my mind was a statement by Bobby Kennedy that said something like this—that the government's harassment for 17 years had served its purpose and that while the law and the courts may not have been serving the Constitution, they had served the purpose of denying freedom of thought, activity and action to those that were following their own path.

I know that this is the purpose of law in the South. In this I could feel something that maybe you cannot feel in any other way: the purpose of the law in the South is to deny Negroes; it is to put them in their so-called place; it is to restrict Negro leadership and the average Negro citizen. But the news today does not stop with this, as you all know from reading the papers. Law may be the official edict of the government of the U.S. but there is also the coming government of the world. I read about a Jomo Kenyatta, too. After years of imprisonment and untold suffering, he has come to be the prime minister of his country. (Applause)

Somehow it is still in the makeup of Man that the torch of freedom will always be picked up by free men whether it be in the colonies outside of England or the colonialism inside the United States.

Civil Rights and Civil Liberties

I came tonight not because of a peculiar or particular political persuasion but in spite of it. We have come a long way in our understanding of the civil rights struggle. We have come to realize that civil rights cannot be obtained until civil liberties are granted to all without qualification. (Applause) A lot of people in the South do not realize this yet. But I will tell you those who have always realized it—the Willises, the Walters and the McCarrans.

In Albany, Georgia, it was months before we recognized that the rights taken away from us were the Bill of Rights. You could not go door to door with educational information without a permit, and permits were not forthcoming.

We can call the roll, state by state, in our Southland and count the legal techniques. Take the use of the injunction in Birmingham. It was this that made it necessary for us to move in Birmingham. An injunction had outlawed the NAACP in Alabama. An injunction had withered the Talladega movement. Now an injunction was enjoining every civil rights group to prevent people from acting in the entire state.

The injunction even stated that anyone hearing of the injunction was barred from working for freedom in Alabama. We have been testing the injunction but it is still there. We're winning a victory in Birmingham but we will not really have won until that injunction has been removed, and not only this particular injunction, but until a curb has been placed on the use of such injunctions....

We have another kind of injunction in the South. It is called the *temporary* injunction. It enjoins you for six months, then they have a day in court and decide that they can't act and so enjoin you for another six months, and then they decide to postpone six months more—and during all this time you cannot move, and can be placed in jail without due process of law for contempt.

The old conspiracy idea is also used in Wallace's Alabama. Students in Talladega were put in jail if three or more of them were to meet.... This conspiracy idea has new touches in Louisiana. They call it *Criminal Anarchy*. One of our students stopped by a jail in order to talk to some civil righters who had been put in jail. They brought some magazines and books, and one of the books was, "The God Damn White Man." As a result, they were put in jail for Criminal Anarchy; they were convicted and sentenced to serve ten years....

Americans must realize that change must come. America has been great because she has made *changes with reason*. McCarranism neither faces the need for change nor offers the solution of reason. McCarranism works out of the context of cowardice and fear.... The ultimate goal desired is a free trade of ideas. Truth is the only ground upon which democratic wishes can be safely carried out.

They tell us in your newspapers about the use of new techniques in the struggle.... In high places they say they want to get Negroes off the streets and into the courts. It bothers me. In Albany, they say they are removing the segregation laws to make it harder for Negroes to break the traditions and receive their liberties and rights.

This will not stop Negroes from demonstrating in Jackson, and it won't stop Negroes in Birmingham, in Albany, in Baltimore, in Washington, or Greenwood, Mississippi. We will demonstrate for freedom. (Applause) We will demonstrate for freedom whether the law is written or whether it is unwritten. Unjust laws grow out of an unjust system. It is not the laws we want to change, anyway; it is the system of segregation that we are going to destroy. (Applause)

As we look over the long struggles we have fought, we realize that the most subtle has been against that legal tomfoolery that is called McCarranism. We have seen how this works in the major cities of Florida. The president of the Florida State NAACP refused to give the names of the members, so he was prosecuted in the courts on the ground that the NAACP was a "communist front." In Louisiana they have a conspiracy act based on the same kind of thinking. What has come out of Washington to quiet the North has seeped into the South to plague us.... We must get rid of it.

The Threat to Whites as Well as Negroes

One of the most important things that has been done to destroy the hope of reconciliation in the Southland is the threat that McCarranism poses to white persons as well as Negroes. Any white person who deals with a Negro on an equal basis is considered guilty.... He is prosecuted as well as persecuted. The Mississippi Sovereignty Commission sits in white colleges to see that teachers do not teach what Mississippi does not approve. Guy Carawan and his wife, Candy, were arrested for going to a Freedom Rally. In Birmingham a reporter for the *Nation* was arrested. Bob Zellner's family was trailed across the state for going to the funeral of one of their relatives.

McCarranism in the South has separated Men of Good Will. It has prevented the communication so badly needed to reconcile racial differences in that strife-torn area.... There are a great many white persons who want to work in the freedom struggle but they are afraid ... of labels, of arrest, of losing their jobs, of being accused of disloyalty to their country, and being subjected to the violence of the Ku Klux Klan. The spirit of the Smith Act and the McCarran Act is used as a big stick to deny freedom of speech and assembly to the entire South.

The spirit of our movement for freedom in the Southland, on the contrary, is to give due process of law to all. There are things we hold in common with other organizations and not necessarily because they hold them. We do not ask the political allegiance of those who support our organization. We struggle for concepts as well as for people. We struggle today for the proper place of the Bill of Rights, not only in the world of today but that it may be lifted into the world of tomorrow, to the level where it will be unchallenged. We prefer the Constitution's Bill of Rights to the McCarran Act's Bill of Attainder, as Justice Black has called it.

We are told that the House Un-American Activities Committee was established to fight Communism. We have seen it used to fight our thrust for freedom in the Southland. The McCarran Act has become an outline for thought-control and a device to stop our activities. Down in Mississippi we don't know much about the McCarran Act by name but we know about the Un-Mississippi Activities Committee that was formed to destroy the Negroes' hopes and aspirations and to keep segregation in the sovereign state of Mississippi. Farther south—but not any deeper—we have the Un-Louisiana Activities Committee. Before we can stop the legal intimidation in the Deep South, we must stop it in Washington. (Applause)

The cross of McCarranism was constructed in Washington, and the segregationists are nailing us to it in Alabama, Louisiana and Mississippi.

We refuse to be crucified on a cross of legal tomfoolery. We are afraid they may extend the McCarran Act until it includes the peace movement, for which they had Dagmar Wilson up to find out how they can do it in. Tomorrow they might be calling up the Fred Shuttlesworths and the Martin Luther Kings to see if they cannot include the whole freedom movement in the South under the McCarran Act. We want to get rid of it now so we won't have to worry about it later. (Applause)

It is strange to us in the South that those who desire civil rights and civil liberties are listed by the House Un-American Activities Committee but organizations not desiring these things are not listed. No one in America can take the House Un-American Activities Committee seriously until it lists Governor Wallace, the White Citizens Councils and the Birchers and, if you will, Sons of Birchers. (Applause)

The danger we feel about this thing is that if they can keep the status quo in the North, what they can keep in the South is the "status Crow." (Applause)

Our Battle Is Against the Power Structure

As we look at the Southland and the world about us, we realize that our battle is not with the leather jacket boys. Our battle is not with those we see in the streets. Our battle is against the power structure itself.

Down in the Southland we sing a song: "I'm not goin' to let nobody turn me 'round, turn me 'round, turn me 'round." McCarthy couldn't turn us around a decade ago. McCarran couldn't turn us around—he has passed off the scene. Willis won't turn us around either. We're on our way to the promised land of freedom for all America, and we won't stop until we enjoy it all together. (Applause) In Birmingham we have broken the back of segregation in the Southland. (Applause) We shall not stop until its back is not only broken but buried deep in the soil of America. We shall not stop until we are able to say, "We shall overcome—not some day—but today." (Applause)

71 ✦✦ ATTACKING DR. DUBOIS AND PEACE INFORMATION

✦✦ The Editors ✦✦

On February 8, 1951, a federal grand jury in Washington indicted the Peace Information Center and its officers for "failure to register as agent of a foreign principal." The indictment charged the Center with acting as a publicity center for, reporting information to, and at the request of, the Committee of the World Congress of the Defenders of Peace and its successor, the World Peace Council. A more specific change was publishing and disseminating in the United States, "at the request of its said foreign principal,... the 'Stockholm Peace Appeal' and related information pertaining primarily to prohibition of the use of atomic weapons as instruments of war. ..."

The Peace Information Center promptly issued a press release in which "they gladly admit that they gathered and publicized ideas and news of action for peace from everywhere they could obtain them ... with the same objects that other Americans have spread information of medical advance, efforts for labor uplift, scientific discoveries, plans for housing, suppression of crime and education of youth."

The Peace Information Center was in existence only from April 3, 1951, to October 12, 1951, when it formally disbanded. During its seven months of active work, the Center collected $25,000 in small donations, public and house meetings, and sales of literature. It printed and distributed 750,000 pieces, of which 485,000 were petitions for signatures to the Stockholm Appeal.

◆◆◆◆◆◆◆◆◆◆◆◆◆◆◆◆◆◆◆◆◆◆◆◆◆◆◆◆◆

THE STOCKHOLM PEACE APPEAL

We demand the outlawing of atomic weapons as instruments of intimidation and mass murder of peoples. We demand strict international control to enforce this measure.

We believe that any government which first uses atomic weapons against any other country whatsoever will be committing a crime against humanity and should be dealt with as a war criminal.

We call on all men and women of good will throughout the world to sign this appeal.

◆◆signed by 500,000,000 people in 75 countries

◆◆◆◆◆◆◆◆◆◆◆◆◆◆◆◆◆◆◆◆◆◆◆◆◆◆◆◆◆

Defendant W.E.B. DuBois

I have faced during my life many unpleasant experiences; the growl of a mob; the personal threat of murder; the scowling distaste of an audience. But nothing has so cowed me as that day, November 8, 1951, when I took my seat in a Washington courtroom as an indicted criminal. I was not a criminal. I had broken no law, consciously or unwittingly. Yet I sat with four other American citizens of unblemished character, never before accused even of misdemeanor, in the seats often occupied by murderers, forgers and thieves; accused of a felony and liable to be sentenced before leaving this court to five years of imprisonment, a fine of $10,000 and loss of my civil and political rights as a citizen, representing five generations of Americans.

This was the comment of the great American scholar, William E. Burghart DuBois, on first sitting in the dock (*The Autobiography of W.E.B. DuBois* (New York: International Publishers, 1968) p. 379.

Dr. DuBois created a problem for the prosecution. No Black person called for jury duty in Washington (or anywhere in the United States, for that matter) would be unaware that one of the defendants was the most famous Afro-American scholar in the country. Those who were college graduates might well have heard him lecture and certainly would have studied one of his books. Were they likely to vote to convict Dr. DuBois?

The defendants noted that the prosecution used peremptory challenges against all prospective jurors who were Jewish, but they were evidently afraid to bar all Black people. The jury finally selected consisted of four whites and eight Blacks, most of whom worked for the government.

From the beginning of the trial, the courtroom was crowded, largely by out-of-town Black and white people. The Black press covered the trial as it stretched into three weeks.

During the Armistice Day recess in the trial, Dr. DuBois, aged 83, traveled to Boston to present his annual address to the Community Church. He said in part:

> The real cause of World War will persist and threaten so long as the peoples of Europe and America are determined to control the wealth of most of the world by means of cheap labor and monopolies. Against this a resurgence of the revolt of the poor will raise a new Russia from the dead if we kill this one, and birth a new theory of communism so long as Africa, Asia and South America see the impossibility of otherwise escaping poverty, ignorance and disease....

On his return to the Washington courtroom, Dr. DuBois and his four co-defendants heard one of their lawyers, Vito Marcantonio, contest the basis for the government's case. In the third week of the trial, the government admitted that it did not allege that the Soviet Union was the "foreign principal" accused in the indictment.

Finally Judge McGuire asked the prosecution: "Suppose you were living in Vienna and published a pamphlet in New York at my expense. The government asks me to register as your agent. I refuse. I maintain that while I agree with your thought I am not your agent and therefore will not register. Is that not right?"

The prosecutor had no acceptable answer, and the argument soon ended. Judge McGuire then said:

> The Government has alleged that "Peace Information Center" was the agent of a foreign principal.... [I]n this case the Government has failed to support, on the evidence adduced, the allegations laid down in the indictment. So, therefore, the motion, under the circumstances, for a judgment of acquittal will be granted.

What did this prosecution cost the United States government? The defense estimated $100,000. The defense committee raised and spent $42,215 to stop the prosecution.

What was the real object of this case? Dr. DuBois maintained:

> The real object was to prevent American citizens of any sort from daring to think or talk against the determination of big business to reduce Asia to colonial subserviency to American industry; to reweld the chains on Africa; to consolidate United States control of the Caribbean and South America; and above all to crush socialism in the Soviet Union and China.
>
> Despite this, most Americans of education and stature did not say a word or move a hand. This is the most astonishing and frightening result of this trial. We five are free but America is not.... It is clear still today that freedom of speech and of thinking can be attacked in the United States without the intellectual and moral leaders of this land raising a hand or saying a word in protest or defense, except in the case of the Saving Few.... Than this fateful silence there is on earth no greater menace to present civilization.

CEASED TO HEAR MY NAME

[M]y experience in this fantastic accusation and criminal process is tending to free me from that racial provincialism which I always recognized but which I was sure would eventually land me in an upper realm of cultural unity, led by "My People." I have discovered that a large and powerful portion of the educated and well-to-do Negroes are refusing to forge forward in social leadership of anyone, even their own people, but are eager to fight social medicine for sick whites or sicker Negroes; are opposing trade unionism not only for white labor but for the far more helpless black worker; are willing to get "rich quick" not simply by shady business enterprise, but even by organized gambling and the "dope" racket.

It was a bitter experience and I bowed before the storm. But I did not break.... I found new friends and lived in a wider world than ever before—a world with no color line. I lost my leadership of my race.... The colored children ceased to hear my name.

◆◆W.E.B.DuBois

72 ·· THE DON JUANS OF THE F.B.I.

♦♦ Meridel LeSueur ♦♦

Meridel LeSueur has been a writer throughout her life, although she was forced to seek many other kinds of work to stay alive during the Cold War.

The Clowns of power play their dangerous and macabre mime of the final death of a class. The old spun cocoons of capitalism at last open and reveal the terrible parturition of masks of terror and utter dissolution. The moguls of power reveal themselves as poor white retarded fathers or possibly school boys in strange and comical configurations.

If they weren't so destructive and dangerous.

The FBI during the McCarthy period played out fantastic and macabre scenarios, concocted in back room—clandestine love letters, innuendos that set neighbors agog, planting clandestine plots, obscene telephone calls, gossip and scandals, creeping into families, splitting marriages.

Getting your files is astonishing. A gossipy epistle was sent out to a lawyer's clientele and bar association and his neighbors that he had had a clandestine love affair with the black militant he was defending. Anonymous love letters were sent. Amazing how a whole city could be set awry, permeated with phychic poisons and infiltrations.

A bizarre drama on the Iron Range was unbelievable. The brother of the chairman of the Communist Party, a breeder of horses, bought an exceptional stallion from a Communist country. This was blown up to an international scandal. For two years the FBI followed the breeding schedule of the "red" stallion. How much money did that cost? Finally he was sold to a Kentucky breeder, who did not understand suddenly becoming a suspected radical, and his innocent stallion the center of an international plot.

In my own experience I discovered a more curious plot, the presence in our city of trained Don Juans whose function it was to seduce women, preferably communist or radical women, or union organizers.... They were so handsome, so adroit, arrow collar men with impeccable styles of seduction. They could even approach you on intellectual grounds. One golden haired, tall, loquacious lover accosted me, saying he was a graduate of Yale and wrote his dissertation on proletarian literature. And he would like to interview me.

I had a dog name Coyote who attacked only FBI men, grabbing their feet before they got in the door. I had him interview Coyote....

They could make you a non person in your community. They could make it impossible for you to make a living. I had a writing class. All who took my class were visited by the FBI. They said, "I have to quit. My husband will lose his job. Even my children will feel it. ..."

I thought I would have a correspondence course and put ads in the liberal and radical papers, got a post office box, and in a month had quite a clientele. But in two months, workers wrote they would lose their jobs; university people were visited. My post office box obviously had been raided, my correspondence opened.

I could not get a job as maid in the bus latrine, or in bars, or cleaning office buildings. I would be there a week and the boss would say, "You're OK but the FBI has been here. I'll have to fire you."

My father, an attorney, found himself blacklisted. Many of his clients, even radicals, were hounded.... My mother was blacklisted even in the Farmer Labor Party. I stopped going to the University Theater because it was so painful to see the intellectuals cringe, be unable to speak to me and I could hear their ulcers growing.

Like many others, we were driven to the wall and my mother got a rooming house to make our living.

For two years two agents sat outside our house. How much did that cost us? I was followed everywhere I went. They were waiting for me even at below zero weather when I got off the bus, offering a ride home and a chance to talk.

They came into my mother's hospital room after the operation when she was dying, wired with tubes. They asked her which of her grandchildren was a communist. She answered them: "Gentlemen, you may think you are looking at a woman the surgeons have taken everything out of. But they did not take out my integrity."

The nurse came in and drove them out. They sat in the hallway until she died.

They came to her funeral and memorial, taking down names and license numbers. My brother had to get permission to come to her death. It coincided strangely enough with the first appearance of the Un-American Committee in the Twin Cities. My son-in-law who was subpoened had his car stolen at the same time and when he got it back, it was bugged.

Later they took the house away from me. They threatened to do this when I was a witness at the Smith Act trials in Butte, Montana. A rooming house is very vulnerable. There were condemnations; everyone who rented a room was suspect, hounded, often lost their jobs. The neighbors became enemies. Obscene phone calls must have taken up a good deal of their time. They were about the most lively and original dramas that they staged.

My children were molested.

But one of the most astounding performances was that of the trained Don Juans. They were so subtle and skilled I am sure there must have been a training program for them. I believe that they needed stoolpigeons for the coming up Smith Act trials. They needed women. They needed black women. They needed labor organizers, and intellectuals, hopefully, trained Marxists, since the trials were of books and ideas.

Once as I got off the bus, the two FBI men were standing outside their car and they took hold of me and held me halfjokingly, even amorously.

"What's a beautiful woman like you.... Why, you could make it big! Hey, do you want a job? You need a job. We'll get you a good job in one of the big department stores in advertising—just waiting for you—a big job. A clever woman like you ... you could make it big. We've been admiring you. You're a real attractive woman, no kidding.

"We'll set up an appointment for you, tomorrow. You had enough of this being without a job, haven't you? Come on, now."

Then there was the oath of allegiance. The first case to test that law was in St. Paul where a black woman with a dishwashing job at the Vets hospital, had signed that she was not and had never been.... They arrested her.

It is a long story but it is important ... the sexual harassment, the terrible nets and webs, the blackmailing of women, torture and long periods of questioning and bullying.

At the university, the intellectuals signed these oaths to keep their jobs, and did not defend those who were prosecuted. Even the radical movement could not at first defend these early victims.

They held her in the city jail for a year ... no place to be long incarcerated. They visited her every day and night. They offered her a job for life. All she had to do was name those behind her and most of them were already named. Just point them out and be on the watch. She wouldn't have to work in those awful places. She would have it made for life. The matron of the jail said she had never seen such an organized attack upon a prisoner. They tried to seduce her. Took her to a motel for a whole week. Played her tapes of her friends squeeling on her, talking about her: "Just give her a drink and she'll talk."

Some white women refused to help her or see her. They said she would betray them all.

They played a phone tape of her lover denying her and fearful she would break.

The matron said, "I don't know where she gets the strength."

I asked her and she said it was Fuchik. He was imprisoned in Czechoslovakia during the fascist war take-over, and they did the same things to him, his friends stooling on him. But he never broke down, wrote these notes; they were sneaked out and published later—and she read them.

The FBI took her by car and rode with her all the way to Alderson Prison for women in West Virginia, propositioning her all the time. Unable to give up the possibility of her being a black stoolpigeon. But they never got her. She never accepted the laden tables of the fruits of betrayal.

When she was released from Alderson, a couple of years later, she was under surveillance in St. Paul, had to report every week. Needless to say, she developed a terrible hatred for the FBI. They needled her when she had to report. They never gave up breaking her down.

Once when they had kept her all day she turned, shouting at the agent—"Drop dead!"

And strangely he did.

After that they gave her a wide berth. She became a legend. She is one of the many unmarked heroines of resistance of that period.

There were many.

They succeeded in getting a couple of stoolpigeons, who appeared in the Smith Act trials as paid informants. One of them in California informed on two husbands, her children, and all her comrades. She got a huge chicken ranch in Washington....

One, an organizer in the restaurant workers union, with a child to support, was cruelly pinpointed. She was given good jobs and then threatened. She was framed sexually and became one of the major witnesses, appearing all over the country, telling tales of caches of arms. Another became a supporter of Hubert Humphrey in throwing out the left from the Farmer Labor Party to facilitate his betrayal of the Party to the Democrats.

One night an old friend, a lovely girl, came to my house and knelt before me crying that she had slept with this man who turned out to be an FBI agent, and she had named all our names.

Then I heard she had been put in the asylum.

Many women disppeared like that.

There was no limit to the sexual cruel phychological warfare against women, writing covert love letters, sending out suspicions, phoning—guilt by association.

Many women were alert against them. They were trying to close the radical book store and went to see one of the women who worked there. She had a balcony above her front door and when they knocked, she came on the balcony with her baby and the pot she was just emptying. When they asked to speak with her, she poured the pot on their heads.

To show the devious and cruel and idiotic plots they spent time and our money concocting, there was the case of the writer, Irene Paull, who made her living as a legal secretary and often had ads in the paper for legal work. They would answer the ads, want to come out and see her, bedevil her on the phone.

They must have figured out the one thing that would agonize a single mother. One day they phoned her at work and told her her son, twelve years old, was molesting one of her neighbor's daughters.

They didn't know Irene.

She left her work and went immediately to the family they had told her of.

She found the family friendly, knowing nothing of such accusations.

They made rumors, circulating in the neighborhood, when she became chairperson of the Rosenberg Committee, in the Jewish community. They said she would never find a job amongst them again. They drove her out of the city.

It was wierd, incredible. But the recent machinations of the CIA have carried this terrible adventurism to more monstrous international arrogance and destruction of even any small assumption of human relationship.

There was an old radical who recently died at the age of 95. She sent for her FBI papers and she was very disappointed, she said to them. She said, "You didn't do your job. I went to many more meetings than you report here. You could have gotten most of this from the newspaper or any street gossip. I was much more radical than you report. And it is my taxes that is paying you for this."

We have now a habit as if there was no history before us. The McCarthy period was not unique in the history of capitalism. We were hanged for struggle for the eight-hour day. We have been murdered in the thousands for forming unions. Tarred and feathered for being against the first World War. We had to drive the back roads in Kansas hiding in the night against the vigilantes. Our books were burned in St. Paul. You were beaten for not standing up for "The Star Spangled Banner." Your house was painted yellow. You were often "accidentally" killed.

The McCarthy period was pretty mild.

And the next period, if we are not careful, will be worse.

But we're not so naive that it can't happen here now. We're waiting for them in all the neighborhoods. We're giving sanctuary now to dissidents in the churches. It won't be so easy....

73 ♦♦ THE ROSENBERG-SOBELL CASE: ULTIMATE WEAPON OF THE COLD WAR

♦♦Helen L. Sobell♦♦

Helen Sobell, who earned her EdD in computer eduction in 1980, led the defense committee for her then husband Morton's freedom for 20 years. With his release from prison in 1969, she turned to political activity at Columbia University where she was employed from 1969 to 1977. She then worked with the Fund for Open Information and Accountability, Inc. (FOIA, Inc.). Today, she is the co-convenor of the Gray Panthers in San Francisco.

Some of the documents in this section or mentioned here were secured from the files of Marshall Perlin, principal counsel in the court proceedings which successfully prevented the unsupervised destruction of FBI files. The rest were received through the FOIA, Inc. in New York City, which assists the public in obtaining such files.

The accusation in the Rosenberg-Sobell case that the Russians had stolen the secret of the atom bomb was used to destroy the trust and admiration felt for a powerful ally who had borne the major burden in the war against Hitler. The spirit of cooperation with the USSR which had won the war against Hitler had to be replaced in the United States with a climate of fear and suspicion of the "Communist Menace." The memory of the Russian War Relief Committees and all other exchanges that had sprung up during the war effort had to be erased in order for the Taft-Hartley Act to succeed.

The sentences of death for Ethel and Julius Rosenberg, and of 30 years imprisonment for Morton Sobell, validated the linking of "spy" and "communist," providing a field day for the media and glorifying the witch-hunters.

The pride and comradeship of those who had given so much at home and abroad were buried in a mushroom cloud manipulated to inflame the attack on the weakened trade unions, the liberals, progressives, Communists, and Socialists who were already in retreat.

Caving In

Joe McCarthy, J. Edgar Hoover, Roy Cohn, and the industrialists were creating Cold War hysteria to suppress all opposition from progressive forces so that they might profit and plunder. Many felt they could protect themselves and their organizations by mouthing the litany of the witch-hunters instead of confronting them with the basic American freedoms of thought and association.

Documents secured recently under the Freedom of Information Act in the Rosenberg-Sobell case show the impotence of the liberal strategy. Gross violations of fundamental rights are revealed by the undercover actions of the FBI and State Department in bugging the national headquarters of the United Electrical, Radio, and Machine Workers of America (UE), in placing a UE lawyer on the Security Index even though he did not meet their own criteria for inclusion, and in photographing and transmitting, from the Security Division of the Department of State to the FBI, names of an ILWU delegation protesting the harsh sentences in the case. In one instance, an FBI informant in the UE national headquarters revealed a discussion favorable to the setting up of a Labor Committee to secure clemency for the Rosenbergs.

We have collected 34,864 pages of documents on the Rosenberg-Sobell case from the New York office of the FBI alone. Even with their "national security" and "confidential informer" deletions, they show the importance attached to undermining the defense committee which was formed, and automatically labelling "subversive" all who spoke out against this injustice.

The Day They Died

On June 17, 1953, Justice Douglas signed an order delaying the execution of the Rosenbergs until the nine justices could review the case in the fall. But, on June 19, 1953, Chief Justice Vinson called the Court into special session and the majority voted not to review the case. That marked the end for the Rosenbergs. They were executed that same night at 8:00.

News of the Supreme Court's decision provoked a flurry of activity among activists fighting for the Rosenbergs' lives. The national headquarters for the UE was the scene of such concern. How do we know? Thanks to an FBI memo summarizing its wiretap surveillance of the union's office that fateful day:

7/9/53

SAC, New York
FRANCIS v. GARDNER
COMINFIL—UE
IS-C

Confidential Informant NY-603-S* advised that on 6/19/53, the following incidents took place at UE National Headquarters, 11 East 51 Street, NYC, reflecting interest of the persons involved regarding the ROSENBERG case:

Informant advised that THELMA SLAPPY, a secretary to JOSEPH DERMODY, UE international representative, had been in Washington, Thursday, 6/18/53, apparently taking part in the ROSENBERG rally at the White House. According to informant, she did not return to New York until 5 a.m. that morning. Informant said she was very upset over the ROSENBERG case.

BILL CAHN, UE Publicity Director, received a message from one JANE SOMERS to the effect that the Supreme Court had vacated the ROSENBERGS' stay of execution. JANE told BILL that there would be mass action in Union Square that evening.

BESSIE KEMP, UE switchboard operator, received a message from a woman named ESTHER (LNU), who advised that the Supreme Court had vacated the stay of execution. ESTHER requested BESSIE to call her friends and prevail on them to send telegrams to Washington. ESTHER said that the telegrams would cost only $1.05 for ten words, and it would be the last dollar they would have to spend on the ROSENBERGS.

RACHEL KLAUSNER, confidential secretary at UE, received a message from one CLARA MULLEN, asking RAE to meet her at the Stuyvesant Casino that evening at 7:30 p.m. RAE declined, explaining that she had been in Washington on the previous day, presumably at the ROSENBERG rally, and desired to get home despite having heard the news of the stay of execution. CLARA pointed out that the meet-

♦♦ WE HAVE NOT FORGOTTEN! ♦♦

¡NO OLVIDEMOS!
A JULIUS Y ETHEL ROSENBERG

ASESINADOS POR EL GOBIERNO DE GUERRA DE LOS ESTADOS UNIDOS PORQUE AMARON Y CREYERON EN LA PAZ

"We have not forgotten the Rosenbergs . . . !! Assassinated by the government of war of the United States because they loved and believed in peace."

♦♦ Credit: Angel Bracho and Celia Calderon, *El Taller de Grafica Popular*, Mexico, 1954. Thanks to the Rosenberg Era Art Project of Montague Center, Massachusetts. The Project is sponsoring a national art exhibit tour from 1988 to 1990.

ing at Stuyvesant Casino was very important and RAE agreed to do her best to make it.

FRED WRIGHT, "UE News" cartoonist, received a message from an unidentified woman advising him that the rally at Union Square for the ROSENBERGS had been set for 5 p.m.

JANE told him that the execution hour had been set at 6 p.m. RUSS cautioned JANE to take it easy and not be too upset. He advised her "to salt the subjectiveness with a little objectiveness". JANE agreed to try. RUSS added that it concerned a lot of things she believed. JANE agreed and commented that she knew it would happen like this.

Extreme caution should be used in disseminating the above information so as not to jeopardize informant's identity.

Paying Tribute

Tribute must be paid to those in the labor movement who acted on the Rosenberg-Sobell case in the spirit proclaimed by one of the attorneys in the Sacco-Vanzetti and Mooney-Billings cases. In 1959, John F. Finerty wrote: "Whenever the public participates actively in righting a wrong it strengthens the courts and all our institutions. I believe that this is happening in the Sobell case today."

In 1954, Louis Goldblatt, acting for the International Executive Board of the ILWU, requested the transfer of Morton Sobell from Alcatraz, as did Albert Pezzati, an executive board member of the International Union of Mine, Mill and Smelter Workers, and Leon Strauss of the Fur Workers, together with others. The general counsel of the United Auto Workers, Harold A. Cranefield, joined in the appeal for clemency for Morton Sobell in 1958. A number of other labor names, Leon J. Davis, Patrick Gorman, Warren Billings (the chairman of the San Francisco Sobell Committee), come to mind, and many others have fallen back into the womb of time. Named and unnamed alike, they stood by their principles in a most difficult time.

A WRONG TO BE RIGHTED?

Editors' note: Published in 27 official publications of labor unions in August, 1959:

"August 16 is a bitter annniversary for Mrs. Helen Sobell, who is now on a speaking tour of California. It marks the beginning of the tenth year of her husband's imprisonment for a crime she says he could not possibly have committed.

"She is a gentle little woman, soft-spoken, persistent and totally dedicated to securing the release of Morton Sobell who was sentenced to 30 years in prison on the charge of conspiracy to commit espionage. 'The only reason our family has been able to survive for these nine long years is because of Morton's innocence and our belief that he will be freed and vindicated when the facts become known,' she said, her dark brown eyes glowing with a faith shared by her two children.

"Her 10-year-old son, Marco, barely knows his father except through prison visits. Her 19-year-old daughter, Sidney, who is completing a course in social work at the University of Chicago, worked as a waitress this summer.

"Their spirits have been buoyed up by the fact that in recent years thousands of people—many of them notable ministers, lawyers, and scientists—have publicly expressed their belief that the Sobell conviction was a miscarriage of justice. Quotations from comments by these people come readily to Mrs. Sobell's tongue. She flips through a sheaf of clippings to document them. For example: a group of theologians and lawyers, including such men as Dr. Reinhold Niebuhr, vice president and professor of Ethics and Theology at Union Theological Seminary, and Edmund Cahn, professor of Law at New York University, made an independent investigation. They characterized evidence against Sobell as 'vague in character and slender in proof.'

"The former Protestant chaplain of Alcatraz, Rev. Peter McCormack, declared after coming to know Sobell on 'the rock,' that Sobell was 'utterly incapable of doing the thing of which he is charged.... Falsely accused, cruelly treated, sentenced on the testimony of a self-confessed perjurer, this man of fine character and brilliant man still suffers within prison walls....'

"Now in Atlanta he works in the prison textile mill for 29 cents an hour. In his spare time he is studying the circulatory system in hopes of inventing a mechanical device to help persons afflicted with hardening of the arteries. 'He is a creative man—he is trying to make the best of the situation—but it is so hard to get the simplest reference materials to him,' his wife, herself a former physicist, said sadly.

"If it is so 'wrong' for Sobell to be in prison, how did he get there? 'My husband was never implicated in any way with the atomic espionage for which the Rosenbergs were convicted,' Mrs. Sobell declared. 'The indictment had already been drawn up against the Rosenbergs when the prosecution tried to get Morton to be a witness, to say the Rosenbergs were guilty. When he refused the prosecution just added his name to the indictment.

"'There was only one witness as far as Morton was concerned on the conspiracy to commit espionage. He was Max Elitcher and he admitted he was "scared to death" because he had perjured himself and he hoped for the best because of his testimony. He was never prosecuted for perjury.

"'The trial could only have taken place in the time of the Korean War when there was such tension and fear,' Mrs. Sobell thinks. 'And then there was the fact that the prosecution in this case included Roy Cohn, who became known as the late Senator McCarthy's chief assistant. Many people feel Cohn's participation was enough to guarantee that a fair trial could not be held....'"

Labor Fights Back

Labor did fight back, crippled as it was, and one of the ways it continued to do so even after the death of the Rosenbergs was through the Sobell Committee, which remained active until Morton Sobell's freedom was secured in January of 1969.

When more individuals and groups surmount the still present fear of confrontation with a governmental body which is nominally its servant, the FBI will lose its blackmailing function.

◆◆ENOUGH BODIES BROKEN◆◆

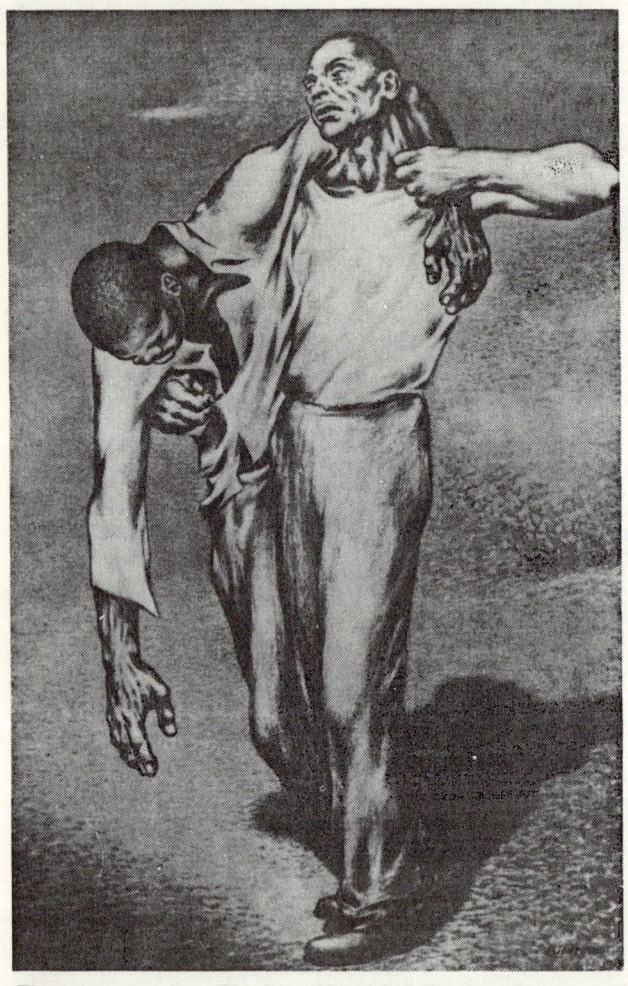

This appeared in *The Best Untold: A Book of Paintings by Edward Biberman* (New York: The Blue Heron Press, 1953).

◆◆ Credit: Edward Biberman; reproduced with permission of Suzanne Zada.

··PART SIX··

FIGHTING FROM BORDER TO BORDER

✦ ✦

The Cold War knew no boundaries in its offensive against the Labor Movement from within and from without.

Active union members and leaders were attacked for moving beyond trade union consciousness toward class consciousness. This marked them the enemies of big business, the government, and those within the labor movement blinded by anti-Communism.

The tactics of repression were everywhere the same: hearings of Congressional witch-hunt committees, firings of workers who refused to become informers, and attempts by unions, the local press, and "civic leaders" to isolate and ostracize militant workers. The Cold War sent a deep, penetrating chill into the homes of countless workers, with women, Blacks, and immigrants as special targets.

Part Six tells fascinating stories of how workers resisted, survived, and even took the offensive in the face of relentless repression: by making a full-length movie about a strike on location in a company town; by heading into the deep South to organize racially-integrated unions; by telling off a panel of Congressmen obsessed with finding "Reds"; by running for office in a Teamsters local in 1970 after being expelled by the leadership.

Part Six closes with startling revelations of behind-the-scenes intrigue, subversion, and influence-peddling by some in the AFL-CIO leadership seeking to export McCarthyism to Latin America, from Chile to Nicaragua.

✦ ✦

74 ♦♦ MINE, MILL, AND SMELTER WORKERS: THE SALT OF THE EARTH

STARTING THE ATTACK

♦♦ **The Editors** ♦♦

After World War II, the CIO leadership set up a three-member committee headed by President Potofsky of the Amalgamated Clothing Workers to decide whether the CIO should set up an "administratorship" over the Mine, Mill and Smelter Workers Union.

Why?

Because Mine-Mill continued the militant spirit of the Western Federation of Miners from which it sprang. Mine-Mill functioned as a most democratic union. It had Black leadership in the top ranks and chartered integrated locals in the South at a time when this was not being done by many other unions. It was a unique union of 120,000 people in the United States, Canada, and Mexico.

The CIO Committee set up a hearing room in the Amalgamated Clothing Workers bank in Chicago and called Mine-Mill's International officers in to be questioned. Potofsky told them: "Let's be realistic ... you know what's going on, with these Taft-Hartley affidavits and this FBI business. We've just got to stop these attacks on the CIO—no matter how we do it."

Working in this climate, from 1947 through 1951, Mine-Mill survived and more, against overwhelming odds. It held fast to its basic jurisdiction in the mining, milling, smelting, and refining industry with a membership of over 100,000. Mine-Mill reached new heights in collective bargaining and new agreements. When it became apparent that raiding CIO unions could not destroy Mine-Mill, the CIO expelled it on charges that its policies paralleled those of the Communist Party.

Mine-Mill President John Clark said in his 1950 convention report: "Raiding is *not* organizing the unorganized. Advocating a wage freeze, as did some CIO union presidents, does not extend the benefits of collective bargaining to the CIO membership. Tying the CIO to a single political party will not secure legislation safeguarding the economic security and social welfare of the workers."

The CIO "awarded" Mine-Mill's jurisdiction in mining, milling, and smelting to the CIO Steelworkers Union and its jurisdiction in brass and die casting to the United Auto Workers. Even that did not break Mine-Mill. It was an old union with strong traditions and strong members.

AN EARLY MINE-MILL LEADER: HUMBERTO SILEX

♦♦Frank Arnold♦♦

Frank Arnold is a member of the International Association of Machinists and the Santa Clara (California) Central Labor Council. He was a founding member of the Southwest Labor Studies Association.

Summarized from "Humberto Silex, Labor Organizer", Southwest Economy & Society, Vol. 4, No. 1 (Fall 1978) by Frank Arnold.

Humberto Selix is one of the unsung heroes of the U.S. labor movement. Born in Nicaragua, he came to the United States in 1920-1921, to San Francisco, then travelled around the country on a variety of jobs. In the late '30s, he wound up in El Paso, Texas. By this time, he had married and had begun raising a family. When the CIO unions started to move into El Paso, they talked to Humberto because he had some previous trade union experience at International Harvester in the Midwest and a number of other places. He became president of the Mine-Mill Union at the Sacco smelting plant in El Paso. He was the leader of a number of strikes in that area, and finally became a full-time organizer.

In 1943, he organized what was possibly the only international labor day in the history of U.S.-Mexican relations. In September 1943, together with a group of trade unionists and progressive political figures in El Paso and its neighbor city, Juarez, CIO unions and Mexican unions organized International Labor Day, where speakers and audience joined on both sides of the border. They marched back and forth across the border, making an impressive show of international solidarity.

In 1948, because of the provision of the Taft-Hartley Act that required full-time trade union employees to be U.S. citizens, the union had to let Silex go. He was in Arizona at the time on an organizing drive. Immediately on his return to El Paso, he applied for U.S. citizenship. He appeared before the judge with a group of others, as is generally done, to be sworn in. The Immigration official called him aside and told him he would be up for a deportation hearing; the first charge was moral turpitude. This charge stemmed from the fact that, several years earlier, he had paid a $35 fine for assault and battery when he got into a fight while on a picket line. The American Committee for Protection of Foreign Born and other groups took up the case and defended him through the Solidarity Committee organized by Mine-Mill. They finally got a full pardon from the governor of Texas, so they could not deport him based on that charge.

The government next tried to prove he was a member of the U.S. Communist Party. Because Silex had close relations with Vicente Lombardo Toledano, the great Mexican Marxist trade union leader and founder of the Confederation of Mexican Workers [see section 23], he was also charged with being a member of the Mexican Communist Party. The U.S. government couldn't prove membership in either of these parties, and finally dropped the case.

But from that time on until the late 1950s, Humberto Silex found it almost impossible to find full-time employment in the El Paso area. He went through a difficult time trying to raise his kids and suffered from depression and isolation during this period. He moved to a small neat house in a working class area with his wife, Maria de Jesus, surrounded by members of his extended family, including 16 grandchildren and 3 great grandchildren. He believes: "The first human right of every worker is a job. Anything that is for the worker is a move in the direction of socialism. The other direction is slavery."

THE UNION IN NEW MEXICO

♦♦ Virginia Derr Chambers ♦♦

During the Cold War, the author was an organizer of women on economic and political issues. Today she is an officer of the Institute for Global Education in Grand Rapids, Michigan, which discusses peace and what happens to Third World countries facing imperialist policies of other nations.

At the end of World War II, my then husband, Clinton Jencks, left the army and we and our two young children moved to Denver, Colorado, where he got a job in a smelter. His union, Mine-Mill, hired him as an organizer, and asked us to go to New Mexico to help organize the workers there. We had an old horse trailer which we loaded all our stuff in, and we went down over the mountain ranges. We arrived in Silver City at night, and my heart sank when I woke in the morning and looked out into what looked like a desert to me.

Later I came to see this terrain and the people there as very beautiful, but it was very much like going to a foreign country for me. What we heard spoken around us was Spanish. English was the business language. The store owners were Anglos. In the restaurants you saw the sign:

> WE RESERVE THE RIGHT
> TO REFUSE SERVICE TO ANYONE

This was a clue that Spanish-speaking people, Indians, and Black people did not go into those restaurants. This area was essentially, and really still is, almost colonized: the Spanish-speaking people do most of the work, the Anglos own most of the land and run the mines, mills, smelters, and service businesses. There have been changes since the union came, but the changes have been as a result of the Mexican-Americans awakening, and, in part, I claim that the Mexican-Americans awoke as a result of the growing strength of the Mine, Mill and Smelter Workers Union in that area.

Mine-Mill had tried to organize the mineworkers there in the '30s. The companies—Kennecott Copper, American Smelting and Refining, U.S. Smelting and Refining, Phelps Dodge—drove the organizers off their property. Mine-Mill took those cases to the U.S. Supreme Court and, just before World War II, the Court found for the union and these union members were paid hundreds of thousands of dollars in back pay.

The Catholic Church had bitterly opposed the organization of workers. But when the people got these awards, the Church called in the leaders and said, "You've got this money now. You should tithe your ten percent. The Church is counting on you."

The union members answered, "Father, you don't want that money. That's Red money. You've told us that's Red money."

And they didn't give it to the church.

It's a wonderful area because the people are like the Italian workers, political Catholics.

Because my husband was a Mine-Mill organizer, our family was ostracized. I cannot tell you how profoundly my two children suffered as a result of that. Shortly before the units of Local 890 were amalgamated, I learned how to write union leaflets and radio programs, how to organize. I had done a lot of this work before I got to New Mexico, but I had never done it consistently, for a trade union, and I had never dealt with Spanish-speaking people. My husband and I both learned Spanish as quickly as we could.

Some of the women literally did not come out of their houses unless their husbands told them they could. Even in terms of going to the grocery store, the men called the tune as to when they went. It was a puzzlement to me because I had always maintained a basic independence of mind and action. Invariably, I went to the union meetings, and right from the word go, I put up my hand and participated. Gradually I got women to come with me, and we always had our say on everything. It was not long—within a few years—before women were attending the meetings and having the right to vote.

In 1948, my husband and I went on a short vacation with our two kids. We went to the only integrated place in New Mexico, a ranch near Taos, in the San Cristobal Valley, owned by two fine progressive people, Craig and Jenny Vincent. People came there from all over the United States. The big ranch house was later burnt to the ground by vigilantes during the McCarthy era. There, we met two people from Hollywood who said they would like to come down and see our area—Paul and Sylvia Jarrico. Paul was a blacklisted screenwriter. Later they did come to Bayard, where the union headquarters was. They said some of the blacklisted Hollywood people would like to do a film about the struggles that were taking place in New Mexico. The membership of Local 890 were asked what they thought, and they thought it was a wonderful idea.

THE LONG STRIKE

♦♦ Clinton Jencks ♦♦

During the Cold War, Clinton Jencks was an organizer for Mine-Mill in Grant County, New Mexico. Today he teaches economics at California State University at San Diego.

When one hundred workers walked off the job at the Empire Zinc Company at Hanover, New Mexico, in 1950, no one knew that this strike would make history.

Most of the strikers were Mexican-Americans. They struck after the company refused to grant the same working conditions to them that prevailed in other mines in the same district. For several months they quietly walked the picketlines. We had organized the several separate local unions into an amalgamated local, and other workers helped with the strike.

The company was trying to starve them into submission. When that failed, management resorted to open scabherding, deputizing gunmen, assaulting strikers, and getting court injunctions against the strikers. As the months wore on, the strike became a symbol of the struggle of the Mexican-American people, of the unity of Chicano and Anglo workers, and of the power of men and women united for dignity and equality. After the local court issued an injunction to halt picketing by the strikers in June 1951, company-inspired violence broke out.

THE INJUNCTION

♦♦ Virginia Derr Chambers ♦♦

When the injunction was issued and the men were forbidden to picket, we had a meeting in a big dance hall.

The women said, "Why can't *we* picket? There's no court injunction against us!"

That meeting lasted from 8 o'clock at night until 4 in the morning. By 7 o'clock that morning, the women—and many children—were on the picket lines, and by 8 o'clock, we were all in jail.

But more women came, and more women, and more women. Women, children ... they arrested so many of us they finally couldn't fill the jail with any more.

The women were keeping the strike alive. One was Anita Torrez, born in 1926 in the farm-mining territory of the Gila Valley in New Mexico. She married Lorenzo Torrez, her schoolmate in elementary and high school. When he returned from the army she joined him in Hanover, New Mexico, where he worked in a mill at Empire Zinc, a lead-zinc property. During the 1950 strike, after the women took over the picketlines, Anita Torrez became a leading force. She fought the scabs, sheriffs, and local and state police.

We were on the lines for almost a year, and there was a great deal of violence against us. We were beaten. Some people's houses were torched by arsonists. I was beaten on a picket line when I saw them knocking a boy around, and tried to interfere. We spent more than 1,200 days in jail, in total.

The strike went on for 18 months. It cost the union $60,000 in fines alone. At times it looked hopeless. But unity was built among Chicano and white workers, supported by their wives and families. The workers finally achieved victory in January 1952, scoring important gains in the settlement.

The Salt of the Earth

While the strike was going on, Michael Wilson, Paul Jarrico's brother-in-law and a blacklisted screenwriter (who had won an Academy Award for his screenplay *A Place in the Sun*), came to Grant County to begin work on the script for a possible film. A group of blacklisted film workers in Hollywood had gathered a little money and started the Independent Productions Corporation. In early 1953, a year after the Empire Zinc strike ended, a crew arrived from California to begin making the film, to be called *Salt of the Earth*.

The Union and Independent Productions co-sponsored the film. There were very few professional actors in the cast—probably the best known in the U.S. was Will Geer. The union president, Juan Chacon, union members, their wives, and their families played most of the parts, acting themselves with a few fictional touches and under different names. (The president in the movie was played by Robert Ames—the crew's carpenter.)

The director was Herbert Biberman, one of the "Hollywood Ten."

When the Hollywood crew arrived in 1953, the people of Grant County welcomed them. A moving picture company! Even though the Anglo community hated the union, "this Mexican union," they were delighted. They thought they were going to get famous, and Silver City was going to get famous.

It wasn't long before the shit hit the fan. Victor Riesel, a syndicated antilabor columnist in New York, reported that Hollywood Reds and union Reds were making an un-American film in New Mexico. Within a short time, the Un-American Committee was inveighing against it. Placards appeared in all the windows of the shops in town saying,

COMMUNISTS GET OUT. WE DON'T SERVE COMMUNISTS!

The editorials in the *Daily Press*, which the union people called "the Silver City funny papers," called for us to be run out of town. Vigilantes organized. The attempt to make the film was attacked on the floor of Congress as "Communist-inspired" by Congressman Don Jackson (R-Calif). Striking for equal wages and working conditions with other miners was an attack on profits, but telling the story of this struggle for dignity and equality to the world in a movie was intolerable! The local radio station seemed to play Jackson's statement every half-hour for days. The Catholic Church in El Paso, 150 miles away, announced that any union member who was Catholic would be excommunicated for participating in the film. The whole Southwest acted as if the atom bomb had either dropped or was about to be dropped.

Those of us who were part of the film-making found it incredible. The violence increased to the point where we could not go out unless union members with a gun went with us. They tried to burn the union hall. Our own car was shot full of holes.

They burned down an Anglo union member's house. There were very few Anglos in the union, and a hatred existed among the larger Anglo community against those few. (The Anglos were mostly in the craft unions, feeling very good about themselves.) Attempts were made to blow up the sound truck, to smash the cameras, to drown out sound by flying small planes over filming areas, to overexpose film by reflecting mirrors mounted on surrounding hills.

Finally, the Immigration people kidnapped the star of the

600 • Part Six •• Fighting from Border to Border

••SALT OF THE EARTH••

Scenes from the film *Salt of the Earth* featuring Juan Chacon and Rosaura Revueltas (top left and right).

•• Credit: Salt of the Earth Photograph Archives, Salvatore Productions.

film, Mexican actress Rosaura Revueltas, and threw her back across the border. They said she'd crossed into the U.S. illegally. Of course, she had not, and that charge was dropped later. The state government threatened to call in the National Guard to keep peace. Instead, they sent for the highway patrol from Santa Fe because the head of the highway patrol offered to come. He was a unique Anglo, a friend of the Spanish-speaking people. A couple of Mexican-American businessmen who owned a few bars met with him. Then we all met together. They said, "You've got to get out; you've got to get out."

So the Hollywood crew left, in a caravan of cars, late at night.

After the film company went back to California, they went through hell to get the film printed. The Hollywood establishment threatened to blacklist any business that processed the film and it was farmed out to various small shops, so they wouldn't see it as a whole. The filming was completed with people from Topanga Canyon who volunteered to do the crowd scenes. Some scenes of Rosaura were shot in Mexico City. But it was finally put together.

Thousands of theaters throughout the United States had contracts to show the film. They were forced to cancel. One suspects it would require the combined powers of the big studios and of the FBI to effectively intimidate so many theater owners over the whole country.

In the meantime, Clint Jencks was arrested by the FBI and charged with having filed a false non-Communist affidavit, for being a member of the Communist Party in 1950 while he had been president of Local 890. Our lives were ground to pieces for several more years. During those years, and since, *Salt* was shown all over Europe, in Cuba, China. It even won an award in France for the best international film of the year. It is a beautiful picture. I feel honored to have been so incidentally a part of it.

UNITED STATES V. CLINTON JENCKS

♦♦ The Editors ♦♦

Harvey Matusow learned how to practice his trade of professional anti-Communist witness by watching the performance of others who appeared before the House Un-American Activities Committee, the Senate Internal Security Subcommittee, deportation hearings conducted by the Immigration Service, state Un-American committees, and similar institutions. One of the important rules was to take the opportunity in each appearance to open up areas for further questioning in later appearances. To assure continuity of employment you had to be able to capture headlines for the government official who subpoenaed you.

On October 6-9, 1952, Sen. Pat McCarran (D-Nev) held hearings of the Senate Internal Security Subcommittee on Mine-Mill. Matusow became the star witness, a role he'd long coveted. The *Deseret News and Salt Lake Telegram* ran a banner headline:

> EX-SPY VOWS RED BOSSES
> ORDERED COPPER STRIKE

In April 1953, just before the 3-year statute of limitations would have run out, the Department of Justice called Matusow before a federal grand jury in El Paso, to testify that Jencks was a member of the Communist Party when he filed his 1950 non-Communist oath. Jencks says:

Both Local 890 and the International Union announced that they considered the indictment an attack on the whole union and its membership. The union mounted a major campaign to defend me. Without the thousands of dollars contributed by thousands of working people, professional people, and other friends, I would have been added to the long list of union militants unjustly imprisoned for refusing to knuckle under and become a part of the system that steals from the poor to give to the rich.

Mine-Mill selected Anita Torrez, the militant picket, to go to Canada to tour the mining towns to raise funds for Jencks' defense. She and her husband, Lorenzo, had both joined the Communist Party at the height of the McCarthy period. She became an organizer for Mine-Mill in the mining town of Superior, Arizona, where repeated organizing drives had failed. Her diligent activities finally brought organization to the Superior district as the Jencks case ground on.

Jencks was brought to trial before a jury in El Paso in January 1954. The United States Attorney presented a series of witnesses who testified that they were former members of the Communist Party and had met Jencks at some Party meetings between 1946 and 1948. Only two witnesses, Reverend J.W. Ford and Harvey Matusow, testified about seeing or talking with Jencks at Party gatherings later than 1948. Both of these witnesses were paid FBI informers.

The government said the Communist Party had dictated a policy to the Mine-Mill officials: resign from the Party publicly in order to take the oath, but maintain a secret membership. There were no Party cards, membership lists, minutes of meetings to prove membership, so the government said it had to establish its case against Jencks by circumstantial evidence (for example, that he had recommended the *People's World*, an allegedly Communist newspaper, to union members).

On the witness stand, Matusow told of a plot by Jencks and Communist labor leaders in Mexico to bring about an international strike that would tie up copper supplies going to U.S. troops during the Korean War.

Jencks told his attorney, Nathan Witt, that the testimony given by Ford and Matusow was sheer fabrication.

Witt demanded that the reports made by Ford and Matusow to the FBI be brought into court, to check whether their written statements made at the time of the alleged meetings with Jencks corresponded with their testimony in court.

The U.S. Attorney objected that the FBI reports were confidential and could not be shown unless Witt could establish beforehand ("lay a foundation") that the statements in them were inconsistent with the testimony in court.

The trial judge denied Witt's motion to see the prior statements, and overruled Witt's objections to several jury instructions. The jury returned a verdict of guilty, and the judge sentenced Jencks to five years in prison. After conviction, attorney Witt filed a motion for a new trial, and began to argue before the judge who had just heard the *Jencks* case.

The judge ordered the lawyer to take the witness stand, then asked him: "Are you a member of the Communist Party?"

Witt refused to answer the question: "This whole proceeding violates the right to counsel guaranteed to my client, Clinton Jencks, by seeking to intimidate or humiliate the lawyer Jencks selected. I therefore claim my privilege against self-incrimination guaranteed in the Fifth Amendment."

The judge announced: "No lawyer who claims the privilege can practice in my court."

That ended that. The judge did not enter an order barring Witt, so Witt had no order to appeal to a higher court. But he could not represent Jencks before that judge.

The lawyers for Mine-Mill appealed Jencks's conviction to

the federal court of appeals. While the appeal was pending, Harvey Matusow made a sworn statement, filed in the Jencks case January 20, 1955 in support of defendant's motion for a new trial, recanting his testimony in this and other cases.

DEPOSITION IN SUPPORT OF NEW TRIAL

I testified that in July and August, 1950, I visited the San Cristobal Valley Ranch in Northern New Mexico, and met the defendant there. While there, I had three conversations with him. I also testified about a lecture given by the defendant at the Ranch ...

It is untrue that on the occasion of this conversation, the defendant said, "It is a good idea, we can use more active Communists out here." The defendant made no such statement....

My testimony relating to the defendant's alleged discussion with "Mexican Communist organizers" concerning a plot to cut off copper production for the Korean war effort was untrue. The defendant made no such statement....

There was no basis for my stating that Clinton E. Jencks was a member of the Communist Party at the time I stated so in court....

I make and swear to this affidavit voluntarily and of my own free will, without having been threatened, coerced, influenced, or intimidated in any way, without having been given any payment, reward, or any thing of value, or any promise thereof; and only for the purpose of now telling the truth, the whole truth, and nothing but the truth, and as I have said, to do what I can to remedy the harm I have done to Clinton Jencks and to the administration of justice.

♦♦Harvey Matusow

Matusow said later:

I concocted the idea of a "plot" when I was in the Air Force. I had read about a week-long copper strike, and then built my story knowing that the strike would make it difficult for the union to deny my charges.

What I didn't say is that the union had accepted the Federal mediator's proposal for a new contract prior to the start of the strike... showing its intent to continue production, but the Kennecott Copper Corp. turned it down. It was after this event that the strike was called.

The Attacks Continue

Jencks immediately moved for a new trial on the basis of this newly discovered evidence. After a lengthy hearing, the Federal District Court denied the motion. Jencks appealed this ruling as well, but the Court of Appeals affirmed both. Jencks then appealed to the Supreme Court.

The government did not wait for the high court's decision in *Jencks*. It had joined the concerted employer attack on Mine-Mill, and instigated the CIO attack on Mine-Mill as part of the Cold War. In this ongoing war, Mine-Mill had to defend itself on seven fronts simultaneously.

* In federal courts against Taft-Hartley oath charges against individual union leaders (Clinton Jencks, Maurice Travis)
* In federal courts against Taft-Hartley conspiracy charges against national union leadership (Ray Dennis and 13 others)
* In NLRB against decertification and orders forbidding use of NLRB (Precision Scientific)
* In Subversive Activities Control Board hearings charging "Communist infiltration"
* In Senate Internal Security Subcommittee hearings
* In protracted negotiations and long strikes forced by employees
* In local unions facing raiding by other CIO unions

Each engagement proved costly to both sides. Goliath had the money and the power, but little David started winning in the appellate courts. The final outcome remained uncertain as this epic drama unfolded on many fronts from Silver City to Denver to Washington.

In May 1954, the NLRB held hearings on its own motion to prevent the union from using the NLRB in any way. The Board rejected Mine-Mill Secretary-Treasurer Maurice Travis's Taft-Hartley oath and decertified the union as bargaining agent at Precision Scientific in Chicago. [*See section 49.*]

Meanwhile, United Steelworkers staff members were trying to raid Mine-Mill locals. When argument failed, some turned to violence. The most serious incident was the beating of Maurice Travis. He was in a Bessemer radio station, waiting in an anteroom to broadcast a union message, when a dozen USW "goons" burst in and beat him severely, destroying one eye. But there was even more in store for Travis. A federal grand jury indicted him in October on the charge of filing false Taft-Hartley affidavits. Within two months Travis was tried, convicted, and sentenced to eight years imprisonment.

In February 1955, the NLRB revoked Mine-Mill's compliance status. In November 1955, the federal court of appeals in Washington unanimously reversed and ordered the NLRB to return Mine-Mill to full compliance status. Then, the Department of Justice subpoenaed Ray Dennis and 13 other Mine-Mill officers, representatives, and employees before a secret federal grand jury investigation in Denver. The issue: whether Mine-Mill had bribed Matusow to recant his testimony in the Jencks trial.

PRESSURE TO RESIGN

♦♦ Clinton E. Jencks ♦♦

While the appeals in the *Travis* and *Jencks* cases were pending in 1956, Maurice Travis and I were summoned to Denver by the International Executive Board of Mine-Mill. Travis had served the Union as International Representative, Secretary-Treasurer, Vice-President, and President. The Board requested that Travis and I resign our positions as International Representatives "for the good and welfare of the Union." Board members told us they were more convinced than ever that the indictments were an assault on the whole union and its membership, an attempt to tame the labor movement and suppress democratic protest through Cold War hysteria. They were frank in telling us that the Executive Board could not stand firm against the mounting attacks. Rival unions were using the perjury cases against us as smear tactics in their raiding attempts to displace Mine-Mill with a "loyal" union that would not have all these problems with government agencies and employers.

Some major corporations had first refused to sign contracts with Mine-Mill because of the union's refusal to comply with Taft-Hartley. When the union complied, charges of filing false non-Communist affidavits were the result. Now these convictions were hanging over the union. Board members told us that, in asking for our resignations, they hoped to strengthen the union's ability to fight off raids, to get the government to let up on attacks against Mine-Mill, and to improve the chances of merger negotiations that were then under way with several other unions.

We resigned, but the strategy did not work. Harassment intensified.

A LITTLE JUSTICE A LITTLE LATE

♦♦ The Editors ♦♦

In November 1956, at a time when Mine-Mill was involved in national negotiations with major mining, smelting, and fabricating corporations, the Justice Department obtained indictments against 14 union officers and leaders in Denver charging "conspiracy to defraud" the government by agreeing among themselves to file "false" Taft-Hartley affidavits. This was similar to the Cleveland Taft-Hartley conspiracy indictments against UE leader Marie Reed and Mine-Mill leader Fred Haug [see section 81].

A month later, however, Mine-Mill won a victory in the case stemming from the NLRB's rejection of Travis's Taft-Hartley oath and the Board's decertification of the union at Precision Scientific. The U.S. Supreme Court decided unanimously:

> The penalty stated in sec. 9(h) is one against the guilty officers. In view of the wording of sec. 9(h) and its legislative history, we cannot find an additional sanction which in practical effect would run against the members of the union, not their guilty officers.

From February to May 1957, the Attorney General paraded paid witnesses before the Subversive Activities Control Board, most of them deserters of Mine-Mill.

Despite repeated red scare headlines on June 3, 1957, the Supreme Court handed Mine-Mill another victory, reversing the conviction of Clinton Jencks and ordering a new trial. Justice Brennan wrote for the seven-to-one majority that Jencks had a right to see FBI reports of informer witnesses.

> The impeachment of [Matusow's] testimony was singularly important [since Matusow admitted]:

"I don't recall what I put in my reports two or three years ago, written or oral. ...."

Every experienced trial judge and trial lawyer knows the value for impeaching purposes of statements of the witness recording the events before time dulls treacherous memory. [The accused was demanding specific documents of statements taken from an actual witness about relevant matters,] and did not propose any broad or blind fishing expedition among documents possessed by the Government on the chance that something impeaching might turn up.

Jencks's lawyers had asked merely that the documents be shown to the judge to determine whether parts should be admitted in evidence. The Supreme Court went further:

> We now hold that [Jencks] was entitled to an order directing the Government to produce for inspection all reports of Matusow and Ford in its possession, written and, when orally made, as recorded by the F.B.I., touching the events and activities as to which they testified at the trial. We hold, further, that [Jencks] is entitled to inspect the reports to decide whether to use them in his defense ... for purposes of discrediting the Government's witness .... Justice requires no less.
>
> The practice of producing government documents to the trial judge for his determination of relevancy and materiality, without hearing the accused, is disapproved....

The government had a choice, Justice Brennan explained: it could prosecute a person for crime and allow him access to all "relevant statements or reports in its possession of government witnesses," or it could keep its information confidential and not undertake the prosecution.

Justice Clark dissented. "Unless the Congress changes the rule announced by the Court today," he said, "those intelligence agencies of our Government engaged in law enforcement may as well close up shop, for the Court has opened their files to the criminal and thus afforded him a Roman holiday for rummaging through confidential information as well as vital national secrets."

Congress took heed of Clark's dissent and quickly enacted what became known as the Jencks Act, stating that a defendant is to be shown reports of earlier statements by government witnesses *only if* the entire document relates to the witness' testimony; otherwise, the trial judge should pick out the relevant portions and show only those to the defendant.

Despite their limitations, the *Jencks* decision and the Jencks Act marked significant steps in protecting the rights of defendants in all types of criminal cases. The FBI and some state investigating agencies thereafter modified their practices and seldom made written records of their interviews with prospective witnesses; this led defense counsel to move for information on the existence of tapes which were sometimes granted.

After the Supreme Court decisions, Harvey Matusow testified for the defense in trials of some Communist leaders, recanting his earlier testimony. He wrote a book, *False Witness*, describing his transformation from liberal youth leader to anti-Communist witness with ambitions to become famous and rich. He charged that a government lawyer encouraged him to embellish his testimony in the prosecution of Communists. For these recantations the federal government charged him with perjury and won his conviction. Ironically, he, not Clinton Jencks, ended up serving a five-year sentence.

A Tremendous Victory for the Whole Country

On June 17, 1957, two weeks after freeing Jencks, the Supreme Court reversed the Smith Act convictions of the leaders of the Communist Party from California in *Yates v. United States*. The Court found procedural unfairness in their case also, and sent it back for retrial.

But the government decided not to retry Clinton Jencks. Rather than permit Jencks's lawyers to see the reports of FBI conversations with informants, it dropped charges. And, with *Jencks* and *Yates* against them, the government decided not to try the *Yates* defendants again and dropped Smith Act charges against almost 100 Communist Party leaders around the country.

The stubborn, courageous, and creative work of labor unions and labor people like Jencks and his lawyers helped put a stop to the whole McCarthy repressive drive.

WHY ME?

Why was I selected for frame-up out of the thousands of militant and courageous rank-and-file union officers? In fact, the *Jencks* case is a small part of a much larger picture. My case was an illustration of what may happen to you if you serve your membership, fail to give in to overwhelming power arrayed against you, if you are not satisfied with what the system is willing to allot to working people. The *Jencks* case is more than that. It was and is part of a more general attack on Mine-Mill, the labor movement, and all sections of the population who work or hope for more economic, social, and political democracy.

The *Jencks* case marked an intensification of a long campaign by government and the mining, milling, and smelting industry to destroy or transform the Mine-Mill union and its predecessor, the Western Federation of Miners. This campaign was only part of the larger campaign to subdue or transform the labor movement. It is sad to have to record here that temporarily some of the objectives of that campaign succeeded.

◆◆Clinton E. Jencks

THE ATTACKS RESUME

◆◆ The Editors ◆◆

In July 1957, the U.S. Court of Appeals in Denver set aside Maurice Travis's conviction for filing false Taft-Hartley affidavits because of procedural unfairness. In January 1958, he was tried for the second time and convicted. This time, the U.S. Court of Appeals upheld Travis's conviction. Mine-Mill lawyers appealed to the Supreme Court which reversed this second convction over the issue, again, of unfairness. The Court held, in January 1961, that Congress had so carefully indicated the place of the act, that the only place defendants could be tried was in Washington. The government quit trying Travis, who had not been a Mine-Mill official for five years by this time.

Mine-Mill was engaged in a nationwide strike against the copper industry when, in November and December 1959, its 14 leaders who had been indicted by a Denver grand jury for conspiracy were put on trial. The judge dismissed indictments against two of them, but nine were convicted by the jury; most were sentenced to three years in prison and fined $2,000. (Three had pleaded no contest.) These convictions were also appealed. In March 1962, the Court of Appeals reversed the convictions and ordered that indictments against two defendants be dismissed, because government witnesses had presented prejudicial evidence that was only hearsay. On retrial, the remaining 12 were convicted again.

In November 1965, the U.S. Supreme Court unanimously reversed the convictions, citing, once again, procedural unfairness. The Mine-Mill defendants had asked the government to produce the grand jury testimony of four key governement witnesses, but the government had refused. The Court said failure to produce this evidence required reversal; the government could produce it in a new trial (384 U.S. 855).

Justices Black and Douglas disagreed. They said there could be no new trial because the underlying law had changed. The T-H oath had been repealed by Congress in 1954, which passed the 1954 Communist Control Act (making it a crime to be a union leader and a Communist.) This had been held unconstitutional in the case of Archie Brown of the ILWU [*described in section 84*]. Therefore, the Mine-Mill defendants could not be fairly tried again. The government did not take up the challenge a third time, dismissing the charges after a 10-year battle.

At the same time Mine-Mill was engaged on these various courtroom fronts, it had to defend itself in administrative hearings and in the halls of Congress.

It began when the U.S. Attorney General petitioned the Subversive Activities Control Board to find Mine-Mill to be a "Communist-infiltrated" organization as defined in the 1954 Communist Control Act. After a series of intermittent hearings in 1957, in December 1961, the SACB Hearing Officer issued his "Recommended Decision" finding Mine-Mill to be a "Communist infiltrated organization."

Meanwhile, in October 1961, the Senate Internal Security Subcommittee (SISC), chaired by Senator James O. Eastland (D-Miss), questioned Mine-Mill officers and staff regarding its mutual assistance pact with the Teamsters Union and the $100,000 loan for strike relief secured by the Teamsters.

Throughout 1962, 1963, and 1964, the Eastland Committee, the SACB, and the Justice Department continued to attack Mine-Mill. But the national tide was turning away from simplistic Red-baiting and union-baiting. In November 1965, the U.S. Court of Appeals sent the Mine-Mill case back to the SACB because the evidence was "stale." In June 1966, the government gave up. The SACB order against the Union was vacated and the Attorney General's petition against the Union was dismissed.

RAIDING MINE-MILL

♦♦ Morris Wright ♦♦

Morris Wright is a former editor and education director for Mine-Mill.

During this entire period of harassment by government agencies in cooperation with employers, Mine-Mill was attacked by other unions. Before this time, there had been some raiding of one union's membership by another, but this had been generally frowned upon and was forbidden by federation bylaws. When it had occurred, usually it was based on a claim that the membership in dispute belonged within the jurisdiction of the raiding union and would be better served by that union in collective bargaining. Both AFL and CIO, and later the AFL-CIO, had committees on jurisdiction that tried to settle such disputes and spare the labor movement the humiliation of intramural fighting.

But after the expulsions and the CIO's "awarding" of Mine-Mill's jurisdiction to other unions, raiding became "respectable," even patriotic. This resulted in degrading standards of unionism throughout the labor movement. Mine-Mill had practically completed organization of its jurisdiction vertically as well as horizontally. The raids broke up the unity thus achieved within individual properties, as well as industry-wide.

What arguments could the raiders put forward to persuade Mine-Mill members to change unions? They could not offer better wages and conditions; Mine-Mill had the best contracts in the industry. They could not convincingly offer better handling of grievances. They could not offer more rank-and-file control; Mine-Mill was a model of union democracy. (John L. Lewis had told Mine-Mill leaders: "You guys are too democratic for your own good. It takes you too long to move, with all of your area councils and industry councils.")

So what was left? Red-baiting—a time-honored employer tactic. As raiding proceeded, its internal logic brought the raiders into ever closer collaboration with employers and their stoolpigeons, antiunion politicians, vigilantes, the antilabor press, and backward workers who identified their interests with the employer.

Two elements of the Mine-Mill membership did not respond to the raiders' appeals. First were those local unions with substantial numbers of Black or Latino members, who identified Mine-Mill with their advancement from dual wage scales and general second-class status on the job. The second were those in the mining camps of the West and Southwest, who were used to being called Reds every time they had to strike, since the days of the Wobblies. Some of these locals succumbed after repeated raids over a period of years. In every such case, the union had been weakened from within by a leader who changed sides.

Should Mine-Mill Merge with USW?

After 1959, Mine-Mill was no longer the dominant union in the nonferrous metals industry, although the union had successfully fought off many raids by the United Steelworkers and others. But it was unable to regain lost membership, and its contracts no longer were significantly superior to those of USW.

By 1967, both Mine-Mill and the USW were struggling to maintain wage standards as the steel and nonferrous metals industries curtailed operations in the U.S. because of imports and sagging prices. Political issues such as U.S. foreign policy that had divided the labor movement 20 years earlier were no longer in focus. Mine-Mill found its energies almost entirely consumed in economic struggles.

In these circumstances, the principal difference between the two unions was in internal democracy. Mine-Mill decided this was outweighed by the advantage of greater unity in planning and bargaining to be attained through merger with USW in 1967. There was some talk of Mine-Mill locals becoming centers of rank-and-file influence within the USW, but people knew that the relatively small and scattered Mine-Mill elements would be lost in the huge USW organization.

What has happened to former Mine-Mill locals since the merger? An example is Local 890 at Bayard, New Mexico. In the early 1940s, unionism in the area had been greatly strengthened by the amalgamation, under the International Union's leadership, of several lead-zinc mining locals with a big Kennecott Copper local there. After the 1967 merger, the USW regional director reversed this move, creating again separate locals at the various mines, mills, and smelters. The reason obviously was to diffuse and weaken the influence of a strong rank-and-file controlled union which had opposed the merger.

Ray Marrufo, a Local 890 oldtimer, described changes in Local 890 when it joined USW-AFL-CIO. He said:

The solidarity that we had in 1949 or 1953 was not there any more.... There were strikes, but no struggles. A struggle exists when there's something to get the people really united around—and when there's leadership. That was really important to us: the International's leadership.

Lorenzo Torres, another oldtimer, described another change, something very important in Mine-Mill's past—the willingness to donate your own time for union business. "That has gone out of existence now. It's getting to where people won't go to shop stewards' classes, unless they're paid their full wages." Torres said this had to do with the view of the union "as part of a social movement. A worker will not sacrifice his time unless he understands that he is able to move things and change things." (Kent Hudson, "Mine-Mill: The Voices from the Mountains," unpublished doctoral thesis, Union Graduate School, 1979.)

Mine-Mill suffered a heavy loss at the huge International Nickel Co. property at Sudbury, Ontario, in Canada. But one small unit in Canada rejected the raid at the Falconbridge mines, and one at Trail, B.C., proudly continued as local unions of the International Union of Mine, Mill and Smelter Workers, and do so today.

THE END

In 1972, I visited Trail, B.C., Canada. There I saw a Mine-Mill local still flourishing. But Mine-Mill is now dead in the United States. It is dead as a result of oath and conspiracy trials, the Un-American Committee, the Senate Subcommittee.... It was like a creature being attacked in the sea by sharks and I watched it. I watched it die.

♦♦Virginia Derr Chambers

75 ‣‣ EFFECTS OF UNION McCARTHYISM ON BLACK WORKERS

♦♦Philip Foner♦♦

For author note, see section 21.

The 1950 CIO Convention

The CIO leadership invited a distinguished Black educator, Dr. Mordecai Johnson, to be the featured speaker at its 1950 National Convention. To the dismay of many delegates, this president of Howard University warned the CIO not to be taken in by the propaganda of the Cold War.

What, he asked, was the "free world" that Truman, Churchill, Franco, Salazar, and other champions of the Cold War professed to be defending against "Communist aggression" inspired by the Soviet Union?

It was made up of Britain, France, Belgium, the Netherlands, Spain, Portugal, Germany, and the United States—every last one of which had "been busy during the last two hundred years securing and sustaining [its own] freedom by the political domination, economic exploitation and social humiliation of over half of the human race." The "free world", in other words, comprised "probably the most ruthless dominators and exploiters and humiliators of human life that ever spanned the pages of history." Instead of bringing economic and political freedom to India, Africa, China, Malaya, Indo-china, and the Near East, they had used their power "to dominate them politically, to exploit their natural resources and their labor, and to segregate and humiliate them upon the land upon which their fathers had died and in the presence of the graves which hold the bodies of their mothers."

Dr. Johnson referred to a part of the world that would later erupt into prominence, Southeast Asia:

Now, suppose you were Indo-Chinese, wouldn't you be amazed at us? For over 100 years the French have been in Indo-China, dominating them politically, strangling them economically, and humiliating them in the land of their fathers.

We [the United States] haven't ever sat down with the French and demanded that they change that system. And in the defect of leadership on our part, they have turned to the Communists, and the Communists have given them leaders; they have trained their troops, and given them money. And now it looks as though they can win.

And as they are about to win their liberty, we rush up to the scene and say: "Dear Brothers, what on earth are you getting ready to do? Are you going to throw yourselves into the hands of this diabolical conspiracy under the false notion they can bring you freedom? Why, they aren't free; we are the free people of the world; we have democratic institutions; we are your friends; we will send you leaders; we will send you ammunition, and we will send you bread."

And they look at us in amazement and say: "Brother, where have you been? Why, if we'd a-known you was a-coming, we'd have baked a cake."

At the time, CIO President Philip Murray praised the Black educator's speech as an "inspirational address that could only come from the soul of a man." But what was the record of Murray and the CIO leadership in their relations with unions that upheld a position practically identical to Dr. Johnson's?

The Case of FTA Local 22

One of the earliest Cold War targets of the CIO leadership was the United Tobacco Workers, Local 22, affiliated with the left-wing Food, Tobacco, Agricultural, and Allied Workers Union (FTA). Local 22 had Communists in leadership.

In the summer of 1947 Local 22 was engaged in negotiations for a new agreement with R.J. Reynolds in Winston-Salem, North Carolina, employing 11,000 workers about equally divided between Black and white, and mainly women. This was the largest plant organized in the South. When management would not sign, the workers went out on strike.

Immediately, the House Un-American Activities Committee (HUAC) began investigating the leaders of Local 22 on the ground that it was a "Communist-dominated union." The investigation made headlines in the Winston-Salem press, but the tobacco workers were not intimidated. Soon the company began evicting strikers from their company-owned houses. On July 1, Paul Robeson, the militant Black performer, spoke and sang at a mass meeting of 12,000 people in Winston-Salem. The theme was "full support for Local 22."

The strike lasted 38 days, and led to a workers' victory. The agreement between Reynolds and Local 22 raised wages and reduced working hours.

Shortly thereafter, Local 22 launched a campaign to register its members to vote. They added 8,000 new names to the rolls. As a result, Winston-Salem became the first Southern city in the twentieth century to send a Black, the Reverend Kenneth Williams, to the City Council.

Then the CIO leadership picked up where HUAC had left off: they set out to raid Local 22, one of its own unions. With funds provided by the CIO Executive Council, Willard Townsend, Black President of the United Transport Service Employees, came into Winston-Salem in 1949 to challenge Local 22 in an NLRB election. At the same time, the company financed a campaign to persuade white members of Local 22 that they owed it to their country to quit a union dominated by Communists. The mayor of Winston-Salem went on the radio to read extracts from the report of the House Un-American Activities Committee on Local 22.

Townsend and his CIO staff of Black organizers won over only a few Black workers. And a few white members were influenced by Red-baiting to vote against Local 22. However, the NLRB election, involving 11,000 workers, went "No union" by 60 votes.

Local 22 continued to exist, but no longer as the collective bargaining agent for the workers at R.J. Reynolds. Thus, the Black tobacco workers were among the first to feel the sting of the CIO's red-baiting drive. That same year, Local 22 leader Miranda Smith became FTA Southern Regional Director and, as a member of the union's national executive board, occupied the highest position in the labor movement any Black woman had held up to that time.

MIRANDA SMITH

Miranda Smith was the daughter of a sharecropper family, born in South Carolina. The family moved to Winston-Salem, the tobacco center of North Carolina. After graduating from high school, she began working for the R.J. Reynolds Tobacco Co., which had been established a century before by the Reynolds family, former slaveowners of the largest plantation in Virginia. Their slaveholding ideology left its imprint on the factory—no lunch facilities, no decent restrooms, no sick leave, vacations, or seniority, no paid holidays or job security.

In 1941 Miranda Smith and some friends asked the CIO for aid in organizing this gigantic plant. They organized Local 22 of the United Cannery, Agriculture, Packing and Allied Workers.

In June 1943, a Black worker died after the foreman denied him permission to leave work to see a doctor. The workers went out on strike and Smith became the strike leader. That wartime strike led to union recognition and $1,250,000 in retroactive pay in the leafhouse and stemmeries, in accordance with the War Labor Board's rule of equal pay for equal work.

After leading the successful Reynolds strike, Smith attended the 1947 CIO convention. She warned that Congress would continue to pass bills like Taft-Hartley until Blacks in the South could vote.

In 1948, Miranda Smith was appointed assistant director of the FTA's Southern Atlantic region. In January 1950 she became the international representative of the Southern Region.

On April 14, 1950, Miranda Smith died at the age of 35 after a sudden illness. The funeral services were held in the largest church in Winston Salem, with thousands gathering in the streets.

♦♦The Editors
World Magazine[1]

Expelling the Pace Setters

When the CIO expelled 11 international unions in 1949 and 1950, charging them with supporting policies that were against official CIO principles, it dealt a severe blow to the struggle for racial equality in the labor movement. Several of the expelled unions were pace-setters for the whole trade union movement in terms of wage scales and conditions won, and in terms of sex and racial equality. This is not to say that Black and women members were fully represented at conventions and in positions of leadership even in these progressive unions. But, in general, these were the unions that had fought longest and hardest for Black employment, Black upgrading, and Black representation in trade union offices. Their fight had forced the more backward unions in the CIO toward an equalitarian position on the issue of Black labor. But in 1949, that record was of no consequence to the Cold War warriors in the CIO leadership.

CIO leaders were only one force attacking left unions and leaders. The United States government was another. One of the sharpest weapons the government had against union leaders was reserved for those born abroad. The most famous target was Harry Bridges, president of the International Longshoremen and Warehousemen's Union (ILWU).

Another victim came from another waterfront union. Ferdinand Smith was a Black leader of the National Maritime Union. He built a long record of achievements for seamen, and contributions to the struggle for equal rights. Then the Truman Administration branded him an "undesirable alien." After a fierce defense by the American Committee for Protection of the Foreign Born, in August, 1951, Smith elected to leave the United States and return to Jamaica, his native land. He told reporters:

> I helped to build a union which enabled sailors to marry and have children and a home just like other workers, instead of being kicked around like bums. For this I earned the enmity of the shipowners and their agents in and out of the government.
>
> [I am confident that] the stormy night of reaction [will pass away, and that the American people will return their government] to the hands of the masses to whom it belongs.[2]

Scores of Black and white members of the NMU gathered to bid Smith farewell, but Joseph Curran, NMU president, was not among them. He had joined the Red-baiters and was now one of the CIO's top anti-Communists.

Truman's Screening Program

Curran did, however, choose to attend another gathering when the Truman Administration launched a maritime "loyalty" screening program, at a conference in Washington, D.C., on July 24, 1950. He was in good company: Allan Haywood, fresh from his work in getting the National Union of Marine Cooks and Stewards expelled from the CIO, was there, as were representatives of "King" Joseph Ryan (lifetime, racketeering president of the AF of L International Longshoremen's Association), representatives of the Justice Department, and representatives of the shipping interests.

On July 31, 1950, the *New York Times* reported that "invitations to the conference pointedly exempted two unions, and in a definite sense these organizations are a target of the resolution. They are the dock union of Harry Bridges and the Marine Cooks and Stewards."

The conference worked out an agreement that became government policy: maritime workers would not be permitted to ship out if they were deemed poor security risks. This provision was soon extended to longshoremen, who were barred from working on military docks if they did not have the approval of the Coast Guard [*discussed in section 53*].

Local police officials sought and obtained the cooperation of NMU anti-Communists in carrying out the screening process. Brass knuckles, clubs and guns were used in Houston, Texas, as the police, Joe Curran's henchmen, and the press collaborated in driving the militant seamen, many of them Blacks, from shipping jobs.

An investigative reporter for the San Francisco *Sun-Reporter*, a Black weekly newspaper, noted in 1952:

Screening is an attempt to drive Negroes from the waterfront and to undermine the unions that have fought for racial equality. I have found that Negroes with key jobs have been the first to be screened.

In April, 1952, *March of Labor* reported that "65 percent of the blacklisted are Negroes. In every union under a screening program, Negroes have been disproportionately penalized." The ILWU *Dispatcher* explained that "Negroes are among the most militant ILWU members, because they have found in our organization the sort of democracy and freedom from discrimination they seldom find elsewhere." A study of the screening process on the West Coast by Robert Friedman concluded that "approximately 70 percent of the screened members of the National Union of Marine Cooks and Stewards have been Negroes."[3]

In the "screening" process, as in the federal government's "loyalty" board hearings for government employees, any activity against Jim Crow was proof of a suspected person's disloyalty. Black workers were asked: "Did you ever have dinner with a mixed group?"

White workers were asked: "Did you ever entertain Blacks in your home?"

Witnesses were asked: "Have you had any conversations that would lead you to believe [the accused] is rather advanced in his thinking on racial matters?"

Attacks on the Marine Cooks and Stewards

The National Union of Marine Cooks and Stewards (MC&S) was subjected to massive and persistent attacks during this shameful period in U.S. history.

First, it was expelled from the CIO.

Then its president, Hugh Bryson, became the first person indicted under the anti-Communist oath provision of the Taft-Hartley Act for being "affiliated" with the Communist Party. He was indicted for perjury and brought to trial on the charge of lying when he signed the non-Communist oath.

The Black community of San Francisco came to Hugh Bryson's defense. A meeting sponsored by Black leaders in the city passed resolutions praising him and his union for their "contribution to racial democracy." The Baptist Ministerial Alliance of San Francisco, representing Black Baptist churches, also pledged full support to Bryson and his union.

Enraged by this support, the NLRB directed the shipowners to cease recognition of the union "as the sole bargaining representative for the stewards' department" aboard Pacific Maritime Association vessels. The employers promptly recognized the "Marine Cooks and Stewards, A.F. of L., Anti-Communists," the brainchild of the segregationist Sailors Union of the Pacific, which refused to admit Blacks to membership.[4]

Pete Edmunds of the MC&S appealed to the Graphic Arts Workshop for help: "We're under attack from all sides—the government witch-hunting, Lundberg's Seaman's outfit raiding us—and, of course, the shipowners using the situation. All we have to go on is the solidarity of our members. Can the artists do something?"

The challenge was to use our art to strengthen pride of heritage and bonds of mutual respect among the Black, Latino, Asian and white workers. After months of research and painting, the walls of the MC&S headquarters were covered with a dramatic depiction of Black history, and later by murals of the Mexican-American heritage, women in U.S. labor, and other theme exhibits. Hal Fontaine, a screened seaman, and Larry Yamamoto, a longshoreman, were two of the painters.

♦♦Irving Fromer, Chair, Graphic Arts Workshop

Black Workers Stuck by MC&S

Few Blacks were persuaded by the AF of L's allegation that the militant Marine Cooks and Stewards was controlled by "Commies." The vast majority remained loyal. A Black member of the union, born and reared in the South, told an interviewer:

The union is my father and my mother and I am the son who will give my life for it. The union has put bread in the mouths of my children. It has given me a home, it has straightened my back so I do not bend to any man. It took me by the hand and said, "Learn to read," and I learned to read. Big words, words they never had in those chicken coop schools. In the union I learned a trade. What would I be down in that country—an ignorant cotton picker? Wherever the union sees wrong, it points it out. It stands up and says, "That's wrong. Do right. Do like we do. Treat your brother right." I been in M.C. and S. a long time. I lost my prejudices. I had them. But I met real brothers here. I met big men who mean what they say. If my brothers sleep in the foc'sles, I sleep with them. My white brothers, my Black brothers, my brown brothers, all of them. We the children of the union, we all together.[5]

Nor did the workers desert the union when the National Maritime Union, at Curran's insistence, raided it. "They supported MCS," declared Revels Cayton, Black business agent, and a dynamic leader of the union, "because of the union's struggle against the shipowners, for democracy, for Negro-white unity, for the fullest dignity for the Negro seamen."

Hugh Bryson wrote emotionally in the April 20, 1951 edition of *The Voice*, the union's organ: "The cornerstone of the very foundation of our great union.... Negro-white unity has proved to be the most effective weapon against the shipowners, against the raiders, and all our enemies."

Expulsion from the CIO had no effect on the equalitarian policies of the expelled unions. UE, Fur and Leather, ILWU, Mine-Mill, Food, Tobacco, Agricultural and Allied Workers, United Office and Professional Workers, Marine Cooks and Stewards, and other expelled unions continued to fight discrimination against Black workers. Their official union journals show their continued determination to insure the civil rights of Blacks and other minority groups.

Finally, however, FTA and UOPWA collapsed in the face of continuous government persecution and CIO and AF of L raids. [*See sections 79 and 47.*] The Distributive, Processing, and Office Workers Union took over many of their locals. This union emerged from District 65, which began life as an organization for Jewish dry goods workers on Manhattan's Lower East Side. It participated in the great organizing drives of the 1930s. Through mergers with other locals, such as the shoe workers, and organization of the city's textile workers, District 65 increased its membership to about 10,000. District 65 began a drive to organize Black workers in New York by appointing Cleveland Robinson, a Black worker, as organizer. First the union recruited a large Black membership. Later many Puerto Ricans joined. A militant left-wing union, it earned a reputation for consistent support of equal rights and got involved in most of the key battles being waged by Black people.

Anti-Red Meant Anti-Black

The evidence is clear that the CIO retreated on the struggle for Black rights in the Cold War era. For one thing, the expulsion of the left-wing unions removed a source of pressure to make equal rights for Blacks a paramount issue. Soon conservative politicians and employers were charging that even the right-wing unions were "Communist-dominated." These unions were not about to champion the rights of Black workers at the risk of being accused of "subversive" activities! They had led the effort to expel the left unions, but that was not enough to save them from the witch-hunters.

Even the NLRB acknowledged that employers made effective use of the Red issue by branding as Communists CIO organizers from ordinarily conservative unions when they tried to include Blacks in the same locals with whites.

Under such attacks, the CIO quickly retreated. Their tendency was to maintain the status quo in collective bargaining agreements. This meant a slowdown in the fight to upgrade Black workers.

In 1949 sections of the Black press accused the CIO Committee to Abolish Racial Discrimination of doing "little or nothing to overcome discrimination against Negroes."[6] The July 9, 1949 edition of the *Pittsburgh Courier* reported that the committee was "serving no useful purpose to CIO union members and hasn't even proved itself to be of nominal nuisance value. It is a nice window dressing for the organization ... but in its present form is doing the unions and the liberal forces of this country a distinct disservice." The story accused Black members of the committee of holding their offices "on a puppet basis" and described as "disgusting" their conduct at the 1949 UAW convention, where they supported Walter Reuther against the demand from Black members for a Black vice-president. "About the only thing missing from the show was a pair of handkerchiefs wrapped around each of the gentlemen's expansive brows."

Even Black committee member Willard Townsend conceded that in the Black community the committee was "recognized not as a committee to do something, but more like a symbol."[7]

Finally someone proposed that the committee publicize discriminatory practices by CIO unions. This was rejected. James B. Carey, committee chairman and president of IUE, declared that the publicity "would injure all unions."[8]

Some determined committee members supported revoking the charters of discriminatory CIO unions. They faced the hoary excuse, long advanced at AF of L conventions against A. Philip Randolph's similar demand, that such action would violate the autonomy of the member unions.

Columnist Ralph Matthews assailed "the new CIO policy which calls for conformity with America's traditional policy of segregation and Jim Crowism," in the February 18, 1950 issue of the *Washington Afro-American*. Racial segregation was becoming so widespread at functions sponsored by CIO affiliates in the South it was the practice to hold most meetings on a segregated basis, and in South Carolina, it was common knowledge, that "CIO union halls ... have Jim Crow toilet facilities."

Two studies, one in 1950 and the other in 1953, demonstrated that, while many CIO unions had Blacks on their staffs as national organizers and international representatives, they served too often either as "window-dressing for the organization" or as "liaison men between white union leaders and Negro workers."[9] This was a one-way channel from the top down, assigned to keep the Black membership in line. One Black union leader admitted bitterly to an investigator:

"Some unions have a Negro on the staff, or a committee to deal with these matters [of race relations]. But they have no power! Their only function is to *take care* of the Negroes, and they don't [even] do that! Having a Negro on the staff is *just a show* for most unions!"[10]

When Black union officials refused to play the assigned roles, they faced the charge of being "Communists" or "Communist dupes." Some were threatened with suspension from office unless they toed the mark. In several instances, particularly in the UAW, Black leaders were removed from office and expelled for their militance.

When union people showed concern for the problems of Black people, the Red-baiters dismissed them with the claim that they were all devised "to further the program of the Communist Party." They said Blacks were being "used" for this sinister objective.

Robert Friedman, who analyzed the problem in 1952, took issue: "If to 'use' is to advance the economic and social status of the Negroes, give them fuller citizenship rights, wage common struggle with them, and elect their representatives to high union offices, then the word has a meaning which the investigator cannot decipher."[11]

It is clear, then, that during the Cold War era, the CIO position on Black labor began to move closer and closer to the stance long associated with the AF of L, bringing with it "growing disenchantment with the CIO in the Negro community."[12] But the CIO leadership was prepared to pay this price for supporting Cold War policies in the labor movement.

NOTES

1. *World Magazine*, March 10, 1984, p. 4.
2. *Freedom*, Sept. 1951.
3. Robert Friedman, "The Attitude of West Coast Maritime Unions in Seattle Toward Negroes in the Maritime Industry" (unpublished MA thesis, State College of Washington, 1952), p. 181.
4. Philip S. Foner, *Organized Labor and the Black Worker (1619-1981)* (New York 1981), p. 286.
5. Friedman, p. 155.
6. F. Ray Marshall, "Unions and the Negro Community," *Industrial and Labor Relations Review*, vol. 22 (Jan. 1964), p. 185.
7. *Ibid.*
8. *Ibid.* at 186.
9. William Kornhauser, "Labor Unions and Race Relations: A Study of Union Tactics" (unpublished MA thesis, University of Chicago, 1950) p. 22; Scott Greer, "Situational Pressure and Functional Role of Ethnic Labor Leader," *Social Forces* (Oct. 1953), pp. 41-2.
10. William Kornhauser, "The Negro Union Official: A Study in Sponsorship and Control," *Am. Jour. of Sociology* (March 1952), p. 446.
11. Friedman, p. 206.
12. Foner, p. 290.

76 ♦♦ NATIONAL NEGRO LABOR COUNCIL

♦♦ Mindy Thompson Fullilove ♦ Charles H. Wright ♦♦

For authors' and source notes, see section 15.

Unfortunately for Black people in general and Black trade unionists in particular, a major shift of national priorities occurred in 1947 that was detrimental to their welfare. Many labor unions, seeking conformity with the Truman anti-Communist foreign policy, sacrificed their liberal-radical elements, many of whom were Black. For example, by 1949, Ferdinand Smith, formerly Executive Secretary of the National Maritime Union, had lost his position in the Union and was arrested for deportation. Another high official in the Union hierarchy, Ewart Guinier, a Black Panamanian, had fallen from power. His power base, the United Public Workers Union, incurred the wrath of the CIO and was slated for expulsion.

The list of other Black union officials and supporters who became expendable by the Cold War included Revels Cayton, William Chester, Thomas Coleman, George Crockett, W. E. B. DuBois, Octavia Hawkins, Charles Hill, Carleton Goodlet, William Hood, Joe Johnson, Sam Parks, Hobson Reynolds, Thomas Richardson, Teresa L. Robinson, and Coleman Young, to name a few. Most of these rebels attracted the attention of either the Senate Internal Security Subcommittee or the House Un-American Activities Committee. The common denominator and chief rebel of the entire group was Paul Robeson, the great singer, actor and public figure.

The prospects for the Black worker seemed very bleak to

these leaders when a group of them met in Harlem in 1949 to organize a fight for a larger share of the economic resources of the United States. In a move to establish a national organization, a call was sent out to other cities for representation, and a meeting was scheduled for June 10, 1950 in Chicago. The purpose was to launch a more militant attack on job discrimination than had been undertaken by other existing organizations. The 900 delegates, black and white, were told that they had a common enemy within the United States and that they also had a responsibility, as U.S. citizens, to try to help change the foreign policy of our government, having gained strength from the struggles of colonial people for their liberties.

The delegates established continuation committees to organize local councils throughout the United States before the next annual meeting. They chose "National Negro Labor Council" (NNLC) as the name of their organization and elected William Hood, Detroit trade unionist, as their provisional president. Cincinnati, Ohio was chosen as the site of the first meeting of NNLC for its historical significance as "the place where Negroes and whites met in the Underground Railroad to help the flight from slavery to freedom."

Black workers had made some progress under the impact of the New Deal. Then the CIO emerged, expressing coalition politics and opening unions and industry to Blacks. This constituted a crucial shift for Black workers. Soon wartime industry's pressing need for workers had a dramatic impact on Blacks, causing them to move into industry on the basis of the new structure established by the CIO. Under mass pressure from the Black community, President Roosevelt issued Executive Order 8802 establishing the first Fair Employment Practices Committee. Later strengthened by Executive Order 9346, the FEPC was a weak but important tool in fighting for job rights.

Postwar Situation

After the war, the CIO brought a new force into being—the trained Black organizers—a force that was ready and willing to move, provided it was given leadership. The need for uniting the Black working class was again discussed. In 1949, those who had been active in the Negro Labor Victory Committee during the war, the trade-union committee of the National Negro Congress, and other Black workers' forms in the New

York area came together in the Harlem Trade Union Council. Ferdinand Smith lost his job with the National Maritime Union and was unemployed. [See section 53.] He became the executive secretary of the Council, whose program included jobs, community service, and Black political representation. It depended on the unions for financial support.

In May, 1949, the Harlem Trade Union Council supported a demonstration for a pier of its own for the Black local of the International Longshoremen's Association (ILA). Black local members took over the ILA offices. Mounted police and white ILA members sought to break up the demonstration and HTUC put up a picket line in support of the demands. In June, 1950, HTUC became one of the sponsors of the Chicago meeting that founded NNLC.

William Hood, recording secretary of UAW Local 600 in Dearborn, issued the national call to the founding convention of the National Negro Labor Council:

Already the determination of the Negro people to fight back against acts of intimidation, terror and mob violence, in legal and illegal form, which has increased with preparation for all-out war, has been demonstrated in many ways. Peekskill, U.S.A. is our answer to those who attempt to cow us. Though Willie McGee and the Martinsville seven died, the victims of jim crow rule, the hypocrisy of white America, a claim of freedom and justice for all stands exposed to all the world. Freedom for whom? Freedom to do what?

Negro Labor Councils are needed to forge unity of Negro and white in the struggle against the mounting mob violence that victimizes innocent Negro men and women and in the struggle to achieve equality as we believe America achieves it.

The convention call unleased a niagara of protests from all parts of the country, especially Cincinnati. A Red-baiting backlash reared up from the leadership of the city's AFL building laborers union and United Steel Workers-CIO. The Cincinnati City Council took a unanimous stand against the convention, saying it was part of the Communist Party's program to enroll Negroes. The resolution was supported by the only two Negroes on the Council. Both the AFL and CIO attacked the NNLC and requested their members to shun the meetings.

In spite of these impediments 1,052 people registered, including 898 regular delegates and 154 official observers. Some 200 others participated.

Opening the Convention

The convention opened at noon on October 27, 1951 with the singing of the "Star Spangled Banner" and the Negro National Anthem, "Lift Every Voice and Sing." More than 15 international unions were represented, including UAW, MMSW, Distributive, Processing & Office Workers of America, ILWU, UPW, United Steel Workers, United Rubber Workers, UE and other CIO unions, and various AFL unions. Delegates came from 22 states, including nine southern ones. One-third of the delegates were women; four-fifths of all delegates were Black.

The first speaker, Victoria Garvin, vice president of DPOWA, opened the Conference saying:

> Our presence here today records still another victory— concrete proof that despite pressure and hysteria the Negro people will remain firm and support genuine struggles for progress. We are indebted to the several Negro ministers, professionals, business men and women, including the management of the Manse Hotel for their encouragement and cooperation. I am especially proud of the hundreds of Negro families in Cincinnati who rejected the red-baiting and opened their homes and hearts to all of us when the white hotels refused us accommodations. These working men and women responded immediately to a mere postcard or telephone call when we told them of our plight. My people would not see us on the streets. Their steadfastness, combined with our unity and strength, had such impact that it made possible the subsequent blow to white supremacy—our last minute breakthrough, interracially, in the major white hotels....

◆ ◆

THREE NNLC LEADERS

The three leading figures in the founding convention were William R. (Bill) Hood, recording secretary of Local 600 of the UAW-CIO; Coleman A. Young, of the Amalgamated Clothing Workers (CIO); and Ernest Thompson, Secretary of the Fair Practices Committee of the United Electrical, Radio & Machine Workers of America (UE-CIO). They were leading figures in the labor movement generally, and among the top Black trade unionists in the country.

Born in Georgia, Hood attended Tuskegee Institute and worked in the South until World War II. In 1942 he moved to

Detroit and got a job first at the Chevrolet Gear and Axle Plant. Hood came into his own when he shifted to the Ford River Rouge Plant in Michigan. His base was the foundry, with its 20,000 foundry workers, mainly Black. He not only challenged Ford but also was outspoken in support of the Smith Act victims and other targets of political repression.

Young, today the mayor of Detroit, was an able, quick-thinking speaker and an experienced organizer and administrator. Born in Tuscaloosa, Alabama, he lived most of his life in Detroit. He worked for the post office but was fired for trying to organize a union. He served several days in the stockade for attempting to get a cup of coffee at an all-white officers' club. After the war, he worked again for the post office but quit when he was refused time off to work for the United Public Workers. He became director of organization for the Wayne County CIO, state director of the Progressive Party, and candidate for the State Senate.

Thompson, known as "Big Train" because he could "deliver the goods" in negotiations, had been a foundry worker in the American Radiator plant in Bayonne, New Jersey. He had led the struggle to build a union there and later to take the shop into the UE. He left the shop to become the first Black organizer for UE and later headed its Fair Practices committee. He was a leading force in the Black caucus of that union and was the theoretician of the NNLC. He wrote the orginial draft of the founding convention keynote address, as well as several other major pieces which set forth the NNLC outlook. In addition to his leading theoretical role, he could travel extensively because of his job with UE and this made him indispensable for taking the word to the people.

♦ ♦

"Big Train" Thompson followed Victoria Garvin. To him fell the honor of introducing Hood, NNLC president:

We say something new is happening. It gets to your bones; it's on the breeezes; it's everywhere. What is it? It's a new wind of freedom blowing from the Seven Seas and touching the hearts of men and women.... This new wind has brought on the scene a new Negro, the sons and daughters of labor. They have come with one song in their hearts—the song of Freedom.

ADDRESS TO THE FIRST NNLC CONVENTION

♦♦ **William Hood** ♦♦

Brothers and Sisters:

This is an historic day. On this day, we the delegated representatives of thousands of workers, Black and white, dedicate ourselves to the search for a new North Star.... We come conscious of the new stage in the Negro people's surge toward freedom. We come to announce to all America and to the world that Uncle Tom is dead. "Old Massa" lies sleeping in the cold, cold grave. Something new is cooking on the Freedom Train....

The Negro Labor Council is our symbol, the medium of expression of our aims and aspirations. It is the expression of our desire and determination to bring to bear our full weight to help win the first class citizenship for every Black man, woman and child in America. We say that these are legitimate aims. We say that these aspirations burn fiercely in the breast of the Negro in America. And we further say that millions of white workers echo our demands for freedom. These white workers recognize in the struggle for Negro rights, the prerequisites of their own aspirations for a full life and a guarantee that the rising tide of fascism will not engulf America....

We wish to say further that the day has ended when white trade-union leaders or white leaders in any organizations may presume to tell Negroes on what basis they shall come together to fight for their rights. Three hundred years has been enough of that. We Black people in America ask for your *cooperation*— but we do not ask for your permission.

Editors' note: At that, a thousand people rose in an ovation.

If 15 million Negroes, led by their alert sons and daughters of labor, and united together and joined by the 15 million organized white workers in the great American labor movement, say there shall be no more Jim Crow in America—then there will be no more Jim Crow.

The Negro Labor Council ... has come into being at a time when democracy needs fearless champions.

Editors' note: Hood linked the movement in this country with the aspirations of colonial peoples around the world and closed by saying that none of the NNLC's objectives would come without struggle. The immediate program he proposed was a national mass campaign for a

Fair Employment Practices Commission. *He called on all those present to take the Council's constitution, preamble and other documents into battle as "battleflags," to make them living documents.*

We move on, united—and neither man nor beast will turn us back. We will achieve in our time, for ourselves and for our children, a world of no Jim Crow, of no more "white men's jobs" and "colored only" schools; a world of freedom, full equality, security and peace. Our task is clearly set forth.

Brothers and sisters, we move on to struggle and to victory!

A TIME FOR NEW JOHN BROWNS

♦♦ **Mindy Thompson Fullilove and Charles H. Wright** ♦♦

Maurice Travis, of the Mine, Mill & Smelter Workers, laid out a new line for the relationship of white workers to Black workers.

I didn't come here to tell the Negro workers of America, or their leaders, what to do. I didn't come to orate about the problems of the Negro people and hand out a fancy custom-built set of answers designed to wash away all problems—like Tide, the Washday Wonder.... What I've got to say is aimed at the white trade unionists....

He pointed out that, although the progress of white and Black were bound together, most white trade union leaders had done nothing to fight for Negro rights. He stressed that white unionists had a responsibility to fight as trade unionists for the rights of Black workers as trade unionists. "More than that," he said:

It's a matter of cold self-interest, self-preservation of themselves and their unions for them to press that fight just as hard as they can. I have been trying to say that when white workers join in campaigns for the liberation of their fellow freedom-fighters, the white workers are helping themselves.

The white workers who are here at this conference have a special responsibility. They have the job of going back to their homes, to their unions, and campaigning for Negro-white unity—not among the Negro—but among the white workers.

He finished by saying:

This is a time for new John Browns to arise, up and down the land. And I am convinced that out of this conference will come a whole army of John Browns. Men who are dedicated not to talk and double talk, but to action. Men of principle and of conscience who are convinced that Jim Crow can be licked, and the time has come to lick it, so that the Negro can take his full and rightful place as first class citizen of this land—with full social, economic, political and civil rights. The time is ripe. Let's go.

The majority of the delegates left the convention full of enthusiasm and drive for the job ahead. The delegates were charged with two major responsibilities: (1) To establish local Councils in those areas of the U.S. where none exists, and (2) to start and extend militant actions on behalf of Negro workers on every front. The group pledged to meet again the following year.

Organizing Local Councils

A week after the National Conference, the NNLC of Greater New York held a "Job Action Conference" where 250 unionists mapped a campaign of serious struggle. There were reports on the building trades, printing, food, railroads, utilities, and other industries. Rudy Christensen, chairman of the Jobs in Industry Committee, reported 250 jobs had been won and he outlined the future struggles.

Right after the conference, Christensen received a letter from William I. Wells, public relations manager for Safeway Stores, saying, "Equal opportunity will be given each qualified applicant."

By December 14, 1951, National Secretary Coleman Young reported that six new chapters were in operation—Flint, Dayton, Pittsburgh, St. Louis, South Bend, and Fort Wayne. Other branches were scheduled for Toledo, Louisville, Milwaukee, Gary and Denver.

♦♦♦♦♦♦♦♦♦♦♦♦♦♦♦♦♦♦♦♦♦♦♦♦♦♦♦

VICTORY IN NORTHERN CALIFORNIA

Struggle opened early on the West Coast with a brilliant victory in California's East Bay. For years, the Key System Transit Lines, the local transport monopoly, had refused to hire Black workers. The NAACP in 1940 had started a campaign in which other organizations joined and which peaked around 1944 with the Bay Area Council Against Discrimination and the Committee for Better Transportation. Delegations and petitions urging immediate hiring of Blacks met a cold and firm refusal by the Key System, which claimed to hire solely on the basis of qualifications. In 1949, the Urban League took up the fight.

In 1951, the newly formed NLC came into the fray, at a time when the Key System was using the false excuse of "not enough qualified drivers" to ask for a cutback in service. NLC pointed out there was no shortage except for the company's refusal to use Black drivers. NLC took the issue to the community through mass meetings and distribution of 15,000 leaflets sharply titled:

IS THE KEY SYSTEM LYING OR JOKING.

The NLC pointed out that the Key System refused to hire Negroes and the mutual harm and disservice to the Negroes and white low income groups resulting from this policy. We also urged people to call, write or visit the personnel manager protesting his jim crow policy.

The time was ripe, the issue was hot, and the people responded.

The Key System was beaten. People were happy to see first one, three, five, ten, twelve brown smiling faces of the Negro drivers manning the Key System busses.

♦♦NLC Yearbook

♦ ♦
♦ ♦

Of the Southern Councils, the Louisville Area Council was outstanding. General Electric was planning to move all its appliance manufacturing to Louisville to a new plant complex called "Appliance Park," at that time the largest of its kind in the world. It would eventually hire 16,000 workers. Feeling that Black workers should have a fair share of the jobs that would open, the Louisville NLC sought to prepare the workers. Their first campaign was a successful struggle with the Board of Education to train Black people for jobs. Four hundred people attended classes lasting 30 to 90 days. Louisville teachers and shopworkers taught the classes according to specifications which UE gathered from craftsmen around the country in GE shops. From the beginning NNLC involved a broad cross-section of the community, including union and church groups, the NAACP, and the Urban League.

In Chicago, the West Side Negro Labor Council went into action with a drive to break discrimination in stores along Madison Street, where there were many Black shoppers but few Black clerks. NLC picket lines, aimed at Woolworth and Scott stores, caused business to drop as much as 85%. Members and non-members alike supported the campaign, urging shoppers, "Don't spend your money where you can't work!"

Most of the Madison Street stores conceded by June, 1953. Scott's hired 10 Blacks, and Woolworth then had 14 Black employees out of 22. At a tea attended by 300 people and backed by 14 cooperating organizations, the NNLC celebrated—and the Scott and Woolworth managers showed up to join in the party!

Taking on Sears, Roebuck & Co.

In each of its 674 retail stores, Sears had an ironclad policy of discrimination against Blacks as sales personnel. As one store put it, Sears had had "several excellent Negro maids and cleaning women ... for many years and [they] had been treated very well." The company never considered upgrading them to decent or dignified jobs.

The fight against Sears was one of the NNLC's first national efforts. Campaigns were mounted in various cities, with picket lines at stores in San Francisco, Cleveland, Detroit, Newark, Philadelphia, St. Louis, and Chicago.

The successful Cleveland campaign highlighted the necessary elements of a successful job fight. The Sears store in Cleveland was near the heart of the Black ghetto, at a busy intersection. The NLC began by writing a letter to the company on May 2, 1952, demanding a statement of Sears hiring policy and employment practices. A second letter two weeks later demanded an interview. To this meeting went a committee of Black and white Council members, including the chairman, Bert Washington, and the executive secretary, Ethel Goodman.

Sears denied there was any segregation, saying that no qualified person had ever applied and refusing to give any special attention to the "victims of jim crow." "We accept applications from Negroes and place them where they are 'best qualified' to serve us and this we will continue to do," was the final position of the Sears management.

The Cleveland NLC executive board and its jobs committee

♦♦JIM CROW MUST GO♦♦

The artist depicted demonstrations during the 1940s against the Uptown Theater in San Francisco.
♦♦Credit: Pele de Lappe.

then drew up a plan of action, agreeing that the first step was to publicize the interview and the second step was to pull together organizational support from the community to demand that black women be hired for sales and office work. The third step was to organize the kind of demonstration in which broad sections of the community would participate.

The NLC issued a news release (carried, however, only by the Black press) and distributed leaflets. A mailing was sent to trade unions, the NAACP, the Urban League, and church and misterial groups asking that they support the demands, whether or not they supported the NLC. The response was greater than anticipated; even white patrons and workers at Sears expressed sympathy with the campaign. Yet, despite letters and telegrams which poured into the store, Sears would not respond.

On August 29, the jobs committee set September 15 as the date for a demonstration at Sears, initiating two weeks of activity. The date was announced in the churches and in a leaflet distributed at Sears asking, "Which Side Are You On?" 20,000 shoppers got flyers asking them not to cross the picketline. The watchword was, "Time for Action Now!" In spite of threats that "The KKK will be there to take care of you," plans for the picket proceeded.

On September 12, Sears began to move. It called the Urban League and asked them to head off the demonstration, promising a conference later. The Urban League refused to intercede. Sears then contacted the Reverend Luther Hill, secretary of the Civic Committee, and asked him to relay the company's offer to the Council. Hill agreed, although he made it clear that he supported the position of the local NLC. To the offer of a meeting "later," the Council chairman replied that the Council was ready to meet and confer with the company any time, but that "the time had passed for talking alone. If such a conference as proposed by the company could be arranged for Monday, before the picketline was scheduled to begin, and agreement was reached in such a conference, then, and only then, would the picketing operation be called off."

Sears protested but, with no choice, agreed to meet. Out of that meeting came Sears' agreement to hire two women who would be referred by the Urban League. Sears also agreed to a continuing policy of employment and training of Negro applicants who would be referred by the Council, Urban League, and Baptist Ministerial Conference, all of whom were represented at the meeting.

What was crucial to the victory with Sears was the careful preparatory work of the Council in uniting the community before going into the struggle. Other groups recognized the militancy and leadership of the Council: the Baptists, for example, gave credit to the NLC in their "family organ."

By the end of 1953, practically all of Sears' outlets outside the deep South had come to terms. Only in Chicago, "main bastion and national headquarters of the Sears empire," did those policies continue in full force. Finally, in the summer of 1954, under pressure from NNLC and other organizations, the home office agreed—if reluctantly—to hire Blacks.

Second NNLC Convention

In March, 1952, President William Hood issued a call for the national council of NNLC to meet in Detroit to discuss plans for the second annual convention of NNLC. Cleveland, Ohio, was chosen as the host city for the meeting for November 24, 1952.

The two-day convention began on schedule in Cleveland's Municipal Auditorium with 1500 delegates in attendance, both Black and white. They came from all states east of the Mississippi and several western states. The twelve local chapters of the 1951 convention had grown to 30. Three bus loads of Black and white youth, 18-25 years of age, came to the convention from Winston-Salem, North Carolina. Mixed delegations came from such die-hard Southern states as Alabama and Florida.

The Council established a Maritime Commission that was directed to call President Eisenhower once he assumed office and demand FEPC legislation as well as revocation of the Executive Order under which Coast Guard Screening was operated. The Council took militant action on many issues affecting the rights of Negro people in America. They recommended the picketing of railroads and airlines to protest discrimination against Negro workers in these industries.

Convention delegates listened to addresses by Capt. Hugh Mulzac, first Negro to command a ship during World War II; Maurice Travis, and Paul Robeson. After recounting the significant successes of the organization, Robeson ended his statement with a timely warning: "The fact that you have been so successful makes the enemy more determined than ever to destroy the National Negro Labor Council. There are too many people depending on this organization for us to allow this to happen. Already, the enemy is here among us ready to do his dirty work. But, I say to you, Hold On! Hold On! Keep Your Hands on the Plow, Hold On!"

The NNLC continued to face problems. On March 10, 1952, the *Militant*, a labor newspaper, reported that a conference of trade union leaders meeting at the Hotel Theresa in New York City voted to expand the Negro Labor Committee into a national organization. This committee was founded in 1935 to operate in New York City. The new group had the suppport of the AFL and CIO, which were represented at the Conference by James B. Carey and Lewis Hines. This move was designed to compete with NNLC for the Negro workers within the AFL and CIO.

The Enemy Attacks

As early as 1951, The House Committee of Un-American Activities (HUAC) began to focus its investigative eyes on NNLC. A subcommittee of HUAC convened a hearing in Flint, Michigan, early in 1952 where a "witness" testified to a Mr. Tavenner that he had been directed by the Communist Party to infiltrate the NAACP, the Civil Rights Congress (CRC), and NNLC.

♦ ♦

NNLC ACCORDING TO HUAC

The NNLC is a Communist-front organization, designed to infuse Communism into Negro life. By accusing established labor organizations of overlooking the needs of the Negro, it hopes to capture more Negroes for Communism. It deals in propaganda to put across its line. One illustration of this can be seen from the following incident:

William Hood telephoned the Ford Motor Co. and asked for an appointment to discuss labor problems affecting Negroes. He sought the appointment as President of NNLC. He was advised that Ford Motor Co. refused to discuss any problem with NNLC. Hood then requested the appointment as Recording Secretary of Local 600 UAW-CIO, a position which he held. After the interview, Hood claimed that NNLC had obtained certain benefits ... being in the main, an agreement to hire Negroes in a bomber plant that Ford was repairing. The Communist NNLC claimed that never before had Negroes been hired in that building. This claim is false, as all Ford workers know; but in making the claim in the *Communiust Worker*, they know that Negroes in other parts of the U.S. did not. The Communists have thereby used the story to convince unsuspecting Negroes that in NNLC they find their only friend.

♦♦**Annual Report**
House Committee on Un-American Activities
82nd Congress 2d Session p.11

♦ ♦
♦ ♦

In the first Issue of NNLC's *Struggle*, William Hood and Coleman Young announced that an agreement had been reached with Manton Cummungs, Ford Motor Company's Director of Labor Relations, to hire stenographers, typists and comptometer operators without discrimination as to race. Gerald Boyd, Executive Secretary of the Greater Detroit Council, announced that Max Shaye, Vice-President of Big Bear Supermarkets agreed to hire and integrate Negro men and women into their chain of stores.

Between the second and third conventions, the Attorney General placed the NNLC on his list of "subversive organizations." When the NNLC held its third convention in Chicago on December 4-6, 1953, 800 delegates and visitors—mostly railroad, automobile, and packinghouse workers—attended. NNLC officers and other representatives were harassed by HUAC investigators and by representatives of some unions.

There were internal problems, too. Some members felt that the Council duplicated the work of the NAACP and should be merged with that organization. The council's position was that the NNLC was the best civil rights organization to deal with special problems of labor.

The question of dual unionism came in for considerable and heated discussion. Council spokesmen pointed out that their three-year experience had disproved the charge. They reported that literally thousands of Negro trade unionists had been motivated by the Council to work within their own unions for better conditions. They cited their experience with the

United Electrical Workers as an example: "During 1952, Local 475, of the United Electrical Workers, recruited 558 members for the Council and brought in 600 in 1953. Representatvies of Local 475 stated that supporting the NNLC does not weaken their union but makes it stronger by bringing Negro and white workers closer together around a common problem and bringing workers closer to the union." An important item on the agenda of the Chicago convention was the railroad industry. The delegates explored many avenues of possible relief for the Negro worker in this important transportation industry. Another area of concern was the South where textile, lumber, and tobacco industries denied Negro workers equality of opportunity for employment and advancement.

As in the two previous conventions, the delegates prepared a brief on behalf of the rights of Negro women workers. Many companies such as G.E., G.M., Chrysler, and Ford, were severely criticized for their practices of hiring Negro women for menial jobs only. The Convention passed a resolution to designate and celebrate Negro Woman's Day as a part of a campaign to insure equal rights for women.

In its stand for civil rights, the Council went on to attack the false charges of Senator Joseph McCarthy, the U.S. Attorney General, and HUAC.

The campaign was all the more necessary after 1954, when HUAC prepared a publication entitled "The American Negro and the Communist Party," attacking NNLC at length. If that wasn't enough, in 1956, the Attorney General petitioned the Subversive Activities Control Board for an order requiring the NNLC to register as a Communist-front organization. The NNLC was one of 23 organizations facing this form of attack. The petition was dismissed by the Attorney General on the ground that the organizations had ceased to exist. None of the organizations ever registered, but only four of them survived. The NNLC was among the 19 destroyed by the harassment of the government and rival labor organizations. [*See section 82.*]

The five-year story of the NNLC represents an important chapter in the bitter struggle of the Black worker for a fair share of the products of his labors. The development of cadre which went on across the nation did not die with the NNLC. Whether it was their high degree of political sophistication or their background as workers, these men and women stayed with the freedom struggle: they were not frightened off by McCarthy.

77 ∙∙ TWO HISTORIC CONFERENCES FOR WOMEN'S RIGHTS

NNLC CONFERENCE OF 1952

♦♦ Mindy Thompson Fullilove ♦♦

For author and source note, see section 15.

The National Negro Labor Council excelled in its work for Black women's rights. Recognizing that the Black woman was at the bottom of the economic ladder, and the Black man could not advance as long as she was kept down, the NNLC sponsored a series of conferences on "Job Rights for Negro Women."

The call to the Chicago conference announced:

[The Black woman] is chained to the lower rungs of the job ladder, forcibly prevented from advancing to jobs of higher skills and pay for performing the same work as white men and women.... The gains of labor cannot be made secure unless the rights of Negro women are won. The fight of the Negro people for their complete equality cannot be achieved unless Negro women are freed to participate fully in the struggle.

That conference was held on March 16, 1952, at the Packinghouse Workers' Center, with Octavia Hawkins presiding over 225 delegates and observers who came from organizations throughout Chicago to map a battle plan. They named as their main targets Sears, Roebuck & Co. and the meatpacking operations—Armour, Swift, and Wilson. They also discussed the situation faced by women in factories and in the school system.

The conference paid homage to Negro women workers and pointed out that too few of them "have been afforded an opportunity to demonstrate their leadership ability in our trade union movement."

The discussion of the rights of Black women was also a highlight of panel sessions. One after another, delegates spoke to the question, calling on the NNLC to take seriously the issue of women's rights and to raise the struggle to a new level. Black women, they said, are at the bottom of the economic ladder and a fight must be conducted to improve their conditions, whether domestic workers or production workers. They must have the right to work anywhere and everywhere.

The last speaker stated:

> The Negro women are on the offensive. And that means we're plowing through. It means if we're on that other seat on the Freedom Train, driving when that other man goes to sleep, we'll awake still going through.... I think we understand it so well, this role of action for Negro women, because the Negro women are so much oppressed, more than all the other people in the whole country.

The resolution detailed the super-exploitation of Black women and called on the union movement to accept the challenge:

* To win job opportunities for Negro women throughout industry, in offices, department stores, public utilities, air lines, etc.
* To support the organization of domestic workers, both in the North and South, and for improvement of their working conditions.
* For job training and upgrading, especially for Negro women and youth.
* The right to play a leadership role in government, industry and the unions, based on demonstrated ability and willingness to give leadership in family and other struggles.

Conference delegates adopted this resolution enthusiastically, pledging to carry forward the struggle for its implementation. Indeed, the National Negro Labor Council fought for these principles until it was frozen to death in the Cold War [*described in section 76*].

UE NATIONAL CONFERENCE ON THE PROBLEMS OF WOMEN WORKERS

♦♦By Vivian McGuckin Raineri♦♦
For author note, see section 44.

By 1953 the United Electrical, Radio and Machine Workers was a battle-scarred but ever-scrappy veteran of the Cold War. It was precisely then—on May 2 and 3 at the Hotel McAlpin in New York City—that UE convened a historic National Conference on the Problems of Women Workers. Many of the 400 delegates were seasoned fighters against the Cold War Inquisition. One of these was Marie Reed of Cleveland Local 735 [*described in section 44*].

This was the first national labor conference of its kind ever held in the U.S. While fighting for its life, UE pursued the battle for equality in industry, and within the union. To UE, the struggles were integral.

Keynote speaker, UE General Executive Board member Rieta Kochert, told the delegates:

We are gathered to further the fine contribution our union has made in the fight for the rights of working women. We gather at a time when world peace, our standard of living, our schools, our Union, our democracy hang in the balance....

[I call upon the UE to] strike a mortal blow against the cruel economic exploitation of women workers.... [W]e seek to wrest actually billions of dollars from the corporations and put it in the pockets of our sisters, our homes and the nation's purchasing power.... [I]t is our intention to win great victories in 1953.... And in our struggle for economic equality, we are bound to make greater strides toward full social and political equality. This is the high road we will take to our complete freedom. This will be our contribution to an America for peace, for progress.

Dorothy Burch, a General Electric shop steward, described the successful campaign for an increase of three and a half cents per hour to bring some women's pay into line with other workers. She said, "[It's] like getting blood from the proverbial turnip." She addressed the other side of the problem as well:

A man can no longer go out and make the wages needed to take care of a wife and family ... so it becomes necessary for women to get into the plants ... and then some of our husbands wonder why we are not the same "little women" we were! UE's fighting slogan will be:

THERE SHALL BE NO JOBS RATED BELOW THE COMMON LABOR RATE FOR MEN!

Florence Romig, financial secretary of General Electric Local 707, spoke her piece as a delegate from Cleveland:

I think it's pretty obvious to all of us that employers' discrimination is used in the main against two groups—the women and the Negro workers, and the company uses this discrimination to bring down all the [pay] rates. The hiring of Negro people, especially Negro women, in industry has been a long, hard fight. In our shop we fought and won the first Negro woman to be hired by the company. Of course, she was put into the cafeteria. Industries like ours like to put Negro people in the lowest graded jobs or the most menial jobs ... we wanted Negro women on *production* jobs. Today we have many Negro women in production jobs, active in the Local and pitching in to help fight discrimination against all women.

Delegates drafted an appeal to take back to their UE locals, and to other organized and unorganized workers:

We the women who work for a living in the electrical, radio and machine industries, suffer a common exploitation, regardless of the companies for which we work, or the unions of which we are members. We are all seeking equal pay for equal work, equal opportunities for training and upgrading, equal rights in hiring and seniority. Divided, we cannot fully succeed. United, we cannot fail. We call upon all women in our industry to join with us in winning from the corporations: all rates for women above common labor rates, full equality in all seniority rights, regardless of sex. United, we can win!

At UE's 18th National Convention later that year, excited women delegates reported on the progress they made when they brought the conference program back home: they got rid of some wage discrimination, speed-up, and health problems. They saw a growing unity between women and men workers, fighting together on the job, striking together on the picketline. Local 639 delegate Margaret McCortney said women delegates "were so inspired that they went out to the other plants and carried our program, by leaflets, to the organized and unorganized shops." Fighting for women's rights isn't a matter of "doing favors" because it "is with the strength of everybody [that] no one in this country will ever lick our union."

Marie Reed emphasized three programmatic points: the elimination of wage rates lower than common labor, fighting for tax deductibility for child care expenses, and bringing more women into union leadership. She asserted:

[Union leadership] is not easy.... [I]t takes time, and one thing women don't have very much of is time. When a man is through work, he comes home and eats his dinner. When a woman is through work, she first buys the dinner, then cooks it and maybe she eats and then she washes the dishes. And when a man needs a clean piece of clothing, he goes to the drawer and gets it out. When a woman needs it, she has to wash it and iron it first. . . .[I]t is tough to hold two jobs, and every woman who works in the shop is holding two jobs at the same time. What that means is that we have to find flexible methods for making it possible for the women to be active.

Fellows, never underestimate the power of women.

78 ♦♦ RED, WHITE AND BLACK IN SOUTHERN LABOR

♦♦ Anne Braden ♦♦

Anne Braden is a journalist and veteran activist in the Southern civil rights, civil liberties, peace, and labor movements; she is also the author of The Wall Between *(New York: Monthly Review Press, 1958).*

The beginning of the end of the Silent Fifties came on December 1, 1955, when Rosa Parks refused to move to the back of a bus in Montgomery, Alabama, sparking a new Black upsurge for human rights that shook the nation.

National media described Mrs. Parks as a "Negro seamstress." She was also, in fact, a leader of the Black community in Montgomery.

Her first memories as a young bride in the 1930s were of her husband and his friends coming home at night, pulling all the shades in their kitchen, and carefully counting money they had collected for the defendants in the famous Scottsboro Case. In the 1940s, she became secretary of the Montgomery NAACP branch and later recalled how she walked door-to-door in the community, urging other Blacks to take the severe risks involved in joining that organization.

She knew and worked with E.D. Nixon, who was not only an NAACP leader but a militant member of the Sleeping Car Porters Union in Montgomery. She was also a good friend of Clifford and Virginia Durr, white natives of Alabama who had gone to Washington, D.C., to help build the New Deal; they had returned to Alabama after Clifford gave up his high-level government job rather than live with President Truman's loyalty oath order in the late '40s.

In August, 1955, Mrs. Parks attended a workshop on civil rights at the Highlander Folk School in Monteagle, Tennessee. There, she expressed the opinion that little would ever be accomplished in Montgomery because "Negroes there are too divided."

In those days, Montgomery buses carried movable signs dividing the front section for whites from the back section for Blacks. On that historic day in 1955, Mrs. Parks, weary after a day's work, sat down on the first row behind the sign. As more whites got on, the driver moved the sign back and ordered her to move.

"I was tired," she said simply later. "I did not see why I should get up so a white man could sit down."

Mrs. Parks' arrest on that day was not the first of a Black person in Montgomery for refusing to abide by seating restrictions on city buses; in fact, there had been two such arrests earlier in 1955. Nor was Montgomery the first city in the South in which a boycott of buses had been tried.

But for some reason that no historian has ever been able to explain totally, the time, the place, and the issue met in Montgomery. Mrs. Parks' arrest was the final straw for a Black community that had lived through years and years of indignities. Outraged, the city's 50,000 Blacks united, and for a year refused to ride the buses.

By the end of the next year, not only were the buses integrated in Montgomery; similar boycotts were in progress in other Southern communities, and mass movements to destroy racial segregation were developing in Black communities across the South. The movement grew steadily and—spurred by the actions of a new Black student generation in 1960—grew to massive proportions in the next decade. That movement changed the face of the South and of America and profoundly altered the history of our country.

What happened in Montgomery in 1955 is remarkable almost beyond belief. We were at a moment in history when virtually every organization in the country that advocated progressive social change and social justice had been destroyed or debilitated. People everywhere were frightened, afraid to go to meetings, to sign petitions. Then suddenly, in the most reactionary part of the country, in the Cradle of the Confederacy, among its poorest and most oppressed citizens, the new movement arose. Its leaders and members had few ties to the labor movement or any other organizing effort.

We can only understand the miracle of Montgomery if we understand what the Cold War at home was really all about, and if we grasp the meaning of the historic position of Black people in America. It is impossible to understand fully the problems and challenges of today unless we know this history—and the legacy of both hope and problems that it gives us for today, beginning in the 1930s, when a people's movement for racial and economic justice developed steadily in the South.

World War II brought rapid growth to the South. Black workers were able to move into jobs previously denied them, and they consistently turned to the CIO, seeing it as a bastion of support for their demands for human dignity. By the end of the war, CIO membership in the South had grown to 400,000.

Action/Reaction

Then the trouble began again. Company managers fired thousands of wartime workers in their reconversion from war to peacetime production. Black and white war veterans returned from the fronts to resume their jobs. Many found that their jobs no longer existed.

In the South, employers decided this was the time to take advantage of the wage differential between North and South. They opened new plants with old ideas about discrimination.

The CIO had other plans. It launched Operation Dixie to organize the unorganized and to kill Jim Crow. The CIO still saw itself as the cutting edge for broad social progress in the nation and saw Operation Dixie as a vision not only of the organization of Southern workers, but as a major thrust for democratic reform in the region. This included voting rights for all Southern Blacks (and for poor and working whites who were also denied voting rights in many places by complicated registration procedures). Social activists envisioned this as a time when progressive politics would create a truly "new" and egalitarian South.

Operation Dixie was a phenomenal success in 1946. In its first year and a half, it increased union membership in the South from 400,000 to 800,000. At one point in 1946, about 20 new Southern locals were affiliating with the CIO every month.

The Louisville Story

After the war, International Harvester opened a new plant in Louisville and, in the usual pattern, hired Black workers mostly as janitors or maintenance workers. But some of the first people hired in the shop, both Black and white, were workers with experience in unions elsewhere. They immediately began organizing for the Farm Equipment Workers Union (FE). Black workers formed a Black caucus, and the FE-CIO campaign stressed the necessity of Black-white unity. The organizing campaign was successful, and later—after FE merged with the United Electrical Workers (UE) in the late '40s—UE issued a pamphlet, *The Louisville Story*, about the organizing drive:

... [FE organizers] explained that the policy of the union was economic equality for all. They explained how the only way to beat Harvester's low wages was to unite the Negro and white workers. They explained how the Southern bosses for generations had played Negro workers against white, and white against Negro. They pointed out that there was a direct connection between this and the fact the Southern workers were the lowest-paid in the country.

Many of the workers had not thought of this before. They had for years been fighting a losing battle with the cost of living, struggling to get along, not knowing why. Now they began to see that in real unity lay hope for better living and a better life. They saw that they could, if they refused to be divided, force the boss to pay them a decent wage.

White workers at International Harvester in Louisville came from backgrounds no different from those of white workers in other Louisville plants at the time, where Blacks stayed in the lowest-paying jobs and were discriminated against by their unions as well as the companies, and where wages for all workers remained low. But the white workers at Harvester were exposed to different ideas—from the FE national leadership, from FE organizers who came to the city, and even more important, from the Black leadership that emerged within the Louisville plant itself. Thus, they developed a totally different understanding of their problems; white workers on a number of occasions walked out of the plant when a Black worker in their department was demoted or denied a deserved promotion, or discriminated against in some other manner. White and Black learned to work together in the union local. A firm unity developed—and, as a result, the Louisville local fought a victorious campaign to end the wage differential that had kept their wages 70 to 90 cents an hour below what comparable Harvester workers were getting in Chicago. By the late '40s, the Louisville Harvester plant had the highest industrial wages in the South.

All over the country workers were demanding some of the fruits of the democracy they thought they had fought for during World War II. They went out on strike in massive numbers in 1946 and 1947.

In Winston-Salem, North Carolina, FTA Local 22 sparked a campaign that elected the city's first Black alderman since Reconstruction. Black men and women led this 10,000-member local in the R.J. Reynolds cigarette plant. In Suffolk, Virginia, union members elected the first Black to public office. In Memphis, FTA led the strongest local CIO Council in the South, which began to challenge the rule of "Boss" Ed Crump.

This situation was obviously a major threat to the powerful few who traditionally ruled the South in their own interests. Not only did unions threaten the low wage scales in their factories; coalitions led by labor threatened their political power at the ballot box. The power structure had to strike back.

Would they have been so successful if the national atmosphere had been different? We'll never know. As it was, the employers and politically powerful in the South had the perfect atmosphere—for them.

The Cold War Comes South

By that time, the Cold War was on, abroad and at home. Every movement for progressive social change was labelled "Communist" and treasonous to the country. This provided the perfect weapon for those who wanted to keep power in the hands of the few in the South. Southern segregationists and anti-union employers were usually the same people. They had always attacked trade unionists and civil rights advocates (who were also usually the same people) as "un-American," "outsiders," "foreigners," "Communists," and "traitors." Such name-calling had always had some effect. But the progressive thrusts of the late '30s and '40s had undermined this form of attack. Too many Reds had been on the picket lines for Red-baiting to work. Now, with a national witch-hunt in full swing, Southern reactionaries were able to tie their kite to a national windstorm. They could pose as upholders of national security and all that was patriotic—not as defenders of a divisive and unjust racial and economic system in the South.

They called in some of the major witch-hunters of the day to help them—the House Un-American Activities Committee (HUAC) and Senator James Eastland's Senate Internal Security Subcommittee (SISS). When the witch-hunting congressional committees came South, their targets were always militant union movements and civil rights activists. In Winston-Salem HUAC called in leaders and members of the powerful FTA local at the Reynolds plant. Those called before HUAC became isolated from other workers and the local was finally destroyed. The plant became non-union and remains so to this day.

In Memphis, Eastland's committee held hearings that produced sensational headlines charging the city's most militant and anti-racist labor leaders with subversion. When the witch-hunt struck, FTA had 2300 members in Memphis, 60 percent Black and 40 white [*described in sections 21 and 79*]. Earl Fisher, a local Black leader of FTA in the 1930s and '40s, managed to survive and rebuild the local that had existed then, although almost entirely on a base of the poorest Black workers. He said many years later:

It was the white workers who got out. The Blacks stayed, but not the whites. Lots of our white members had begun to see how divisions kept them down. But the red-baiting scared them, and they forgot. Other unions came along and said they'd set up all-white locals, and that's where they went. They had stood up to getting hit in the head, and even being called "nigger-lover." But they couldn't stand being called traitors.

Southern reactionaries and the national witch-hunters had help from within the labor movement itself. Between 1946 and the early 1950s, the national CIO leadership totally surrendered to the anti-communist witch-hunting atmosphere. By 1949, it had expelled its most militant unions, charging them with being Communist-led. Invariably these were the unions, such as FTA and Mine, Mill & Smelter, that were carrying the main thrust of organizing in the South. And invariably also, they were the unions that took the most uncompromising stand against racism and for Black-white unity.

In the South, local white union leaders who had never agreed with the CIO stand for racial justice seized this opportunity to get rid of all those—Black and white—who did. Local

♦♦ WE SHALL OVERCOME ♦♦

This woodcut was done during a civil rights workshop sponsored by the Graphic Arts Workshop of the San Francisco Bay Area.
♦♦ Credit: Louise Gilbert.

witch-hunts within the labor movement soon followed the national CIO purge. Local activists were brought up on union charges and accused of being Communists and subversive. Some of them, of course, *were* Communists. Everyone knew that much of the early work of organizing the CIO in the South had been done by Communists for the reason John L. Lewis had stated. But in the internal witch-hunts of the Cold War in the Southern labor movement, every unionist who stood for racial justice was labelled a Communist.

Across the South, Blacks were pushed out of local union leadership. Their most vocal white allies were pushed out of the labor movement entirely. Union membership in the South stopped growing as racists launched purges in one Southern community after another. The CIO nationally abandoned all commitment to Operation Dixie when it pledged its allegiance to the Cold War instead. Progress first stopped short, then took a dramatic turn backward until the CIO was ready to declare that Operation Dixie was over in 1953. The promising coalition of progressive forces—the Black movement, the labor movement, and some white intellectuals—was crushed by anti-communist witch-hunts. Southern workers, for the most part, remained unorganized—and no significant organizing efforts took place again for more than a decade.

Sparks of resistance remained—individuals here and there who kept on fighting, helping to fuel the fires of new movements that came later. But as a movement, the social forces that were challenging the status quo in the South in the '30s and '40s disappeared in the early '50s. Nowhere was the devastation wrought by the Cold War greater than in the South.

Even where unions continued to exist, they were on the defensive throughout the '50s and early '60s, losing strike after strike, due to internal union weakness and lack of community support. New national CIO policy discouraged progressive groups throughout the South. The CIO withdrew cooperation from the Southern Conference for Human Welfare in 1946, contributing to that group's demise in 1948. The Southern Conference Educational Fund (SCEF) emerged as a successor, but had no ties to what remained of the labor movement in the South. The CIO likewise cut its connections with the Highlander School, which went on to become a vital training center for civil rights activists, but without a base in organized labor during the 1950s. The CIO withdrew support from the National Committee To Abolish the Poll Tax, which went out of existence in 1947. The Southern Negro Youth Congress was destroyed. The NAACP, at the national level, gave in to the witch-hunts of the late '40s and early '50s and encouraged its local branches to engage in their own purges of people accused of being "subversive."

The Significance of the Montgomery Movement

It is in this context that we can understand the significance of the new Black movement that started in Montgomery in 1955. The Cold War was actually a well-organized and very efficient attempt on the part of those in power to keep the rest of us under control. But the oppression of Black people in our society, especially in the South, was so severe that they just could not be kept under control. Their need for freedom and justice was so strong that, beginning in Montgomery, they burst through the straitjacket that had been imposed and organized anew.

In so doing, they ultimately broke the straitjacket for everybody. In seeking to force this society to make room for them and meet their needs, they stretched the society for us all. It was the new Southern Black movement—joined ultimately by many whites who saw its issues as their own—that finally broke the Cold War pall and got the nation in motion again in pursuit of social justice.

The interplay of old and new forces in the South in the '50s explains much that has happened in our country in the last 35 years. The movement that started in Montgomery set the South on fire and changed its social and political patterns forever. It also spread across the country, began to move the nation as a whole in a more humane direction, and actually set the national agenda for a brief time in the activist 1960s. It focused attention on the racist nature of the entire society and thus provided a setting in which the struggles of other people of color—Native Americans, Hispanics, Asian-Americans—could gain attention. And it gave rise to the other movements that shook the nation in the '60s and beyond—the mass movement to abolish the House Un-American Activities Committee, the movement against the Vietnam War, the women's movement, the environmental movement, the drive for the rights of disabled persons, the movement for the rights of gay people. Most of the initiators of all these movements were people whose lives had been changed first through their association with the civil rights movement.

Where Was the Labor Movement?

And yet it is also a fact that the Black freedom movement of the '50s and '60s was weakened by the circumstances that had destroyed the movements that preceded it. When the new movement looked around for support, there was no Southern labor movement—which should have been a natural ally—to provide that support. When it looked for white allies, they were not to be found in union locals. Eventually, some white Southerners made significant contributions to the Black-led civil rights movement—ministers, teachers, other professionals, women, students. But the mass movement that might have developed for both racial and economic justice through an alliance of the new Black movement with a labor movement involving significant Black leadership, was an impossibility at that time. Some national labor leaders supported the civil rights cause, but Southern civil rights activists did not even seek support from Southern unions. Such an approach would have been unthinkable in most places. In Birmingham, for example, the relatively strong Steelworkers Union was under the control of the Ku Klux Klan; white unionists everywhere either opposed the civil rights upsurge, or ignored it.

Another related effect of those Cold War years on the new civil rights movement was the fact that the witch-hunts had created an atmosphere in the country that closed the door to asking some very basic questions about the society. The new civil rights movement was crippled by the fact that this was a time when one could not question our economic system. The rampaging anti-communism of the '50s had made capitalism sacred. Thus, one could not suggest that our economic system might have flaws without being labelled a traitor.

The Economic System Is Not Working

Yet, this economic system was obviously not working for Black people. How in the world could the movement really deal with the oppression of Blacks without questioning economic injustice? The battle of the lunch counters, and for the vote, were critical struggles; they were a beginning, an opening wedge. But there were built-in limits on how far they could go in actually changing the conditions of the lives of the masses of Black people. And when Black activists began to realize that, there came a period of frustration and fragmentation of the movement.

Later the Southern freedom movement did move on to economic issues—in the late '60s, again bursting through the straitjackets imposed by those who wanted to keep control of the society. And when it did, the real repression came down: the murder of Dr. Martin Luther King, Jr., and all the other counterattacks on Black organizations and Black organizers that marked the late '60s and early '70s. The movement reeled under these attacks, and for a critical moment lost its moral initiative. But by then the massive momentum of the early '60s had already been lost in a splintering process.

I think it was for this reason that the movement was not able to stand up to the massive attacks of the late '60s as well as it might have if the civil rights forces had not already begun to splinter because of the disillusionment and frustration of many activists. To a large extent, this disillusionment and frustration occurred because—although Jim Crow was on its death bed, and the vote was being won—the basic conditions of the lives of the majority of Blacks were not changing.

Thus, the Cold War not only stopped progress in the South temporarily in the late '40s and early '50s. It also stretched its icy hand into the 1960s, ultimately blunting the tremendous mass movements of that decade. It thus also determined the history of this country from 1970 to 1984—among other things, setting the stage for Ronald Reagan to get into the White House. This would have been impossible if the Freedom Movement had continued into the '70s as strong and united as it was in the early '60s.

And yet, even though it was blunted in the early '70s, the Black freedom movement so changed the atmosphere in the South—broke the police state, and won the right to organize—that it became possible in the late '60s and '70s for Southern workers to organize again. And new union drives did indeed develop in that period. There were some important breakthroughs—for example, the J.P. Stevens campaign; the successful effort of Steelworkers to organize the massive Newport News, Virginia shipyard; and electrical workers organizing in South Carolina. There have been, and continue to be, new thrusts by the United Furniture Workers in the South, by hospital workers, and by workers in many other low-wage industries. Invariably, the new union organizing of the '70s got its impetus from Black workers who had gained entry into industries previously closed to them, such as textile, because of new laws won by the mass struggles of the civil rights movement.

A Joint Mass Movement

But by the time these new union drives developed, the civil rights movement, as it had existed in the '60s, had already been weakened by the attacks on it—and sometimes when the new Southern unions looked to the civil rights movement for allies, *it* was not there in any cohesive form. That joint mass movement of Black people seeking freedom and a labor movement seeking economic justice—the movement that all our history teaches us could be the key to social progress for the South and this country—has yet to develop.

The South and its politics have always been pivotal to developments in the United States as a whole. That is because the issue which undergirds our entire existence as a nation—the oppression of people of color, and organized resistance to that oppression—has been sharpest in the South. Thus, although what we call the South (actually 11 Southeastern states) is a relatively small part of the nation geographically, what happens there has generally set the direction of the country at any moment in history.

The vision that Dr. Martin Luther King, Jr. was beginning to project to the nation in his last years was of a movement that joined the moral force of an assault on racism and racial injustice with a challenge to the basic economic inequities of our society. That was the meaning of the campaign he led in Memphis, in support of Black garbage workers fighting for equal rights within the union there, and it was the meaning of the Poor People's Campaign, in which he was seeking to unite the poor across racial lines at the time he was killed.

There have been a number of efforts to lay that vision before the nation again—recently, the work of the Coalition of Conscience that was created to unite diverse forces in the 20th Anniversary March on Washington on August 27, 1983, and the Rainbow Coalition campaign led by Jesse Jackson in 1984. These are efforts to organize a joint movement like the one destroyed in the Cold War period.

But this time there is a qualitative difference. Black leadership was a key element in the movements of the '30s and '40s, but much of it developed at the local level and was usually ignored by the media of the time (and by many historians since). Today, as a result of the civil rights movement, there is a very visible national Black leadership that cannot be ignored and that gives new impetus and strength and potential to efforts at coalition-building in the 1980s.

Despite the difference in the two periods, however, the years of the Cold War in the South offer dramatic lessons for today. The Southern social-justice movements of the '30s and '40s were crushed by the combined thrusts of racism and anti-communism, and these two ideologies were inextricably intertwined. They have left the South with the weakest labor movement in our nation. Even today, only 14 percent of the Southern industrial work forces are members of unions; in some Southern states, the numbers are only 6 or 7 percent. And in January, 1984, wages of Southern industrial workers were still only 83 percent of those in non-Southern states.

The question for the 1980s and beyond is whether we can finally build in the South and in the nation that illusive coalition of our society's rejected people—Black, Brown, Yellow, Red, and White, women and other workers—a coalition that will wage a simultaneous assault on both social and economic injustice, and will wage this battle in both a moral and political arena. Whether we can do that may well determine whether this decade will lead us in the direction of a more democratic and just society, or whether in this time of both domestic and international crisis, we will move toward greater division, scapegoating politics that set white against non-white, and ultimately a garrison state.

ACKNOWLEDGMENTS

I am indebted to my good friend Mike Honey for much of the detailed information on Southern labor history contained in this article. [*See sections 21 and 79.*] The quotation from Earl Fisher was obtained in a 1970 interview with me. The material on International Harvester in Louisville is mostly from my own memory, as my husband and I worked for the union that represented the workers in that shop in the late '40s and early '50s. An excellent account of the work of this local is included in a study by Mindy Thompson, *The National Negro Labor Council: A History*, American Institute for Marxist Studies, Occasional Paper #27 (1978). [*See section 76.*]

79 ⋄⋄ FOCUS ON MEMPHIS: UNION HALL TO CITY HALL

⋄⋄ Michael Honey ⋄⋄

See section 21, page 168, for author's note.

The issue of segregation in the home of the CIO set off the most bitter confrontations between Local 19 of the Food, Tobacco & Agricultural Workers and Memphis CIO director Red Copeland. In 1946, Copeland's assistant, Lawrence McGurty, insisted on enforcing national CIO policy against segregation. The best place to start? Desegregate the CIO hall. Copeland responded by firing McGurty.

In 1947 the CIO moved its office to a new building, which it alone controlled. Segregation in the union hall remained strictly against CIO policy and Copeland could no longer claim that segregation had anything to do with landlord pressure. Now he claimed that left-wingers were raising the issue only to further their "communist" ideology. The confrontations grew more bitter. Finally Copeland got the CIO to pass a resolution banning National Maritime Union delegate Red Davis and Local 19 business agent Ed McCrea from the building. By 1949, the CIO Council had purged Local 19 members and other leftists so it could change hall policy without "helping the Communists."

The CIO hall remained segregated.

Local 19's Strong Black Leadership

The FBI and local police followed every move of Local 19 and infiltrated the union with informers. The local produced the strongest and most independent black union officials in Memphis, and the FBI considered them Communists. Indeed, some of them were. Henderson Davis, a black worker with a family of ten children, became one of the local's early leaders. With almost no formal education, he learned literacy and other skills in the labor club of the Memphis Communist Party. John Mack Dyson, who became the Local's first President in 1939, likewise learned organizing skills in the Communist Party. In 1948, he became an elector for Progressive Party candidate Henry Wallace. He also helped bring Paul Robeson to Memphis in support of the Wallace campaign.

Other black leaders in Local 19 did not belong to the Party, but respected the civil rights and union work of its members. Radicals and non-radicals alike worked together in the union. They all agreed on the need for a strong rank and file, a militant union, and opposition to segregation.

More than any other Memphis union, Local 19 developed a strong core of black officers and shop stewards. Shop leaders like William Lynn, Leroy Boyd, Allison Stokes, and George Isabel carried the main weight of the union's activities in the postwar period. The union did not depend on a charismatic leader, but on a solid rank and file.

Together, black shop workers broke through the old strictures of segregation. George Isabel, for example, became the first black electrician at the Buckeye Cellulose plant. He forced the company to break down its segregated job system by threatening to quit and taking the other workers out with him. Isabel's threat succeeded because the Buckeye company knew Local 19 meant business. The union carried out an impressive ten-day strike there in 1947, with an integrated picket line and negotiating committee. The strike won the first major wage increase for low-wage workers in Memphis after World War II.

Local 19 continued to lead the Memphis labor movement in wage increases after the war, and won every one of its postwar elections. Why? First, according to union leaders, because the local had a solid core of black supporters. Second, the union also demonstrated a remarkable display of unity between black and white workers.

At Buckeye, the largest Local 19 shop, whites made up

nearly half the workers. Many at first resisted plant-wide seniority, which would allow blacks to bid on all jobs. They also resisted getting rid of segregated facilities. "The bathrooms, the water fountains, even the time clocks were marked 'white' and 'colored'," according to George Isabel.

White workers, however, came to accept the union's success in tearing down the walls between the restrooms and integrating all facilities. The union opened jobs in every single department to black and white alike. Racial wage differentials came to an end.

Local 19 held integrated union meetings at the Buckeye Plant every month. It developed a strong grievance procedure, with union leaders in every department. As a result, blacks and whites developed a strong sense of common purpose. The integrated officers and staff of the union proved that union members, working together, could defeat Jim Crow.

Copeland's attacks did not stop Local 19 and radical activism. In 1949, left-wing organizers in the United Furniture Workers Union led a bitter eight-month strike at Memphis Furniture. Communist Party district organizer Red Davis used the opportunity to set up classes in Marxism-Leninism for the workers. Later, left-wingers circulated the Stockholm Peace Appeal aimed at ending the Cold War and U.S. intervention in Korea.

Red Copeland charged "treason."

Because of its integrationist policies, and because Communists provided important leadership in the union, Local 19 came under heavy attack in the postwar period. Red-baiting became the standard tool of those who opposed the union.

According to Leroy Boyd, however, red-baiting proved almost useless with black workers. "Anytime a white man spoke up for black rights he was called a Communist. We knew that," said Boyd.

Ed McCrea, white business agent for the union in the late 1940s, was indeed a Communist. According to Boyd, "He had the people behind him. He was a good negotiator and stood up for his rights. The Communist thing was used to scare off the white workers. We knew that, too, and stood behind Ed."

But, hearings by Mississippi Senator James Eastland's Senate Internal Security Subcommittee (SISS), along with the launching of an extensive Red-baiting campaign by local CIO leadership, the Urban League, and local black ministers, put Local 19 to a severe test.

Red Copeland and Steelworker district director Earl Crowder gave Eastland star witness testimony. Copeland told how the CIO undertook the fight against "communism" in Memphis long before Senator Eastland, but regretted that, "with the exception of the Memphis Urban League, we have never been able to enlist the support of other Memphis organizations in the fight."

Meanwhile, the CIO Council resolved that "We do not believe that Communist sympathizers should be permitted to roam our streets.... To us there is no difference between a communistic sympathizer in Memphis and one in Korea." As long as Local 19 existed, the CIO concluded, "there is a danger of communism spreading in Memphis." They could not destroy Local 19, but could expel the Local, and they did.

Eastland concluded that Local 19, "instead of being a labor organization ... is, in reality, a Communist organization and that Negroes who belong to it are dupes." Local 19's black officials, he added, "are dumb."

These attacks did not shake black workers from Local 19, but they led FTA international officers to pull Ed McCrea from Memphis, believing the adverse publicity from the SISS hearings had undermined his effectiveness.

The media publicity, combined with the purge in the CIO, served to effectively remove the strong white allies of black militancy from the Memphis labor movement.

Media attention, blacklisting, and the red scare eventually drove Communist activists such as Red Davis, Ed McCrea, and Lawrence McGurty out of Memphis. The repressive climate gave them little choice but to leave the union brothers and sisters they had worked with to build a solid CIO in Memphis. FTA Local 19 remained under continuing attack by the CIO, SISS, and the Urban League. The Local went into a period of decline as its leading members became victims of the Cold War. Under the combined weight of the 1950's red scares, the segregationist movement, and a new anti-union climate, Local 19 had almost ceased to exist.

By the end of the 1960s, veteran black union activist Earl Fisher had built the union back up to 1200 members, often using his own money for organizing expenses. Fisher hooked the local to a number of international unions, whoever would provide the best support.

In an interview in 1972, shortly before his death, Fisher told Anne Braden of *The Southern Patriot* that the union's strength still remained with its members. "No international reps come to tell us what to do," he told her. "All our leaders, like myself, come from the shops—so they understand the workers' problems. We train our own leaders."

In stark contrast to Local 19's internal democracy stood the dictatorial power of "Boss" Ed Crump whose political machine had run Memphis since World War I. For decades, neither blacks nor union organizers who stepped outside Crump's rules could last long in Memphis.

Crump held onto his power partly by maintaining a cooperative relationship with AFL unionists. He provided them with patronage jobs, particularly as building inspectors. He allowed AFL unions to organize along craft lines to their hearts' content, as long as they did not try to organize any of the mass production industries. Crump assumed that AFL unions would not tamper with the Memphis system of racial segregation or with Crump's political machine.

Crump was right. AFL leaders had no inclination to associate with, much less organize, black workers or white industrial workers in low-wage sweat shops, lumber mills, furniture companies, cotton compress and cotton seed oil plants—all of which formed the base of Memphis' economy.

The AFL's cozy relationship with Boss Crump left Memphis' black workers with few allies in the white community and the limitations of the electoral process served to keep blacks "in their place" as well.

Memphis was unlike most southern cities, however. It did allow blacks to vote, if only under Crump's rules.

Crump controlled black voters by paying their poll taxes. He raised the money through kick backs from Memphis vice establishments and from donations gathered from business supporters and patronaged city employees. Crump also bought white votes for candidates of his choice. As a result, Crump kept a strong hold over elections in Memphis, Shelby County and the state of Tennessee, as well, from the 1920s until the late 1940s.

SOMETHING NEW WAS BORN IN 1946

A change came with the rise of the CIO. During the election primary in 1946, FTA Local 19 and other CIO unions provided foot soldiers to monitor the Crump machine at the polls. This paved the way for an open political challenge to Crump in 1948.

In that election, the CIO served as the political base for Estes Kefauver, who ran for the U.S. Senate in the Democratic primary against a Crump candidate. During the primary, Local 19 mobilized black voters in Memphis. It was the only organization capable of doing so. The local helped swing the black vote in Shelby County in favor of Kefauver. It was the first election defeat for Crump since 1915!

During the general election, Local 19 supported Rev. D.V. Kyle, a black minister who ran for Congress on the Progressive Party ticket with a white woman—something unheard of in the Delta. As part of the Progressive Party campaign, Paul Robeson and Henry Wallace appeared at an unsegregated Memphis political rally of over 2,000.

♦ ♦

The Legacy

Red Davis, a Memphis native and long-time veteran of the NMU and the Communist Party, worked for many years as a stalwart in the Memphis CIO. Looking back, he felt that the Red Scare provided an ideal cover for efforts to destroy the growing movement for equal rights for black people. Segregationists appealed to white workers to maintain racial purity in the name of opposing "communism"—an appeal that worked in the context of the Cold War.

According to Davis, the Red Scare drew white support away from the civil rights movement and thwarted change in white working class thinking about racial questions. By driving the left out of the labor movement, union officials stifled dissent. Soon, few white workers dared to speak in favor of civil rights for fear of being labelled "communist." Furthermore, local officials used the Red Scare to suppress the most militant black working class leaders.

By the late 1950s, most union locals in Memphis had nothing to do with the civil rights revolution brewing all across the black South; many locals actively opposed that revolution.

80 ·· THE CIO AND AFL MERGE IN 1955

♦♦ The Editors ♦♦

More workers went out on strike in 1952 than in any year since 1946, including teamsters, locomotive engineers and railway conductors, telegraph and telephone operators, oil refinery workers, and especially 650,000 steelworkers, making a total of 887,000 strikers. All these work-stoppages occurred while U.S. troops were fighting in Korea.

In 1953, new CIO President Walter Reuther and new AFL President George Meany faced the new Republican President Eisenhower, as well as militant workers demanding an increase in their real wages and working conditions.

Such demands required labor unity. But in this period, from 1951 to 1953, there were 1,245 cases of raiding between AFL and CIO unions, involving 350,000 workers. The AFL filed 791 complaints with the National Labor Relations Board, challenging the right of CIO unions to act as collective bargaining agents for certain shops, and the CIO filed 936 such complaints against the AFL. The AFL leaders spent $11.5 million on organizing raids and bringing action against the CIO.

At the same time, some unions were going the other way. Wanting to strengthen their positions, the CIO Packinghouse Workers Union and the AFL Butchers and Slaughterhouse Workers Union merged, and many CIO and AFL bodies passed resolutions on the need for labor unity. In early February 1953, the CIO executive board named a committee of officials headed by Reuther to meet with an AFL committee headed by Meany, to discuss unity. Reuther said: "The CIO wants a united labor movement with all the Communists and racketeers kicked out", and recalled that the CIO had "rid itself of nine Communist unions some years ago."

By June, 1953, some progress had been made in AFL-CIO talks, but no settlement had been reached on jurisdictional disputes and a two year no-raiding pact was not to go into effect until January, 1954.

Then, nineteen years after it had left the AFL over the issue of industrial unionism, the CIO adopted a program at its 1954 convention, looking toward "fair and honorable unity with the American Federation of Labor, to a continued drive to organize the unorganized, and to domestic economic and social legislation designed to end stagnation." The convention noted that raiding had virtually ceased.

On February 9, 1955, the Unity Committee finally reached agreement on the creation of a single trade union center. All AFL and CIO unions would automatically become affiliated to the new labor federation, at the same time retaining their constitutions and organizational integrity. The agreement recognized both craft and industrial principles of organization. Discrimination because of race, color or religion was prohibited in the organization. The leaders of the federation promised to fight against all forms of corruption and against Communist Party influence.

The seat of all authority in the AFL-CIO would be the national convention, which would meet biennially, not annually, as in the CIO. An Industrial Union Department would be set up within the new AFL-CIO, co-existing with Building & Construction Trades Department, the Metal Trades Department, and other old-line craft structures.

At the point of merger, the combined membership of the AFL and CIO was less than 15,000,000 of the country's 62 million workers, less than 25 per cent.

The First Constitutional Convention of the AFL and CIO took place on December 5, 1955, in New York, attended by 1,487 delegates representing 13.7 million organized workers. The convention proclaimed the creation of the AFL-CIO composed of 138 national and international unions (108 from the AFL and 30 from the CIO), 93 state labor councils, 490 central labor unions and local industrial councils, and 146 federal labor unions and local industrial organizations. The 31 CIO unions formed an Industrial Union Department headed by Walter Reuther. The terms of the merger did not provide for merger of parallel AFL-CIO unions or restructuring to eliminate more than one union at an enterprise.

New York Governor Averell Harriman told the convention that U.S. trade unions had done more to combat "Communist subversive activities" in the country and abroad than any other organization in the USA.

Convention resolutions urged unionists and all workers to work in defense of civil rights, especially those of the Negro people, and called for the organization of unions, above all in the South and in the mass production chemical and paper industries where they were almost non-existent. The convention pointed to the need for more independent political action by unions at election time, and stressed that they would support those candidates who spoke out against the Taft-Hartley Act, state "right-to-work" laws, and racial discrimination, and who favored tax reductions.

Certain differences emerged at the convention on foreign policy questions. Most of the CIO union leaders, headed by Reuther, supported the government's foreign policy but recognized the need for negotiations on the most pressing international problems. The presidents of the clothing and hotel and restaurant employees' unions advocated rejection of the Meany pro-administration position-of-strength policy and called for efforts to resolve the problems of disarmament. The convention finally passed a compromise resolution: it condemned the 1955 Geneva conference of foreign ministers, but underscored the possibility of new negotiations; it supported the government's official foreign policy, while condemning colonialism. It opposed cooperation with Soviet trade unions, and took no position on what kind of aid, economic or military, should be given to other countries.

A few days later, AFL-CIO President George Meany told a conference of the National Association of Manufacturers that there was so much in common between the views held by labor leaders and employers that it was stupid for them to fight each other. Furthermore, he said: "I never went on strike in my life, never ran a strike in my life, never ordered anyone else to run a strike in my life, never had anything to do with a picket line."

Some union members evidently did not get Meany's message, as statisticians recorded 28 million man-days idle due to strikes in 1955 and 33,100,000 man-days idle in 1956, involving 2,750,000 workers in 1955 and 1,900,000 workers in 1956. (*Historical Statistics of the United States, Colonial Times to*

1957.) Collective bargaining in 1956 and 1957 won wage increases of five to 11 cents an hour for five million workers in the automobile, steel, construction, transportation, aircraft and aluminum industries.

But the promise of a new, exciting organizing effort did not materialize, and by the end of the 1950s, the AFL-CIO lost 1.5 million members when it expelled the teamsters, bakery workers, and laundry workers on charges of corruption.

During the same period, the condition of the expelled progressive unions continued to worsen. Some merged with related or stronger unions. By 1960, only four with a total membership of 300,000 remained in existence: UE, ILWU, Mine-Mill, and ACA (American Communications Association), and the latter two were prepared to merge if they could find an international that would take them in.

81 ♦♦ UNITED STATES vs. MARIE REED

♦♦ **Vivian McGuckin Raineri** ♦♦
For author note, see section 44.

In 1956, the U.S. Justice Department assigned investigators to draft a complex plan to try to put Marie Reed, her husband, Fred Haug, and six other Cleveland workers in federal prisons.

EIGHT INDICTED AS RED PLOTTERS

the *Cleveland Plain Dealer* whooped on Jan. 24, 1957. Marie Reed and Fred Haug headed the list of alleged conspirators. The indictment "marked the first time the government, in its attempt to break the Communist hold on unions, charged union officials with conspiracy with members of the party to violate the Taft-Hartley Act."

A federal grand jury charged Marie Reed Haug with four counts of perjury for allegedly filing false affidavits in 1951, 1952, 1953, and 1954 that she was not a member of the Communist Party while still an official of UE Local 735. Fred Haug was charged with two counts of perjury for filing false non-Communist affidavits while he was an official of the Mine, Mill and Smelter Workers Union in 1952. Six other Clevelanders were accused of aiding and abetting Reed and Haug in signing the affidavits. The indictments also named as co-conspirators eight national and state leaders of the Communist Party. These eight people were not indicted or arrested, but anything they said or did could be discussed in the trial, in their absence, and could be used to convict the eight defendants under the conspiracy charge.

The indictments were the result of a "secret investigation" conducted by the Justice Department, aided by the Cleveland Police Subversive Squad. They set in motion one of the most vindictive persecutions in U.S. labor history.

The Haugs charged:

Our case has become one of sheer persecution for our ideas. We are innocent of all these fantastic charges that have been filed against us. We repeat we did not file any false affidavits. We did not conspire with anyone. We believe that the people of good conscience in our community will be repelled by this double attempt to crush our little family. Therefore, we are confident of being vindicated.

UE Local 735, which had fought so hard against assaults by Fawick Airflex and Judge James C. Connell, said nothing about the indictments. It had ceased to exist, a victim of the Cold War Inquisition from without and fears that UE was on the skids from within. In September, 1956, a majority of the 1,500 members of UE Local 735 voted to affiliate with the International Association of Machinists. Nationally, fifty thousand members of UE opted to disaffiliate from UE in this period. But now officers of IAM Lodge 2155, formerly UE Local 735, condemned the indictment against Reed as "persecution for union activity." They urged their 1,500 members to give her "full support."

The Trial: 1958

The United States Government was in no hurry to bring this case to trial. As government lawyers worked on their facts, they realized they had nothing against one defendant and had to dismiss the indictment against him. They could not begin to prove the perjury charges against Marie and Fred Haug, and had to drop those charges also.

By January 8, 1958, the remaining indictment was broader, weaker, and therefore easier to prove:

That from on or about May, 1949, and continuously thereafter up to and including the date of the filing of this indictment, in the Northern District of Ohio, ... and elsewhere, James West, Andrew Remes, Hyman Lumer, Sam Reed alias Louie Ladman, Eric Reinthaler, Marie Reed Haug and Fred Haug ... unlawfully, wilfully and knowingly did conspire with each other and with Gus Hall, John B. Williamson, Stephen Mesarosh, also known as Steve Nelson, Sidney Stein, Martin Chancey, Frank Hashmall, Joe Brandt and Anthony

Krchmarek, co-conspirators but not defendants herein, and with ... other persons unknown, to commit offenses against the United States ... by conspiring to unlawfully, willfully and knowingly make, use and file and cause to be made, used and filed with the National Labor Relations Board, ... false affidavits of non-Communist Union Officer ... well knowing that the statements ... in said affidavits that the affiants therein were not members of or affiliated with the Communist Party USA were false....

The Haugs were charged with "overt acts" of signing and filing affidavits. To establish the "conspiracy," other defendants allegedly "maintained communications" between persons, issued "Communist Party instructions," received "a Communist Party directive," and transported "a member of the Communist Party to a meeting. ..." Integral to the "conspiracy," the government claimed, was the making of "false" or "pretended" resignations from the Communist Party, the adoption of "aliases," use of "secret codes" and other "deceptions" to conceal membership in the CP and "conceal the existence and operations of said conspiracy."

None of the defendants were charged with the actual filing of false affidavits. They were only charged with *conspiring* to file them; at least one overt act in pursuance of the conspiracy had to be shown. Nor did the overt act have to be unlawful in itself, but could be one which *tended* to promote the alleged conspiracy. It could simply be mailing a letter.

Fred Mandel, attorney for Reinthaler, said that "based on the trial," Reinthaler had been fired from his job as apprentice machinist for the Wean Equipment Company. Reinthaler, a machine gunner in France and Germany in World War II, was a Purple Heart holder with a 20 percent disability due to war injuries.

The defendants pleaded not guilty. The Haugs denied they were members of or affiliated to the Communist Party when they signed the affidavits or any time thereafter. The case was based completely on the testimony of FBI informers, some of whom made a career of going around the country, testifying at trials and Congressional hearings. The government lined up nine of them for the Cleveland trial: Fred L. Gardner, William G. Cummings, Arthur F. Strunk, Halbert Baxter, Nello John Amadis, John A. Hull, David Garfield, John Edward Janowitz and Frank Peoples.

Proud History

It was a heyday for the newspapers. As in years previous, Reed's Vassar College link was prominent: "Educated at Vassar College, long dominated leftist UE activities here." Fred Haug was portrayed as "a huge raw-boned man with a bellowing union-hall voice." The "power of both slipped as the tide turned against leftist wings in Cleveland labor circles," said the *Plain Dealer*. Other defendants did not rate such extravagant language.

Reed testified in her own behalf. Under questioning by Stephen Young, her attorney, her achievements over many years were disclosed. Reed attended Vassar "in large part" on a scholarship; she graduated with honors in 1935. She worked for the Young Women's Christian Association, then for the American Youth Congress. Reed joined the Communist Party in spring of 1935 while still in college. After Pearl Harbor, she got a job as an automatic screw machine operator for Fairchild Corporation in Queens, New York. Reed joined the UE there and took the union's offer of a job in UE District 6 in Pittsburgh, Pa. To carry out her responsibility for organizing women workers in support of the war effort, she prepared a manual explaining government Office of Price Administration regulations; it was used widely throughout the country.

In Pittsburgh, she met and married Fred Haug. He, too, worked for the UE and when in late 1943, he was transferred to Cleveland UE, she became a field organizer for the union. She was a member of Local 735 and ran for and was elected as business agent in mid-1944. She was elected, and re-elected every year thereafter. Reed negotiated contracts for the local with the Electric Controller Company, Wellman Engineering, Notch & Merryweather, Ohio Electric, Electroline Manufacturing, and National Tool.

Reed was one of the few women union business agents in the country, became the first woman treasurer of the Cleveland CIO Council (CIUC), and was a member of the State CIO Civil Rights Committee.

Her testimony continued: "In the years from 1944 through about 1948 I would say it [*the Communist Party*] was helpful to me in my union work ... from the point of view that in going to meetings I would sometimes get my perception sharpened about some of the problems that were faced by working people. And that helped me in my union activities."

Was she ever directed by the Communist Party?

"The union membership would decide," Reed asserted, "what the union should do. And as far as my personal position was concerned, it was directed by my conscience, my belief in what was morally right. And I felt that I had that right as a member of the Communist Party or otherwise."

Reed told the jury that her UE local had submitted a resolution against compliance with Taft-Hartley, but events dictated a different necessity and by the time the convention vote occurred, the UE, in order to use the NLRB, voted at its September 1949 National Convention to comply with the law. She said she left the Communist Party in 1949, and signed the Taft-Hartley affidavits after she dropped her membership.

U.S. Attorney Canary twice asked Reed:

Q: Is Joe Kres a member of the Communist Party?

A: Sir, it is a matter of conscience with me. I am perfectly willing to discuss any of the defendants in this indictment, but I just—as a matter of conscience, I can't discuss any other individual. I can't do it.

Q: You mean you refuse to answer?

A: It's a matter of conscience with me, sir.... I can't answer the question.

Canary tried again later, and got the same response.

Canary told the jury in summation that the defendants "became a part of this unwholesome thing to maliciously defeat the law of the land." A conspiracy, he said, does not have to "mean assembly of lots of people." It may be ". . . something that they have in their minds, not as you and I talk, but in their minds is an important thing in this case." Canary took umbrage at negative portrayals of informers. What goes on in the minds of conspirators, he said, "goes on deviously, hiddenly . . . and let me ask you how else would an organization such as the FBI, charged, mind you, with the safety and security of this country, how else can they keep track of an organization such as that except by the use of men and women such as Cummings, Strunk, Peoples, people like that." Further: ". . . why don't they [defendants] then do what people like Garfield, Gardner, Amadis are willing to do? Why don't they come to our side once? Why don't they come to the side of law and order? . . ."

Defendants' attorneys termed the conspiracy charge "legalized guilt by association," and informers as "the most dangerous kind of witness," willing as they are to testify for a price.

David Scribner, co-counsel for the Haugs, said the position of the prosecution was "a very interesting one. They say, well, the fact that she [Reed] resigned is suspicious. If you resign you are obviously a member of the Communist Party, and if you don't resign obviously you are a member because you haven't done anything to indicate you have changed your association with the Communist Party, and the Prosecution's position on this is that you are crucified if you do and you are crucified if you don't." Reed, he told the jury, "is to be admired, and you saw her, observed her as a witness, for answering questions frankly, honestly and truthfully. ..."

The jury began its deliberations on January 28. It took eight and one quarter hours to find the defendants guilty. Judge Paul C. Weick released them on bond.

Marie Reed was shaken:

I never expected a guilty verdict. I thought I had convinced the jury that I had not been a member of the Communist Party since 1949. This is a body blow. This is a temporary setback to civil liberties but I am sure we will triumph in the end.

Sentence

On a record-cold February 20, the judge sentenced the defendants. Judge Weick lectured:

It's a good thing for all of you that you were not convicted in Russia.... Over there the accused confesses to these crimes. If there is no confession they kill the accused persons or send them to far-off places where the weather is much colder than it has been here in Cleveland.

Marie and Fred Haug stood arm in arm. Weick sentenced each defendant to 18 months imprisonment and a $2,500 fine.

Afterward, Marie Reed Haug said:

The outcome of this case has been a great shock to me. The whole logic of my life forbids me to be a party to anything underhanded. I left the Communist Party and signed the affidavits in good faith. To do otherwise would endanger the life of my union and the future of my daughter. I hope my reputation for truthfulness will be restored.

The trial judge denied the motions for a new trial. The Haugs asked attorney Jack G. Day to join in their appeal to the Sixth Circuit Court of Appeals.

A MONSTROUS PROCEEDING

It was a touching case.... [T]here was a little girl involved [their daughter], and frankly, I thought the whole proceeding was monstrous. I thought the test oaths were reprehensible and contrary to the basic elements of this political system, and I thought there was no proof ... [I]t seemed to me they were convicted on a lack of evidence. That's anathema to anybody who has a civil liberties bias.

As for Reed:

It was unusual to find a lady in the labor movement who was a Vassar graduate ... [S]he had this terrific commitment to trade unionism and I would gather from her background that this was unusual. It might have been more conventional and more nearly predictable that she would be found in the Junior League rather than in the vanguard of the trade union movement, and particularly with a union which was very militant.

♦♦ Jack G. Day
Appellate attorney for Marie Reed

In February, 1960, the U.S. Court of Appeals for the Sixth Circuit upheld all of the convictions. The defense lawyers filed a petition for a writ of certiorari with the U.S. Supreme Court in May. Four Justices were needed to vote to have the Supreme Court consider the case. They were not found. The defendants were on their way to prison.

Each of the defendants had to face many personal problems before entering federal prison for 18 months. The Haugs had a special concern: What would happen to their small daughter, Lucy Marie?

They were determined that she not be deprived of both parents at the same time.

They appealed to Dr. Benjamin Spock, who was then at Case

Western University Hospital. Reed asked him to make a statement, and he was perfectly willing to do that.

Also, the lawyers found a case where two business partners were allowed to go into prison sequentially so their business wouldn't collapse. "Our argument was that it was even more important not to have the child be alone and the judge went along.... [I]n some ways it was tougher but it was a lot better for Lucy."

Prison

Reed served her time in the Alderson Federal Women's Reformatory in West Virginia. She continued with the post graduate course work she had begun at Case Western Reserve University in the late 1950s, and edited the prison newspaper. She encouraged women prisoners to write about their life experiences. She undertook a survey of women's work histories and how they related to their criminal histories.

She served 14 months, celebrating her 46th birthday in prison. Always a woman of style, Reed departed from Alderson wearing a coordinated prison-made outfit which included a big, floppy blue hat. It was made for her by another prisoner, Lolita Lebrun, a political prisoner for 26 years. She was one of four Puerto Rican Nationalists who, on March 1, 1954, entered the gallery of the House of Representatives in Washington D.C., unfurled the Puerto Rican flag and, shouting, "Libertad para Puerto Rico!," fired shots into the ceiling. Ricocheting bullets wounded five Congressmen. Lebrun told the court at the subsequent trial that there was no intent to kill or hurt anyone. She was released in 1980.

On Marie Reed's release from Alderson in 1963, she sought readmission to Case Western.

At first the university refused, on the ground that she was a felon.

Reed persevered, aided by liberal faculty and attorney Jack Day, who told a college administrator that he could "count on it" that Day would sue for her admission if necessary.

When the administration changed its mind, Reed quickly went to work, turning her survey on women prisoners into her master's thesis. Reed stayed on at Case Western after earning her M.A. and PhD. Ultimately she was appointed a professor of sociology and Director of the University Center on Aging and Health.

82 ⋄⋄ SUBVERSIVE ACTIVITIES CONTROL BOARD ATTACKS

⋄⋄ **The Editors** ⋄⋄

Congress amended the Subversive Activities Control Act of 1950 by enacting the Communist Control Act of 1954. The 1950 Act had provided for proceedings before the Subversive Activities Control Board against "Communist-action" and "Communist-front" organizations. The new Act provided for proceedings before the SACB against labor unions on the charge that they were "Communist-infiltrated." This Act subjected unions and their officers to lengthy administrative proceedings in which union people would never be able to describe their actions to their fellow citizens sitting on a jury, as in a criminal case. Decisions would be made by hearing officers appointed by the President. Penalties for being found a "Communist-infiltrated" organization were severe, including ineligibility to use the NLRB.

In 1955, Attorney General Brownell filed the first petition under the Act to have Mine-Mill declared a "Communist-infiltrated" organization, alleging the group in leadership used the Union for "Communist-inspired purposes". [*See section 74.*]

During this period, Brownell also moved against the United Electrical, Radio & Machine Workers of America (UE) on the same ground. When these hearings before the SACB were suspended in 1958, four UE locals sued, charging that they were subject to injuries from allegations in the Attorney General's petition without an opportunity to defend themselves. The union won, then lost, and lost again. After the union took the case to the Supreme Court, the Justice Department abandoned the proceeding, because they said certain key witnesses were not available.

Mine-Mill was not so fortunate. The SACB held on May 5, 1962, that the Union was "Communist-infiltrated," and found the Union "has consistently taken positions in opposition to the domestic laws and the programs of the federal government in the field of communism." The order made Mine-Mill ineligible to use the NLRB and required that all Union publications be labeled: "Disseminated by a Communist organization."

During this time, the Attorney General also asked the SACB to require several active union leaders to register as members of "Communist action" organizations, including Ralph Nelson, a founder of the International Woodworkers of America, and Louis Weinstock of the Painters Union-AFL.

Three years later, in November 1965, the Supreme Court unanimously destroyed the primary purpose of the 1950 Act by holding that leaders of the Communist Party could not be required to register as members of a "Communist action organization" because that would violate their constitutional privilege against self-incrimination. If Communist leaders could not be fined or imprisoned for failure to register, how could union leaders be penalized?

Soon after this Supreme Court decision, the Court of Appeals sent the Mine-Mill case back to the SACB. The thaw was on.

Finally, in June 1966, the Department of Justice filed a joint motion with the union to vacate the SACB order and dismiss the Attorney General's petition against Mine-Mill. After eleven years, what was left of the union won!

In 1967, the Court of Appeals held that the Communist Party, as an organization, did not have to register with the SACB because of its privilege against self-incrimination. The government did not even seek to appeal to the Supreme Court.

That marked the end of the Subversive Activities Control Board, finally done in by the combined staunch resistance of its intended victims, both individuals and organizations.

83 ✦✦ STEELWORKERS IN BUFFALO: A PERSONAL PERSPECTIVE

✦✦Joseph Cantor✦✦

The author admits he carries with him the fear he learned during the Cold War: "Even now, when I talk on the telephone, I automatically think someone is listening. I work for a midwestern state in a forward-looking department under a fairly decent governor, but there is still a lot of right-wing thought in state government. If I were to use my own name as author of this chapter, I'm afraid it might come back to haunt me on my job, so I am using a pen name. All other names have also been changed to protect their identities, except for public officials."

When I made my appearance at the federal courthouse for the Buffalo hearings of the House Committee on Un-American Activities (HUAC) on October 2, 1957, the marshal loudly boasted how he had served a subpoena on "this steelworker in apron strings."

It was true. I was working night shift at Bethlehem Steel Company and days I looked after the kids while my wife, Esther, was out working. When the marshal knocked at our door, I had our three children in tow: Sam, then six months old, Fanny, who was six, and Warren, who was three.

The marshal's mocking tone was a harbinger of HUAC's customary tactic—destroying a person's self-respect and standing in the community by adopting a posture of intimidation in a theatrical setting, with maximum hoopla and local press coverage. Maybe that is why they became known as the House

UnAmerican Committee; their activities were truly unAmerican! This character assassination served the larger strategic goal of HUAC—to eradicate all progressives and Communists from the labor movement, especially in a basic industry such as steel. They were aided by Philip Murray, followed by David McDonald, as Presidents of the United Steelworkers of America (USWA), who opened up the attack on Communists in steel after World War II.

Cleaning Out the Commies

Many Communist Party members, notably current general secretary Gus Hall, were instrumental in organizing the Steelworkers Organizing Committee, SWOC. Some had been forced out as early as 1937, but the campaign to purge all radicals from the USWA intensified after World War II. An official history of the union by Vincent Sweeney, a former editor of the union newspaper, proudly states that the Steelworkers played a prominent role in "cleaning the commies out of the CIO."

The broad brush of anti-communism painted all critics of the International leadership red. John Barbero, now vice-president of Local 1462, remembers how he was Red-baited during a local union campaign. A phoney letter supposedly written by the Communist Party of Western Pennsylvania endorsed Barbero. Even though the candidate denied the authenticity of the communication, the disclaimer had little impact in the intensely anti-dissident political environment. Barbero recalls:

At every meeting you went to you were "out of order." No matter what you had brought up, [the local president] ... had such a well-organized machine it was "sitdown and shut up"; and he had the goons in the hall to enforce it. An opposition candidate who asked for the right to speak would be thrown out on the floor.

To many of the British immigrant workers at Stelco's Hilton Works in Hamilton, Ontario, America's fear of communism was quite extreme. For instance, in Philip Williams Nyden's PhD thesis, "Rank-and-File Insurgency in A Large Industrial Union: A Case Study of the United Steelworkers of America" (University of Pennsylvania, 1979), George Raine, a long-time activist at Local 1005 and a British immigrant, states:

In Britain, if I was a communist member I could stand up at my local union meeting and say, "I'm a member of the Communist Party and this is our view. ..." That's perfectly acceptable in England, France and Italy. But for hell's sake never do that in North America.

Industrial Concentration

This situation in steel coincided with the outbreak of the Cold War generally. Progressive and communist organizations countered as best they could. One approach was "industrial concentration." Radicals were encouraged to become steelworkers (and workers in other basic industries), so they could organize the rank-and-file to take back the unions from the labor bureaucracy. The Communist Party supported this program, as did the Labor Youth League, the Socialist Workers Party, and other socialist parties with Trotskyist leanings. There was even a movement afoot in radical ethnic and Zionist organizations to "colonize" in steel. I read an article in *Commentary* about the experience of one such Zionist "colonizer." (The term "colonizer" was adopted by people working in the program at the time as kind of a slang shortening. In retrospect it is misleading, with superiority connotations.)

When someone suggested I become an industrial worker in the industrial concentration effort, I was ready to go! I was born poor and remained poor: I wanted to improve my lot and the lot of other workers. I believed that workers had to regain control of *their* (*our*) unions, *their* (*our*) lives, *their* (*our*) government. Even though I had worked my way through City College of New York and had a Bachelor of Science degree, I believed that by working in industry with the workers, I could change the nature of things. So, the idea of industrial concentration was attractive to me. I would become a steelworker!

Besides, I needed the money. In my field of social work, only the lowest paying jobs are open to college graduates, And I had no way to get a master's degree. I might have sought white-collar work, but I had a family to support. I had worked at several factory jobs before coming to Lackawanna, and I knew I could make more money as a laboring man than in an office.

On the application form for employment at the Bethlehem Steel Company in 1952, one of the questions was about educational background. I said I had attended Public Schools 58 and 118 in New York City, and Stuyvesant High School. I did not mention having attended college, because I didn't want a supervisory job but a laborer's job. I was hired as a laborer.

I went into the mill as we all did, feeling that the working class needed to develop class consciousness that it was lacking. The mill in Lackawanna at that time employed 20,000 workers of various racial and ethnic backgrounds. However, the black and chicano workers were assigned to the coke ovens, the open hearth furnaces and other such dirty, unhealthful and dangerous jobs. I was assigned to the segregated, lily-white strip mill, along with all the other young white workers.

What did I feel when I first walked into the mill? Awe, and confusion. Here I was, a city boy from New York who had worked in small factories in the garment industry, walking into a huge mill crowded with machines, cranes and steel. I didn't know what to expect. At the same time I felt: here I am, starting out to work among basic workers, in solidarity with them. These conflicting feelings included a bewilderment that is difficult to describe even now.

In the mill I learned what it means to be a worker, a proletarian. There was an uncanny solidarity I encountered working at the huge machines with other laborers and we soon developed a hostile attitude toward "the company." I have carried that solidarity with me ever since, and at least one of my sons is carrying it with him today.

When I arrived in Buffalo, I met with a single individual whose name I had been given who was the Communist Party contact. He was also a Jewish guy from New York who had come up to Buffalo and become a factory worker several years before. He was the district organizer for the clandestine portion of the Party; I found out later that there was also an open section of the Party.

In those years the Communist Party was under attack by the establishment with all of its apparatus of FBI, police, spies, you name it. The government had indicted its leaders under the Smith Act. Therefore the Party was forced to work in a clandestine manner to be effective. At one level, some of its leadership went totally underground, changing their identities. At my level, the industrial concentration program was conducted with at least some secrecy. Our parents did not know why we had left and our friends didn't know where we had gone.

Colonizers in Steel

Soon I met some of the individuals I was going to be working with in steel and we got closer and closer together. Our backgrounds were varied. I had met the left through the International Workers Order (IWO), a fraternal and cultural organization for workers with many ethnic affiliates which provided an inexpensive group insurance plan. [*See section 61.*]

And a friend of my mother's turned out to be a Communist. I got to know her and her daughters; they introduced me to several people on the left, and I went with them to social affairs. Then when I was at City College, I participated in the strike in 1951, led by the Young Progressives of America. Eventually I joined the Labor Youth League, and went to meetings of the Communist Party as well. I can't recall ever formally signing a membership blank or receiving a membership card, or having been formally recruited in any way. That may have been Party policy in the days of the Smith Act. I studied Marxism at the Jefferson School in New York.

Now that I was a steelworker in Buffalo, I got really close to two fellow concentrators I'll call Joe Smith and Matty Zucker. Joe's father had been active in the National Maritime Union on the East Coast. Joe came to New York and became an automobile mechanic and a Communist. He worked in the strip mill, as I did; we were in the same local and worked very closely together, so we befriended one another on the job, not just off the job. Joe was a real down-to-earth guy with a wide breadth of knowledge and understanding. He was well-liked on the job, and very highly respected. He was a WASPish kind of person, but very working class.

Matty Zucker was a huge hulk of a guy, a real worker, born in Hamtramck, near Detroit, the son of a laborer. I don't recall what brought him to New York, but he got active in the American Labor Party there, and then in the C.P. He was older than the rest of us, and the salt of the earth. He probably had the longest political history of any of us; his parents were active in the left. Matty worked in the coke ovens, not in the strip mill. He worked hard. He was a very astute guy, and the informal leader of the group. We all looked up to him for advice, and he was a very warm-hearted and understanding person. Matty was Ukrainian; that was an integral part of his being.

Neither Joe nor Matty had gone to college. Another member of the small colonizers' club that I was in I'll call Charley Soble. He had a master's degree in history or economics. And another fellow I'll call Lou Poller. He was also Jewish; his wife was not. Lou was less of a working class guy than the others, and had some difficulties as a worker. He was a college graduate, but I don't recall what his field was. Some of the other colonizers were Italian. Some had been workers in light industries or in service jobs.

All of us had families with at least two children, so we did a lot of things together as families. We went on picnics together, and one time, Matty took us all up into Canada to a festival of Ukrainian culture where they were celebrating Taras Shevchenko.

I started as a laborer in the strip mill at Bethlehem and eventually went to the pickle house, where I moved up to the top position of welder operator after five long years. I didn't need a bachelor's degree to obtain these jobs and I couldn't see anything wrong with omitting it from my application. My pay jumped 25 percent in a short time, and went even higher with piecework.

About 1954 it began to appear that big business and Congressional reactionaries had targeted the Steelworkers Union. They sought to discredit the motives of Communists and others working in basic industry and the labor movement. They said the motives of the left were ulterior: to "take over," to foster strikes, to assist "foreign powers," to weaken the economy, etc. In reality, Communists and other progressives were *forced* to work in a clandestine fashion—they were being banned from the unions and subjected to harassment, isolation and being discredited on the job. Their motives—*my motives*—were quite the opposite of what they were said to be.

How We Worked

When we first moved to the area, we lived in Buffalo, and our club of colonizers met in a semi-clandestine fashion, since we sensed that we were being watched and followed, and we didn't want the FBI to know that we were working together, or whatever. We frequently met in a park, or we would take circuitous routes to go to the home of someone we didn't even know. Eventually my family and I moved to nearby Lackawanna, and our small club met in each other's homes, usually at night, depending on the shifts we were working. They were very informal, very friendly meetings. We would discuss our experiences in the mill, union politics, what was going on in the local, and what positions we should take on various issues. Then we would get into theoretical discussions about the Party and politics, and Marxism; frequently we studied some article and discussed it.

But always, from the beginning to the end, there was a fear of being observed walking into the door of another colonizer. And it turned out that we all were under surveillance, although we didn't know it then. For example, our neighbor admitted that she and her husband had spied on us, and that she used to take down license plate numbers of the cars that pulled up at our house. So we were only kidding ourselves: the FBI knew pretty much what was going on and so did our neighbors, although there may have been times when we were successful in fooling them. There was one time, for example, when we went for a week of meetings with some top people in a safe house to discuss not only various political questions, but to get some education in Marxism.

Inside Our Club

We made decisions at the club level with regard to what to do in the trade unions, in steel and so forth; these decisions were made collectively. However, some decisions were not made by us. For example, we were told whether we should contact each other, who the contacts would be, etc. But as far as the work went, we made our own decisions. There was really no formal discipline in our club that I can think of; it was more in terms of self-discipline and formal criticism at meetings. If people felt an error was made, there would be criticism and self-criticism; you were expected to criticize yourself. There was no physical discipline or monetary discipline; it was meted out in the form of verbal criticism.

The concept that was laid down for us when we went into colonizing was that this was a lifetime commitment, and that any changes that were going to occur among the workers in terms of radicalizing them was going to take a long time. Our main job was to become workers, to become trusted, to become involved in the life and work. And we did that with some success. While, theoretically, we were trying to establish ourselves and in time build a movement, in fact what we were doing was just surviving, meeting, and fighting various grievances and problems within the plant and the union.

Of course, you didn't have to make the workers militant. They already were. They walked out at the drop of a hat when they felt the company was screwing them. Many of the workers were also radicalized from years of struggle and the efforts of Communists and Socialists in earlier years. However, as for *becoming* Communists or Socialists, that was another story. There were some indigenous socialists; there was a lot of class consciousness among many of these workers; they had class solidarity. But what was difficult was to get them to think beyond bread-and-butter issues to study formally or to organize into working class political organizations.

The other problem was not to tip our hands, since we were kind of underground. No one functioned as an open "Party" member in the shop or in the union at that time. Our idea was to attempt to win over the workers through formal alliances and friendships, to educate them and eventually to recruit workers into the Party. We hesitated in trying to recruit any of them at the time, or even give them radical literature. That was apparently the job of the "open" section of the Party in Buffalo and its environs. Little of that really went on. There were some rare instances, but several times it turned out that people we were attempting to recruit had at one time been Party members or had some affiliation with the Party or were involved with left organizations. Between 1952 and 1957, however, we didn't recruit anyone into the Party.

Usually we left our club meetings feeling good, in the sense that we had an opportunity to meet with other Communists who were doing similar kinds of things; we had an opportunity to get some questions answered, and to socialize a little. I must say, I usually left the meetings feeling much better than when I arrived.

Frequently we'd bring our wives along, and the wives would also get together, mainly to socialize. Eventually there was a women's club formed of Communist steelworkers' wives working, not just in our local, but in other places as well, wives of industrial colonizers. Until then they felt that they had been left out.

In my case, however, since I was very active in the community, my wife could be a part of the work and she did feel a part of it. Esther participated very much in the Point Street Home Owners' Association, helping to organize in the community. She got to know the people, and that was the main thrust of what we were trying to do: not only to become workers in the factory but really to become workingclass steelworkers and live the lives of steelworkers, which is basically what we did, and what Esther did, too. I think in that sense she felt good about it. She still cherishes the friends she made and the things she did as a steelworker's wife.

Back in those days, the wives of steelworkers stayed home and took care of the kids, although some women worked outside the home for wages. And so the colonizers' wives, in the main, also stayed home and took care of the kids. Of course, during periods of recession, steelworkers' wives had to go out and work because the husbands had no income. My wife was one of the women who worked when she had to. She went to work in a dog biscuit factory one time, to earn some money when I was laid off. During strikes—and there were strikes in steel in those days—many women would also work.

The colonizers' wives got together separately and began to talk and to see the need for getting together more formally. They would discuss Marxist works, current issues, Party affairs, in addition to planning for community work in schools and the Democratic Party, and for family affairs and education. They worked to forge ties between black and white women. It was unfortunate that no real formal program for the colonizers' wives was organized at first. Their specific needs and problems hadn't been considered, and there was no program to help them in various ways, as there was for the men. A lot of them were young and inexperienced, and could have used some guidance and some help, in addition to making them feel they were part of this thing.

Later, occasionally we would all get together, men, women and children to celebrate a holiday, to give some progressive cultural life to the kids (such as folk singing) in an organized way, in addition to what each family could do. Later on, we even organized the kids as they got a little bit older, to talk about such things as the similarities of holidays, like the winter holidays of Christmas and Hanukkah, to develop an understanding and appreciation of black music such as blues and jazz, of history, and those kinds of things.

Setting the Stage

Life in Lackawanna, New York, however, continued on as it had for decades. It was a company town of the Bethlehem Steel Company. But it had a long history of struggle, beginning with the great steel strike of 1919 and continuing through many strikes in the '30s while the Union was being built with the help of the Communists and other radicals. I learned of these struggles directly from the old timers who had lived through them.

Although the lot of the average Lackawanna steelworker had improved, he still had to struggle economically to keep his head above water. He faced layoffs, national strikes, local walkouts and wildcats over local issues that took wages out of his pay check. In this period, however, there was a wonderful feeling of solidarity among the working people. I experienced it on the job and in the union. I noticed a high level of resistance to the Company's divisive policy, in spite of all the efforts of the lackeys of the Company and the establishment, in and out of the Union.

By 1955, the International and its local cohorts had been only partially successful in throwing out the progressives. Many remained at the local level. The rank-and-file, especially the old-timers, had become militant and some even radicalized during their years of struggle to establish and maintain their union. Workers filed hundreds of grievances, and walkouts and wildcat strikes were common in the '50s, as they had been throughout the Union's history. The actions of the rank-and-file were in sharp contrast to the sellout policies and the anti-progressivism of the labor bureaucracy, whose mission was self-enrichment through labor peace at any price. This solidarity of workers expressed itself in local ethnic organizations, community organizations, and political organizations. Nyden's PhD thesis on rank-and-file insurgency within the union notes that:

The first rank-and-file electoral challenge to the International leadership occurred in 1956, when the Dues Protest Committee (DPC) built an organized opposition to the International administration.... [T]he DPC gained strength by pursuing broader issues such as leadership accountability to the membership, honesty in elections, increased local union democracy and better shop-floor union representation.

Although this grassroots challenge failed, by the mid-1960s, membership dissatisfaction with the leadership of the International had grown even further. Poor contract settlements, lack of membership voice in International union affairs and the USWA President's extravagant personal life style were objects of criticism.

In this political environment another International officer successfully defeated the incumbent President. This "palace revolt" only changed the personal leadership style; the structure of the International administration and the nature of its policies changed little. The rank-and-file reform movement, thus, continued to grow and challenged the new International administration in the 1969 elections. However, organizational weaknesses of the 1969 insurgency, like those of the DPC campaign in 1956, hindered the ability of the union dissidents to build a viable union-wide grassroots movement.

In addition to working on the job and within the union, I was elected chairman of the Point Street Home Owners Association. One contractor had built a so-called low-cost housing development, using prefabricated materials. However, he left out insulation in the attic and had not put a storm drain in the back of the property, so there was a problem of flooding. All of us who had bought houses in this development were steelworkers mortgaging our lives away on 30-year loans. We had a fantastic feeling of community, and we organized together to get the City to require the developer to put in the needed minimal additions. And we insisted that the City government provide adequate services to protect this new development in the shadow of the steel mill.

I was also working successfully with others to build an independent movement in the Democratic Party, becoming secretary of the local ward club. All seemed to be going well for Esther and me, although the FBI and the anti-Communists had been working to isolate some of the other colonizers. They had not been successful with Esther and me.

Then came that knock on the door. It was part of the effort to break the back of the rank-and-file movement, as well as to destroy the successes of Communists and progressives such as myself among basic industrial workers within our unions and communities. The vehicle was HUAC, but it involved the use of all of their forces in every sector of the unions and society. Their ultimate victims were the workers, their families, their union, and the common people generally.

The 1957 HUAC Hearings

When HUAC brought its road show to town, it created quite a stir. Of course the hearings were rigged so that the mere appearance of a witness led to denunciation and ostracism by friends and neighbors due to the fear promoted by the local anti-Communists and the press. The hearings were indeed Star Chamber proceedings, to which most witnesses were called solely because of their associations. The hearings also provided quite an education for this naive, starry-eyed socialist—on the nature of power, and on human nature. I suppose I expected the parade of informers. I did not expect the turncoats. Some refused to be informers but nevertheless used the occasion to demonstrate their "loyalty" by cooperating with HUAC in every other respect, even to denouncing their pasts and swearing allegiance to the Cold War.

The role of the Committee was to "expose" the ulterior motives of Communists and progressives. How better to do this than by building on the fear and hatred of intellectuals! Union workers had mistrusted college students since the '30s, when football players and fraternity boys had been recruited to walk through union picketlines as strikebreakers. So the Committee focused on questions intended to show that there were many *college graduates* working in basic industry, "intellectuals" who had nothing in common with their fellow workers, except perhaps some secret "sinister" motives. My college degree was flaunted by the Committee to prove what they portrayed as my ulterior motives as a steelworker. Their line was that no decent college graduate would voluntarily give up the white-collar world for a blue-collar job, so anyone with a B.A. and a union card was not to be trusted.

In all, seven workers at the Lackawanna Plant of the Bethlehem Steel Company were "uncooperative witnesses" before HUAC. Two resigned before they could be fired; five of us were fired.

There were three "charges" against me and the others:

1. *Falsification of application of employment.* Some of us were college graduates and did not note that on our applications. (When I was hired, nobody even looked at applications. They needed men, and here was a warm body with arms and legs. The Company developed this into we "had something to hide.")
2. *Security risks.* There was no security check at Bethlehem Steel in Lackawanna! There were no "sensitive" jobs, even if the steel was supplied to defense industries. (I worked in a cold sheet-steel milling operation that manufactured sheet steel mainly for auto bodies, appliance housings, etc.) The Company made no effort to demonstrate how our working in steel posed a threat to "security"; it was enough to justify our discharges if it alleged we were members of the Communist Party or other organizations defined as "subversive" by the U.S. Attorney General's office.
3. *Conduct detrimental to the Company's business interests.*

This was the failure to "cooperate" with HUAC, to act as an informer, to "name names" of friends and associates. This led a spokesman for the American Legion "Americanism" committee to label us "traitors" at a public forum on HUAC in the nearby town of Orchard Park.

The local union leadership was aligned with the Company almost throughout our ordeal. And the Western New York District Director's office not only did not come to our support, but participated in attacks on us for not cooperating with HUAC. Finally, due to our perseverance, the International Union was forced to step in through the office of the General Counsel, who at that time was Arthur Goldberg. He assigned his associate, David Feller, to the case. While the union bureaucracy was right-wing conservative, the general counsel's office could be characterized as liberal. They would defend us so long as we could prove we were not "tainted," i.e., not subversive.

So what did these Union liberals do? They issued a statement:

STATEMENT OF THE UNITED STEELWORKERS OF AMERICA

"The United Steelworkers of America has a deserved reputation as a labor organization which exists to preserve and protect the interest of workers in its jurisdiction within the framework of the Constitution and democratic traditions of our great country and our own democratic constitution.

"The position of the United Steelworkers of America on the question of communism has always been clear. We recognize that the Communist Party is a branch of an international conspiracy which, in the words of the Steelworkers' constitution, is opposed to the democratic principles to which our country and our union are dedicated. The members and supporters of the Communist Party and any fascist or other totalitatrian organization [are] barred from holding office [or being members]....

"Our Union is equally constitutionally dedicated to the protection and extension of our democratic institutions and civil rights and liberties. This is specifically provided as one of the objects of our organization in Article II of the union's constitution.... We emphatically deny and reject the notion that it is necessary or desirable to limit our constitutional principles in order to effectively fight the Communist conspiracy....

"[W]e have another important principle, which must always

guide our action as a union.... We have a legal and moral obligation to protect the employment rights of the employees under [union] agreements.... To permit unilateral abrogation ... of our agreements at the request of outside parties, whatever the motive, would undermine the basic bargaining principle upon which our union must always insist.

"These three principles ... provide the necessary guide for our union in establishing a policy in the few situations ... where members of our union have invoked the Fifth Amendment in response to questions relating to Communist Party membership.

"1. We ... deplore the excesses in this area which investigating committees and agencies of government have engaged in. We ... support a code of fair practices and procedures for legislative investigations and government security programs.

"We equally deplore, and warn our members against, the obvious program of the Communist Party and its agents to induce innocent people who have no legitimate fear of prosecution to invoke indiscriminately the Constitutional privilege against self-incrimination.

"2. If a member of the union invokes his constitutional privilege ... in ... an inquiry into Communism, the local union ... should investigate whether there is sufficient evidence from which to conclude that he is ineligible to retain his membership. If such evidence does exist, it is the duty of the local union to take appropriate action in keeping with our constitutional provisions and democratic procedures.

"3. Invocation of a constitutional guarantee, standing alone, cannot be the basis for loss of membership in our union or for failure of the union to protect employee rights under a collective bargaining agreement, including the right to be free from unilateral and arbitrary disciplinary action or discharge."

At a pre-discharge hearing the International Representative, who wielded all the power, read only that part quoting the union's constitution. He failed to quote the other part of the statement which supported the Fifth Amendment.

Five Fight Back

The five of us who were fired formed a support and defense group to fight back against the company and the local (and district) union organization. The reaction in the community was interesting. Many of the workers who were anti-Communist in their expressed viewpoint were still personally empathetic and even protective of us.

Who would speak out against HUAC in 1957 in Lackawanna or even in Buffalo?

The ACLU, but only with a weak voice, although some of its attorneys provided private support. Robert Fleming, who had organized the Catholic Lawyers Guild in Buffalo, was extremely helpful to us. He represented one of the steelworkers in the hearings, and without a fee. However, the ACLU and all the other lawyers recommended that we come forward as good citizens, take the First and Fifth Amendments to protect ourselves at the hearings, but in every other way, act respectful toward the Committee, and level with its members about our backgrounds.

We appeared at the hearings with a "defensive" posture. I now think we should have taken the offensive. We should have treated the Committee with the same contempt they showed for the Constitution and the Bill of Rights.

Church leaders, some rabbis, ministers and lay people provided support and also spoke out publicly. A private Jewish welfare organization provided financial and other support. Of course, the local progressive unions and organizations themselves were under attack and caught up in their own defense, so they could provide little help. The real support came from individual rank-and-filers and community people. They held no positions of power, no platforms from which to speak, and no bullhorns to amplify their voices. But their support of us individually did enable families to survive. These wonderful few provided sufficient encouragement to the victims so that at least some of us decided to try to fight back.

What role would the big press play when American freedoms were under attack? We had to wait two months after the hearings to see. The *Buffalo Courier-Express* response was platitudinous. An editorial on December 15, 1957, in commemoration of the (then unofficial) Bill of Rights Day, supported the use of the Fifth Amendment privilege and applauded the Board of the Council of Churches in Buffalo and Erie County resolution specifically supporting the First and Fifth Amendments.

Most of the press favored HUAC, but some small papers, such as suburban Orchard Park's local newspaper, supported us, praised our resistance, condemned HUAC, and called for its demise. The *Buffalo Evening News* published letters defending "unwilling witnesses" and the Fifth Amendment, by the local

ACLU chairman and a local minister, who wrote: "To deprive a man of his job and then fail to process his grievance because he makes use of his God-given and constitutional rights is in my opinion a throw-back to the methods of the Inquisition."

McCarthyism Robs My Family

The impact on my family took varying forms. The loss of income resulted in economic hardships. The struggle to fight back robbed my time, energies, and emotions. My wife, Esther, bore the brunt of it, having to work to provide some support to the family, with a baby at home to be cared for. I assumed some responsibility for the children but I was preoccupied with my defense. We faced ostracism in the community, although some of our neighbors became even closer, offering solace and support. We could not have survived without the help of one neighbor in particular. He had fled Franco Spain as a young man, and had a brother, a Loyalist, who was killed in the Civil War. We will always be indebted to him and his family; they understood McCarthyism.

The impact on the children was reflected in varying ways. Fanny, the oldest, was shunned by some of her playmates; others taunted her about her father. She suppressed her fears and anxieties for almost eight years. When she was 15, she developed nightmares and an unexplained, uncontrollable fear of dying. We finally went to a professional family counselor. By then, Warren had become the "little man," the stalwart member of the clan. At age 13 at a counseling session to discuss Fanny's problems, Warren managed to bring to the surface the real source of our problems: the scars from the hearings and the firing. Because of all the stress I was under during the hearings, I treated our youngest, Sam, harshly. It took many years for him to come out of his hostility toward me in particular and authority in general.

◆ ◆

A BIG WIN

The government was after the Cantor family and the families of the other fired workers. When we applied for unemployment compensation, it was denied because we had been discharged "for cause" by the Company. We appealed the decision. In a surprising decision, the State Examiner ruled that the company had not fired me for "just cause" and awarded me unemployment compensation. The landmark decision decried firing in response to McCarthyite tactics by HUAC and took the Company to task for the firing.

♦ ♦♦♦♦♦♦♦♦♦♦♦♦♦♦♦♦♦♦♦♦♦♦♦♦♦♦♦♦ ♦

Fighting the Union and the Company

We five filed grievances to get our jobs back. The grievance procedure under the Union Local's contract called for a number of steps of appeal in a company disciplinary action against an employee. The first two steps were at the shop level, but the third step was a hearing before the plant manager with top Union leadership.

At the pre-discharge hearing held by the Company, the role of the Union began to unfold. The Local and the District refused to take our case to the third step, and the Local leadership forced a vote by the Local membership against our defense. Under union rules, we appealed to the International staff. We weren't exactly heartened by the International's position, reported in the local press: "The ... men have the right to their day in court, regardless of anybody's personal feelings. We don't want to make martyrs of these men."

The third step hearing occurred on December 4, 1957, with management continuing to hammer away at me for neglecting to state that I had attended college on my job application. I was told that my HUAC appearance "had an adverse effect on the Company and its employees as well as members of Management and the stockholders.... However, it should be clear that we do not question your right to invoke the Fifth Amendment. However, the fact that you refused to answer questions in this matter warrants a reasonable conclusion that you are a security risk."

On my behalf, I read at length from *The Fifth Amendment Today*, a book by Erwin Griswold, Dean of Harvard Law School, who explained that a person who takes the Fifth Amendment is not automatically guilty of something. I also quoted Supreme Court Chief Justice Earl Warren about the abuses of congressional investigations through their wide-ranging intrusions into private lives.

The International Union official representing me sought to corral me and make me "stick to the points that are pertinent." But I continued to spar with the management representative.

At the hearing's conclusion, my grievance was denied.

The International then put its cards on the table: If we wanted to get reinstated, we needed Union support. The Union had a price: We would have to swear we were not Communists at a rehearing of the Third Step Grievance in February, 1958.

How to Proceed?

What should we do? There was no easy answer.

We five discussed it, collectively and individually. I underwent great struggle within myself to arrive at my decision. I decided on a pragmatic approach, and so did one other worker. We would both deny membership in the Communist Party. We *did* create a dilemma for the Union. They wanted capitulation. We refused to turn against our brothers. And we refused to become informers or to cooperate with the anti-communist falange. We played a legalistic game and in doing so built a platform for civil liberties.

Our union counsel, David Feller, had the same dichotomy in his thinking that was reflected in the statement of the Steelworkers Union. He wanted me to confide in him, and I told him I had lied when I said I had never been a member of the Communist Party. He was a decent guy, a liberal, and a member of the Arthur Goldberg team of lawyers out of Chicago. Once I conformed to what the Steelworkers Union wanted and said I was never a Communist Party member, Feller did not try to push me to name names.

We forced the International to step in and make a statement on our firings, which, while basically anti-Communist, did advocate a half-way civil liberties position, i.e., job protection for those victims of HUAC and McCarthyism who would swear (under oath) they were not Communists. This was an advanced position for the Steelworkers Union in those dark days of McCarthyism. It also allowed us to provide support to the other three fired workers at a later date.

After negotiations to establish my position, the International requested a rehearing of Step Three. This was merely a formality, because the deal had already been clinched between the International and the Company. Once we agreed to swear "under oath" that we "were not now members or supporters of the Communist Party," we put the International on the spot, and they persuaded the Company to reinstate us to our jobs. Knowledgeable attorneys outside the Union had assured us that swearing "under oath" at a private hearing of this type, i.e., a labor grievance meeting, has no legal significance, and we could not be prosecuted for perjury as in a court proceeding or even a Congressional hearing.

Shortly after this rehearing, the Company reinstated us.

The *Buffalo Evening News* printed USW District Director Molony's declaration that our reinstatement "resulted from scrupulous adherence by the United Steelworkers of America to principles adopted in 1955 pertaining to invocation of the Fifth Amendment on questions of Communist affiliation." To the press, Molony waxed eloquent about the Union's carrying out its duty "to protect and extend our democratic institutions and civil rights and liberties and thus to perpetuate the cherished traditions of democracy." We knew then and there how he had acquired the nickname, "Baloney Molony." He had been in the forefront of the local Union's bureaucracy to deny us Union protection.

After I was rehired by the Company, I had some really bad experiences. One guy threw a wooden four-by-four over a pile of steel that just barely missed me. It could have hit me on the head and maybe crushed my skull. I found out who did it. He was a vicious anti-Communist. And I couldn't fight on the job because I would have been fired. On the other hand, there were workers who came up to me and befriended me because they felt I had been wronged, and felt close to me. This included a wide range of people.

The Next Phase of the Struggle

With a weak but partial victory, our struggle at Bethlehem Steel began a new phase: solidarity of those who were reinstated with those who were not continued. The outcome would determine how much we had gained by our pragmatism!

Our purpose was to try to continue to challenge the labor bureaucracy on their anti-communism. We were determined to try to bring the message to the rank-and-file, and to continue to involve the community in the fight-back effort. This was occurring against a backdrop of the national struggle against McCarthyism, which began to see successes in the courts and, to some degree, in the unions.

I sent out a letter to all the folks who had been supportive of our efforts to get reinstated, thanking them for their help and explaining my feeling that some basic democratic procedures had been violated during my fight for reinstatement. I urged them to continue supporting the other three who had been discharged for taking a more principled position.

In May, 1959, Smith, Soble and Zucker filed a lawsuit against the Company and the Union in the federal court. In a statement about the suit to the rank-and-file, distributed to several thousand workers at the gates of the mill, the brothers described the background facts, their unsuccessful appeals to District Director Molony and International President McDonald, and their demand for a court order that the Union take their grievance through arbitration or that the Company pay them each $75,000 in damages for the unjust firings. They charged an agreement and conspiracy between the Company and the Union that injured them "in the free exercise and enjoyment of rights and privileges of a citizen of the United States," namely the right to refuse to bear witness against oneself. They attached a letter to their statement:

We want to point out especially that we have sued the Union only because it was unavoidable in view of the position taken by the Union leadership in refusing to process our grievance past 3rd Step. Even so, we are not suing the Union for money but only that they fulfill their obligations to us, as they should to all their members, by processing the grievances according to the provisions of the contract. The fact that the Union filed a grievance in the first place shows that the firings were unjust and a violation of the contract by the Company.

The Company did not want its undemocratic linen washed in public. Neither did the Union. They asked their lawyers to use delaying tactics to avoid the basic issues in the case. Company and Union lawyers asked to have the case moved from Pennsylvania to the Western District of New York. In 1960, the court agreed and the case was moved. In 1961 in Buffalo, the Company called each of the plaintiffs to answer questions under oath. In these depositions Company lawyers asked the three men questions geared to "reveal" their associations and memberships in progressive organizations. HUAC had asked many of the same questions at its 1957 hearings. Other questions came from information supplied directly by the FBI or indirectly by HUAC.

The three workers refused to answer such questions, saying

the Company was pursuing a strategy to trap them. The nominal purpose of the depositions was to prove they had been fired "with cause," *i.e.*, that the three were members or supporters of the CP and had refused to answer questions at the HUAC hearings because of their membership.

The Union was silent as the Company tried to turn the screws on the discharged workers one more time.

THE BASIC QUESTIONS

Whether the appearance of a witness before the House UnAmerican Activities Committee constitutes a discharge for cause when the worker relied on the Fifth Amendment privilege?

If so, whether a Bethlehem steel worker may sue the Company directly or must proceed through the grievance machinery of the Steelworkers Union contract?

Whether a worker can compel a trade union to process a grievance for him in this situation?

...And, of course, there is the overall civil liberties problem as to whether reputed membership, recent membership or even present membership in the Communist Party bars one from employment in a steel mill.

♦♦Victor Rabinowitz, attorney for the three
Memo to a civil liberties group

No Answers

We will never know the answers to these questions because the plaintiffs were forced to drop the case by an interesting twist. Since this was a civil suit and the workers were the plaintiffs, they could be compelled to answer the Company's questions or lose the right to proceed. As a result, two of them dropped out of the case and the third failed to appear at the deposition ordered by the judge. The case was closed and justice was not done. It was not even put to the test, just bogged down until the underlying issue was buried.

While this was going on, the back of the rank-and-file movement in steel was broken. The attack on progressives was successful in Lackawanna, and throughout the steel industry.

The Dues Protest Commitee, an insurgent group within the USW, took up issues of dishonest elections, poor workplace representation, discrimination, and collaboration of top union officials with company representatives. Rank-and-file steelworkers were also rejecting Union President David McDonald's campaign to create a "mutual trusteeship" between workers, stockholders and employers. According to Philip Nyden's PhD thesis on rank-and-file insurgency within the steelworkers, this philosophy came to symbolize much of what progressive rank-and-file union members came to oppose in the next 20 years. At the 1954 Constitutional Convention, McDonald explained his philosophy:

> The days of the Andrew Carnegies and people like him are gone. The great corporations of our country are no longer owned by small family groups. Hundreds of thousands of stockholders own the great corporations of America, particularly in the steel industry.... Those stockholders ... employ a group of managers. Those managers are simply employees of those corporations. Then there is another group of employees, known as the working force. Both of these groups have this mutual trusteeship who operate this steel company, or all of these steel companies. This is their mutual trusteeship and in the operation of this mutual trusteeship they are obliged to give full consideration to everybody involved.

Summing Up

The Company succeeded in silencing the workers in Buffalo by firings and threats. The labor bureaucracy succeeded in maintaining its stranglehold on the Union. By the time HUAC was through with Buffalo in 1957, it had succeeded in driving out of union activities those workers who were essential to the struggle to democratize their locals and build them into effective representatives of workers' interests. Without the participation of progressives and Communists, the union degenerated into class collaboration, doing the company's bidding at the expense of the workers. This was best exemplified by the special no-strike agreements negotiated in later years while working to increase worker productivity.

By 1964, our Party club was no longer in existence. Some folks had left the Party and joined a new group, Progressive Labor; some had remained. I was out of steel and had drifted out of the Party because I could not accept Party discipline and broke ranks over being rehired. I was still in touch with a lot of Communists and PL'ers, although I had gone back to college to get a degree in chemistry.

When I left the mill, I wondered whether I had been successful in industrial concentrations, and if not, why not? I concluded that we had made pretty good friends with our fellow workers, in spite of the fact that some of us had college educations. We were respected and liked. Some of our guys became leaders in their locals, or on the job; I don't mean just union officials, but leaders. One guy was an officer in his local. So in the main, it seemed to me to be working, until HUAC hit. Then it all fell apart because HUAC and the FBI were successful in raising the spectre of an "underground" group of "traitors".

I have never seen an evaluation of the industrial concentration program or colonization by the Communist Party or any other political group. Many people gave a good part of their lives to such programs which deserve a critical analysis.

HUAC Returns to Buffalo

In 1964, in Washington, D.C., an informer appeared before HUAC and I think also before the Senate Internal Security Sub-Committee and related his experiences in Buffalo. Immediately we all began to sense that something was in the wind. Then HUAC announced it would return to Buffalo.

Would this be a replay of 1957, when the community rolled over and played dead? Maybe not, because this time the UnAmericans were going after progressives at the University of Buffalo, a force that was silent in 1957.

We began to talk informally with University people about resisting the Committee. By then, I had graduated and had a job as a chemist, and my wife was attending college there. After awhile we got together and discussed whom we might contact. Eventually we brought into being an ad hoc organization called the Buffalo Committee to Oppose the House Un-American Activites Committee. I was instrumental in the formation of this group, helped to bring some of the people together, contacted others, and was a very active organizer.

I must say I was leading kind of a schizophrenic life at that time, since I had a whole circle of friends through my job who knew nothing of all this, while I was working very actively with a lot of university people and industrial workers against

HUAC. We called people; we circulated and distributed leaflets; we had a campaign of writing protest letters to the government.

Then Esther and I received notices from HUAC saying that we had been "identified as having been ... member[s] of the Communist Party" and that a subcommittee of HUAC would soon be meeting in Buffalo. "At that time," the notice said, "if you so desire, you will be afforded an opportunity to appear as a witness."

By now, however, the situation was a little different than it had been in '57. The Committee had been forced to adopt rules that were somewhat protective of witnesses. This was due to the valiant efforts of many "unfriendly" witnesses, their lawyers, and others who opposed the Un-American Committee and its hearings.

We learned that in an executive (private) session of the Committee, our names were mentioned by a paid informer, saying we had attended a party sponsored by persons who happened to be Communists (some attending actually were members of the Progressive Labor Party). Of course, we *did not* appear at the HUAC "meeting". And when the paid informer testified in public session, he was cut off by the Committee counsel just prior to naming our names. We were never subpoenaed to testify at those hearings.

And the mood of the country was changing. Alexander Meiklejohn and other civil libertarians had been struggling over the years to defeat HUAC and the other McCarthyites in their effort to stifle democracy and mold the US in their own image. Many victories were being won by the civil liberties movement, including the cases of some colonizers and other steelworkers in Gary, Indiana, who were subpoenaed by HUAC in 1958 and won their cases in the U.S. Supreme Court in 1963. Efforts to abolish HUAC were also taking hold in the U.S. Congress.

This time, labor unions joined our broad-based coalition in support of "unfriendly" witnesses and in opposition to HUAC, in addition to the University community and the community at large. In a largely Catholic city, liberal Catholics, including one lawyer who subsequently became Dean of the University of Buffalo Law School, joined in the struggle in opposition to very powerful elements in the Church.

This time HUAC was greeted with contempt, both from those subpoenaed to appear, and from many in the community. Subpoenees took the position that HUAC was contemptuous of the Bill of Rights and deserved to be treated with contempt. If anyone was going to be accused of contempt of Congress, there would be adequate grounds for the charge!

The trip to Buffalo by HUAC was one of the last hearings that it held outside of Washington, D.C., and one of the last hearings it held before being abolished by Congress. Even its chairman at the time, Rep. Edwin E. Willis (D-La.), avoided the Buffalo hearing because he "was detained by other business in Washington."

The opposition to HUAC had a very powerful impact on the community. It resulted in an outpouring of civil libertarian sentiment that was to be felt for many years to come.

THE END FOR HUAC

♦♦ Frank Wilkinson ♦♦

Frank Wilkinson is Executive Director Emeritus of the National Committee Against Repressive Legislation (NCARL), the successor organization to the National Committee to Abolish HUAC.

One highlight of the Buffalo hearings was the appearance of a most unlikely HUAC opponent: actor Sterling Hayden. In the 1940s, Hayden had availed himself of HUAC's proffer to informants: "name the names we give you, and we'll see to it that you are not blacklisted!" In the intervening years, however, Hayden not only recanted, he asked the National Committee to Abolish HUAC to call upon him to appear against HUAC "whenever and wherever needed." So we called upon him to speak in Buffalo, and he added his prominent voice to the growing opposition to the Committee.

The National Committee to Abolish HUAC was organized in 1960 by Southern New Dealer Aubrey Williams; philosopher Alexander Meiklejohn; Quaker Clarence Pickett; and retired Wall Street banker James Imbrie, who had broken away from his conservative background in the Henry Wallace campaign of 1948. The going was painfully slow. It took five years to get an abolition petition prepared by Meiklejohn and Professor Thomas I. Emerson formally introduced in Congress by Rep. Don Edwards (D-Cal.) in 1965. This led to a grassroots, Congressional District-by-District campaign for abolition.

Following the 1964 Buffalo hearings, HUAC made one final public effort outside of Washington, the Stamler-Hall-Cohen hearing in Chicago in 1965. By then, it was unsafe for HUAC to venture away from the more protective House Office buildings. Opposition to HUAC became contagious, deeply influenced by the rising civil rights struggles in the South. When five Black students in Greensboro were arrested for a sit-in at a Woolworth store, white students led protests against Woolworth stores on the West Coast. Within three months, thousands of students besieged HUAC in San Francisco's City Hall.

In addition, there was a succession of legal challenges to the Committee's violations of the First Amendment: 53 individuals chose jail, if necessary, to register their contempt of HUAC. The early fight-back by labor was joined by a wide coalition of community forces.

By 1975, the vote in Congress to abolish HUAC was overwhelming, conservatives joining liberals to elminate an embarrassment to the Congress. Finally, after 38 years and more than 3,500 subpoenaed persons, the witch-hunt was ended on January 14, 1975.

THE FATAL QUESTION

♦♦Joseph Cantor♦♦

That knock on our door in Lackawanna in 1957 ultimately sent me not only out of steel, but out of the world of rank-and-file unionism and into the white-collar world. But the lessons learned there live on, and the respect for the workers and their families whom we got to know and love will sustain us for the rest of our lives.

Had it not been for that knock on our door, and on the doors of other progressives, who knows what eventually might have happened in Lackawanna, in the Steelworkers Union, and in the U.S. steel industry?

Anti-Communism, business unionism, and class collaboration prevailed in the steel industry. But Lackawanna was a bustling, vibrant steeltown even in the dark days of McCarthyism.

Who could foresee that the victory of the Cold Warriors would lead to the defeat of *all* workers and turn Lackawanna into a ghost town within 20 years, as Big Steel transnationals ran away to non-union countries, leaving behind an army of unemployed steelworkers?

What did all the anti-Communism get the USWA?

84 ♦♦ ILWU COMMUNIST SLAYS THE SON OF TAFT-HARTLEY

♦♦ **The Editors** ♦♦

The Taft-Hartley non-Communist oath of 1947 did not last very long. It did not sit well, even with anti-Communists, because it violated the basic right to have political ideas and affiliations and to keep them to yourself if you want to. Besides, the wording of the oath was so vague that nobody felt safe from attack. And it was one-sided: employers' representatives did not have to swear they were not members of the KKK, White Citizens Councils, or the Right-wing anti-Black States' Rights Democratic Party of 1948.

In 1954, Congress passed the Communist Control Act. One section abolished the requirement that labor leaders swear they were not members of, or affiliated with, or supporters of the Communist Party. The '54 Act simply made it a crime to be a member of the Communist Party and an elected union official at the same time, or for five years after leaving the Party. (29 U.S. Code sec. 504.) The stated purpose of the section was "to protect the national economy by minimizing the danger of political strikes."

Archie Brown, a colorful leader of the West Coast International Longshoremen's and Warehousemen's Union, challenged this new provision. Brown had joined the Communist Party in 1929 and the Longshoremen's Union in 1936, fought with the Loyalists in Spain as a member of the Abraham Lincoln Brigade, and ran for the San Francisco Board of Supervisors three times from 1939 to 1959. He was a leader of the movement to kick HUAC out of San Francisco in 1960, along with students from the University of California-Berkeley, and other labor and liberal people.

Archie Brown ran for the Executive Board of Local 10 of the ILWU in San Francisco and was easily elected in 1959, 1960, and 1961. He also openly stated what was no secret, that he was a member of the Communist Party.

In 1961 he was arrested for "knowingly and wilfully serving as a member of an executive board of a labor organization ... while a member of the Communist Party." He answered that this section of the '54 Act was forbidden by the U.S. Constitution because it punished a person for beliefs, not for acts, and it punished without trial, based solely on membership in an organization. Brown and his lawyers said this made it an illegal bill of attainder like the laws confiscating the property of Catholics and Protestants charged with treason during the religious strife in feudal England.

During Brown's trial, the defense tried to tell the jury that the local executive board had never called a strike, and that the union had not been involved in any strike since 1948.

The Government moved to strike this from the evidence, and the judge would not permit the jury to hear these facts.

In 1964, 14 years after the Supreme Court upheld the Taft-Hartley oath in *A.C.A. v. Douds* [*described in section 38*], the Supreme Court held that Brown was right. The vote was 5 to 4, and the opinion was by Chief Justice Warren.

He went through the history of bills of pains and punishments and bills of attainder in England and in colonial America. He pointed to their basic flaw: that the legislative body decided precisely who was guilty—e.g., all members of the Communist Party and all who had left the Party within five years when they ran for union office. This law violates the basic idea of trial by jury to determine individual innocence or guilt. It gives members of Congress the power to convict individuals in advance of jury trial, which is very unwise because Congressmembers are "peculiarly susceptible to popular clamor" and unable "to try with coolness, caution and impartiality, ... especially in those cases in which the popular feeling is strongly excited, ..." (*United States v. Brown*, 381 U.S. 437, at 445 (quoting 1 Cooley, *Constitutional Limitations* 536-37 (1927)).

♦♦ WHO, ME? ♦♦

This unsigned cartoon graced the back cover of *Censored News of Your America* (Vol. 1, No. 1) published by the Civil Rights Congress in September 1950.

Other Repressive Laws Also Died

The Taft-Hartley non-Communist oath, and its successor Communist Control Act prohibition were only two of the myriad governmental restrictions placed on Communists and non-Communists who refused to be anti-Communists during the Cold War.

Churches and other nonprofit organizations had their tax-exempt status questioned or lifted.[1] The NAACP, as well as the CP, faced state laws requiring its members to register with authorities in states where everyone knew this would result in loss of employment and, perhaps, even of life. The Supreme Court said this was unconstitutional many times.[2] Lawyers for Cuba were ordered to register as foreign agents.[3] Public employees in Arizona had to take a state non-Communist oath; they, too, won in the Supreme Court,[4] as did lawyers and activists challenging the Louisiana Un-American Activities Committee.[5] It wasn't until 1958 that progressive artists like Rockwell Kent were able to get passports,[6] and Communist Party leaders Herbert Aptheker and Elizabeth Gurley Flynn won theirs after a trip to the Supreme Court in 1964.[7] Military discharges based on pre-induction political activities and memberships were declared unjustified in *Harmon v. Brucker* [8] in 1958. In 1959, the Veterans Administration restored payments to a disabled veteran whose benefits they had stopped after his conviction under the Smith Act.[9] Social Security benefits were denied to employees of the Communist Party; in 1956 these benefits were restored.[10] Blacklisting of performers began to die out after John Henry Faulk won his damage suit against blacklister AWARE publication and most of the award was upheld in 1964.[11]

Some areas tried to deny public housing to people who would not sign non-Communist oaths,[12] and even unemployment compensation to employees of the Communist Party[13] (which had helped pass the first unemployment compensation act). Many states made it impossible for radicals to get admitted to practice law by means of non-Communist oaths and "security checks."[14]

But by the late 1960s, these remaining federal and state laws and practices were finally falling into disuse, after being repeatedly declared unfair, unnecessary, and/or unconstitutional.

NOTES

1. *First Unitarian Church of Los Angeles v. Los Angeles County*, 357 U.S. 545 (1950). *Re Fellowship of Reconciliation*, 202.5, 8 CIVIL LIBERTIES DOCKET 97; 10 DOCKET 27 (1964).
2. See *Bates v. Little Rock*, 361 U.S. 516 (1960).
3. *Rabinowitz and Boudin v. Kennedy*, 376 U.S. 605 (1964).
4. *Elfbrandt v. Russell*, 384 U.S. 11 (1966).
5. *Dombrowski v. Pfister*, 380 U.S. 479 (1965).
6. *Kent v. Dulles*, 357 U.S. 116 (1958).
7. *Aptheker, Flynn v. Secretary of State*, 378 U.S. 500 (1964).
8. *Harmon v. Brucker*, 355 U.S. 579 (1958).
9. See *Wellman v. Whittier*, 259 F2d 163 (CA DC 1958), 254.1, 4 CIVIL LIBERTIES DOCKET 46 (1959).
10. *Matter of Bittelman, Mindel, Foster*, 1 CIVIL LIBERTIES DOCKET 56, 93 (1956).
11. *Faulk v. AWARE*, 253 NYS2d 990 (NY Ct. of App. 1964).
12. *Housing Authority of the City of Los Angeles v. Cordova*, 279 P2d 215 (Cal Ct of App 1955), *certiorari denied* 350 U.S. 969 (1956).
13. *Communist Party v. Catherwood*, 367 U.S. 389 (1961).
14. E.g., *Konigsberg v. State Bar of California and Committee of Bar Examiners*, 353 U.S. 252 and *Schware v. Board of Bar Examiners of New Mexico*, 353 U.S. 232 (1957), and see *In re Terrence Hallinan*, 421 P2d 76 (Cal Sup Ct 1966).

85. ♦♦ EXPELLED TEAMSTER FIGHTING FOR DEMOCRACY

♦♦Jack Weintraub♦♦

Jack Weintraub, retired president of Teamsters Union Local 85 and heavy-duty driver, is a veteran of many progressive struggles in the San Francisco Bay Area. He was an early and consistent supporter of the United Farm Workers and an unfriendly witness before the House Un-American Activities Committee.

During the fall and winter of 1970-71, the administration of Teamsters Local 85 in San Francisco in a series of actions removed five opposition members from the union, four by permanent "suspension" and one by issuing a withdrawal card over his protest.

We fought the expulsions and the sustaining decision of the executive board of Joint Council 7 of the IBT all the way to the General Executive Board of the IBT. It took us a year and a half.

When the weight of a bureaucracy is used to deny the rights of an individual, one seeks vindication in the courts, particularly if the offending bureaucracy is in the public sector of the community. But when the bureaucracy of a 2,200,000-member trade union is used to deny individual rights, the problem is more complex and resolution of the problem more unlikely.

There was an initial contradiction inherent in the situation: the members expelled were an active threat to the local administration's policies. Had we been submissive, there would have been no need to expel us. By the same token, we were the people most likely to resist the expulsions. The conflict, instead of being resolved by the expulsions, was intensified and broadened.

THE OPPOSITION FIVE

The five of us were known in varying degrees throughout the labor movement and in political circles. All of us disagreed with the 1970 IBT policy in regard to the United Farm Workers, AFL-CIO. Ray Talavera and I had also been consistent and outspoken advocates of closer communication between the leadership of the Teamsters locally and the leadership of the ILWU local unions, and between the stewards and the rank-and-file membership of both unions. All of us had walked the picket lines, not only of our own union, but of many of the unions in the Bay Area—the Department Store Clerks, the Typographers, the United Farm Workers, the ILWU, and many more.

One of our number had been one of the local leaders of the Peace and Freedom Party. Another had been Northern California Coordinator of Labor Liaison for the California Democratic Council. We had participated in various city, county, state, congressional, senatorial and presidential campaigns. In short, we were not obscure in personality or in activity.

The Charges

Talavera was the first to be charged with violation of the Teamsters' constitution and by-laws. He was charged with having violated the constitution, first, by calling Richardson, Local business manager, a liar, and second, by inciting violence against Richardson in the course of an incident related to an unauthorized strike and picket line in San Francisco.

John Ryan, an owner-driver, represented Talavera before the executive committee of Local 85 sitting as a trial board. The next day, Richardson issued a withdrawal card to Ryan.

Ryan protested: Why was this action taken?

Richardson replied: You "asked for it."

Harry Orr, Tony Baeza, Bob Quilici, and I were charged with aiding alleged pickets in an unauthorized strike, and I was further charged with having taken a leading part in these events by chairing a meeting during which they were organized. Specifically, I was charged with having violated the section of the IBT Constitution that prohibits any member from entering into "any action which is disruptive of or interferes with the performance or obligations of other members of local unions under collective bargaining agreements." (1971 Const. p. 126)

The charges against Talavera were based on the following incidents:

One: It was disclosed at a regular membership meeting that the executive board had taken unilateral action in relation to property on Fulton Street and the property adjoining it.

Talavera rose to protest that Richardson had exceeded his authority.

Richardson replied that the property in question had been recommended as ideal by a committee of which both Talavera and I were members and which Talavera had chaired.

Talavera replied that the statement was a lie.

Richardson shouted frantically that he wanted it entered in the minutes that he had been called a liar.

When I joined the debate from my seat, I was hastily cut off as soon as I mentioned the name of Jack Dooling, an attorney who had been acting as real estate consultant and broker for the union.

Two: In May of 1970, members of Teamsters Local 208 from Los Angeles were attempting to force the California Trucking Association to grant amnesty to some of their activists who had been fired for displaying excessive enthusiasm in an unauthorized strike. They had hoped to force the amnesty by disrupting the flow of freight in the San Francisco Bay Area. The Southern Pacific piggy-back yard was "rendered inactive" in San Francisco. Teamsters from San Francisco, Alameda and Contra Costa counties in the Bay Area, supporting the Los Angeles Teamsters in great mass, swarmed to the "pig yard" when word spread that Tim Richardson was going to try to reopen it.

Richardson was not alone. He was preceded by hordes of police, in street clothes and in uniform, by representatives of the employers, and he was accompanied by muscular "heavies."

Realizing that his show of force had momentarily caused apprehension among the assembled teamsters, Richardson took advantage of the pause to shout to his cohorts to leave him, that he was safe among his fellow members. Plowing into their midst, he used the pause he had created to engage in shouting arguments with various pickets. Out of this incident grew the second part of the charges against Talavera, who certainly was present but could hardly have been considered a threat to anyone under the circumstances.

Strategy and Support

From the time we first were presented with charges pressed by Tim Richardson, business manager of Local 85—from the time that Richardson declared he was going to press charges against Talavera—we tried to guess whether Richardson and his administration really meant to go through with it and really expel us. We also had to determine the exact reasons why our expulsions were necessary to the Richardson administration because that would affect our decision on how best to fight for reinstatement.

The question whether we should fight the expulsion or remain outside the union never was given serious consideration, if it was raised at all. All of us automatically assumed that our new situation was a continuation of our struggle for trade union democracy and to make the trade union truly representative of its membership vis-a-vis the employers.

The struggle for reinstatement did not follow a blueprint but it did follow an overall strategy that was developed and refined as the struggle progressed.

Immediately upon being expelled, we took our cases to the Northern California Committee for Trade Union Action and Democracy (TUAD). We asked for support and that our cases be publicized. We were well received and given constant support from that organization. We contacted various trade union rank-and-file organizations for the same purpose and, each time, we were well received.

We did all in our power to make our cases a *cause celebre*. The purpose in doing this in the trade union community was to exert pressure on the leaders of the Teamsters in this indirect manner.

No teamsters in Joint Council 7 believed that the charges against us represented the real reasons for the trial. The history of J.C. 7 is full of cases of varying degrees of support of wildcat strikes and unauthorized walkouts. This has always been regarded by the officialdom as solidarity, although sometimes and to some degree misplaced. Because of recurring instances where the officials wished this support to evidence itself, there had been an understandable reluctance on their part to punish "unauthorized" support of unauthorized walkouts. In addition, overt support was being provided the Los Angeles pickets by many Bay Area locals.

Most of the officials of Bay Area Teamster locals gave tacit approval to the sweep of rank-and-file support. Tim Richardson went much further. He introduced one of the leaders of the Los Angeles pickets, named Murietta, from the platform at a meeting of Local 85, allowed him to address us, then, in effect, closed the city of San Francisco in supposed support. It did not seem logical for Richardson to try us for attempting to do what he claimed he did better than we could have.

The next consideration that came to mind was that we were being removed from the scene because, as a group, we represented meaningful opposition and possible defeat for Richardson in the next Local 85 election. Although there was merit to this consideration, further reflection made us doubt that it was the only, or perhaps even the major, reason for our trials. Incumbents had never resorted to expulsions in order to stay in office before. On the other hand, there is always a first time.

A third consideration was that, as a group, we represented meaningful opposition to the employers. Since a great deal of money is at stake for the employers in their constant drive for maximum exploitation of their employees, it is reasonable to assume that they exert every influence and even spur whichever of their agents are available within the union to neutralize or eliminate the threat radical workers pose to their future profits. In short, we constituted a threat to the system of accommodation established between the employers and the incumbent officers and the combined wrath of both camps demanded and necessitated our expulsions.

In essence, we feel we were expelled because we championed a program the employers feared, and because we were capable of mobilizing enough support for ourselves and for the program within the union membership to enable us to move it forward in some degree.

THE STRUGGLE FOR REINSTATEMENT

We waged our struggle for reinstatement in four arenas: in the internal union bodies outlined in the International Constitution and the local's by-laws, in the relationships we continued to have with the members of the local union, in the federal and state judicial systems that heard our lawsuits, and in the trade union community that got interested in our cases. These struggles were conducted concurrently.

The IBT Trial Procedures

The trial procedures specified in the union constitution leave much to be desired in the way of democracy. The executive board of the local union becomes the trial board. Its decisions are not subject to question or ratification by the membership of the local union. Appeals of the decisions of the local union's trial board are to the executive board of the Joint Council of Teamsters, to which the local union is affiliated. Decisions rendered by this body can be appealed to the General Executive Board of the International. And the last appeal is to the next International Convention.

These trial boards are far from conversant with rights of individuals under common law. They are composed of political people who are there because of political victories. Their decisions are bound to be highly political and have little bearing on questions concerning justice or the rights of individuals.

In our case, the relationship of forces on the Joint Council Executive Board that would hear our appeals gave us no hope. Richardson could expect strong support from one or two of the seven members. Although the remainder usually opposed him on many issues, and at times looked favorably upon us, we saw no possibility that they would identify with us in this particular struggle against a seemingly entrenched local union power.

The union constitution prohibits representation at trials by anyone who is not a member of the IBT, and of the same local as the member charged.

John Ryan represented Talavera before the local union's board. Then he was issued a withdrawal card. He continued to represent Talavera through all the appeals, including his own.

Orr and I represented each other at each hearing. We stated that we were not going to endanger any other member's status. Baeza, facing each board alone, gave the same reason for not having representation.

Knowing that we were on an uphill course, we pursued the procedures as specified. Not only did the IBT Constitution demand that we exhaust all internal remedies. Common law and the consciences of our brothers and sisters within the IBT demanded that we exhaust all internal remedies. This took a considerable period of time.

In the meantime, we received partial protection from the Landrum-Griffin Act, the same act that had inspired the section of the IBT Constitution we were alleged to have violated. Under Landrum-Griffin, we could not be taken off the job by the union unless we were expelled for "non-payment of dues."

We made visible and overt attempts to pay dues. Before witnesses, we repeatedly attempted to give the secretary-treasurer of the local union our dues money. We wrote checks in varying amounts that were finally accepted on a temporary basis but not cashed. I sent money via Western Union. In that manner, a dated receipt was obtained even though the telegrams were not cashed. We suspected we were "suspended" instead of "expelled" so that later we could be expelled on the dues strategies.

Petitions and Work in the Local

Although we were prevented from attending union membership meetings, our relationships with the membership continued on the job and in the hiring hall. Since most of us continued to be employed on jobs under labor contract, we enjoyed a new relationship with our employers now that we had been expelled. In case of a grievance with the employer, we could call on the union representatives to enforce the contract. Or we could exercise a dual option, going directly to government agencies to represent us. The employers were uneasy about this arrangement and were loathe to test us. They adopted an official "hands off" policy.

We continued to publish leaflets and petitions addressed to the membership of Local 85, in which we tried to arouse them to respond to our plight as expelled members. We asked them for money in order to continue our struggle. A few responded. We asked them to sign a petition demanding our reinstatement. Several hundred of them responded.

Our best responses from the membership came when we proposed a program relating to pensions and job security and policing of the labor contract by union representatives. We could measure this response, in part, by the money sent to the Teamsters Defense Fund that was established to support our efforts.

We found that when we attempted to focus attention on our problem primarily, we encountered minimum response. Each teamster had problems enough and if our problem was presented as an additional one, it was evaded. We found our best response when we consistently hammered away on the problems most important to the membership and proved that our reinstatement was a step toward their solution.

In the election of officers of Local 85 in the spring of 1971, we conducted a consistent campaign against the policies and program of Richardson in his bid for reelection to the office of recording secretary and business manager of the local union.

As the election campaign moved into the final stages, many members came to us and asked our advice. Richardson's only opponent, Andy Leonard, had certain differences with us and he had other differences with Richardson. We were in a similar position but we recognized Richardson as the threat, not only to us, but to the best interests of the union. Therefore, we advised those who asked not to vote for Richardson.

The Legal Battle

Immediately upon being expelled, we separately and collectively sought and acted on legal advice. After considering alternatives, we decided to move on all fronts, including the legal front. We found ourselves constantly trying to explain our position to our supporters.

As an example, one complained bitterly about the fact that we were suing the local union. "But that means that you're suing me!" he cried. "Why? I'm on your side!"

"That's true!" he was answered, "and we appreciate it. We appreciate that when we were expelled, you protested loudly on the floor of the meeting. We appreciate that you donated a lot of time and money to our defense. We appreciate that you signed and distributed petitions demanding our reinstatement. We appreciate that you campaigned against Richardson and helped defeat him in his bid for reelection. This you did as an individual and as part of an unofficial group. It was heroic and moral. But it cannot be denied that you are a member of an organization that kicked us out and for that organization's inability to prevent the injustice, you must bear the guilt, the responsibility and financial cost if we win our suit."

This argument went over like a lead balloon.

Yet we thought we had a responsibility to try to win in court—not only for ourselves, but for others. Would our responsibility be satisfied if we were to be reinstated? What about others who may be similarly persecuted later? Would they endure the expense, the harassment, the anguish and apprehension for the satisfaction of being reinstated? What would repay the wives and families of those who may be expelled as they see their economic and social welfare endangered and yet must stand helplessly by while the battle that concerns them so closely goes forward in an arena from which they are excluded? Who would do what we did? Wouldn't they take a look at our experience and decide that the effort was not compensated by the return?

If we could set a legal precedent, we thought it would be worthwhile.

Attorney Lloyd McMurray took Talavera's case into federal district court, suing Richardson, Local 85, Joint Council 7 of the IBT, the International Brotherhood of Teamsters, and several John Does. McMurray asked Judge Wollenberg to order that: 1) the local's elections in 1971 be delayed until Talavera's status as a candidate could be determined, and 2) the local be ordered to abide by the constitution and by-laws in its relationship with us and with Talavera as a candidate for office.

The judge refused to take any action at that time and the elections proceeded.

Victory in the Election

Leonard defeated Richardson by a narrow margin! Meanwhile, our appeal to the IBT General Executive Board went forward.

After many months, McMurray went back to federal court. He added to the original plea a demand for general and special damages, exemplary damages, attorney's fees and court costs.

Attorneys for the Joint Council argued that the court had no jurisdiction in the matter because the alleged specifics were not violations of federal law and because due process within the IBT had not been exhausted. (A panel appointed by the IBT

General Executive Board had conducted an appeal review of our cases but, to our knowledge, had not yet given a recommendation or an opinion.)

This time Judge Wollenberg ruled that the specifics of the case came within the jurisdiction of his court as possible violations of the Taft-Hartley Act as amended by the Landrum-Griffin Act. He further ruled that due process could be considered to have been exhausted in view of the long period of time spent in pursuing remedies within the IBT. (The question of delaying the union elections was stipulated by all parties as being moot since the elections had already taken place.)

A peculiar debate developed around the request that Judge Wollenberg order the union to comply with the union constitution and by-laws. Duane Beeson, representing the union, protested that such an order would be redundant, since both the constitution and by-laws provided procedures for discipline if their terms were violated.

Wollenberg agreed that this was so and asked McMurray why he should duplicate the implied orders.

McMurray answered that the court's order was necessary because the union refused to follow its own procedures when Talavera was involved.

Wollenberg suggested to McMurray that the proper procedure would be to catch the union in the process of violating the constitution and by-laws and then come to the court for relief.

McMurray, in a voice raised to exasperation, stated they had found such a situation, brought it to Wollenberg, and Wollenberg wouldn't do anything claiming that, since the election process had started, it was too late to stop it.

Wollenberg took the matter under submission.

McMurray then prepared similar complaints for Baeza, Orr, Ryan, and me (excluding the complaints relevant to the elections), and filed them in the San Francisco Superior Court, setting up a situation by which we could pursue relief in federal and state courts simultaneously.

Victory in the International

On April 5, 1972, the General Executive Board of the IBT reversed our expulsion by the local union, and reversed the decision of the joint council upholding the local's action!

Immediately we dropped our legal suits because they would have had the effect of diverting us from the struggle against the employers. We did this as a matter of political consideration, not because we felt we were fully vindicated.

Our lawyer, Lloyd McMurray, credited our victory on the totality of our efforts: organizing and leading the membership of Local 85, defeating Richardson in his bid for reelection, pursuing appeal procedures within the union, marshalling labor movement and community support for ourselves, and carrying through our legal efforts.

Shortly after reinstatement, Talavera ran for the position of Local Union Business Manager against Richardson and incumbent Andy Leonard, and won. He was Red-baited by Richardson and most of the other officials throughout the election campaign and his term of office.

Talavera lost to Richardson in the subsequent two elections. Richardson died of a stroke early in his second term. Talavera won the next election against James Baker, who had completed Richardson's term. At this writing (May, 1985) Talavera is still Business Manager of Local Union 85.

I rose through the ranks of leadership also. In 1976 I was elected to the post of Local Union Trustee. Within the three-year term of office, I was advanced by the Local Union Executive Board to the office of Vice President, and then to President of the Local Union. In the next election, I was re-elected to the Presidency by an overwhelming majority.

Ironically, as the results of the 1976 election were being tabulated, Richardson realized he could not continue to fight against us, and proposed that he and I work together "for the benefit of the union." Although Richardson's politics didn't change, he and I became a team, working together against the employers.

86. ◆◆ A PLUMBER GETS CURIOUS ABOUT EXPORTING McCARTHYISM

◆◆Fred Hirsch ◆ Virginia Muir◆◆

This section is told from the first-person perspective of Fred Hirsch, a long-time member of Plumbers & Fitters Local 393. Virginia Muir is area steward of Office and Professional Employees International Union, Local 29. They live in San Jose, California.

Space limitations forced extensive cuts in the text. Interested readers can refer to the source material presented at the end of the section, with each source numbered from 1-143. Numbers in the text refer to these items.

I'm a union plumber in San Jose, California. Right after the 1973 coup in Chile, I became interested in what U.S. unions were doing in Latin America. Because of events in El Salvador, Nicaragua and almost every country in the news south of the border, my interest—call it curiosity—is ever more intense.

I was propelled into action by the terrible crimes and suffering levelled against the Chilean workers in 1973 for having elected a president who opened a door toward self-determination and socialism. I helped organize a local committee in solidarity with Chile. Because I was on the bench and had some time to kill, our labor subcommittee gave me the task of assembling a packet to prod our Central Labor Council into action. The job meant researching information that was brand new to me and startling to all union people who looked at it carefully.

We had shared the notion that U.S. labor had a policy of solidarity with workers who were hurting abroad. We found the very opposite—a world of betrayal. We just couldn't believe it.

As a plumber I'm primarily a mechanic. Things have got to fit together. We lay out a job, take our measurements, cut and fit the material and, if it doesn't work out, we're down the road and back on the bench. We can't get away with covering up misdeeds with rhetoric.

Neither should officials of the AFL-CIO.

In looking at Chile, I found that any concept of solidarity was at odds with the work of the AFL-CIO arm in Latin America and the Caribbean, the American Institute for Free Labor Development (AIFLD). In effect, their measurements were all cut to fit the needs of the companies and government officials that inflicted unspeakable suffering on the workers. I had to remeasure. Something was drastically wrong. If the AFL-CIO was part of the betrayal—why? And why didn't union people here seem to know anything about AIFLD's impact on workers in Chile and in other countries?[1]

I learned from books and from interviews with a few remarkable people. I discovered that the AFL-CIO has been involved in the disruption of Latin American labor movements. This has been done, not by our members, but by certain top officials in concert with corporate America and government agencies. I learned that the transnational corporations (TNCs) manipulate our government and our unions to serve their commercial interests and to control workers in Latin America.

That's how my investigation began.

The Bottom Line

Today, in labor's ranks, and among many elected officials, there is a growing realization that opposing U.S. policy on Chile or Brazil or Central America or South Africa is not just do-goodism. People are beginning to see that any aid to the corporate drive for dominance abroad puts the wealth created by our hands and brains into super-profit foreign investments. This decapitalizes our basic industries and stifles modernization. The result: plant shutdowns and whole runaway industries in garment, shoe, light electrical, steel, and others.

Outside the war industry, the greatest corporate profits are grabbed by picking clean the low-wage, underdeveloped countries, taking their resources and labor. The increasing rate of profit in such places runs more than double our domestic rate.[2] The annual rise coincides with the growth of U.S. labor involvement abroad:

$2.9 billion in 1960
$7.6 billion in 1970
$18.5 billion in 1980

At the present rate, it won't be long before foreign profits outstrip domestic profits. In mid-1985, counting new investments, foreign profits reinvested, and subcontracts abroad, U.S. corporations invested more abroad than at home.[3] Such investments are backed by U.S. government insurance, foreign aid grants and loans, and needless, dangerous military costs. And we pick up the tab for all of it while the TNCs dodge taxes on foreign profits. [*See section 99.*] It costs us millions of jobs and is transforming our country into an underdeveloped nation.

In short, a corporate Fifth Column has emerged inside our labor movement, helping to undermine our economic future by the export of our jobs and national wealth. This has been done for resources and pittance wages abroad, controlled through gross repression. The director of AIFLD, William Doherty, gave a rationale for its actions in 1969:

> David Rockefeller ... decided we had a lot to gain from cooperating in Latin America ... and that we would try to throw away some of the classic concepts of how labor views management and how management views labor.... What we did was set up the AIFLD in cooperation with management.[4]

In 1980, David Rockefeller, chair of the Council on Foreign Relations (CFR), told why: "Five or ten years ago our earnings from Europe were greater than Latin America and Asia, now Latin America has become the most important contributor. It's really very exciting."[5]

The mutilated corpses of hundreds of thousands of Latin Americans testify that it has not been a voluntary contribution.

Research into the Roots

To make this study accurate, names will be named and light shed on some individuals and groups that would prefer to remain in the shadow. There is much still to be studied, measured and drawn before it is all reconstructed. I can't present statistics very often—foreign policy is mainly a world of relationships and code phrases that often mean the opposite of the words used. To reveal even as much as we have done here has meant checking hundreds of sources as the source notes indicate. I've attempted to avoid pointing a finger without accurate documentation. I have also learned that several key labor leaders who accepted the official line changed their minds when they finally discovered some of the hidden facts.

My studies show that workers in this country have long been concerned about working conditions and unions in other countries. For generations, most workers were immigrants or first generation Americans. When they saw the "heroic support" of European workers for the U.S. government in the Civil War against slavery, early U.S. labor unions made several efforts to join international labor organizations and movements after 1866.[6] But international labor solidarity was dealt terrible blows by worker killing worker in World War I along national lines[7] and by anti-Communist hysteria against the new "workers' state" established in Russia in 1917. Efforts to develop structures for international labor solidarity did not gain much headway in this country until World War II, when U.S. worker/soldiers fought alongside British, French, and Soviet worker/soldiers.

At the end of World War II, CIO officials and labor leaders from the Soviet Union and many other countries formed the World Federation of Trade Unions (WFTU) to oppose any new "imperialist scramble for power," and to organize world-wide as "one of the most potent instruments of world peace and a tower of strength to the United Nations."[8] [*See section 23.*] But the peace was already imperiled by the dropping of atomic bombs on Hiroshima and Nagasaki and by a scramble for markets and power. By 1949, the CIO was deliberately split asunder and yanked out of the WFTU to create the International Confederation of Free Trade Unions (ICFTU), which excluded Left unions in the "West" and unions in socialist countries. There was to be no united nations in the world labor movement.

In the Beginning Was the Council on Foreign Relations

Long before labor started to develop effective structures for international solidarity and action, the U.S. transnational corporations had filled their similar need. The TNCs formed the Council on Foreign Relations (CFR) in 1919. Wall Street admirers of the British empire joined founders from the National Civic Federation, including AFL leaders who bartered "respectability" for limiting union goals in industrial organizing and rejecting socialist politics. In 1939 the exclusive CFR had 570 members, all pledged to secrecy in CFR matters.[9] It included the sons of the robber barons, their lawyers and servants in government, academia, media and church. The members held the stolen riches produced by 200 years of black slavery, contract labor, immigrant poverty, indentured servitude, strike breaking, and child labor in the mines, mills and fields. Within that pack of highly-schooled inheritors were an incongruous few union leaders artfully selected by CFR's board of directors. Most important among them to receive the gratuity of CFR membership was David Dubinsky.

◆◆◆◆◆◆◆◆◆◆◆◆◆◆◆◆◆◆◆◆◆◆◆◆◆◆◆◆
DAVID DUBINSKY AND HIS PALS

As much as any person of his time, Dubinsky locked top officials of the AFL and then of the AFL-CIO into a policy of government-financed Cold War corporate service abroad. By 1932 Dubinsky won the presidency of the International Ladies Garment Workers Union (ILGWU-AFL) in bitter battles with the left and secured his position through secret deals with employers. Praised as "America's finest exemplar of class collaboration and free enterprise"[10] for shepherding the garment industry through two generations of labor peace, garment employers introduced Dubinsky to high society, where he basked in the reflected glory of the Rockefellers, Aldrich of Chase Bank, and Lamont of J.P. Morgan. By 1939 he was a rising star in labor and a trusted member of the Council on Foreign Relations.[9-11]

Dubinsky hired Jay Lovestone, top Communist Party defector, to fend off the left in ILGWU, and then paid Lovestone's costs to similarly divide the United Auto Workers (UAW), where Irving Brown joined his crew. Eventually Dubinsky boasted that his colonizing influence helped hand the UAW presidency to Walter Reuther.[11, 12]

Dubinsky's CFR cronies needed an anti-Communist labor presence to defend their European interests prior to U.S. entry into World War II. Alleging concern for "Soviet firing squads," Dubinsky gave them Lovestone and the resources of the 500,000-member Jewish Labor Committee to organize and work with European refugees during and after the war. The group formed for this project became the Free Trade Union Committee (FTUC), the official foreign policy arm of the AFL from 1943 until the merger with CIO in 1955.[11, 13] With Serafino Romualdi added to Dubinsky's staff, FTUC became a "veritable recruiting office" and a "well known system of intelligence agents," according to insiders. In postwar years, FTUC finances arrived in stacks of crisp, new $100 bills from the CIA.[12, 14, 15]

Dubinsky's weighty CFR policy role continued in the AFL-CIO Executive Council past his 1966 retirement, executed through Jay Lovestone, International Affairs Dept. director until 1974. Dubinsky brought top officials in AFL-CIO foreign policy into the closed chambers of CFR: Lovestone, Ernest Lee (retired Marine Colonel who succeeded Lovestone in the International Affairs Department); Irving Brown (key operative in Europe, Africa and ICFTU, currently director, International Affairs Department); Michael Boggs (Brown's assistant); Serafino Romualdi (ex-AFL Inter-American representative, founder of ORIT, explained below, and founding director of AIFLD); William C. Doherty, Jr. (AIFLD Executive Director). Tom Donahue, AFL-CIO Secretary-Treasurer, is a CFR member. Lane Kirkland, AFL-CIO president, has sat on CFR's board of directors since 1976.[9]

♦ ♦
♦ ♦

What is CFR?

CFR calls itself a "non-partisan and non-commercial organization studying the international aspects of America's political, economic, strategic and financial problems", such study leading to "actions the U.S. or elements in the U.S. should take about particular problems or questions in the world." CFR seeks to create "an intellectual product that is functionally relevant to the concerns of those who are or will be in operating positions, both public and private, in international affairs."[9, 17]

CFR membership is roughly 40% business executives, financiers and corporate lawyers; 20% top media, education, foundation and church people; 16% government, military and intelligence officials; 21% scholars; 2% journalists; and 1% top AFL-CIO men.[18]

Hardheaded businessmen don't single out union officials without a reason. Leading scholars of CFR say: "Members of the ruling capitalist class ... are in control of member selection, program and staff.... The fact that the Council [is] open to some people who are not already members of that class should not be regarded as a compromise of class.... Rather, it may be more reasonably taken as one of the mechanisms of class dominance."[18]

CFR is unmatched in raw power. Top journalists call it "the real State Deparment." *Newsweek* says it is "the foreign policy establishment of the U.S." CFR scholars say, "With access to the most sensitive and highly confidential state secrets, CFR can render 'de facto control over the state.'" It is also known as the primary power base of the CIA.[18, 19]

Council members slide in and out of government. Allen Dulles was on CFR's board for 42 years, moving from a law firm representing I.G. Farben in Nazi Germany to take a sensitive job in the Office of Strategic Services (OSS). He then designed the plan for CIA and became its longest serving director. In rare candor, Henry Kissinger once told CFR leaders, "You invented me."[21] That truth also applies to OSS, CIA, AIFLD, State's Agency for International Development (AID), and an array of ex-presidents, presidential candidates, and diplomats.[20, 21, 18]

Detailed CFR economic studies determined the territories needed for U.S. corporate expansion and led the Council to cooperate in World War II to defeat expansionist Axis imperialism and then to lead the charge in the Cold War. CFR cynicism was clear in its position that "Formulation of a statement on war aims for propaganda purposes is very different from formulation of one defining the true national interests."[18] Empire-building, not anti-fascism, was clearly CFR's prime interest:

> To the degree that the U.S. is the arsenal of the democracies, it will be the final arsenal at the moment of victory. It cannot throw the content of that arsenal away. It must accept world responsibility ... a measure of our victory will be the measure of our domination after victory.[18]

The machinery to implement CFR interests in Europe and Africa was well-oiled and operational. However, Latin America, rich in resources and cheap labor, posed another problem: how could U.S. "responsibility" and "domination" take root anywhere if not in the Western hemisphere? It soon became clear to CFR policy-makers that a new organizational form was required to accomplish this goal.

Serafino Romualdi became the central character in building this new organizational form. Inter-American representative of the AFL after World War II, Romualdi brought to his job credentials gained from his experiences in OSS intelligence and propaganda activities, work in Dubinsky's ILGWU and FTUC coteries, and letters of introduction from top CFR people in finance and the State Department. Romualdi approached Latin American labor officials to undermine the Latin American Confederation of Labor (CTAL), which included the CIO and was a WFTU affiliate. His pockets lined with government cash and contacts, Romualdi's anti-Communist campaign attracted labor officials ready to represent "inter-American" unionism. By 1951, he had put together ORIT (Inter-American Regional Organization of Workers) and became the regional organization for the ICFTU.[28, 29]

To balance his credibility in approaching labor officials, Romualdi got an endorsing letter from Norman Thomas, Socialist Party presidential candidate in the U.S. Romualdi had that letter broadly published in the Latin American press, charging CTAL was a "federation dominated by fifth column labor organizations of communist totalitarian states."[27]

◆◆◆◆◆◆◆◆◆◆◆◆◆◆◆◆◆◆◆◆◆◆◆◆◆◆

LET'S COME TO TERMS

Many people south of the U.S. know from experience that an organization called *"Inter-American"* must include the U.S. and that never occurs without dominance, if for no other reasons than our size, numbers and wealth. They prefer *"Latin American,"* even to include the English-speaking Caribbean states. Otherwise, they use *"American,"* meaning the whole hemisphere.

"Multinational corporation" connotes an equality among the nations involved with the company. In Latin America the popular view is that companies based in more than one country are really one-way operations: they take labor and resources

from the host country while the corporate owners grow rich back in the developed countries. Therefore, companies that cross borders to exploit are called, not *"multinational,"* but *"transnational."*

♦ ♦

ORIT's Reputation

From the outset, Latin American workers learned to distrust ORIT as an AFL creation and a creature of U.S. corporate domination. Even Romualdi admitted that workers' struggles took a backseat to ORIT work, which "... mainly consists of efforts to prevent totalitarian forces, especially communists, from controlling unions from whence they could sabotage production and transportation of raw materials."[30]

An ORIT training manual said about the same, warning against "agitation to nationalize the industry now in the hands of foreign interests."[31] A U.S. Senate study notes that workers of the region see ORIT as "an instrument of the U.S. State Department."[32] The official historian of the Swedish Labor Federation expanded on this point: "[The AFL-CIO] ... saw the situation entirely in terms of the Cold War. [They used] a form of bilateralism which was equivalent to 'colonialism' ... and crowned their work by completely dominating ORIT, [putting] it at the disposal of American foreign policy. ORIT has given the ICFTU a very bad name in Latin America."[33]

Certain monies used by Romualdi came from the AFL-CIO. Other money, came from the FTUC office clandestinely. Another conduit for CIA cash was through some International Trade Secretariats (ITSs). There are 17 ITSs, most organized early in the century, all tied loosely to the ICFTU. An ITS is an international grouping of unions or federations covering a single trade or industry, designed as an instrument of solidarity through which unions could assist their counterparts in other countries. Throughout the 1950s, Romualdi learned to use the ITSs to cover for ORIT as it became increasingly discredited.

CIA → U.S. FOUNDATION → U.S. UNION → ITS

ITS funds in Latin America largely came from U.S. unions, which received money from a group of sham foundations established as cash conduits by the CIA. This conduit system was exposed in Congress by Representative Wright Patman in 1964 and in 1967 became a national scandal in the major media. The scam was organized by then CIA Director of International Organizations Cord Meyer, Jr. (CFR), reportedly the man who directly supervised Jay Lovestone.[34, 35, 36]

Some cases of CIA funding can be readily substantiated, to the Retail Clerks (now UFCW), Communications Workers (CWA), Newspaper Guild (ANG), Public Workers (AFSCME), Oil and Chemical Workers (OCAW). We may never know how much money went into CIA-Labor activity, but a well known columnist pegged it at "around $100,000,000 a year."[37, 38, 39]

The International Federation of Petroleum and Chemical Workers (IFPCW) was an ITS formed directly by the CIA. From its start in 1954, the CIA paid salaries in the Secretariat's headquarters not far from the headquarters of OCAW, its U.S. union sponsor. People abroad were told that its $350,000 budget came from OCAW, but such contributions were never reported to OCAW membership. Samuel Butler (CFR) audited IFPCW books for "accuracy" while heading one of the foundations used as a conduit. For years OCAW president O.A. Knight quietly received checks for IFPCW use.[35, 9]

After the 1968 publicity, the director of CIA clandestine services, Richard Bissel (CFR), said "We need to operate under deeper cover." A new arrangement was engineered by retired Marine Colonel Ernest Lee (CFR), son-in-law of George Meany, then AFL-CIO president. While ITS money still comes through U.S. affiliate unions, the role of the secret CIA conduit is now taken by AIFLD, which receives *its* funds from the State Department.[35, 40, 41]

The quickest way to see how the system operates is to study how it worked in one country.

United Fruit is Bitter Fruit in Guatemala

In the 1980s, workers in the U.S. started reading in the news about deep trouble in Guatemala—strikes, killings, death squads. The trouble began in 1954 when Jacobo Arbenz, Guatemala's president, moved his country beyond accepted U.S. limits toward labor and land reform. He proposed that his government take over 225,000 acres of unused United Fruit-owned land and give it Guatemalan peasants for essential food production.

Assistant Secretary of State for Inter-American Affairs, Adolph Berle, asked Nelson Rockefeller to tell U.S. President-elect Eisenhower (CFR) about the proposed change in land use. Ike dubbed Arbenz a "communist puppet."[18]

Meanwhile, Romualdi had been trying in vain to turn Guatemalan unions away from Arbenz. He used ORIT sponsorship and U.S. funds to set up a dual union, the National Union of Free Workers (UNTL). Soon some of his UNTL people were charged with carrying guns and several hundred found it better to leave for Mexico, where Romualdi greeted them and enrolled them in the CIA's "Liberation Army," led by a Ft. Leavenworth-trained Guatemalan colonel, Carlos Castillo Armas.[42, 43]

George Meany then published an open letter to Arbenz; he cited the presence of Guatemalan officials in "bogus peace campaigns, communist youth congresses [and] cultural gatherings" as proof of the "subversive activities of the Guatemalan section of the world communist party." Meany warned Arbenz of "many workers' groups ... willing and anxious to break the shackles of communist domination."[44] There was no extensive or informed debate in the AFL prior to Meany's letter.

CFR director and CIA chief Allen Dulles and his brother, Secretary of State John Foster Dulles, then sold Eisenhower on a military coup. Richard Bissell (CFR/CIA) and Frank Wisner (CFR/CIA) were in charge of operations, with Richard Helms (CFR/CIA) in a minor role; CIA station chief for Guatemala was John Doherty.[42]

In June, 1954, bombers supplied and flown by the CIA, along with Romualdi's workers' group as the "liberation army," attacked the Guatemalan government. After ten days of siege, Arbenz was overthrown and left the country. Castillo Armas took power and put United Fruit back in the saddle, with Meany proclaiming that the AFL "rejoices over the downfall of the Communist controlled regime."[27] This ended land reform and liberal labor codes in Guatemala. Even Romualdi noted: "A wave of anti-communism threatened to sweep away the labor movement itself." That wave destroyed democracy and labor rights, assured more than 30 years of corporate profiteering, and led to the killing of at least 30,000 Guatemalans by successive military regimes.[45, 46]

AIFLD's Shadowy Origins

Romualdi tried to thwart revolution in Cuba, but failed. This story has been spelled out in detail.[47, 27, 28, 48, 35]

Before the revolution, Cuba's economy had been wholly dependent on U.S. corporations. With Castro's first steps toward economic independence, the CFR and the U.S. government demonstrated immediate hostility. IT&T, Standard Oil and United Fruit felt threatened by nationalization. Their answer? To push our government into the Bay of Pigs invasion. Fully 12 of the 14 top decisionmakers in the CIA Bay of Pigs fiasco are to be found on the exclusive CFR lists.[49, 9]

When Eusebio Mujal of the Cuban Federation of Labor fled to the U.S., he found not just a home but a welcome mat for membership in the selective CFR. Other CTC officials loyal to Mujal became the backbone of the AFL-CIO Latin American apparatus.

With the success of the Cuban revolution, it became clear that ORIT was neither sharp nor strong enough to do what the TNCs needed. Direct control by AFL-CIO officials seemed to be the answer in Latin America. An instrument for training leaders and molding labor to fit the corporate need came on the agenda—The American Institute for Free Labor Development. AIFLD was not planned by labor representatives, but by government and business consultants. It was designed to serve a corporate establishment bent on expansion abroad in cheap labor havens where, as in Cuba, people were expressing new demands for national dignity and their rights as workers. Such demands could not be confronted directly, but could be attacked as "communism" under the new strategy of "counterinsurgency."

The information coming from AIFLD sources about its origins is contradictory enough to make one wonder about its true history.[51, 35, 9] AIFLD's Director, William C. Doherty, said the American Institute for Free Labor Development "got under way in 1962, but only after three years of discussion within the executive council of the AFL-CIO."[4] Victor Reuther said, however, such policy-making was "hush-hush," done in conjunction with the State Department and other agencies with "no discussion beforehand with the executive council members. There was not even a pretense of democratic process."[50]

AIFLD arose, according to Doherty's timetable, "in 1962 after some three years of discussion" about the best structure the AFL-CIO could devise to fit the program laid out in print by the CIA. That program was formulated by an unnamed group and written down by Generals Richard Stilwell (CFR) and Edward Lansdale (CFR). It became the primer of counterinsurgency. The two men were known in the highest security circles as "effective operators ... with, for and in support of the CIA" who saw that "the time had come ... to form a massive paramilitary international power under para-civilian leadership and a monstruous cloak of security."[19] Various writers have charged and speculated about the CIA ties of AIFLD officials. The truly ominous conclusion is that the U.S. labor movement, with or without knowing cooperation, was used to flesh out a blueprint drawn by the CIA.[35, 52]

AIFLD: Out of the Brainstorms of the CIA

The Stilwell-Lansdale program was titled *Report of the Special Presidential Committee to Study Training Under the Mutual Security Program,*" May 15, 1959. It urged that the "National Security Council be seized with" a long term effort to "influence the thoughts, habits and attitude ... of the middle billion ... and ... the institutions that bind them together." It exhorted "greater efforts to identify, train and groom the foreign leadership cadres in all key sectors and provide guidelines for closer relationships with and support from the private sector."

I'm going to quote a lot from the Stilwell-Landsdale Report to give an inside perspective on how and why an entity like AIFLD was created to suit corporate needs and, with that, government interests.

Certain of their power, the CIA generals demanded that the State Department take: "a primary interest in the totality of programs to build the national leadership of foreign countries.... Action must be taken at the Washington level ... to elicit greater attention on the part of private institutions operative in the foreign field to the development of indigenous leadership."

A new "private institution" had to be built and CIA agents couldn't do it all alone. The two CFR generals wanted to give the CIA much more:

> The starting point ... is knowledge of the attitudes, aspirations and pulse of a selective cross-section of the populace ... knowledge of the background views and factors which motivate the leadership elite; knowledge of the extent to which community of interest among government, armed forces and people is lacking; knowledge of the opposition and nature of the weaknesses it exploits; ... extensive personal contacts with all strata of society can alone provide such knowledge. This is the first and key responsibility of the Country Team; the routine of reports, inspections and administration must be subordinated thereto....

Without pretense about "national security," CIA generals wanted the development of leaders with "standards comparable to our own; through these leaders to insure the kind of stability and growth that constitutes the basis of our aid [and to] promote closer orientation and communications between the U.S. and the recipient country [for] pursuits involving foreign business."

The monumental attempt to restructure and subordinate nations around the world under CIA direction had nothing to do with planting seeds of democracy. Trade union and government sector work was to interface with a truly sinister reorientation of foreign armed forces to become:

> the only cohesive and reliable non-communist instrument available to fledgling nations.... Those who lead or who are destined to lead must ... acquire qualifications and attributes beyond the criteria which identify the successful commander in combat.... they represent too great an investment in manpower and money to be restricted to such a limited mission....
>
> Properly employed, the army can become an internal motor for economic growth and social transformaiton ... with a high degree of discipline, dedication and political moderation ... [it] will probably, as a unit, accede to the reins of government as the only alternative to domestic chaos and leftist takeover.[19]

The action framework blueprinted by the CIA generals had no precedent in U.S. military thinking. It reflected the thoughts of a prime backer of AIFLD, current chair of CFR David Rockefeller. He wrote in 1966:

U.S. investors seek no special favors ... they look for stability ... and for evidence that threats of expropriation will not cast an ominous shadow on capital investment....

Private enterprise in all parts of the hemisphere [is] encouraged to stimulate and ... to win the active support of as many people as possible in creating broader understanding of the role of business and private enterprise. [Most important are] leaders in forming public opinion—educators, intellectuals, professional men and women, labor leaders and clergy.[53]

In 1965 George Meany, President of both AFL-CIO and AIFLD, mirrored Rockefeller's thoughts in stating the Institute's goal to: "help the Latin American labor movement become full fledged partners with management and their national governments."[54] AIFLD itself stated its corporate aim: to build unions in which workers "will be assured of representation [and] need not resort to the more radical means of violence and revolt." AIFLD seeks to train "national leadership" for political and social stability on the TNC notion that "true development is dependent upon investment."[55]

The Report turned in by Stilwell and Lansdale was tied down by George Cabot Lodge, son of Henry Cabot Lodge, who figured prominently in covert operations from Greece to Vietnam. Both father and son are leading CFR people. In 1962 George Lodge was Assistant Secretary of Labor under Arthur Goldberg.

◆◆◆◆◆◆◆◆◆◆◆◆◆◆◆◆◆◆◆◆◆◆◆◆◆◆◆◆
◆ ◆

ARTHUR GOLDBERG:
FROM CIO TO SUPREME COURT VIA AIFLD AND OSS

Goldberg held a union job briefly while studying to be a labor lawyer. He became counsel to the Steel Workers Union, wrote the first anti-Communist clauses into CIO bylaws and hobnobbed with the elite of the Chicago CFR. He landed in the wartime job as chief of the Labor Division of OSS. Goldberg's most flattering biographer says that in OSS he "worked at a job that was singular—even for that singular organization—the job of a labor spy.... He organized spy networks." Before the end of World War II, he was asked to write the legislation needed to create the CIA.[22, 23]

In 1948, with a fascination for intelligence and psychological warfare and with the help of Walter Reuther and the Dubinsky group, Goldberg became chief CIO counsel. He was said to be CIO president Phil Murray's "chief of staff and formulator of policy," and his talent was needed to prepare the cases and establish the internal procedures to expel the left unions from the CIO and divide the WFTU. Goldberg's complaint against the expelled unions was that "a group had captured control and were doing things the members did not understand."[24]

He served as counsel for the United Labor Planning Committee during the Korean War, helped Reuther into the CIO presidency, and then took credit as the architect of the 1955 AFL-CIO merger, writing a constitution empowering the AFL-CIO Executive Council to expel left unions and locking foreign affairs in the grip of the FTUC clique. The merger enhanced labor unity but opened up an era of government/labor collaboration in foreign affairs no longer obstructed by the old CIO-AFL conflict.[25, 26]

Boosted by Dubinsky and preaching labor-management-government cooperation, Goldberg became Secretary of Labor and used that post to help form a labor/management group that moved AIFLD off the drawingboard, funded openly by the State Department. President Kennedy then lifted Goldberg to the Supreme Court; President Johnson sent him to the United Nations as Ambassador.

♦ ♦

Lodge's Views on "Responsible Unions"

Young Lodge produced a unique book on labor foreign affairs "*Spearheads of Democracy.*" Ironically, this scion of the social register was in a stew that unions were "seriously infiltrated with communists." Lodge preferred to see unions abroad used as "the first line of defense against communism." He made much of developing "the responsible labor leader... of today [who] may well be the president or prime minister of tomorrow."[56, 57] The book was developed in a 19-member CFR study group that included Cord Meyer, the CIA executive who set up covert funding through sham foundations. Two other CFR members who took part in the pre-publication process, were Romualdi and Michael Ross, with the AFL-CIO Department of International Affairs.[56, 9, 42]

In the preface of the book, Lodge offered his boss, Goldberg, "special praise for his successful efforts to rid the CIO of communists." The premise of the book: that "we are involved in a total war ... against communism" demanding tight central control of AFL-CIO foreign affairs. This was shortly established when Jay Lovestone (CFR), previously known as the "grey eminence," took full control of that department.[56]

Parts of Lodge's book read like an instruction manual for AIFLD. It urges: use of the international banks to finance special projects, cooperatives and housing; close liaison with the ITSs; establishment of national, regional and U.S. training centers; linking up with exchange visit programs; funding through State's American Institute for Development (AID); working to control peasant movements; coordinating through labor attaches with union "credentials that will open many doors closed to others"; prohibiting all contacts with unions in socialist countries and tying it all up with backing from the TNC giants.[56]

All of this became the practice.

Lodge pleaded that anti-union companies "draw a very sharp distinction between ... labor problems in the U.S. and what they are abroad." He urged them to see "responsible labor unions [as] essential social insurance ... against the shocks of radical change" abroad. Like a snake oil pitchman, Lodge sold "responsible unions" as a "hope for evolving a stable economic relationship ... [and] protecting against political upheaval and expropriation."[58,56]

As one might guess, soon after AIFLD cut the pattern, AALC, the African American Labor Center and AAFLI, the Asian American Free Labor Institute, emerged. Now there is even the Free Trade Union Institute covering southern Europe. They are all "spearheads," but not of democracy.

Was the Rank and File Bypassed in Creating AIFLD?

At the time AIFLD was created, not even a handful of U.S. union members knew what was going on. The ranks of labor have had their hands full with here-and-now economic problems. AFL-CIO foreign operations have had little or no relation to the expressed will of the membership. By and large, rank-and-file workers have not been accomplices to the murder, misery and political repression facilitated by agencies like AIFLD. In fact, a 1960 University of Chicago study, available to but ignored by AIFLD, concluded: "U.S. union representatives in dealings with Latin American unions act ... on most issues, without the guidance of an enlightened union membership.... The unions operate ... without the support of a well informed membership in this area."[32]

According to Roy Godson, reponsible for training international labor specialists at Georgetown University, a school used extensively by AIFLD and all U.S. foreign service agencies, "A handful of AFL leaders assisted by several of their staff constituted the AFL foreign policymaking elite." Victor Reuther simply said the AFL-CIO foreign policy was "a vest pocket operation.... The membership was not really involved." Lane Kirkland, now AFL-CIO president, wrote in 1975: "I reveal no secret when I say that this interest [foreign affairs] has been somewhat top heavy in the labor movement. It has not reached down to the local level."[59, 50, 60]

Now, some CFR elite are at the top of the AFL-CIO, selling labor foreign policy, which the State Department is buying. Goldberg's phoney attack on left unions for "doing things the members did not understand" have come full circle.

AIFLD Takes its First Steps

In 1960 the CWA-PTTI pilot program for training Latin Americans, funded by the State Department, showed promise. The AFL-CIO, with $20,000 of questionable origin, pursued a feasibility study to start an institute. The project was favored by a contribution from the Michigan Fund, one of the CIA phantom foundations.

A business advisory panel was then formed to firm up tripartite participation in AIFLD as a corporate, government, labor joint venture. Romualdi listed Eric Johnston, a natural, as the number one man in that group. Johnston headed the U.S. Chamber of Commerce in 1946 when it led the Red scare, with massive circulation of pamphlets on "Communist Infiltration." Then, as president of the Motion Picture Association, he enforced the House Unamerican Activities Committee Hollywood blacklist to erase any hint of pink on the silver screen or in the Hollywood unions. He was no apprentice at the job. Johnston had served in Siberia in 1919 during the U.S. Army's first anti-Communist intervention. In the '30s, Johnston fought CIO organizing drives with anti-Red fervor and, in the '40s, did a stint with Rockefeller's OIAA in Latin America.

Yes, the advisory panel gave AIFLD the green light.[27, 63, 64]

In 1961 AIFLD became a non-profit Delaware corporation, enabling it to receive foundation money legally. George Meany became president and J. Peter Grace chair of the board of directors. This group included George C. Lodge; Berent Friele, Director of the National Foreign Trade Council; Juan Trippe of Pan American Air; Charles Brinkerhoff, Director of Anaconda Copper and First National City Bank; William Hickey, President of United Corp.; Henry Woodbridge of True Temper—each of them CFR, and, of course, Eric Johnston. Of 25 non-rotating members of the AIFLD board, 12 are found on CFR member lists. More recently, 15 of 28 were CFR, at a time when the board had only 12 elected labor officials.[27, 9, 65]

Who Bankrolled AIFLD?

Arthur Goldberg hand carried AIFLD's first $100,000 grant from the President and put together a Labor Advisory Committee on Foreign Assistance to regulate and assure all future government funds. The group was more than two-thirds government officials. AIFLD then opened its doors in June, 1962 and Meany could brag of having "a working agency of the U.S. government, working with its expenses paid."[12, 27, 35, 40, 36, 61, 62]

From that point forward, over 90% of AIFLD money has come from AID. The rest comes from labor sources and contributions from among over 90 of the biggest TNCs on the Institute's list of corporate sponsors. A reasonable estimate of AIFLD expenditures, including its varied projects through the years, would be over $150 million. One reason for an estimate, not an exact figure, is Victor Reuther's insistence that published "AIFLD funds were only the tip of the CIA iceberg." Meany, discussing the open funds, tried to laugh off the intelligence link with: "When you get that kind of money, why do you have to go running to the CIA?"[50, 12, 35]

◆ ◆

J. PETER GRACE: WITHOUT SELFISH PURPOSE

The Chair of the Board of his family enterprise, W.R. Grace Co., is no ordinary unionbuster. Oh, J. Peter Grace has been known to break a strike or two—one in Peru cost three workers their lives. He also runs a string of non-union subsidiaries in the U.S. In 1960 he countered an organizing drive by UAW with threats to fire strikers[66] and a leaflet saying "No one needs a union partner in his pay envelope."

A year later he was chums with Meany, organizing the overlords of Latin American trade and investment to join him on the AIFLD board. Grace saw AIFLD as a "joint venture of free men ... working together for a common goal without selfish purpose." The goal: "cooperation between labor and management and an end to class struggle." How? "Teach workers to help increase their company's business [and] promote democratic free trade unions, to prevent communist infiltration, and where it exists, get rid of it."[67, 63, 69]

Grace is a leader of the U.S. Council of the International Chamber of Commerce. He is also president of the 1,000-member U.S. branch of the highly secret Catholic society, the Knights of Malta, a group liberally sprinkled with CIA and CFR people: William Donovan, World War II head of OSS; William Casey, Reagan's CIA Director; Alexander Haig; William Simon and William F. Buckley. It also includes Jeremiah Denton, a most dedicated anti-union Senator, and a supporter of AIFLD funding.[70]

Grace's company has shifted from Latin American trade into chemicals. By 1980 the biggest stockholder was the Frick Group of West Germany, which grew fat financing the Nazis and taking over Jewish-owned enterprises.[70] A top executive in his German subsidiary is Otto Ambrose. J. Peter Grace wrote of his "deep admiration" for Ambrose in a letter recommending him for a visa to this country. Ambrose had an entry problem based on his war-time position in I.G. Farben and on his conviction at Nuremburg on charges of slavery and mass murder. He had been head of inmate labor for I.G. Farben at Auschwitz death camp and ran all poison gas operations.[70] The usually talkative Grace has evaded reporters' questions on the matter.

After 19 years on the AIFLD board, Grace resigned to become President Reagan's chief cost cutter, to slash even bigger holes in the safety net of social legislation.

AIFLD's Modus Operandi

AIFLD's approach to training follows a basic pattern, varying only to meet local customs. It uses ORIT and the ITS contacts to establish training centers at the local level, the national level and, grouping countries, at the regional level. The training is in practical skills, business style unionism, and anti-Communism. The unionists who are most influential or promising rise from one level to the next in seminars lasting from three days to two weeks.

Country Program Directors select prize proteges and put them on the payroll for 7 to 12 weeks of training in the U.S. These trips are preceded by a week of special orientation at an ORIT facility in Mexico. AIFLD training typically includes such courses as "The Open and Closed Society," "Recognition of and Defense Against Infiltration and Front Organizations," and "Countering Extremist Offensives."[72]

AIFLD TRAINING PROGRAM

By 1982, 393,481 unionists had been part of this AIFLD training program. Of those, 3,197 had the special treatment in the U.S. *These figures are greater than the number of Latin Americans and Caribbeans trained under U.S. military programs.*[67, 71] U.S. policymakers seem to know that the destiny of nations, for better or worse, can be determined by the organized working people.

Unionists brought to the U.S. are methodically chaperoned on visits to union, corporate and government facilities. In the first decade, AIFLD graduates stayed on the payroll for nine months after U.S. training. Now many go onto their own union payrolls, funded through AIFLD; others are kept secure in AIFLD or ITS jobs.

In 1959 the Stillwell-Lansdale Report described AIFLD's system best, saying it called for developing "comprehension of the complex nature of subversive forces at play ... full knowledge of the means of counterattack [and] appropriate elements

... trained for unorthodox warfare." These CIA generals laid out both rationale and process:

> The less developed nations ... are not capable of sharply identifying priority needs in ... labor.... The Country Team [needs] manpower analyses ... procedures for identification and grooming of future leaders ... orientation visits [with] carefully programmed extra-curricular activities [and] careful handling ... in transition from native habitat to the American scene. Painstaking attention ... to adapt the individual for the return home [and] continuing contact with the key decision maker, actual or potential, is self evident.

The S-L Report called on the Country Teams to provide "adequate biographic registers, personal contacts ... lists of promising candidates in all sectors; and priorities within lists."[19]

AIFLD's personal contact list of trainees alone now is almost half a million. Applicant forms for its many special projects ask outrageous information and have been filled in by countless unionists. Some of the 32 questions on one form to be filled out by interviewers of workers applying for housing are: internal organization of the union; internal friction among leaders, between leaders and members; is the applicant interested in power, prestige, influence? (stated, known, suspected?); attitude taken in response to questions on matters of importance; does the person accept guidance and orientation?; political and ideological connections; photograph if possible.

Why such information? The situation in Chile provides a clue. The Chilean Country Labor Team invested heavily in maritime unions. A June 20, 1974 broadcast told of a Valparaiso port union leader "producing lists of workers to be shot, jailed or fired." A Chilean magazine mentioned a Pinochet general with "a complete file on workers and unions in the capitol."[73, 74] The military used such lists mercilessly.[68, 94, 95, 97, 98]

The S-L Report calls for "leadership cadres [to be] capable of influencing the direction of unofficial programs to cover priority gaps." Such capability has been described in several nations, but in Chile indelible tracks were left when gross U.S. intervention was proved in Congressional inquiries after the 1973 coup against the Allende government. A Senate report shows the CIA had "a number of political action operations aimed at ... organized labor [including] combatting the principal communist-dominated labor union in Chile [with] two projects worked within organized labor."[77] Much more was done than stated. The only CIA tool in the unions was AIFLD's apparatus, which had "trained" over 9,000 Chileans—79 in the U.S.

WILLIAM C. DOHERTY, JR.:
HIS MOUTH IS FULL AND RUNNING OVER

Fast-talking, burly Bill Doherty (CFR) took over AIFLD in 1965. His guiding words for the AFL-CIO agency have been:

"The key question of our time is the future road of [Latin American] revolution: toward communist totalitarianism or toward democracy ... all other questions must remain secondary."[78]

Neither gross exploitation nor assassinations of workers divert his pursuit of Reds.

Enno Hobbing was staff man for the Council on Latin America, a CFR creation. Hobbing, who worked closely with John Doherty, CIA station chief in Guatemala during the 1954 coup, praises Doherty's AIFLD: "American private investors favor the ... AFL-CIO investment ... as a means of reducing communist influence in unions."[4]

Bill Doherty acknowledges Hobbing's praise: "We are collaborating with the Council on Latin America ... to make the investment climate more attractive and inviting to them."[76]

In 1974 Bill Doherty visited the Santa Clara County Central Labor Council to get our Council to rescind a resolution questioning AIFLD. The powerful, experienced debater had foot-in-mouth problems. He denied the AIFLD role in the 1965 overthrow of democracy in Brazil, which he had bragged about in the past. He also insisted AIFLD had no "in country programs" in Chile during the bloody 1973 coup against Allende, but couldn't keep from boasting of support of CUPROCH, the "professional unions" identified by Allende as leading the destabilization. And he laughed off the question of CIA connections.

The Central Labor Council stood its ground and sent Doherty away emptyhanded.

Brazil

Events cry out for investigation and analysis of every country on each continent where AIFLD and AFL-CIO "Instutes" touch the lives of workers. Our focus and space limits lead us to start with Brazil.

Discussing AIFLD graduates who returned to Brazil on AIFLD payrolls, Bill Doherty said: "They became intimately involved in ... the clandestine operations.... [W]hat happened in Brazil ... did not just happen—it was planned and planned months in advance ... [T]he trade union leaders ... actually trained in our Institute ... were involved in ... the overthrow of the Goulart regime."[77]

Another time he said: "AIFLD has never been involved in the overthrow of any democratically elected government ... AIFLD had no connection with the 1964 coup in Brazil."[78]

These statements directly contradict each other. One must be an outright lie.

The first statement was made in 1965 when there was not much resistance or questioning of labor foreign policy and Doherty could reveal pride in his role. The second statement came in 1974. The Chilean coup had evoked a rumble of dissent at the local level in U.S. labor. Doherty was sent all the way from Geneva to stop the first open revolt in a Central Labor Council against AIFLD based on its role in the 1973 overthrow of Allende in Chile.

Why would Doherty falsify his answer? He could not convincingly deny "clandestine operations" in Chile if he admitted AIFLD's role in Brazil.

In 1961, there were about $1 billion in U.S. investments in Brazil, a nation the size of the U.S., rich in natural resources with a population in 1961 of 100 million. The CFR guardians of U.S. foreign investment and trade were not letting such a treasure trove slip from their grasp. Serious tension began to build in 1961 when A.A. Berle (CFR) of the State Department offered $300 million in aid for Brazilian support of the planned Bay of Pigs invasion of Cuba.

Affronted, Brazil froze relations with the U.S.

A thaw began only after a visit from U.N. Ambassador Adlai Stevenson (CFR). When our Ambassador to Brazil, Lincoln Gordon (CFR), relayed to Washington concern about "communist infiltration in the labor movement," among students and in government, things started to move. President Kennedy sent his brother, Robert, to warn Joao Goulart, Brazil's president, that U.S. aid depended on his government "putting its house in order."⁷⁹

The problem was that U.S. corporate leaders were unnerved about Goulart's policies. David Rockefeller, then Vice President of CFR, told West Pointers that U.S. bankers had decided early on that Goulart had to go. Goulart's offense was that he won overwhelming support for policies of Cold War neutrality, increased relations with the socialist world, Brazilian control of Brazilian resources, limitation of foreign profit to 10%, and giving labor its greatest independence in recent history.⁷⁹

In 1961 Colonel Vernon Walters arrived as Embassy military attache in Brazil. Walters had been liaison to Brazilian forces in Italy during World War II, was on intimate terms with the officer caste, and helped set curriculum and procedure in their Superior War College (ESG). In all, he worked to bind Brazil's military to the Pentagon.⁷⁹ The U.S. Information Service in Brazil built a staff of 231 people. They took surveys and published anti-administration tracts, books and even a labor monthly, *The Worker*.

As if from nowhere, in 1962 the Brazilian Institute for Democratic Action (IBAD) sprang up, led by a Brazilian with no traceable background in public or professional affairs. IBAD members were largely businessmen tied to the TNCs, many of whom were trained at the military's Superior War College. IBAD spent $20 million in 1962 bi-elections, to little avail, as Goulart's party grew in strength. Among IBAD's cash sources were U.S. Steel, Standard Oil, Hanna Mining and General Motors. When asked if CIA backed IBAD, the U.S. consul general said, "I don't know who else would have been funding them." To get IBAD backing, candidates and organizations had to pledge to switch all party loyalties to IBAD, to fight communism, and to defend foreign investment. IBAD boldly rented the editorial pages of Rio de Janeiro's paper for 90 days.⁷⁹

At least two ITSs were actively working against the elected administration—the International Federation of Petroleum and Chemical Workers (IFPCW), and the Postal Telephone and Telegraph International (PTTI). One IFPCW report to AIFLD describes efforts to isolate activists seeking nationalization of oil and strong economic measures against the company. The leader of Rio's oil workers even stated that IFPCW "does not operate with autonomy in Brazil. It only executes the programs of AIFLD ... which, for its part, receives the imperative influences of not less than sixty large American companies and the vigilance of the CIA."[79, 80]

The PTTI operation was led by William C. Doherty (CFR) until he went with AIFLD. The gap he left in the PTTI staff was filled by Richard Martinez, fresh out of a real union in New Mexico. Martinez mistakenly started organizing workers in IT&T until he was reprimanded. He was then sent to New York for orientation and training in clandestine activities at several CIA "safe houses." Once returned to Brazil, Martinez claims, "I was taking orders from the CIA, carrying a briefcase full of money to pay off people in labor." Martinez also said that "John McCone ran the labor operation from the U.S." McCone (CFR) was then CIA Director. Two of the groups Martinez carried cash to were the Democratic Trade Union Movement in Sao Paolo and the Democratic Resistance of Free Workers in Rio. Both, according to a Brazilian congressional inquiry, had "come under the influence of IBAD."[81, 79]

In 1963, when IT&T was nationalized in one state in Brazil, President Goulart was threatened with a cutoff of U.S. aid until an outlandish compensation was paid. When Hanna Mining, the U.S. third largest iron producer, was ruled out of a claim in Minas Gerais, the State Department was even quicker than the company to issue an official protest. Hanna Mining's counsel happened to be John J. McCloy, former head of the World Bank and then chair of the board of both Chase Manhattan and the mighty CFR.[79, 9]

In the fall of 1963, AIFLD director Romualdi visited Sao Paolo with Berent Friele (CFR). They met with Governor Adhemar de Barros, a key anti-Goulart plotter. He told them of plans for a coup, which they then discussed with Ambassador Gordon. As part of the plot against the government (Romualdi said "to bring it down"), AIFLD rapidly set up a program to train 33 Brazilian unionists in the U.S. and under Histadrut auspices in Israel. (Histadrut is the Israeli Labor Federation befriended early on by Arthur Goldberg.) The 33 returned as "graduates" on AIFLD payrolls under an arrangement that our General Accounting Office (GAO) said, "Substantially preclude[s] all ... effective control or monitoring capacity."[27, 22, 82]

The State Department suspended most of $600 million promised Brazil through AID. About $100 million continued to be allocated in an "islands of sanity" strategy. The funds bypassed the Goulart administration and went to various state governors and agencies organizing for the overthrow. Funds also continued for labor manipulation and training, police training, and military assistance.[79]

In mid-March 1964, Goulart acted to nationalize Brazil's oil industry. Immediately Thomas Mann (CFR), Assistant Secretary of State for Latin America, urged that protection of investments and fighting communism be seen as our primary national interest. The CIA, acting through Brazilian technocrats and business people tied to the TNCs, rapidly staged demonstrations led by middleclass women. Ambassador Gordon made a quick trip to Washington, returned and called in his staff to plan contingencies for the oncoming coup. Vernon Walters, with the coup declaration in hand, wired the details to Washington a week before it occurred.[79, 52]

Vernon Walters was commonly thought to be the coordinator in center stage of the officers plotting the coup. One faltering supporter of Goulart, a general eager to end up on the winning side, went to Walters to denounce the leftists and secure his future. Probably through Walters (and certainly through the CIA), the plotters were assured of U.S. military supplies if needed, immediate U.S. recognition of the new government, and the presence of an aircraft carrier group offshore to insure victory.[79]

On March 31, 1964, the governor of Minas Gerais announced on radio that "The revolution to save Brazil from communism" was on. The troops were mobilized in trucks supplied by Hanna Mining. The one general who led resistance was soon captured and brought to the War Ministry. Vernon Walters was already there. The next day, June 1, Goulart surrendered the government, rather than commit the nation to civil war.[79]

♦♦♦♦♦♦♦♦♦♦♦♦♦♦♦♦♦♦♦♦♦♦♦♦♦♦♦♦
♦   ♦

THE TAKE OVER

The CGT, the only national workers federation, called a general strike to oppose the coup. Their meetings were staked out and, within a few days, 7,000 trade union and political prisoners were rounded up. The military seized control of 456 unions and councils and replaced leaders with AIFLD graduates and their followers. A wage freeze was imposed, striking became a capital crime, and torture and death squads became commonplace for a generation. Thus, the

Stilwell-Lansdale words became reality in Brazil. With comprehensive U.S. coordination, the military acted to "accede to the reins of government."[52, 83, 84, 79]

♦ ♦

Vernon Walters was at the home of his close friend, Marshal Castello Branco, when Branco was announced President. U.S. recognition came immediately, along with an emergency loan of $50 million at two percent.[79] Within a week the new military dictatorship received a wire from ORIT pledging support.[52]

Between 1964 and 1968 U.S. profits from Brazil multiplied 15 times. By 1971 Senator Frank Church noted, "We have pumped $2 billion (in tax money) since 1964 to protect a favorable business climate of investment that amounts to $1.6 billion." He felt that such funds should be invested here to provide jobs for U.S. workers. In the ensuing years investment and aid to Brazil tripled.[79]

In the first year after the coup, AIFLD expanded operations at the pleasure of the generals. But even a little trade unionism is dangerous under a military junta. By late '65—after clashing with authorities, the AFL-CIO admitted the dictatorship "has recently become an authoritarian regime." Still, on April Fool's Day, 1966, dictator Castello Branco was joined by AIFLD chief Doherty on a platform to applaud the second anniversary of (in Doherty's words) Brazil's "Democratic Revolution."[27, 85]

The toll taken on the working people of Brazil is startling:

1960—the poorest 50% shared 17.4% of national income
1980—the poorest 50% shared 12.6% of national income
1960—the richest 10% took 39.6% of the national income
1980—the richest 10% took 50.9% of the national income[86]

Now—after 20 years—Brazil's labor movement is getting into stride. Its growing unity and power has shaken the government back on the road to democracy. At the pace shown in 1984-85, it will not be too long a road. Also in 1985, General Vernon Walters, later Deputy Director of CIA, was appointed U.S. Ambassador to the United Nations by Ronald Reagan.

Chile: On the Hit List

We turn next to Chile, where a Brazilian expatriate said of the September 11, 1973 coup, "I felt I was living a Xerox copy of Brazil in 1964." Indeed so, but the destruction of the Allende government of Chile entailed much more institutionalized terrorism and violence.[68]

The destabilization process began in 1970 at the request of IT&T, when $1.1 billion U.S. corporate bucks were invested in Chile. It is a matter of record produced by admissions in Congressional hearings that killing Chile's democracy in 1973 was made possible by external forces. It was done with what Richard Bissell (CFR) of CIA clandestine services called, "A comprehensive effort ... with ... separate operations designed to support and complement one another and to have a cumulatively significant effect." Those factors were: gross electoral manipulation, financing the media for propaganda and disinformation, political conspiracy, military connivance, labor penetration, coup de etat, and bloodthirsty cruelty.[91, 92, 93, 94]

All this has been documented in other published works. Here we will show some of the work of the AIFLD network in labor penetration.

In 1970, President Nixon (CFR) ordered his National Security Council to face down Allende's nationalization of IT&T and the copper transnationals by making "the economy scream," and the AIFLD network began to move seriously. At this time, Robert O'Neill was AIFLD Country Program Director in Chile. His role merits major scrutiny not possible in this section.[106, 107, 108]

AIFLD brought the number of trainees to 8,837 by 1972, with 79 graduated from "studies" in the U.S. By early '73 those trained in the U.S. jumped to 108.[95, 96, 85]

Doherty has denied activity in Chile during the Allende period. What do AIFLD records and contracts reveal? Coordination and subcontracting with seven ITSs in that period. Funds were supplied by the State Department and dispensed to the ITSs through appropriate U.S. unions, i.e.:

- International Transport Federation (ITF) through the Brotherhood of Railway & Airline Clerks (BRAC)
- Postal, Telephone & Telegraph International (PTTI) through Communication Workers of America (CWA)
- International Federation of Petroleum & Chemical Workers

(IFPCW) funded directly, but working with Oil, Chemical & Atomic Workers (OCAW), Glass Bottle Blowers and Sailors International Union (SIU)
* International Federation of Commercial, Clerical & Technical Workers (FIET-French initials) through Retail Clerks International (RCIA—now UFCW)
* International Federation of Free Teachers Unions (IFFTU) through the American Federation of Teachers (AFT)
* Inter-American Federation of Textile, Garment & Leather Workers (FITITUC) through Textile Workers Union of America (now part of Textile & Garment Workers (TGWUA))
* Inter-American Federation of Entertainment Workers (FITE) through the American Federation of Musicians (AFM).[99]

Some of these organizations, using government funds through AIFLD, worked in Chile to promote destabilizing political strikes that occurred among truckowners, shopkeepers, textile workers and among professionals in the mines, banks and Chile's national airline, LAN CHILE.

Two million Chilean workers were members of CUT, 90% of the work force. They were responsible for the ever-increasing electoral victories of Allende's Popular Unity, but there was still room for trouble. Wage increases were granted where they were most needed—to the lower paid workers. That left middleclass-oriented professionals vulnerable to the appeals of the AIFLD network. In a poor country with a thriving black market, the millions of dollars spent to promote strikes went a long way. Ray Cline (CFR) of State Department Intelligence said some of the cash "was intended for financial support of small businessmen and truckers."[15, 12, 91, 100, 101, 102, 103, 104]

The tragic hero of Chile was the man workers called Companero Presidente, Salvador Allende. His loyalty to constitutional and formal democratic processes limited chances for popular armed defense of his elected government against the formidable force of the United States, in collusion with local corporate power. But when he was surrounded in the national palace, La Moneda, and under pinpoint bombardment, he levelled a machine gun in desperate defense. At that final moment, Allende focused on the single most important factor that made the overthrow of the Popular Unity government possible without bringing in the U.S. Marines overtly:

Workers of my country, I want to thank you for the loyalty you have always shown, for the trust you have placed in a man who has only been the mouthpiece of the great aspirations of justice, who gave his word to respect the constitution and the law and was faithful to his promise.... I am speaking to the members of the professions, those patriots who a few days ago were continuing to struggle *against the revolt led by the professional unions*, that is, the class unions which were trying to hold onto the advantage granted to a few of them by the capitalist society. [Emphasis added.][105]

Within a few moments, his body was viciously torn apart by bullets, according to his widow who later viewed it.

The new military junta immediately outlawed the CUT (and 1,279 unions in Santiago alone) and attempted to form a new national body, CNT. Wenecslao Moreno, one of Romualdi's first contacts in Latin America, was reported "in the highest rank of leadership in the effort to replace the CUT." The report also said Moreno was "identified as a CIA agent."[109]

Alfredo Montecinos, President of COMACH (Chilean Maritime Confederation) was taken to a concentration camp, because COMACH had become too militant under his CUT-oriented leadership and had fallen away from AIFLD. The military replaced Monecinos with Eduardo Rios, who went on to become a prime speaker abroad for the junta and was praised as "heroic and very positive" by Pinochet's subsecretary of the Ministry of Foreign Affairs. He was introduced as a visitor to the 1975 AFL-CIO convention.[110]

Within four months of seizing power, the junta led by General Augusto Pinochet killed 20,000 and jailed 30,000, many of whom suffered unspeakable torture. William Colby (CFR), then head of CIA, said the junta's executions did "some good" in reducing the danger of civil war.[87, 88]

What other government officials and corporate leaders on the CFR list were involved with the intervention in Chile?

- Henry Kissinger, National Security Adviser
- Melvin Laird, Secretary of Defense
- William Rogers, Secretary of State
- Edward Korry, U.S. Ambassador to Chile until 1971
- Charles Meyer, Assistant to Kissinger
- Richard Nixon, U.S. President
- John McCone, Director of IT&T
- Harold Geneen, President, IT&T
- Viron P. Vaky, Assistant Secretary of State—Latin America
- Richard Helms, CIA

- William Colby, CIA
- J. Peter Grace
- Juan Trippe, former President, Panama
- Ray S. Cline, State Department Intelligence
- Deane R. Hinton, National Security Council on International Economic Policy
- Timothy Stanley, IT&T
- Ralph A. Dungan, U.S. Ambassador to Chile until 1970
- Arnold Nachmanoff, Senior Adviser on Latin American Affairs
- Jack Kubisch, Assistant Secretary of State for Inter-American Affairs, 1973
- Nathaniel Davis, U.S. Ambassador to Chile 1973
- Thomas Mann and McGeorge Bundy, Interdepartmental Commission to Manage Chilean Elections[89]

The original junta was composed of military men long and intimately tied to the U.S. military. Pinochet had been military attache in Washington for ten years and had been trained extensively at our Ft. Gulik in Panama. By 1973 some 4,000 Chilean officers were trained in U.S. military assistance programs. The importance of such contact was outlined in 1971 by Secretary of Defense Melvin Laird (CFR): "It is important for us to bear in mind that the military is the only cohesive group in many countries of Latin America ... they are very important."[90, 143]

Is There an Echo in Here?

Six months after the coup, the military tried to stem future problems by announcing a "reorganization of the whole system of union organization of marine and port workers." A BRAC and AIFLD report for that period indicates cooperation in "technical advice re general reorganization."[111, 12] Ernesto Vogel, a rightwing Christian Democrat CUT leader in Santiago's municipal transport system, was a guest at an AFL-CIO convention[115] after he spoke in favor of Pinochet's December 1973 Decree Law 198, saying it was "extremeley favorable to the development of trade unions in the country.... This is an indication of how well workers understand the sacrifices the soldiers have made to rescue the country from the claws of Marxism." Law 198 prohibits any political activity by unions, permits meetings only for information and internal business and only held with previous notification to the police; it bars union elections, collective bargaining and limits the time a union rep can spend away from his/her company job.[113, 114]

◆◆◆◆◆◆◆◆◆◆◆◆◆◆◆◆◆◆◆◆◆◆◆◆◆◆◆◆◆

ONLY A TEMPORARY SETBACK

Luis Figueroa, president of the militant CUT, saw things quite differently. In 1975, he characterized AIFLD activities as "thirteen years of massive social espionage."[116]

One year after the coup Figueroa told a Stockholm audience:

> The North American AFL-CIO led by George Meany is proven to be an instrument of imperialism. It is precisely with money from the AFL-CIO that the military junta now seeks to create new Chilean unions that are docile in the face of the dictatorship.[117]

Figueroa told me he wanted to do nothing that might offend union members and other workers in the U.S. He was certain that, as the world and U.S. workers learned the facts, the solidarity would be forthcoming to help his brothers and sisters regain democracy in Chile.

At one moment Figueroa would verge on tears about the defeats, and in the next would be filled with hope and unshaken faith that September 11, 1973 marked only a temporary, if tragic, setback for his people.

◆◆◆◆◆◆◆◆◆◆◆◆◆◆◆◆◆◆◆◆◆◆◆◆◆◆◆◆◆

AIFLD did reopen its programs. Its seminars were even announced in the Pinochet-controlled press. Its network agents did try to reorganize the Chilean labor movement in general and several industries in particular.

It failed miserably. The former CUT continued to work clandestinely until new forms developed that are currently building rapidly toward unbreakable unity. The junta found that even a little trade unionism is too much to permit under conditions of fascism. International solidarity even carried ORIT to oppose the junta.[50, 118, 119, 141, 120]

With increasing repressive measures against the working-class, even most of the puppet leaders emplaced by Pinochet into unions have turned against the dictatorship. By 1979 the

AFL-CIO was at the point of agreeing to worldwide boycott of Chile. It sent AIFLD board chairman J. Peter Grace to meet with Pinochet and he defused the boycott.[121]

Chile now has been reduced to economic desperation. The TNCs once again dominate the economy, but general work stoppages and mass demonstrations are increasing in tempo. It will not be long. Hopefully U.S. workers will move the AFL-CIO to join the labor movement of the world in effectively demanding the reestablishment of human rights, union rights and democracy in Chile—and in terminating the Pinochet nightmare.

Today in Nicaragua

Nicaragua suffered almost half a century of Somoza dictatorships, from 1933 to 1979. The repression was in place long before the Cold War growth of the doctrine of national security. While any political element that challenged the regimes was labeled "Communist," the Somozas really sought no justification. They simply sacked the economy, made room for fruit, coffee and other TNCs, and maintained stability with the iron fist of the U.S. Marine-trained National Guard.

Union organizing had been mostly clandestine in nature except for the Confederacion de Unificacion Sindical (CUS). CUS was founded with the help of AIFLD and was the only group permitted to function under Somoza. It was what Latin Americans call a "yellow union," raising no social or political demands but only the narrowest economic requests.[122]

In 1979 the Nicaraguan people finally shook off the Somoza regime at the cost of tens of thousands of lives. The revolution was led by the Sandinista Front for National Liberation (FSLN), supported by the widest possible unity. Before the overthrow of Somoza, and since, the CUS has remained aloof from the revolutionary process. Its membership has shrunk while all other unions have grown and thrived, organically part of the revolution.[123]

The U.S. corporate elite views Nicaragua as a threat to stability and transnational dominance. The Reagan administration mounted a Cold War red scare, launching a CIA war through the use of the Contra army led by Somoza's old National Guard.

AIFLD FOR THE CONTRAS

AIFLD supports the CUS and other miniscule dissident groups opposing the Sandinistas. It functions as a public relations sounding board to help the Reagan administration pull our Congress behind the CIA contra war.

William Doherty drew up a paper to "document how the Sandinista government has all but destroyed the free trade unions in Nicaragua." His sheet was enclosed with a cover letter from Lane Kirkland and circulated to all unions nationally, making them the direct target of AIFLD disinformation.[124]

Succeeding groups of union delegations visiting Nicaragua have challenged the AIFLD document, even as have CUS leaders.[125, 126] In April 1984, nine labor lawyers went to Nicaragua to investigate, and returned to prepare a 62-page report challenging every detail of the Doherty sheet as "flawed ... a grossly inaccurate and misleading document." Their work has been published by the National Lawyers Guild, and appears in the appendix to the Congressional Record.[143]

In El Salvador: AIFLD and Resistance

In 1979, U.S. ruling circles were shocked by the successful revolution in Nicaragua and immediately moved to stem that same potential in neighboring El Salvador, where a military-led oligarchy has ruled with farcical elections since 1933. Their tactic was to push a highly controlled agrarian reform plan in order to deprive revolutionary forces of support in the countryside. AIFLD became the linchpin of that U.S. policy.

AIFLD had been ousted from El Salvador after placing an undesirable Country Program Director (CPD) in charge of its 1972 program. This was Torres Lazo, a Nicaraguan who had been a top prosecutor for Anastasio Somoza. (An AIFLD CPD must be a U.S. citizen. Lazo allegedly gained his citizenship without living in the U.S. the required five years.)[127]

Through the efforts of "leaders" it was funding in the campesino organization, Union Comunal Salvadorena (UCS),

AIFLD regained entry to El Salvador in 1979. An outside auditor found "misappropriation of funds the rule, not the exception" in UCS. When AIFLD gave assurances of "complete faith and confidence in your honor," adding, "the important thing is to smooth the path for the entrance of the Institute," UCS leaders did so.[127]

By March 1980, AIFLD had a plan ready for agrarian reform devised by Roy Prosterman, the same plan designed as part of the Phoenix pacification program in Vietnam. The plan was instituted concurrently with a state of siege suspending all civil law in El Salvador. The Phoenix plan took at least 20,000 lives in Vietnam. At least twice that number have been killed in tiny El Salvador.[128] This phoney agrarian reform gave AIFLD a foothold and has been used to fabricate support for U.S. military and economic aid to a government that rules by oppression, death squads and mass murder.

Doherty was the AFL-CIO spokesman to Congress, calling for increased millions for the Salvadoran government up until 1983. He paraded two Salvadorans, one from UCS and one from a construction union, to show Congress that Salvadoran labor supported U.S. meddling in their country. Doherty claimed his men represented 500,000 workers. In fact, the last Salvadoran census lists only 76,578 recognized union members in that country.[130]

The Salvadoran Committee of Trade Union Unity, which documents its affiliation of 85 percent of the nation's union members, is a firm component of the FDR-FMLN, the popular revolutionary forces.[131, 132] In 1983, it supported Alejandro Molina Lara, a Salvadoran unionist, on his successful U.S. solidarity tour.

Lane Kirkland tried to throw up a roadblock, sending out a letter saying that before AFL-CIO bodies offer an audience to representatives from abroad "their authenticity should be verified by the Department of International Affairs." An unsigned letter smeared Lara as "a known kidnapper and assassin" and his union as "worse than the PLO." The source of the new McCarthyism was the AIFLD.[133, 134]

The AIFLD/AFL-CIO alignment with the Reagan administration's desperate moves in Central America has triggered new expressions of organized resistance all over the U.S. Top officers of 21 national unions initiated the National Committee for Democracy and Human Rights in El Salvador. This committee has visited El Salvador, had success in gaining release of imprisoned unionists, and published well-documented reports generating opposition to U.S. government policies against the people of El Salvador.[135, 136]

Walter Reuther: "It is Fatal to Resist Communism by Courting Reaction"

Walter Reuther was United Auto Workers president from 1946 to 1970. Unlike Dubinsky and Goldberg, Walter Reuther never could quite break his ties with his socialist family background. He rose from the ranks in organizing battles with the auto makers, an authentic voice of his coworkers. He forged unity with the left and then turned on that unity.[137, 29, 138, 21, 22] *[See section 42.]* Victor, his brother and righthand man, directed UAW's work in foreign affairs. Walter once told Victor something that was to live with him all his life: "It is fatal to resist Communism by courting reaction."[50]

Though sharing Meany's anti-Communism and signing on with AIFLD, Reuther pulled out over events in Brazil. In 1966, when Meany shut the AFL-CIO door to East-West dialogue in the International Labor Organization, he and Reuther locked horns. At that moment, Victor Reuther gave the press information on the AFL-CIO connection with the CIA. Meany seethed and Victor, pressed for more detail, told reporters "a more appropriate time will come."[18, 141, 50, 12]

When Walter Reuther violated AFL-CIO doctrine by planning a UAW-Soviet auto worker exchange visit, Meany had his State Department people quash the visas. Reuther felt ready to confront Meany policy. He demanded a full-blown hearing on AIFLD at the August 1966 AFL-CIO Executive Council meeting. His assistant, Jack Conway, said, "A strong effort was made to get this off the agenda—by the CIA, by Hubert Humphrey [CFR], by Robert Kennedy [CFR] and others." Reuther and Meany agreed to this.

Reuther was totally surprised at the meeting to find that AIFLD had been put back on the agenda. Unprepared, Reuther tried to table discussion and said, "The CIA is something you do not discuss publicly ... it should be by a small subcommittee. ..." A glowing report was presented and passed, topped by a vote labelling dissent to the Vietnam War as "disruption" which is "aiding the Communist enemy."[12, 15, 141]

Reuther prepared to pull the UAW out of the AFL-CIO. He issued a series of administrative papers criticizing AFL-CIO policies, still without airing the CIA issue. For this, *he* was criticized in the press.[139, 50, 140] All but isolated in the AFL-CIO Executive Council, he was its only member to support Dr. Martin Luther King, Jr. in the 1968 Memphis labor marches. He was the only AFL-CIO Council member at the funeral following Dr. King's assassination in April. After Robert Kennedy's assassination in June, the UAW withdrew from the AFL-CIO, and Reuther formed the Alliance for Labor Action (ALA) with the Teamsters and several small unions. Its four million members called for an end to the Vietnam War and new unity with "progressive forces in and out of labor." Along with other top leaders of UAW, Reuther became a regular signer for demonstrations to end the war. Union members began responding in increasing numbers.[141, 50]

Every union person I've discussed this with agrees that, if large sections of the labor movement had entered the anti-war movement, it would have meant an end to the Meany/Dubinsky/Lovestone grip on AFL-CIO foreign affairs—if not on the leadership itself. In 1968, that same estimation was held at the highest level about stability of power in the overall establishment: the 12 CFR people in the President's 14-member Senior Advisory Group on Vietnam agreed that "the divisiveness in the country was growing with such acuteness it was threatening to tear the U.S. apart."[18, 141]

The Question of Violence

One day in the fall of 1968 the Reuther brothers crashlanded in a chartered Lear jet at Dulles Field in Washington. Somehow the altimeter brought them in 82 feet below the proper glide angle. They survived. Walter told Victor, "I guess this wasn't intended to be our time." I met and talked with Victor Reuther about this and he said, "Yes, I always thought somebody intended that to be our time, but I can't prove it."[50]

By April of 1970, polls showed a growing anti-war majority that had become increasingly workingclass in character. The Meany group, although losing its grip, leapt to call for "the full support of the American people," when Nixon bombed Cambodia in early May. Instead, unprecedented, broadbased demonstrations erupted nationwide on this issue. Nixon called the demonstrators "traitors" and two Black students were killed in

Mississippi and four white demonstrators at Kent State in Ohio.[141]

Reuther's timing was finally right. On May 9 he was polishing off arrangements for a first-ever conference jointly sponsored by the United Nations and a union—the UAW—on the question of violence. He called Victor about strengthening a protest message condemning the war and calling for a coalition of new dimensions against international and domestic violence. He then left his office for the conference site in northern Michigan.[141]

His plane was one of the safest small planes made—an M43eJ Lear jet—chartered from the same company he used in 1968 when he crashlanded. The plane hit treetops at 9:28 p.m., taking the lives of Walter Reuther and five others.

Victor says the altimeter "read too high." A writer intimate with the Reuthers said part of the instrument was "installed upside down." The Transportation and Safety Board found ". . . the evidence is not conclusive." One reporter who tried a prompt investigation found "a strange lack of cooperation." No sufficient investigation was ever made.[24, 50, 142]

Resistance in U.S. Labor is Growing

Future historians will be able to detail the toll taken by the government/corporate collaborators of the CFR in the AFL-CIO. While rarely bloodying their own hands, their work has set back workers' struggles in many countries at a cost of uncounted numbers of lives, in Guatemala, Chile, Nicaragua, El Salvador, etc. They have mined the road to peaceful coexistence and have undermined the international labor unity that can effectively wage peace.

Each of their divisive thrusts has drawn both blood and opposition. Guatemala sparked protest in the UAW. That protest became massive with Vietnam and, were the protest not beheaded when Reuther was killed, the Lovestone legion might have been routed. It was with Chile that detailed understanding of AIFLD began to take root.

AIFLD's actions in Central America have raised opposition to new levels. Dozens of labor solidarity groups have formed across the country. A heavy number of Lane Kirkland's Executive Council are members of the National Labor Committee on Human Rights and Democracy in El Salvador. That group is comprised of 23 international union presidents representing nearly half the rank-and-file of the AFL-CIO! The Labor Network on Central America articulates opposition through nationwide distribution of its Labor Report. The West Coast has seen the growth of the Committee for International Support of Trade Union Rights (CISTUR) with 55 unions and councils affiliated. CISTUR's *News and Action Bulletin* gives its affiliates and subscribers a constant flow of information reflected in resolutions that weaken the ideological grip of the CFR clique on a local, state and even national level.

The rising opposition has forced AIFLD, in particular, to turn its government-funded intelligence talents against the rising opposition in the AFL-CIO. As AIFLD agents turn on the dissenters, their McCarthy-style Red-baiting has a chilling effect on some sectors, while angering others who become even more bold.

The CFR clique in the AFL-CIO lays claim to the words "pluralism," "democracy" and "free trade unionism," but it was anti-Communism which put them in bed with the transnational bosses. It is anti-Communism which keeps them there, dividing workers abroad and thereby smoothing the way for the corporations to export our jobs to cheap labor havens. The residue of McCarthyite anti-Communism also divides the opposition and retards the ultimate ability of our dynamic and proud union movement to take control of union foreign affairs.

With a new, genuine internationalism, our unions will reflect the needs of the members. We will—in the not-too-distant future—join the ranks of unions of all other nations in the quest for a world free from exploitation, unemployment and, finally, from the threat of nuclear war.

SOURCE NOTES
1. Susanne Jonas, "Trade Union Imperialism in the Dominican Republic," *NACLA Latin America and Empire Report*, Vol. IX, No. 3 (April 1975), p. 13.
2. Ernie DeMaio, *World Trade Union Movement* (WFTU Monthly Review), No. 1 (1983).
3. *Statistical Abstracts of the United States 1981*, Table 1492.
4. Hearings, Subcommittee on Inter-American Affairs of the Committee on Foreign Affairs, House of Reps., 91st Cong., July 20, 1969.
5. *New York Times*, 11/19/80, p. 1.
6. Philip S. Foner, *History of the Labor Movement in the United States Vol I*, (1947), pp. 409-417.

7. Ray Ginger, *The Bending Cross: A Biography of Eugene Victor Debs*, (1949), pp. 328-332.
8. Matthew Josephson, *Sidney Hillman: Statesman of American Labor*, (Doubleday, 1952), pp. 647-650.
9. Council on Foreign Relations rosters and By-Laws.
10. Albert Vorspan, *Giants of Justice*, (Thomas Cromwell, 1960).
11. David Dubinsky and A.H. Raskin, *David Dubinsky: A Life with Labor*, (Simon and Shuster, 1977).
12. Joseph C. Goulden, *Meany*, (Atheneum, 1972).
13. Max D. Danish, *The World of David Dubinsky*, (World Publishing, 1957), p. 270.
14. *Chicago Daily News*, 3/15/53.
15. George Morris, *CIA and American Labor*, (International, 1967).
16. CFR By-Laws, (Jan. 1945), p. 1.
17. CFR Annual Report, (1973), pp. 83-85.
18. Lawrence H. Shoup and William Minter, *The Imperial Brain Trust*, (Monthly Review Press, 1977).
19. L. Fletcher Prouty, *The Secret Team: The CIA and its Allies in Control of the World*, (Ballantine, 1973).
20. Albert E. Kahn, *The Plot Against the People*, (Lear Pubs., 1950), p. 227.
21. *Newsweek*, 10/2/72, p. 40.
22. Robert Shaplen, "Profiles," *New Yorker*, 4/7/62.
23. Richard Dunlop, *Donovan: America's Master Spy*, (Rand McNally, 1982).
24. Jean Gould and Lorena Hitchcock, *Walter Reuther: Labor's Rugged Individualist*, (Dodd, Mead, 1972).
25. Philip Foner, *Organized Labor and the Black Worker*, (Praeger Pubs., 1976), p. 315.
26. Joseph Rayback, *A History of American Labor*, (MacMillan, 1966), p. 426.
27. Serafino Romualdi, *Presidents and Peons*, (Funk & Wagnall, 1967).
28. Ronald Radosh, *American Labor and U.S. Foreign Policy*, (Vintage, 1969).
29. Bert Cochran, *Labor & Communism*, (Princeton Univ., 1977).
30. *AFL-CIO News*, 1/28/56.
31. Fanny S. Simon, *Teaching Methods and Techniques in Labor Education*, (ORIT, 1968), p. 14.
32. *Survey of Alliance for Progress Labor Policies and Programs*, U.S. Senate Comm. on Foreign Relations Staff, GPO, 7/15/68.
33. Ake Wedin, *International Trade Union Solidarity: ICFTU 1957-1965*, (Bokforlaget Prisma Pubs., Sweden, 1973), pp. 32, 53, 69.
34. Drew Pearson columns 2/16 and 2/24/67.
35. Hearings, Committee on Foreign Relations, U.S. Senate, 91st Cong., Aug. 1, 1969.

36. *Washington Post*, 2/26/67.
37. William Grieder, *Washington Post*, 5/21/69.
38. Paul Jacobs, *How the CIA Makes Liars out of Union Leaders*, (Ramparts, May 1967).
39. *New York Post*, 2/24/67.
40. Report to the Committee on Foreign Relations, U.S. Senate, by the Comptroller General of the U.S., Aug. 4, 1970, pp. 39-44.
41. Senate Foreign Relations Committee press release #66, Aug. 26, 1970.
42. Thomas Powers, *The Man Who Kept the Secrets*, (Pocket Books, 1979).
43. *The Federationist*, Sept. 1954.
44. *Inter-American Labor Bulletin*, Feb. 1954.
45. David Graham, "Liberated Guatemala," *The Nation*, 7/17/56.
46. Marlise Simons, "Guatemala: The Coming Danger," *Foreign Policy*, Vol. 43, (Summer 1981).
47. Robert J. Alexander, *Organized Labor in Latin America*, (The Free Press, 1965), pp. 164-168.
48. Dan Kurzman, "Lovestone's Cold War: The AFL Has Its Own CIA," *The New Republic*, 6/25/66.
49. Carl Marzani and Robert E. Light, *Cuba vs. the CIA*, (Marzani & Munsell, 1961), pp. 21-25.
50. Victor Reuther, *The Brothers Reuther*, (Houghton Mifflin, 1976).
51. Milton Bracker, *The Grace Log* (W.R. Grace Company magazine, Spring 1963).
52. Philip Agee, *Inside the Company-CIA Diary*, (Penguin Books, 1975).
53. David Rockefeller, "What Private Enterprise Means to Latin America," *Foreign Affairs*, Vol. 144, #3, (April, 1966), pp. 408-414.
54. Proceedings of the Sixth Constitutional Convention of AFL-CIO, Vol. II, p. 108.
55. "A Union to Union Program for the Americas," *AIFLD booklet*, 1982, pp. 4,5.
56. George Cabot Lodge, *Spearheads of Democracy: Labor in the Developing Countries*, (Harper and Row, 1962).
57. George C. Lodge, "U.S. Aid to Latin America: Funding Radical Change," *Foreign Affairs*, Vol. 47, #4, p. 745.
58. George C. Lodge, "Revolution in Latin America," *Foreign Affairs*, Vol. 44, #2, (Jan. 1966), pp. 195, 196.
59. Roy Godson, *American Labor and European Politics—The AFL-CIO as a Transnational Force*, (Crane, Russak, 1976), pp. 51-53.
60. *Free Trade Union News* (AFL-CIO International Affairs Department, May, 1975).
61. Sidney Lens, "American Labor Abroad: Lovestone Diplomacy," *The Nation*, 7/5/65.

62. Comptroller General Report to Congress, 12/29/75, pp. 6,7.
63. *Who's Who in America*, Vol. 24.
64. Eric Johnston, *America Unlimited*, (Doubleday), pp. 173-184.
65. AIFLD public relations pamphlets.
66. Jack Scott, *Yankee Unions Go Home: How the AFL Helped Build an Empire in Latin America*, (New Star Books, 1978), p. 224.
67. "AIFLD: A Union to Union Program for the Americas," *AIFLD Booklet*, (9/16/65).
68. Deleted from earlier draft.
69. *U.S. News and World Report*, 3/19/84, p. 60.
70. *San Jose Mercury*, 1/10/80, p. 10E.
71. Miles Wolpin, "External Political Socialization as a Source of Conservative Military Behavior in the Third World," *Studies in Comparative International Development*, (1974), (Comparison of figures leads to obvious conclusions).
72. *Covert Action*, July 1979, p. 28.
73. AIFLD housing interview form.
74. *Que Pasa* (Chilean magazine), 10/24/74.
75. Senate Hearing, Committee to Study Governmental Operations with Respect to Intelligence Operations, Vol. 7, 12/4 and 5/75, pp. 9, 12.
76. Senate Hearing, Committee on Foreign Relations, New Directions for the 1970s, Foreign Assistance Act (of 1967), 90th Congress, first session, p. 1096.
77. Mutual Broadcasting System program, 7/12/64, (Labor News Conference).
78. Doherty at Santa Clara County Central Labor Council, 7/1/74.
79. Jan Knippers Black, *United States Penetration of Brazil*, (Univ. of Pennsylvania, 1977).
80. Eugene Methvin, "Labor's New Weapon for Democracy," *Reader's Digest*, (Oct. 1966), pp. 21-28.
81. Interview with Richard Martinez, Oct. 1982.
82. Comptroller General Report, 5/20/68, pp. 29, 30, 48, 72.
83. Robinson Rojas, *Estados Unidos en Brazil*, (Prensa Latinoamericana, Chile, 1965), p. 174.
84. "Torture in the Eighties," *Amnesty International Report*, (1984), p. 62.
85. *AIFLD Report*, Vol. IV, #5, May, 1966.
86. *Brazil Labor and Information Center Newsletter*, No. 5, (Feb. 1984), p. 2.
87. *Le Nouvel Observateur*, 3/4/74, p. 82.
88. Victor Marchetti and John Marks, *The CIA and the Cult of Intelligence*, (Dell, 1974), p. 19.
89. Names taken from various Congressional Hearings on Chile, cross-checked with CFR Rosters.
90. "Training Programs for Foreign Military Personnel: The Penta-

gon's Proteges," *NACLA Latin America and Empire Report*, Vol. X, No. 1, (Jan. 1976).
91. "U.S. and Chile During the Allende Years," Hearings, Subcommittee on Inter-American Affairs of the Committee on Foreign Affairs, House of Representatives, GPO 1975, p. 302.
92. "The ITT Co. and Chile 1970-71," Report to the Committee on Foreign Relations, U.S. Senate, June 21, 1973, pp. 1-20.
93. CFR Study Group Minutes, 1968.
94. "Covert Action in Chile 1963-1973," Staff Report of the Select Committee to Study Governmental Operations with respect to Intelligence Activities, Senate.
95. Eduardo Labarca, "Chile Invadido," *Editorial Austral*, Chile, 1968.
96. CLASC (Conference Latino Americano de Sindicatos Christianos) Report of Second National Congress (Christian Democratic Party), Sept. 1966.
97. *Boletin Informativo*, #50, Casa de Chile, Mexico, 11/4-11/1974.
98. F. Sergeyev, *Chile, CIA, Big Business*, (Progress Pubs, Moscow, 1981), pp. 223, 224.
99. Letters and Reports to Regional Operations Division, Dept. of State, signed by Angelo Verdu, on AIFLD stationary, 8/10/73.
100. BRAC report, Section A, April-June 30 1973, No. 1 (SG).
101. Interviews with Anibal Severino and Rodolfo Ortega in June 1975.
102. AIFLD report to Dept. of State 9/10/73, submitted by Gerald O'Keefe, Dir. of Intl. and Foreign Affairs for RCIA, Section D, p. 3, Organizing Programs.
103. *NACLA* news release (mimeo), Nov. 1973.
104. Chilean Christian Democratic Party document, 12/31/71.
105. Recording 9/11/73, available Casa de Chile, Mexico.
106. Hortensia Allende speech Yale Univ., 1975.
107. AIFLD Report, April, 1975.
108. *El Siglo*, 9/7/71.
109. *Chile Boletin*, #6, 12/1-7/73, Files of Casa de Chile, Mexico, p. 8.
110. *El Mercurio*, 7/7/74, *CUT Boletin Informativo* #2, 6/6/74.
111. BRAC-AIFLD Report, 4/1—12/31/74, p. 28.
112. BRAC-AIFLD Subgrant report for 7/1—12/31/73.
113. *La Prensa* (Chilean magazine), 12/31/73, p. 3.
114. *La Tercera*, 12/23/73.
115. Proceedings AFL-CIO Convention, 1977, pp. 332, 333.
116. Speech, Mexico City, March 1975.
117. Speech, Stockholm, 9/11/74.
118. *La Patria*, 10/21/74.
119. *Agencia EFE*, Spain, 12/23/73.
120. *AFP*, Oslo dateline, 10/8/74.

121. Council on Hemispheric Affairs press releases, 12/15/78, 12/19/78, 1/2/79, and 1/19/79.
122. Frank Arnold, "Nicaraguan Labor and the AIFLD," at the 6th Southwest Labor Studies Conference, San Francisco State Univ., 5/1-3/80.
123. Robert Lopez, "Nicaraguan Trip: a report to the UAW by an International Representative," 11/79.
124. Lane Kirkland, Letter to all State and Local Central Bodies, enclosing 12-page Doherty "documentary."
125. American Labor Education Center, "Face to Face: An Inside View of Labor in Nicaragua."
126. Labor Network on Central America, Report of the West Coast Trade Union Delegation to Nicaragua, "Nicaragua: Labor, Democracy, and the Struggle for Peace."
127. Carolyn Forche and Philip Wheaton, *History and Motivations of U.S. Involvement in the Control of the Peasant Movement in El Salvador: The Role of AIFLD in the Agrarian Reform Process, 1970-1980.*
128. "Land Reform as a Counter Insurgency Program like the CIA's Phoenix Operation in Vietnam," *Inter-Press Service*, 7/25/80.
129. U.S. Government Memorandum, Reply to Jonathan Silverstone, 8/8/80.
130. William C. Doherty, Statements to House Appropriations Committee, Subcommittee on Foreign Operations, 2/25/81, and to the House Subcommittee on InterAmerican Affairs, 3/11/81 and 2/25/82.
131. Brief Summary of the Situation in El Salvador, CUS, Nov., 1980.
132. Ronald Duarte, *Un Amargo y Decepcionante Balance*, (Federacion Unitaria Sindical de El Salvador, 1984), pp. 4, 5.
133. Lane Kirkland, letter, 3/24/83, and unsigned letter circulated by Ed Collins, AFL-CIO Region 6 Director.
134. Labor Network on Central America Background Paper, #2, 11/84, p. 4.
135. "El Salvador: Labor, Terror and Peace," A Special Fact-Finding Report by the National Labor Committee in Support of Democracy and Human Rights in El Salvador, Summer, 1983.
136. "Labor Campaign for Jailed Salvadoran Unionists," above source, Fall, 1984.
137. Roger Keeran, *The Communist Party and the Auto Workers*, (Indiana Univ. Press, 1980).
138. Bert Cochran, *American Labor in Midpassage*, (*Monthly Review* Press, 1959), p. 177.
139. Thomas Braden, "I'm Glad the CIA is Immoral," *Sat. Evening Post*, 5/20/67.
140. John Herling, *The Right to Challenge*, (Harper and Row, 1972), coverleaf.

141. Philip Foner, *American Labor and the Indo-China War*, (International Publishers, 1971).
142. Interview with journalist William Allan, 2/28/82.
143. U.S. Labor Lawyers' Delegation to Nicaragua, "*Are Nicaragua's Trade Unions Free? A Response to the American Institute for Labor Development (AFL-CIO) Report, 'Nicaragua, A Revolution Betrayed: Free Labor Persecuted,'*" Dec. 1984. Excerpt in Congressional Record—House April 8, 1985, #2188-2189.

••PART SEVEN••

WHERE DO WE GO FROM HERE?

◆◆◆◆◆◆◆◆◆◆◆◆◆◆◆◆◆◆◆◆◆◆◆◆◆◆◆

Strikes and lockouts are making news today, in city after city. Workers carrying picket signs, families waiting in line for free meals, farmers at auction sales fill our TV screens. Blue-, white-, and pink-collar workers are meeting at union halls to discuss rumors of plant closures, contract negotiations, and, sometimes, plans for organizing. They are registering to vote and joining political action committees to stop small companies from going under and transnationals from abandoning old U.S. plants while building new ones in nonunion areas all over the globe.

No one who works for a living in the United States today feels secure. If they have made it, they are not sure they can keep it. Traditional union members face attacks on traditional contract clauses.

The authors in Part Seven take us from the grape boycott to the graveyard shift to a debate at an AFL-CIO convention. They keep returning to problems of race and sex discrimination, the need for affirmative action, and for action by Congress. They describe their work for peace, and to revive their unions.

Finally, many voices propose actions for the future—in the shops, communities, and legislatures—to put a stop to the Cold War unleashed after World War II. They have no easy answers. They are determined to build a new and unified movement for peace, jobs, and justice to face the 21st century.

◆◆◆◆◆◆◆◆◆◆◆◆◆◆◆◆◆◆◆◆◆◆◆◆◆◆◆

87 •• ILGWU ORGANIZER MURDERED: WHY?

◆◆ **The Editors** ◆◆

From "Justice Sought in Lozano Case," Labor Today, *June 1985, reprinted with permission.*

On June 8, 1983, Rudy Lozano, an organizer for the International Ladies Garment Workers Union and a key figure in Chicago Mayor Harold Washington's campaign, was gunned down while playing in his kitchen with his 2-year-old son. The murder sent shock waves through Chicago's progressive and labor communities.

One of Lozano's major areas of work had been with rank-and-file union members, helping them convince their labor unions to defend the rights of all workers, including the undocumented. In 1979 he became an organizer for the International Ladies Garment Workers Union, concentrating on organizing the unorganized, especially immigrants working in sweatshops in Chicago.

When he met workers employed by the Del Rey Tortilla factory, they asked him to help them start a union. By the end of 1982, they had forced an election for representation in this shop. Del Rey fought the workers all the way, calling in the Immigration and Naturalization Service to detain and deport rank-and-file leadership.

The workers and the community responded with a boycott to bring pressure against the company. Eventually, they forced the company to recognize the union.

By 1983, the 31-year-old Lozano had become the Director of

Organization of the ILGWU in the Chicago area and a board member of the Hispanic Labor Council. He was also a national board member of the National Alliance Against Racist and Political Repression, and a founding member of the National Congress of Unemployed Organizations.

His work also led him into an independent political organization in Chicago's 22nd ward. He became a candidate for the city council, and came within 17 votes of forcing a run-off election against the Chicago Democratic machine incumbent. When Congressmember Washington was elected Mayor in April 12, 1983, he appointed Lozano to his new administration's Transition Team. Two months later, he was slain.

By early July, 1983, Gregory Escobar was arrested and charged by police, but many questions remained.

Was Lozano's success in unifying Hispanics and Blacks for political reform, which posed a challenge to the entrenched and powerful "machine," the motive for his assassination?

Did Lozano's fight against the exploitation of undocumented workers cause the employers to see him as a danger to their operation?

Were the threats from specific individuals before and during his campaign connected with his death? (The State's Attorney's office has refused to question the individuals who made threats on his life and the lives of his family.)

The Commission for Justice for Rudy Lozano asked Representative John Conyers, chairman of the Congressional subcommittee on crime, to conduct a federal investigation of Lozano's death.

Editors' note: In the spring of 1987, Congressman Conyers (D-Mich) promised an investigation, official or unofficial, depending on the availability of federal funding.

88 ·· ORGANIZING FEDERAL WORKERS

♦♦Vivian McGuckin Raineri♦♦

During the Cold War, Vivian McGuckin Raineri was a member of the United Office and Professional Workers of America (UPOWA). Today she is a journalist and a member of the Newspaper Guild.
  See also sections 44 and 81.

> Times are tough for public workers,
>   every day it's something new.
> Layoff threats and hiring freezes,
>   freezes in our wages too.
> Paychecks pounded by inflation,
>   budgets cut down to the bone;
> We've got to stand together,
>   it's no time to stand alone.
>
> ♦♦"Public Workers Stand Together"
> Words by Paul McKenna
> Tune: A Miner's Life

Federal workers are the people who make the government of the United States work. Yet, down through the decades, they have been maligned from all sides.

There are two million federal employees in the USA today, not including postal workers, top management and part-time workers. Thirty-five percent are organized, considerably above the percentage in private industry; 1.2 million are men, 743,000 are women. The women make 63 cents for each dollar earned by men. Hundreds of thousands of federal workers in lower pay grades earn less than workers doing the same jobs in the private sector, sometimes $1,000 less per year. They do clerical and office work of all descriptions in all of the government offices across the nation; they are mostly white collar. It is workers in the blue-collar categories who bring much of the militancy to the ranks of organized government workers; they identify more closely with the trade union movement as a whole. White-collar workers are now making this identification in increasing numbers.

The growing militancy among federal workers in the 1980s is also an outgrowth of the crusading traditions of the United Federal Workers and its successor, United Public Workers of America [*described in sections 22 and 48*].

UPWA's main rival was the American Federation of Government Employees; AFGE today is the principal union of federal workers—in the Social Security Administration, Immigration and Naturalization Service, Department of Labor, National Labor Relations Board, Veterans Administration offices and hospitals, Customs, State Department. They are the civilians who work on military bases. They build and maintain nuclear submarines, work in aeronautical and space agencies, work for the Department of Agriculture, help ships navigate the Panama Canal, run fish hatcheries, inspect mines and do custodial work to keep federal public buildings clean.

They carry out controversial policies and must depend on Congress to change such policies. They are subject to the caprices of the President; he issues executive orders and can rescind them at will. Government workers do not have the right to strike. They cannot take part in partisan political campaigns under the Hatch Act. The only political right they have is the right to vote and to express personal opinions. They walk a tight line.

> The papers slander and insult us—
>   call us lazy parasites.
> They say we're only civil servants,
>   and servants have no civil rights.
> They turn the populace against us
>   with the lies they fabricate.
> Let's tell our side of the story,
>   then we'll set the record straight.
>   ♦♦"Public Workers Stand Together"

By its 20th National Convention in 1968, the American Federation of Government Employees was reportedly the "fastest growing union in the AFL-CIO." The first woman national representative and the first Black woman national representative were hired and for the first time, a blue-collar AFGE member headed the District of Columbia department. Increasingly, Blacks and women won leadership roles in AFGE lodges, and some rank-and-file members argued for using the strike as a weapon to gain equitable treatment, but they were quashed by the top union leadership.

In 1970, the AFGE convention was ready to vote to delete the no-strike clause from the union constitution. And the union fought Nixon's proposal for a "stabilization" wage freeze that would have thrown 100,000 federal workers out of work. Congress rejected Nixon's freeze and the political clout of labor got credit. AFGE formed its own political wing: the Committee on Federal Employee Political Education (COFEPE). A voluntary organization parallel to AFGE, COFEPE's main purpose was to register and get voters to the polls and to do voter education through exposing candidates' records.

AFGE's 1972 National Convention was tumultuous. Delegates were outraged that national president John Griner had personally endorsed Nixon, apparently in exchange for the president's acceptance of the Wage Grade Bill. The convention was described as "one of the greatest shakeups we ever had," ending in a "near riot." The delegates rebuffed the national leadership on many resolutions and proposals, paving the way for a Women's Department, revitalizing the Fair Practices Committee, and starting rank-and-file formations, including a Minority Coalition and a Hispanic Caucus.

> Workers in the private sector,
>   we're no different from you.
> We work hard to feed our families,
>   pay our rent and taxes too.
> It doesn't matter who we work for,
>   we're all workers just the same,
> But the rights you take for granted,
>   we're still fighting to obtain.
>   ♦♦"Public Workers Stand Together"

The 1980s

In the 1980s, times are tough for federal workers. But they are fighting back, in the face of a government freeze on hiring, closure of agency offices, cutbacks in programs, new "economy" drives, continuation of "contracting out," and affirmative action thrown to the winds by the Reagan administration.

One active AFGE woman told me federal workers resent implications, sometimes boldly stated, that government employee unions "are not real unions." They want to become involved with labor federations and boards on state and local levels. They work to build alliances with the public they serve on issues of common interest, convinced that "both we and the public must watchdog the government." For example, hundreds of Social Security Administration offices were scheduled to be shut down or consolidated in the mid-'80s under a "systems modernization" plan. Not only were SSA workers' jobs on the line but most of these offices were in poorer parts of towns with little public transportation. The local people will have difficulty traveling to other offices, as they found when the West Oakland, California, office was closed in January, 1985. AFGE got wind of the "consolidation" plot, let Congressmembers in on it, did research to show the impact of such closures on the communities, and called press conferences. Congresspersons were upset when offices were scheduled for closure in *their* districts. The upshot: the Social Security Administration said it was all a misunderstanding. The danger continues, however, with SSA plans to close many field offices and reduce the force by 17,000 workers by the year 1990, as the number of seniors soars.

It's a constant struggle. J. Peter Grace and his President's Private Sector Survey on Cost Control has declared war. [*See more on J. Peter Grace in section 86*] The enemy: "Government waste." The Grace Commission conducted a slick multi-million dollar campaign to get public support for the proposition that government *equals* waste, but there's more than cost-cutting involved. Their philosophy puts the corporations in *all* the drivers' seats: Contract out—to corporations like Grace's and others in the Fortune 500 that make up most of the commission. Cut wages and benefits of federal workers—making it easier to follow suit in private enterprise. Call anything that doesn't suit you "waste"—like Social Security offices, like federal retirement benefits. Then call the cuts "reform."

President Ronald Reagan beat the drums for it. In the Congress, Citizens Against Waste lobbied for support of the Grace Commission's 2,478 recommendations and claimed (in April, 1985) to get 1,000 calls a day from the public. Newspaper columnist Jack Anderson co-chaired Citizens Against Waste with Grace.

Its proposals cover just about everything. They would terminate federal regulation of oil pipelines, exempt hydroelectric projects from federal licensing, reduce federal financing of rural electric cooperatives, and phase out the entire Rural Electrification Administration.

Attack and Response

The wages, retirement and health benefits for federal workers—all this is at stake. That's one side. The other side, a federal worker said, "is the basically anti-people, anti-democratic thrust of this attack." So AFGE is also busy on the legislative front.

Paired with this is organizing the unorganized. This is difficult when the work force is declining and a mood of despair and cynicism seeps into the workers' ranks. "We're trying to change the perception among some that we are apathetic," asserts one worker. "Members of Congress tell us that the more active our union is the better they can push a lot of our issues." So AFGE sends out legislative alerts, holds legislative conferences in Washington, D.C., calls on local legislative representatives, holds training seminars on the Hatch Act as well as collective bargaining.

In the San Francisco Bay Area, a Federal Labor Coalition organized across union lines. The Coalition formed spontaneously when "cutback" mania hit Washington, D.C. and the Congress. It brings together union friends and union rivals. A Social Security worker may sit next to a person who works for the military and refers to "the Commanding Officer" or the "Commander in Chief," rather than "Reagan" or "the President," like everybody else. "Yet when it comes down to the average member, they're just fellow federal employees and it's fascinating to see all these workers trying to do a job while these ridiculous changes in procedure come down and we're told that thousands of us won't have jobs by 1990."

Besides AFGE, some of the unions in the Coalition are the National Association of Letter Carriers, American Postal Workers Union, National Federation of Federal Employees, National Treasury Employees Union, National Labor Relations Union, and Union of Compliance Officers (of the Department of Labor).

The Hatch Act frightens federal workers. There is a general sense that if an issue is political, federal employees better keep hands off. That is why the hardworking unionist who gave me all this information then asked me not to use her name. "When you're fighting apathy, that all unions fight against, and have the added burden of the Hatch Act, it's rough. You've got to be a legal wizard to figure out the ins and outs. We have to teach federal workers what they can and cannot do."

So insidious is the Hatch Act that many federal workers must be convinced that it's not against the law to march in labor parades and protest demonstrations.

While walking precincts or licking envelopes for partisan officeseekers is forbidden, federal workers always did voter registration. In the mid-'80s, however, even this was challenged. After the 1984 election, AFGE president Kenneth T. Blaylock and the national presidents of the two postal unions, Moe Biller and Vince Sombrotto, faced Hatch Act violation charges for their endorsement of Mondale; four years earlier, when PATCO endorsed Reagan, no such charge was made.

Suppose the wife of a federal employee is an active Democrat and holds a fundraising party in her home. It has been ruled that the federal employee/husband does not have to leave the house for the duration of the party, but he may not lift a finger to help his wife, nor wash a single dish. Or suppose several federal workers have a car pool and for the convenience of one rider they stop at the polls on election day to let her off. Charges were brought that the federal employee driving the car was engaged in driving people to the polls; this case actually went to court.

Where to draw the line? How to figure out what can be said in a newsletter? What can be posted on a bulletin board? How about the publication of negative remarks about management when management ultimately is the President? "Every election time we have interminable discussions about whether this or that is all right; it's so complex that even our experts can't give us total assurance."

Charting a New Course

The 29th Biennial Convention of AFGE in August, 1984, adopted a Report on National and International Affairs:

The American Federation of Government Employees has long understood that our vision must extend beyond our bargaining units to the world around us. Our goal of fair benefits and wages for our members is not different from the goal of fair benefits and wages for all workers. Our desire to eliminate discrimination in the federal workforce cannot succeed if discrimination persists and is accepted in the larger society. Our attempts to secure job security for federal and District of Columbia employees is meaningless if our very existence is threatened by foolhardy foreign policy.

In international affairs, AFGE condemned the Reagan administration for cutting social programs while pumping more and more money into new generations of nuclear weapons; it spelled out that military production costs jobs as compared to the number of jobs that could be created in the civilian sector.

The 1984 policy statement noted, too: "While the Reagan administration builds for war, churches and communities throughout this country build for peace." It urged its members to participate in freeze rallies and vote for pro-freeze and pro-labor candidates, and to pressure Congress. It urged the U.S. government to negotiate a bilateral, verifiable nuclear freeze; to join the Soviet Union in a pledge never to use nuclear weapons first; to oppose nuclear arms production. It decried U.S. government support of the government of El Salvador, opposed U.S. intervention in Nicaragua, calling upon the AFL-CIO to "actively oppose this policy. ..." It opposed expansion of U.S. military bases in Central America, maneuvers in the Caribbean and military aid to Honduras, Costa Rica and Guatemala. AFGE called for the elimination of apartheid and the institution of majority rule in South Africa, and pledged not to invest in corporations that do business in South Africa.

In national affairs, AFGE called for addressing the fundamental "deeprooted structural problems" of unemployment and poverty, stating its belief that:

[T]he federal government should take responsiblity for ensuring full employment, focusing on conversion of wasteful defense spending to jobs for peace.... AFGE councils, in particular, will take an active role in budget priorities under their jurisdiction and form coalitions with relevant constituency groups.

The federal workers called for enactment of "universal, comprehensive national health insurance" and pledged that until such passage is won it will take legislative and community actions to oppose cutbacks in Medicare and Medicaid.

It's hard sometimes for government workers to "make the

government work" under rules and regulations they consider wrong or unfair. This includes concern among some Immigration and Naturalization Service (INS) workers about harassment of the Mexican community. Some rules are also seen as unenforceable and put INS employees at great risk. This is the beginning of union members' outreach into the Mexican community and building of alliances to counter unjust laws or rules. The 1984 AFGE convention went on record supporting "an effective but humane immigration policy which fully protects the civil liberties of all people who live and work in the United States." It opposed the Simpson-Mazzoli bill and exploitation of the undocumented, and sought a "humane and consistent immigration policy for refugees from repressive regimes such as El Salvador, Guatemala and Haiti." The convention joined the INS Council (national bargaining council of INS-AFGE locals) in opposing the national identification card for the undocumented.

> In conclusion, fellow workers, we must organize
>   for power.
> "Solidarity forever" is the watchword of the hour.
> Let's fight back in opposition against the bosses
>   and the press,
> Build a workers' coalition and march onward to success.
> ♦♦"Public Workers Stand Together"
> Words by Paul McKenna
> Tune: "A Miner's Life"

SOURCES

The author wishes to acknowledge use of the following sources:
1. "AFGE—Federal Union. The Story of the American Federation of Government Employees," By Jack and Lorna Nevin. © 1976 by the American Federation of Government Employees.
2. "The United Federal Workers of America—The C.I.O. and the Organization of Federal Workers," by Rhonda Hanson, Graduate Research Paper, Department of Labor Studies, University of the District of Columbia. September, 1984.
3. "Songs for Labor," AFL-CIO Publication No. 56. December 1983.
4. Federal Service Labor-Management Relations Act.
5. Interviews with union members, news reports.

89 ♦♦ ORGANIZING TEAMSTERS IN THE 1980s

♦♦ Ron Teninty ♦♦

Teamsters Union business agent Ron Teninty, of Local 315 in California's Contra Costa County, gave this report at the 1982 Symposium on The Right To Earn A Living presented by Meiklejohn Civil Liberties Institute in Oakland, California.

Organizing is being developed within the Teamsters at all levels, from the International all the way down to the local unions.

The International is basically working in metropolitan areas such as Long Beach and Los Angeles. Currently, the International is working jointly with the International Longshoremen's and Warehousemen's Union to organize on the waterfronts down there. Today it is cheaper to bring a product into Los Angeles and truck it up to the San Francisco Bay Area than to ship it up, because of the difference in labor rates and because of non-union competition. The conference is working with the Longshoremen in Los Angeles, not only on the waterfronts, but also in the warehousing industries. They're organizing on a company-wide basis, taking on one company that has facilities within that conference or within the state, not in just one location. We have found out too often that if you try and organize one location, the company simply shifts production to other locations and stymies your organizing effort.

Joint Council 7 is made up of all the Teamster locals in

Northern California. It also has an organizing program that's just now getting underway with one full-time person and a part-time person who are coordinating the activity. They've sent out letters and information sheets to all the locals in the area to identify those facilities that would be targets for organizing. Funding is coming in from the conference and from the International, and from the Joint Council. As soon as they have picked a target, they will mount an intensive organizing campaign.

Most of the organizing goes on from a local level, and it differs from local to local. Some local unions have full-time organizers on staff whose responsibility it is to organize. Other locals don't have organizers at all, and rely primarily on their business agents and some executive board officers to do the organizing for them.

My local does not have a full-time organizer. As a result, business agents try to organize in what you might call "spare time." The problem with this is that it's very difficult to organize if you don't have the time to do it. We have learned that you can't organize very well on a part-time basis. It's just too damn difficult. I am the one primarily responsible for most of the organizing in our local. To give you an idea of how difficult that is, I also represent 900 members in 14 different installations in our geographic area. Needless to say, I spend most of my time putting out fires in the areas I service, as compared to organizing.

In our local, most of the organizing comes from people phoning in, saying: "We've got a problem. Here's what the issue is. We'd like to talk to somebody because we want to get organized." Most of these people think the Teamsters are going to come in with some kind of magic wand, and they're gonna be able to sit back and wait for the work to be done. Then they'll all become Teamsters, have better wages and better working conditions, and have to pay dues.

For those who aren't familiar, organizing is a 24-hour job that requires you to constantly make contact with people, sit with them, spend time in their homes. I'm finding out that organizing nowadays is even more of a family activity than it is an individual worker-by-worker activity. Most frequently what you find when you organize people who are working is that they have a problem going home and telling their families that they're getting organized, or they're going to vote for a union, or they're going to go out on strike and become unemployed.

Labor's major problem today, of course, is unemployment. Obviously, unemployment in our system is manufactured, and it has been manufactured on the old Phillips Curve Theory, which says that in order to control inflation, you have to create unemployment so that you won't have to increase prices. Of course, that system does work, even though it's an inhumane system. By creating unemployment you create competition for labor; you drive labor prices down, and companies can increase their profit without an increase in prices.

Avoid Going to the Board

I have found it's best to avoid going to the National Labor Relations Board and petitioning for an election. That system just doesn't work. It is a long-term system. It takes anywhere from eight to twelve weeks to even get an election, and sometimes even longer, depending on how much money the employer is willing to spend to fight you. In our area there are numerous anti-union or union-busting law firms that are more than happy to go down to the Board and pick up the names of the people or the companies who've had a petition for an election filed against them, contact those companies and say, "For [whatever charge] we can come in and see to it that you don't have a union." One of the more notorious firms in this area has 50-some attorneys sitting in an office in San Francisco spending most of their time fighting unions. About half of them spend their time fighting organizing drives.

To go through a Labor Board election, you have to go through hearings. The employer will fund the appeals system, and by the time you finally get to an election, the employer's had an unlimited amount of time to work on the people.

If you have people out there waiting to take your job in a minute, probably for half the rate you're already making, which is obviously cheap, then you're already scared. You're trying to figure out how you're going to walk out on strike with your new union, or how you're going to enforce your demands. The employer knows and uses this. The game is now psychological. We don't find too much of the game anymore where the employers send out the goons and start busting heads and using some sort of threatening tactics to keep organizers off the job. Most employers use very sophisticated techniques.

Unfortunately, for the most part, they work.

Today, of the elections that go before the Board, unions are winning 43 or 44 percent. That's a far cry from what was going on eight or ten years ago.

So, what I find to be most effective is to go in and meet with people—usually it's a very small core group—and tell them to keep it as absolutely secret as possible. I do go through the process of getting pledge cards, or authorization cards. Those are little documents that say "I want Local 315 to represent me in bargaining over the terms and conditions of a contract." Those cards are used to get the Board interested, because the Board says you have to have at least one-third of the affected bargaining unit sign cards before they will spend the taxpayers' dollars to get involved in an election. I go through that process, not so much to convince the Board that I have enough people for them to get interested, as to give people a sense of commitment, to make them feel they've committed themselves to the organizing drive. Then I try and organize those people to go out and get the people who didn't show up.

Move Fast and Be Prepared To Strike

I try to do this as quickly as possible, usually within a 2-to-3 week period, in hopes that the employer won't find out.

Another reason I have them sign pledge cards is to protect the advocates if the employer does find out and thinks he has an opportunity to take action against them. This shows the Board that the organizing drive was in effect prior to the time the employer started firing or disciplining people. Then if it seems to be the only way to do it, I can start using the Board and the courts to enforce the workers' rights to organize without employer discipline or threats.

After I get the employees somewhat organized, I will do everything possible to talk the workers into striking for recognition immediately. To me, that's the most effective way of making an organizing effort work.

Generally, I'll tell the employer, "Look, I have a vast majority of your people signed up. They want me to represent them. I want to get recognition from you in writing, and I want to sit down and work out a contract within the next two or three days."

Most of the time the employer says, "Who the hell are you? I gotta call my attorney," or "Get the hell out of my office."

And I tell them, "OK, I'm leaving, but as I leave your office, your workers are coming with me."

I've done that four or five times now, and it works. I've had two of the five call the bluff and say, "OK, go." I went and the workers started coming out with me. We didn't even get out the door. The employer was calling me back into his office and telling me to hold on a minute.

Naturally, I tell the people to stand around and don't do anything until I get back out. The people see themselves supporting each other—actually see it happening. It gives them a real strong feeling for what's happening. It gives them a sense of community.

More importantly, it doesn't give the employer time to get ready. If you go the long way, the employer has time to set up scabs to come in and take over the jobs, time to set up the psychological war, time to start figuring out ways to move production, time to start stockpiling. They have just too many ways to build and eventually bust the strike even if you win the election.

Once you win an election, you then have the problem of negotiating the damn contract, and I'll tell you, that's even harder. Trying to win a contract after you've won an election is like trying to pull teeth, particularly now. You know that the only weapon you really have is taking your labor and moving out on the street, although, frankly, there are a few other innovative tactics I'm finding more successful than that, like keeping the labor on the place and making sure production doesn't get out.

But then again, you have to build that kind of energy and militancy within your group. I'm not saying this is something I've been able to accomplish on any kind of a large scale because I'm one of those people that have lost more than I've won, but I'm learning from the losses and I'm finding out that the only way to win, at least right now, in this kind of economy, is to hit first and hit quick. Don't give the employer time to do something about it. Plus, given my other responsibilities in servicing the members I represent, this strategy works best with my schedule.

Now, in terms of developing other kinds of tactics that I think would work, the name of the game is monopolizing labor and labor prices, especially within industries. To give an example, eight years ago, 90 percent of all the trucking industry in this county was organized by the Teamsters. When you had an organizing drive going on, and you put a picket sign up, you could depend on nine out of every ten trucks not crossing the picket line. That put tremendous pressure on somebody we were trying to organize. Teamster contracts were pretty good contracts, mostly because of the kind of stranglehold we had on trucking when it came to putting up that picket sign.

Today we have about 40 percent of the trucking industry organized, largely because of deregulation and, of course, unemployment. Because of that, we have much more trouble organizing.

Concentrate on Certain Industries

We need to identify certain industries where we think we can win, or that have a certain amount of organization already. Then, we have to figure out which employers in our area are in that industry and do some research on them. We have to find out which employer would be the best to hit and concentrate all our effort on that one employer, win there, and then march throughout that industry, instead of going out and scattering.

I come from a general local, as opposed to a craft local—that means we cover everything from A to Z. It's crazy for us to be out organizing this little lumber yard over here, then this little office staff over here, and then this little trucking outfit over there. We put a lot of time and energy and money into organizing drives. The truth of the matter is that when we finally do get a contract, we find ourselves getting our asses kicked three years down the road, or in concession bargaining because there is so much damn non-union competition. Realistically speaking, you could bargain yourself out of the industry. That's what makes a scatter approach so difficult.

By concentrating on certain industries, we can also set up organizing committees from among the rank-and-file members and agents we already have to service those industries. You can provide a more intensive organizing effort by utilizing those resources.

Once you start winning, it has a tremendous impact on other employers and other industries because the word gets around quick. Believe me, when you're successful and the tactics you're using are working, people know you're not afraid to strike, because you've struck and you've won. So right off the top, instead of saying, "I'm gonna get me some fast-shooting law firm," employers are looking at it from the position of, "Uh-oh, if I don't do something quick, I can lose my business." There is a big difference between putting them on the defensive and giving them time to develop an offensive.

Until we begin reducing unemployment and creating a better climate for workers in this country, we'll have to use these kinds of tactics. We're not going to be able to use the National Labor Relations Board and the election process. The Board decided that it is OK now for lawyers for companies to go in just days and hours before the election and put out a bunch of lies. They can just blatantly say anything they want to say. That's perfectly legal now, where it wasn't legal six months ago. Of course, unions can do the same thing, too, but employers are the ones that are hanging the paychecks over our heads, just hours before elections. So let's concentrate on industries, and let's hit 'em, and hit 'em fast.

90 ✦✦ AFFIRMATIVE ACTION

IRONWORKERS FOR UNION DEMOCRACY

✦✦ Leonard McNeil ✦✦

Leonard McNeil retired from the ironworkers in 1987 after 14 years and presently works for the American Friends Service Committee as Program Associate with the Peace and Justice Youth Outreach Project in Oakland, California.

We organized the Ironworkers for Union Democracy (IFUD) in Ironworkers Local 378 in Oakland, California, out of a need for greater union democracy and representation. We felt that the union leadership is not qualified to speak to the interests of minorities and women or the membership as a whole.

Organized labor (AFL-CIO) has traditionally endorsed the principle of equality in theory, but it has never waged a strong and persistent struggle against race and sex discrimination in its own ranks. The history of the trade union movement has demonstrated that all too often it has not rallied to the support of victims of discrimination, and in fact, has been party to the very discrimination it claims to abhor.

This failure to wage a principled struggle against inequality has left an organizational vacuum that has been filled by independent Black, minority, and women's caucuses throughout U.S. history. Today there are many examples of such forms: the American Federation of Teachers' United Action Caucus, Teamsters For a Democratic Union, Miners for Democracy, the Coalition of Black Trade Unionists, the national Center for Trade Union Action and Democracy, and the Coalition of Labor Union Women. In the building trades, the independent forms include the United Construction Workers Association in Seattle, the United Community Construction Workers in Boston, Fightback in Harlem, and IFUD.

IFUD is a multiracial, rank-and-file group. Our members are journeymen who came through the traditional apprenticeship program, and trainees. The trainee program was instituted as a result of a suit brought by several Blacks charging Local 378 with discrimination. The federal district court ordered the union to establish a trainee program, which existed from 1970 to 1976. It was established specifically to bring Black workers into the trade, but other minorities—Filipino, Japanese, Latino—benefited as well. Barry Luboviski, a white ironworker, played a very large part in recruiting minorities.

Before becoming ironworkers, a few IFUD members were involved in community struggles, the civil rights and student movements and the anti-war (Vietnam) movement, and thus brought with them political consciousness and organizational abilities.

IFUD members were also involved in important affirmative action struggles before IFUD materialized. After the court's consent decree expired, there was no special program for bringing minorities into the trade, so we set out to do our own recruiting. We visited community organizations representing different minorities, displayed our tools and presented a slide show. We explained the qualifications and the nature of various aspects of the trade. In 1978 there was a construction boom in the Bay Area, and the apprenticeship program opened for an unprecedented second time in the same year. At that moment, getting into the trade was on a first-come, first-served basis.

As a result of our recruiting efforts, we brought the first women into the trade, as well as the majority of the people who enlisted in the fall of 1978. "Our" recruits stood in line with other applicants in a driving rain on and off for three days just to sign up!

We established very effective recruiting, but we did not have a support network to address the problems of apprentices, and to prevent the eventual weeding out of most of the minorities and women. To counter the mass exodus, we set up a tutoring program and kept the apprentices informed of their rights.

When the Joint Apprenticeship Training Committee "dropped" a Black woman from the apprenticeship program, we directly challenged the union's program. As the Ironworkers for Union Democracy, we came to the defense of Mosetta Reynolds, a mother of two. We put together a political and legal fightback on the basis of race and sex discrimination, testified in her behalf, and raised money. We won the case! Ms. Reynolds was reinstated and given credit for the time she was out of the program.

Shortly afterward, we sponsored a banquet to honor Brenda Mallory, a Black woman who was the first female to complete the apprenticeship program in Local 378. One hundred thirty ironworkers, friends and supporters came to pay tribute to Ms. Mallory, who received a certificate from the mayor of Oakland, plaques from IFUD and the Coalition of Black Trade Unionists, and flowers. No elected officials from the union attended the event.

IFUD started a rank-and-file newsletter called "The Loadline" to provide a voice for our concerns and reach others, particularly other minorities and those who did not attend meetings regularly. Our purpose was to inform the rank-and-file about issues concerning us all as union members, as ironworkers, and as minorities. This is particularly necessary in a trade like ours where people move frequently from job to job. "The Loadline" carries articles about the apprenticeship program, job stewards, affirmative action, union contracts, health and safety, and the non-union offensive.

The union leadership initially ignored the newsletter. Then followed hostility and outright opposition. In one particular union meeting, the newsletter was Red-baited. A white ironworker stood up and said he had had an experience in New York with a similar newsletter that was supposedly funded by the Ford Foundation and the CIA, of all things.

At one point the business agent called Bill Sorro, a Filipino member of the caucus, and me to discuss the newsletter. He charged that "The Loadline" was divisive and causing dissension within the local. As an alternative to "The Loadline," he suggested that regular meetings be set up to discuss our views. While we recognized the need for dialogue, we did not want it to take place at the expense of the rank-and-file newsletter, which we have always recognized as an independent vehicle for democratic change in our local.

The union printed a newsletter that came out after "The Loadline." It is called, coincidentally, "The Local Line," and has never tried to educate the membership on the importance of

♦♦ YOUNG WORKER ♦♦

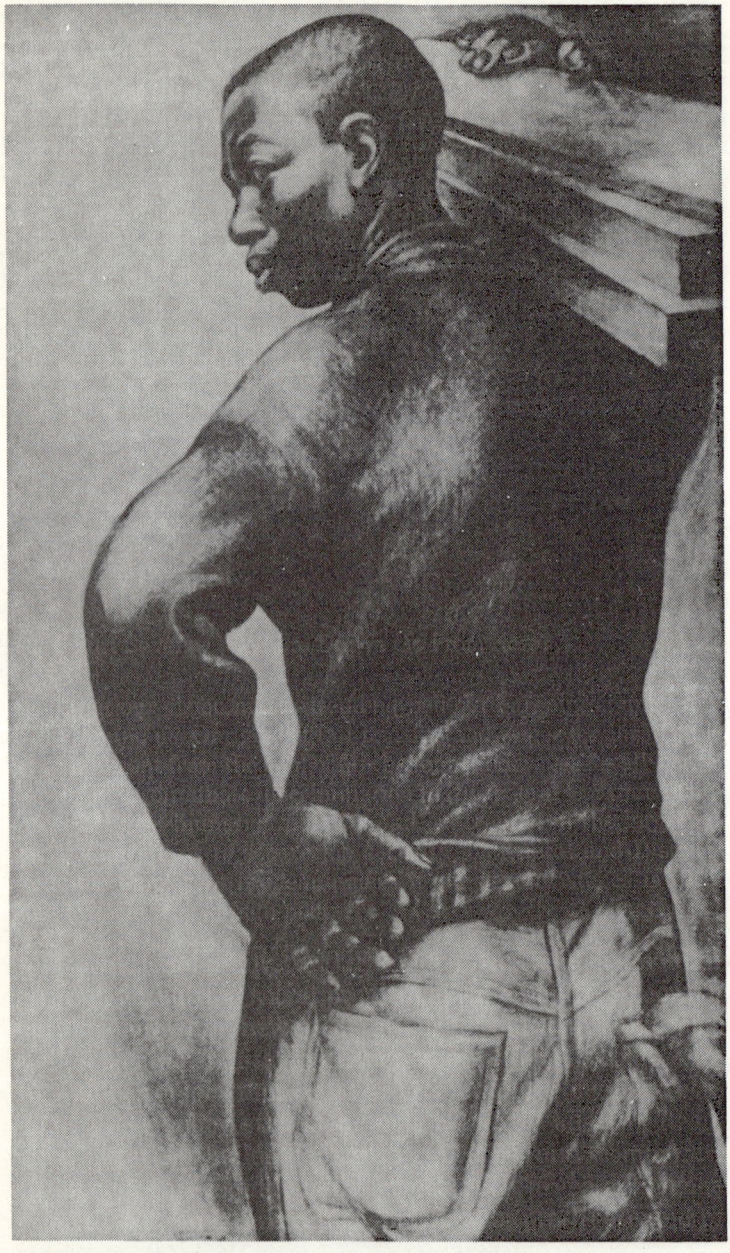

A 1954 image in wolff crayon by Charles White.

♦♦ Credit: Charles White, collection of Dr. R. Martin, courtesy of Heritage Gallery. Print provided by Reinhard Schultz.

affirmative action, nor has it done much to educate the membership on trade unionism.

IFUD has supported residency requirements: those living in the large metropolitan areas, like Oakland, should get a proportional share of the construction jobs. The building trades unions have resisted this because more women and minorities would come into the trades, since the large cities have a high percentage of jobless minorities living where much of the construction takes place.

Local 378 has a dispatch system that is undemocratic and inherently discriminatory. It allows the employer to call 50 percent of new hires by name, which, in practice, usually means that women and minorities and those white ironworkers not in the "clique" will be less likely to be selected.

After IFUD recruited a significant number of minorities, the union took steps to change the process of entering the trade. A motion spearheaded by the leadership passed to strengthen the conservative base of the local by giving retirees the right to vote on all matters.

The union now has an entry process that is exclusive and inherently discriminatory, in contrast to the more democratic system of first-come, first-served. Under the present structure one has to apply to initially get on a list of applicants. Then the applicant must obtain a subscription letter from the employer that guarantees him/her six weeks work in order to get indentured in the trade. Women and minorities do not have access to the employer, who decides who gets into the trade. Even white applicants are victimized by this undemocratic process, because not all have fathers, uncles, cousins, or close friends who, as foremen and superintendents, can be instrumental in securing subscription letters.

As often as not, women and minorities must confront the triad of employers, unions, and federal agencies that are less and less committed to monitoring and enforcing affirmative action.

As a rank-and-file caucus, IFUD has waged the fight to get our union to support affirmative action, but we have not succeeded in getting the local to take positions that go beyond lip service.

Two important affirmative action cases were the focus of our activities in the local—when Allen Bakke attacked affirmative action in education at the University of California at Davis, and Brian Weber led an assault on affirmative action against

Kaiser Aluminum and the United Steel Workers in Gramercy, Louisiana. In both instances, we raised the issue of unity and how in particular the Weber case represented an attack on collective bargaining.

In neither case were we able to persuade the local to defend affirmative action by filing friend of the court briefs when these cases were in the U.S. Supreme Court. Indeed, there was not one building trades local that filed an amicus curae brief in favor of affirmative action.

Since Black workers have come into the trade, our union leadership has done nothing substantive to challenge the racist character of the local. This same leadership has, instead, paternalistically done favors behind the scenes for some minority ironworkers, expressing a reluctance to "antagonize" the white membership.

The building trades unions have been conspicuously absent among organizations opposed to the Reagan administration's dismantling of affirmative action, and thus have not taken a principled position in protecting women and minority trade unionists.

Soapboxing for Affirmative Action

Three very significant, interrelated statements provide a good starting point for discussing affirmative action in the building trades. First: the only time in U.S. history when Black people had full employment was during slavery! Second: there are basically two kinds of employers in regard to women and minorities—those that hire them in menial positions, and those that don't hire them at all. Third: the oldest grievance women and minorities have against the trade union movement is exclusion from employment. These statements lead to a conclusion: organized labor's best hope for turning back the reactionary employer offensive of today lies in the vigorous and principled support for and involvement of women and minorities, the constituency it has traditionally failed to represent. To turn back the rightwing assault against workers, the trade union movement must address the longstanding question of race and sex discrimination. This will bring the unity that is imperative to advance the cause of labor.

WHAT ARE THE FACTS?

Today, after decades of confrontations, demonstrations, hometown plans, consent decrees and executive orders, Black workers still are minimal recipients of the $280 billion a year construction industry, and programs for women have largely benefited white women, who have not played much of a role in opposing the racial discrimination against nonwhite women. Today women in apprenticeship programs in the building trades number less than 2 percent. In 1980, there were fewer Black construction workers than there were Black doctors and lawyers (1980 census). There are more Black accountants, proportionately, than Black carpenters or electrical workers. By 1984, the percentage of Black construction workers had actually decreased (Bureau of Labor Statistics). In Chicago in 1980 60 percent of the contractors doing federal work failed to meet the established minority hiring goals. Nepotism is common in the building trades, and it continues unabated in this period of economic downturn, which historically brings with it an intensification of racism.

Attacks on Affirmative Action

The ideological offensive against affirmative action has focused on four major areas: opposition to quotas, opposition to lowering standards, championing individual merit, and alleged reverse discrimination. Many foes of affirmative action contend the demands of women and minorities are stretching the Constitution beyond reason. They claim these demands run counter to competition, and the idea of rewarding ability and hard work, individual freedom, and responsibility.

Quotas designed to keep people out have been used against women and people of color. We must distinguish between the reprehensible quotas of old, designed to limit access and establish a ceiling on the entry of minorities and women, and today's quotas, which open access and establish a floor. When you agree to goals, you need criteria to measure progress, just as in a car you have a speedometer to measure speed.

Without guidelines in affirmative action, a bleeding heart employer can say, "Well, we did the best we could to hire women and minorities, and now we have moved on to other priorities." Before we accept this kind of statement, we need data indicating that Black unemployment is being significantly reduced, that lily-white and all-male unions and occupations are being integrated, that the differences between male and female and white and minority incomes are being eradicated.

Opponents often charge that affirmative action leads to "lowering standards." The inherent assumption is that oppressed people and women are inferior and less qualified. People are denied opportunities, and then criticized for lack of experience.

When a disproportionate number of young minority men were drafted in the Vietnam War, they were given on-the-job training to teach them to kill to protect "our" interests in Southeast Asia. In the same war, when the U.S. government faced a manpower shortage, it took steps to rectify the situation. To provide more cannon fodder, the government lowered test standards to allow youth to enter the military despite inferior educations. There was no outcry when standards were lowered so that minority youth could be blown to bits, maimed, wounded and exposed to agent orange!! There are no inferior people, just inferior opportunities.

Opponents of affirmative action say that "individual merit"—one's knowledge, experience, and talent—should be used to determine opportunities.

The bottom line of race and sex discrimination is that it denies decent housing, quality health care, educational opportunities, and employment to its victims. This means that special burdens and obstacles are placed on women and minorities that prevent them from competing, or, when they do compete, require them to do so at an enormous disadvantage. This means that merit has not been fully and fairly employed. In virtually all aspects of society, power in this country has remained white and masculine. Doesn't this mean that those who have had opportunities—in jobs, education, training—have had them without facing competition from women and minorities?

"Reverse discrimination" is the most insidious argument against affirmative action. It asserts that non-whites have received more help than other ethnic groups (Jewish, Polish, German, English, Italian), pitting racial minorities (non-whites) against white ethnic groups.

Many white people in the U.S. ask, "Why don't the minorities be American like the rest of us? My ancestors also had it rough, but we all made it by working hard."

If working hard were the criteria for success in this country, there would probably be a different group of people running it! Minorities have done the hardest, dirtiest, most dangerous and menial work on farms, in factories, and in mines and mills. They have also done much of the hard personal service—taking care of the children, the sick, and the elderly.

In this nation, people often measure the problems and progress of all people of color by the success of European immigrants in adapting to the United States. These immigrants of the 1800s fled their former countries because of economic or political repression, but the color of their skin spared them the treatment as inferiors that was meted out to Black people who came to this country in chains, or other non-whites who became Americans as colonized and conquered peoples. Minorities have not yet become an integrated part of the U.S. culture and political community. The European immigrants who "made it" by working hard forced the non-white workers into lower-paying unskilled jobs. In fact, these white immigrants rose on the backs of non-white people.

Affirmative action is not reverse discrimination. It is a method of accelerating the goal of placing women and minorities in the same position they would have been in if there had been no discrimination. It is similar to an ancient principle of equity, requiring restitution after something has been stolen from someone. Its purpose is not to take away jobs from anyone. It is to ensure that minorities and women get a fair share of the jobs. It is a cure for past discrimination, in the tradition of the 13th, 14th and 15th Amendments to the Constitution after the abolition of slavery.

Affirmative action is based on the same sense of justice as seniority. The seniority system was instituted to end favoritism in hiring, promotions and pay. Affirmative action was instituted to end the favoritism enjoyed by white males in this country.

Some people say that workers who get jobs because of affirmative action will suffer from this "unearned advantage," which could lead to a loss of a sense of self-worth. If this were the case, the mental health field would have millions of white male clients to prescribe for and send to asylums!

White people cannot point to any form of systematic oppression imposed on them because of their race. Affirmative action will not place white males where minorities and women are today economically. It will not place them in a position in which their jobless rate is three times the rate of Black workers; it will not reverse the median incomes ($8,967 Black; $15,401 white in 1984); and it will not impose a disproportionate and genocidal maternal death and infant mortality rate on white women and children.

The trade union movement has always looked down on scabbing. Scabbing can bring a person immediate advantage, but destroys the long- run advantages of solidarity in the union. Gaining an advantage from discrimination is like scabbing. It sacrifices the interests of the entire working class for individual, selfish gains. And I think you will notice that the opponents of affirmative action do not spend their time attacking race and sex discrimination itself. Instead, they come out against the policies and programs that would eradicate such discrimination.

Unions Need Affirmative Action

The labor movement needs affirmative action for many reasons. First of all, discrimination acts to hold down *all* wages, hurting the pocketbooks of all trade unionists. Employers extract extra profits from all non-union workers, and from non-whites and women workers who are non-union in particular. These profits support reactionary policies and conservative candidates. Second, affirmative action unites workers of different races and sexes against company attacks, rather than allowing the employer to split workers along racial, minority group, or sexual lines. In the midst of the rightwing corporate attack on working people, the general needs of white workers can only be met to the extent that the special needs of women and minorities are met simultaneously. Third, affirmative action brings new militance to the labor movement. Minorities and women as a whole have developed a progressive outlook because of the nature and character of their struggles against race and sex discrimination. They have greater insights into the inequalities that exist, and are prepared for active responses.

Fourth, labor needs allies. A multiracial union that includes women is in a better position to establish community ties and political relationships outside of labor, as it takes concrete action to fight racial injustice, diescrimination against women, and other undemocratic practices. For example, building trades unions in the San Francisco Bay Area have been waging a fight against the California Transportation Department (CalTrans). Under the current Republican administration, CalTrans awarded a $43.6 million contract to a non-union contractor from Oregon who established business enterprises allegedly headed by women and minorities which it runs as non-union fronts. The building trades are trying to muster support for their campaign by rightfully accusing CalTrans and R.A. Hatch of discrimination and opposition to affirmative action. But these are the same building trades unions that have long excluded women and minorities, and their campaign has been met with some skepticism.

Fifth, workers need jobs based on affirmative action for our cities. Up till now, construction workers have demanded jobs only for themselves. Today they are confronted with a growing anti-union drive and massive unemployment. They must ask themselves: Where is the most pressing need for housing, mass transit, schools, freeways, hospitals, infrastructure repairs? The answer: the cities where people of color live are in dire need of repair at a time when there is a terrible need for jobs. It seems only natural that the unions and those who live in the cities should work for these common goals.

Sixth, affirmative action can bring millions of workers into the union movement. We must remember that slavery prevented the growth of unions and ask ourselves: Are the unemployed going to be used to strengthen the employer or organized labor? The seventh argument for affirmative action is simply that it is the law, and discrimination can be costly. For example, Local 542 of the Operating Engineers in Philadelphia fought affirmative action in the courts for 11 years before losing in 1982. Its membership had to pay the victims of discrimination $1.5 million.

THE LAW OF AFFIRMATIVE ACTION

♦♦ William J. Brennan, Jr. ♦♦

On March 25, 1987, the U.S. Supreme Court upheld (6-3) the affirmative action plan of Santa Clara County, California in Johnson v. Transportation Agency, Santa Clara County, California. *The opinion clearly stated that minorities and women can benefit from voluntary plans by employers to change the composition of the workplace in industries like construction (referred to by Leonard McNeil) and transportation (referred to in this landmark case). Justice Brennan wrote the Court's opinion.*

We ... hold that the [County Transportation] Agency appropriately took into account as one factor the sex of Diane Joyce in determining that she should be promoted to the road dispatcher position. The decision to do so was made pursuant to an affirmative action plan that represents a moderate, flexible, case-by-case approach to effecting a gradual improvement in the representation of minorities and women in the Agency's work force. Such a plan is fully consistent with Title VII [of the 1964 Civil Rights Act], for it embodies the contribution that voluntary employer action can make in eliminating the vestiges of discrimination in the workplace.

... [In *United Steelworkers v. Weber* (1978) we] upheld the employer's decision to select less senior black applicants over the white respondent, for we found that taking race into account was consistent with Title VII's objective of "breaking down old patterns of racial segregation and hierarchy."

... [Here the] Agency has identified a conspicuous imbalance in job categories traditionally segregated by race and sex. It has made clear from the outset, however, that employment decisions may not be justified solely by reference to this imbalance, but must rest on a multitude of practical, realistic factors. It has therefore committed itself to annual adjustment of goals so as to provide a reasonable guide for actual hiring and promotion decisions.... The Agency has no intention of establishing a work force whose permanent composition is dictated by rigid numerical standards.

... [T]he Agency adopted as a benchmark for measuring progress in eliminating underrepresentation the long-term goal of a work force that mirrored in its major job classifications the percentage of women in the area labor market.... The Plan therefore directed that annual short-term goals be formulated that would provide a more realistic indication of the degree to which sex should be taken into account in filling particular positions. The Plan stressed that such goals "should not be construed as 'quotas' that must be met," but as reasonable aspirations in correcting the imbalance in the Agency's work force... women were most egregiously underrepresented in the Skilled Craft job category, since none of the 238 positions was occupied by a woman.

The Agency's Plan emphasized that the long-term goals were not to be taken as guides for actual hiring decisions, but that supervisors were to consider a host of practical factors in seeking to meet affirmative action objectives, including the fact that in some job categories women were not qualified in numbers comparable to their representation in the labor force.

By contrast, had the Plan simply calculated imbalances in all categories according to the proportion of women in the area labor pool, and then directed that hiring be governed solely by those figures, its validity fairly could be called into question.

91 ⋄⋄ UNITED FARM WORKERS USE THE BOYCOTT

⋄⋄ Suzanne Meehan ⋄⋄

The author prepared this report on the 1984 boycott by the UFW-AFL-CIO for the Center for Labor Research and Education, Institute of Industrial Relations, University of California, Berkeley. She thanked the Rev. Fred Eyster of the National Farmworkers Ministry for a lengthy interview.

"The United Farm Workers and the Grape Boycott" appeared in Labor Center Reporter, No. 132 (November 1984).

Editors' note: The story of the organization of migrant farm workers into the United Farm Workers of America—AFL-CIO is an exciting tale of heroic dimensions that has been told in many books and articles. Here we focus on only one of the unique features of the UFW: its extensive, and frequently successful, use of the consumer boycott as a tactic.

We told the growers and we told the Deukmejian administration that if they shut down the law, we would return to the boycott. Now it's time for us to place our faith in the court of last resort once again—with the grape boycott that symbolized the farm worker's struggle during the 1960s and '70s.

This is how Cesar Chavez, president of the 22-year-old United Farm Workers of America, AFL-CIO, described the union's decision to initiate a new boycott on table grapes. What does Chavez mean by a "shutdown" of the law and to what extent does this shutdown affect grape workers? To answer these questions we must look at some of the legal and historical background of the new grape boycott.

In 1973, the UFW's contracts with grape growers came up for renewal. Instead of signing new contracts with the UFW, several growers signed contracts instead with the International Brotherhood of Teamsters, triggering a jurisdictional dispute between the two unions. The UFW called for a boycott and a strike. The strike was called off when two of its members, Juan de la Cruz and Nagi Daifullah, were killed; de la Cruz was killed on a picket line. The boycott was maintained until 1977.

In 1975, the California legislature passed the Agricultural Labor Relations Act (ALRA), making California's agricultural labor laws unique in the United States. Aside from guaranteeing agricultural workers the right to bargain collectively, one of its most important features was the creation of the Agricultural Labor Relations Board (ALRB), whose function was the enforcement of the ALRA. Among the powers granted to the Board was the power to issue complaints. A person or group may make an unfair labor practice charge to the ALRB and after examining the charge, the Board has the authority to issue a complaint against the party charged. The complaint states the charge and issues notice of a hearing either before the Board or one of its members, or before an agency designated by the Board. The party charged with an unfair labor practice then has the right to file a response to the complaint and to present testimony at the time of the hearing.

The legal recourse of the ALRA and its enforcement agency the ALRB might make it seem that the resort to a consumer boycott is at best unnecessary, and at worst an indication of the union's unwillingness to participate in the usual procedures governing labor/management relations in the U.S. But Chavez and the farm workers claim that this is not the case and that they had no alternative to invoking a boycott. Why?

Since his election as governor of California in 1982, George Deukmejian, in keeping with his conservative politics and his political campaign debt to the growers (90 percent of the growers' campaign contributions went to Deukmejian), has argued that the ALRB is strongly biased toward deciding cases in favor of the UFW. His administration has taken several steps during the last two years to counter this perceived bias. Among them:

♦ In 1982, ALRB's budget was slashed 26 percent, resulting in

a backlog of cases which cannot be processed due to lack of necessary personnel.
- David Stirling, general counsel for the ALRB and a Deukmejian appointee, has consistently moved to centralize the appeals process, causing further backlogs in the system. Stirling has also initiated far-reaching changes in procedure that could result in a substantial decrease in the amount of money a company must pay in back pay to workers who win an unfair labor practice dispute.
- In June 1984, Deukmejian vetoed a $1 million legislative appropriation to hire investigators to help reduce the backlog of more than 1000 cases (*Los Angeles Times* July 12, 1984).
- In the summer of 1984, Deukmejian appointed attorney Jyrl Ann James-Massengale as chair of the ALRB. James-Massengale has represented growers in several disputes before the ALRB.

According to Chavez, these actions have gutted the laws which previously protected farm workers. The ALRB's failure to enforce the law has resulted in claims by the UFW that 36,000 workers who have voted by secret ballot to be represented by the UFW have not yet been able to sign contracts with growers, and that 6,300 farm workers owed over $72 million in back pay by growers have yet to receive that money. The union estimates that while the number of uninvestigated charges has more than doubled under the Deukmejian administration, the number of complaints going to growers has been cut by more than half. These figures refer to all farm workers and not specifically to grape workers, but the figures for the grape workers are no better. According to Arturo Rodriguez, general manager of the Grape and Tree Fruit Division of the UFW, approximately 400 unfair labor practice charges filed by grape workers in the last three years have yet to go to the ALRB complaint stage. Another 46 cases, involving $32 million in back pay and benefits, which are at various stages of the legal process, show no signs of being resolved within any reasonable length of time.

A New Kind of Boycott

The new table grape boycott will be based on a strategy that the UFW has developed in a long and bitter struggle it has been waging against the Salinas-based Bruce Church, Inc., the nation's second-largest lettuce grower. In 1977 the UFW was certified as the bargaining agent for the employees at Bruce Church. In 1979, the employees at Bruce Church went out on strike and the UFW initiated a boycott against Church's brand-name lettuce, Red Coach; contract negotiations broke down for the last time in 1980. After declaring the boycott against Church, the UFW organized boycott action against Lucky Stores, Inc., one of the largest retail food chains in the U.S., and a major purchaser of Bruce Church lettuce.

The UFW's tactics in the boycott against Bruce Church represent something of a departure from those used in the first grape boycott. The union has established a Direct Marketing Department, which uses sophisticated mass marketing techniques to target households in areas close to chain stores such as Lucky's that carry Red Coach brand lettuce. These households receive repeated mailings from the union which introduce the union, explain the boycott, and appeal for support. One of the union's strategies is to attempt to counteract "the bad image of the union that growers and their allies have tried to create in the minds of farm workers and the general public."

On December 12, 1983, the ALRB ruled that Bruce Church was guilty of bargaining in bad faith with the union, a ruling that could result in substantial back-pay awards to the unionized farm workers employed by Bruce Church. In January 1984, Lucky Stores notified Church that it would no longer buy Bruce Church lettuce. While Lucky's claimed that its decision to stop purchasing Church's lettuce was due to the ruling by the ALRB, this decision was surprising to food industry officials. One official, quoted in the *Los Angeles Times* on 1/14/84, said, "I cannot figure it out. Most employers believe the state agency is run by pro-union appointees of former governor Jerry Brown, and for Lucky's to drop Bruce Church because of that board's ruling against Church is amazing." This would seem to indicate that Lucky's, financially hurt by the boycott, used the ALRB ruling as an excuse to discontinue its purchase of Red Coach lettuce. More recently, McDonald's fast food chain announced it had stopped buying the shredded lettuce used on its hamburgers from Freshcon U Vegetable Processing Co., the sister company of Bruce Church, Inc. While McDonald's claimed that the move was purely a "business decision," Roberto de la Cruz, a UFW lobbyist in Sacramento, said that some McDonald restaurants had in fact been boycotted. It seems possible that McDonald's "business decision" was motivated by its fear of jeopardizing its reputation and volume of business by becoming a target of a UFW boycott similar to the one against Lucky's.

While the boycott against Bruce Church has not yet been won by the UFW, the decisions made by Lucky's and McDonald's indicate that the new strategy, which will now be used for table grapes, shows much promise. However, it is important to remember that the ultimate success of any boycott lies with us, in our roles as consumers; we are the judge and jury in this "court of last resort" and our verdict will be rendered by the decisions we make in the grocery store. It seems only logical that people who would not cross a picket line would not violate a union boycott.

92 ·· IS THERE LIFE AFTER THE MILL CLOSES DOWN?

♦♦ The Editors ♦♦

In 1982 Bethlehem Steel closed its plant just southeast of downtown Los Angeles in an area already suffering from high unemployment.

This crisis led Steelworkers Oldtimers Foundation, established in 1964, to work with the L.A. County Federation of Labor and community members to develop the Coordinated Community Food Bank & Emergency Services Program and the Steelworkers Welfare Action Unemployed Council. Based at United Steelworkers Local 1845, this project provides monthly grocery distribution, hot lunches, rent and mortgage assistance and counseling services for the unemployed and their families in Huntingdon Park, Bell, and Maywood. (Healthcare benefits for most workers were simply terminated when the mill shut down.)

"When I learned of George Cole's vision of a community center that would meet the practical needs of the unemployed," said Susan Franklin Tanner, "it struck me that, as so often happens, the cultural needs of the community were being overlooked. Culture is rarely seen as fundamental to human survival. Yet, as an artist, I know it is not a frill, but rather a necessity." Tanner turned this knowledge into the Theatre-Worker's Project, which provides theatre and writing and workshops for children, teens and adults taught by professional actors, directors and writers. It brings professional theatre performances into the community and takes community members to see performances at major Los Angeles theatres.

TheatreWorker's Project is funded in part by the California Arts Council, a state agency, and the National Endowment for the Arts, a federal agency, and is sponsored by the Steelworkers Oldtimers Foundation, George Cole, program director.

END OF AN ERA

♦♦ "Franco" Curtis ♦♦

The following poem was written by "Franco" Curtis, who worked in the 10 Inch Mill at Bethlehem Steel near Los Angeles for two years, before the plant closed. He is a member of USWA Local 1845 and the TheatreWorker's Project. © by TheatreWorker's Project, Susan Franklin Tanner, director. All rights reserved. (And see "Burial of Old Beth" by Lloyd R. Andres in section 6.)

They didn't like us
because our fathers worked
        in jobs not respected.
Our mothers lived
        in small houses.
We did not have
        our own bedrooms.
We responded by
        rebelling,
        using drugs,
        stealing,
Fighting in a whole
        of an outcast
        collective.
We matured
        in San Quentin.
We did not mature
        in death
        by a bullet,
        an overdose.
We matured
        in factories
        of chemicals
        heating steelpipes
        standing over large
        vats of molten lead.

Working in mills
>of molten steel
>in the boring
>assembly lines
Installing back seats
>in an automobile
>we could not buy,
>installing permanent
>injury to our backs.
Trying to raise
>a family
>that's future would be different
Only to find
>that the factories
>and mills would close
>and
Our children were
>in competition
>with those who
Did not like us
because our fathers worked
>in jobs
>not respected.

♦♦THEATREWORKER'S PROJECT♦♦

Singer Bruce Springsteen, who contributed $10,000 in the fall of 1984 to the food bank for unemployed workers based at United Steelworkers Local 1845 in the Los Angeles area, joins Director Susan Franklin Tanner and members of the union's Theatre-Worker's Project for this group photograph. Springsteen participated in a poetry workshop with the unemployed steelworkers.

♦♦ Credit: Jim Kottra.

93 ◆◆ PRESSMAN'S BLUES

◆◆ Jim Ginger ◆◆

Jim Ginger is a journeyman pressman and member of the Executive Board of Graphic Communications Union Local 388 in Oakland, California. He wrote this poem while serving out his apprenticeship.
  © 1987 by James F. Ginger

I got the blues this mornin.
I got the black red yellow & cyan blues
'Cause I'm a printing pressman
& every day I pay my dues.

I'm a 4 color printer.
Print post cards & travel brochures
I print lots of pretty pictures
Of my favorite places & yours.

From San Francisco to Yellowstone,
New Mexico & Grand Teton,
From London to Hawaii,
Florida to New York City,

All the places I used to go
Before I started printing.

I got the blues this afternoon
I got the red yellow black & cyan blues,
Cause I ain't had a real vacation
Since I put on my workin shoes.

I finally got apprenticed
After seven long years in the trade
I knew I'd be a pressman
I thought I had it made.

Then the foreman came to see me
Said "I found you a real nice spot.
There's an opening on the night shift.
Do you think you can fill the slot?"

That was 3 years ago come May Day—
& I've seen many a pay day
But at midnight when I'm workin late My lovers just keep slippin away.

I got the blues this evenin
I got the all-night printing blues
Printing blue skies & sunsets
While outside looms the moon.

They put us on overtime
We start at five in the afternoon
We're done at 4 in the morning
Which is either too late or too soon.

Because the whole damn town is sleepin
There's not a thing to be done
Tho' I'm still wired from workin
I sit quietly til the dawn.

Force myself to roll over
Cover my head to keep out the sun
Sleep right on thru the mornin
Til the middle of the afternoon.

Wake up with leg cramps
Sore feet & an aching back
With just time to read the paper
Before I'm back on the printing track.

I get the blues at midnight
I get the red yellow black & cyan blues
Cause my press just won't run right
& it's no longer even news.

I got static in my paper
Can't get a sheet through the press
By the time I get it going
Lord but the color's a mess.

& then somethin starts to squeakin
I can't find it yet
My press's steady drumming
Interrupted by a jazz clarinet.

When I finally find that bearing
I get it nice & wet
Then I'm printing oil spots
Have to stop the press.

When I get it started up again
The register is shot
My screens are turning solid
I can't hardly find a dot.

Inks have gotten tacky
I was down too long
So I add some water to the plates
Try to get the color back where it belongs.

Then a sheet runs through sideways
Smashes all 4 blankets
Balls up the delivery
But I didn't even notice
Cause I was adding ink.

Then I see I'm marking
Both sides of the sheet
Smearing up the printing
From Waikiki through Wall Street.

I shut down & look around
Scrub the transfer cylinder
About to start back up again
When I see a sheet of paper wrapped around a form roller.

I got the blues
I got the red yellow black & cyan blues
I got paper in the rollers
& it's 20 after 2.

I got static in my paper
Water's turning alkali
Plates are getting sensitive
The ink's starting to emulsify.

This song goes on forever
It just don't never stop
If it ain't one thing it's another
You just keep printing til you drop.

94 ♦♦ WOMEN AND UNIONS: TODAY AND TOMORROW

UNION WOMEN

♦♦ Carolyn J. Jacobson ♦♦

Carolyn J. Jacobson is managing editor of the Bakery, Confectionery & Tobacco Workers News *and is also president of the International Communications Association. Emilie Stoltzfus assisted her on the article, "Women at Work," published in* The AFL-CIO Federationist, *April 5, 1986, from which the following material was excerpted.*

Today, two of every five union members is a woman. More than 7 million women belong to unions, compared with 4 million a decade ago.

Women are beginning to emerge in leadership positions in the labor movement, but not yet in proportion to their numbers in the workforce. They do fill high level staff positions in the AFL-CIO, as well as in affiliate unions. Leading women include Joyce Miller, president of the Coalition of Labor Union Women and a vice president of the Clothing & Textile Workers, and Barbara Hutchinson, a vice president of the Government Employees. Both serve as AFL-CIO vice presidents. Women are also top-level assistants to both AFL-CIO president Lane Kirkland and secretary-treasurer Thomas R. Donahue. Women presidents of affiliated unions include Linda Puchala of the Flight Attendants, Colleen Dewhurst of Actors' Equity and Patty Duke of the Screen Actors. The nation's largest local union is also headed by a woman—Sandra Feldman, president of the 85,000-members Teachers Local 2 in New York City, and Betty Tianti was installed as president of the Connecticut AFL-CIO last fall.

With the gains in female membership, union officials have become more sensitive to women's concerns, CLUW president Joyce Miller points out; male union leaders recognize "that there is a potential for organizing women."

In their 1985 paper "Union Maids: Unions and the Female Work Force," Richard B. Freeman and Jonathan S. Leonard noted that the biggest organizing gains in women workers have been in the public sector and white-collar occupations. From 1973 to 1983, "the proportion of females organized in the public sector more than doubled to attain near equality with the proportion of males." In the private sector during the same period, the decline in proportion of unionized women was less than among men. The study also found that "women are as organized as men among white-collar workers, but are less organized than men among blue-collar workers. Because of female concentration in white-collar jobs, however, women constitute 58 percent of white-collar unionists."

An AFL-CIO survey of more than 200 recent representation elections conducted by the National Labor Relations Board found that unions won 50 percent of the elections in which women made up 75 percent of the bargaining unit but only two-fifths of the elections in which fewer than half the workers were women. A Bureau of Labor Statistics survey showed that in 1985 women workers under union contract had median weekly earnings of $347, compared with only $262 for nonunion women. Union pay scales for women even topped the rates of nonunion male workers, whose median weekly earnings were $315 last year. The male-female wage differential was about the same for union and nonunion workers.

The Freeman-Leonard study indicates that unions have brought marked gains for women in white-collar jobs. They also have done better for women in the public sector than in the private sector, particularly in blue-collar jobs. Women's blue-collar jobs predominate in the lower-paying apparel and garment industry, while blue-collar men are chiefly employed in the traditionally higher-paid auto and steel industries. In 1984, 80 percent of the women in the workforce filled 20 percent of the Labor Department's 427 job classifications. The most common occupations for women were in expanding, low-paying dead-end jobs—secretarial, bookkeeping, nursing and cashier work. Thus, despite collectively bargained contracts, unions have made limited progress in altering institutionalized wage differentials.

A New Approach

In organizing campaigns, unions are aware that bread-and-butter issues may not always be a strong enough motivating force for women in certain white-collar sectors. Some white-collar, professional and technical workers place improvement in the scope and content of their jobs ahead of improvement in wages, benefits and working conditions. "They want more participation in decision-making," observed Anne Nelson, director of the Institute for Women and Work at Cornell University. Organizers now emphasize these issues and employ new and creative techniques appropriate to the particular bargaining unit. The AFL-CIO's recent report on "The Changing Situation of Workers and Their Unions" acknowledges this point and encourages organizers to devote more resources to this challenge.

Recent successful organizing campaigns involving large numbers of women illustrate this different approach.

* The SEIU District 925 organizing campaign and fight for a first contract at the Syracuse, N.Y., office of the Equitable Life Assurance Society is one example. The battle centered on issues involving new office technology. The union won substantial protections in the area of health, including breaks during the day from work at video terminals and periodic safety checks of the machines.
* The use of new organizing techniques also came into play at the Yale University campaign for clerical and technical workers. The organizing victory led to the negotiation of a first contract in January 1985 by the Hotel & Restaurant Employees. The 2,600-member unit, predominantly female, was solidified by a three-year drive, culminating in a 10-week strike that focused attention on the low-level wages in historically female-dominated jobs.
* AFSCME has organized large numbers of female employees by stressing the need to correct wage and benefit disparity in predominantly female classifications.
* The Hospital & Health Care Employees are for the first time

mobilizing to organize women who work in private homes and do not meet each other, nor report to a central location.
- Since early 1983, a union coalition of the SEIU, Food & Commercial Workers and the Food & Allied Service Trades Department has been conducting a nationwide drive at the Beverly Enterprise nursing home chain. Employees at these facilities are mostly women. In early 1985, the union victory rate was 70 percent.

But labor's foes have not been idle. In recent years, "unionbusters" have developed specialized strategies appealing to women to keep unions out of the workplace. Unions are finding that in some cases women entrants to the labor force are difficult to organize because they feel grateful just for having a job. Another roadblock to organizing is the large number of part-time workers. One of every four women in the labor force works part time.

Some Statistics

Although more than 50 percent of all women work outside the home, only 13.2 percent of those in full- or part-time jobs were union members in 1985. In 1977, 15.7 percent were union members. Comparable figures for male workers showed a drop from 29.6 percent in 1977 to 22.1 percent in 1985. Even so, the proportion of male workers in unions has not kept pace with the proportion of female workers in unions. The female proportion of union members increased from 19 percent in 1956 to 41 percent in 1983, according to the Freeman-Leonard study.

Women are entering the workplace in record numbers. Even so, the fastest growing place for women is in the ranks of the poor. Today, they face many of the same challenges that confronted women who entered the workforce a decade ago: the continuing struggle for pay equity, finding work in jobs traditionally filled by males, guaranteeing job safety, and balancing home obligations with work.

The notion that women work for "pin money" is a myth. The fact that women remain in the workforce for an average of 34 years and typically hold full-time jobs should convince skeptics that most women workers aren't temporary employees. The number of families maintained by women grew more than 84 percent between 1970 and 1984. In March 1984, 10.3 million families—16 percent of all U.S. households—had as their principal support women who were divorced, separated, widowed or never married. The single female heads of households have higher unemployment, lower education attainment, more dependent children and lower earnings than other labor force groups.

Last year, government statistics showed that 13 million women, of whom 4.2 million are non-white, were living in poverty. The number of poor people in families headed by women jumped by 25 percent in the past four years.

Because women comprise three-fourths of the elderly poor in the United States, deep Reagan cuts in food stamps and Medicare are particularly hard on those who are old and female.

In 1984 more than three out of five women maintaining families had children under 18. Reagan has consistently sought to require all recipients of Aid for Families with Dependent Children to seek employment. At the same time, he has seriously hampered their ability to work by cutting funds for inexpensive child care and for job training.

Coalition of Labor Union Women

The Coalition of Labor Union Women was founded in 1974 to seek affirmative action in the workplace, to strengthen the role of women within their unions, to encourage political and legislative activities and to organize unorganized women. CLUW has grown from 10 chapters and 5,000 members in 1974 to 75 chapters and more than 18,000 members in 1985.

Although increasing numbers of women hold union office, many still are in lower level positions due to discrimination, lack of training and encouragement and a lack of a substantive agenda to give them a stronger voice in the labor movement. CLUW works to assist women in gaining skills to move up in their unions.

CLUW's Center for Education and Research is undertaking the Future of Work Project and the Collective Bargaining Clearinghouse & Monitoring Project. CLUW's goal is to bring together representatives of the labor movement, women's organizations, civil rights organizations and public policy decision-makers to develop research and education policies and strategies that will address these concerns. The project will document collective bargaining progress in four major areas: pay equity and wage parity; job access, training, promotion and upgrading jobs; child and dependent care programs that assist working parents in coping with work and family responsibilities; and policies to correct the adverse effects of automation on women's job skills, pay, promotional opportunities and health. CLUW publications on these and other issues are used widely.

Organized labor has long been a leading force in the fight for women's rights in the legislative arena. It actively lobbied for the 1963 Equal Pay Act and the 1964 Civil Rights Act, milestones in the continuing fight for equal rights. A coalition of union and women's groups spurred passage of the Pregnancy Disability Act in 1978 after the Supreme Court ruled that discrimination because of pregnancy did not amount to sex bias. Two major victories for women in the 98th Congress—expansion of pension rights for women and improved enforcement of child support obligations—had the strong backing of organized labor.

CLUW TAKES ITS STANDS

♦♦ The Editors ♦♦

The following is based on articles in the AFL-CIO News, *for November 15, 1986, and in the* WREE-View, *for November/December, 1986.*

Over a thousand women delegates focused on work and family issues at the fourth biennial CLUW convention in St. Louis in 1986. The union members represented women assembly line workers and telephone operators, teachers and airline stewardesses, childcare workers and nurses' aides, computer operators and secretaries, farm workers and miners, truck drivers and garment workers.

The convention passed 30 resolutions on workplace, national and international issues.

On workplace issues:

♦ National health care
♦ Workplace safety and no industrial homework
♦ Affirmative action and pay equity
♦ Ending sex-based discrimination and sexual harassment
♦ Affordable child care and parental leave

On international issues:

♦ Opposing spending for the Strategic Defense Initiative ("Star Wars")

- Opposing U.S. interference in Central America
- Opposing apartheid in South Africa

On national and solidarity issues:

- Supporting the Hayes Quality of Life Action Act [*see section 97*]
- Supporting locked out USX steelworkers, 5,000 striking TWA stewardesses, and United Farm Workers grape boycott [*see section 91*]

Work and Family

The time-consuming and costly task of child care has traditionally fallen to women. As more of them enter the workforce, the need for accessible and inexpensive child care has become increasingly apparent. In 1984, the House Select Committee on Children, Youth & Families reported that almost half of all children under six had mothers who worked. The Women's Bureau reported that six of every 10 women—or about 19.5 million—with children under age 18 were in the labor force in 1984. Furthermore, almost 70 percent of all married women workers with children at home are employed full time. Despite the obvious need, the United States remains the only industrialized country in the world without a national child care policy. Congress adopted comprehensive child care legislation in 1971 but it was vetoed by President Nixon.

The limited progress made in securing child care can be attributed to unions and collective bargaining. The management-oriented Conference Board reported that only 1,800 of the nation's six million employers provide child care. Those that do tend to be large, high-tech corporations, banks, insurance companies and hospitals. Unfortunately, women predominate in occupations that are most resistant to employee benefits, including all child care, according to the Congressional Caucus on Women's Issues.

For the few employers who provide child care programs, the advantages include decreased absenteeism and employee turnover, heightened morale and motivation, and increased ability to attract employees. *Business Week* noted that "the outlay for child care is more than offset by the savings from higher productivity and less turnover."

EMPLOYER IN-KIND DONATIONS

Recognizing the needs of workers for adequate child care and the Employer's limited ability to fund a child care facility, the Employer agrees to provide any or all of the following to any child care center providing services to 10 or more children of its employees:

1. All necessary furniture and equipment for the child care facility.
2. Professional and consulting services to the child care facility including legal service, accounting, personnel support and insurance advice and protection.
3. Use of a section of the employee cafeteria at mealtime by the childcare facility.
4. Use of the employee medical facility in case of illness of a child or a staff member of the childcare facility.

The Employer also agrees to finance a training program annually, available at no cost, to any family day care provider serving at least one child of an employee.

♦♦Proposed contract language
NY/CLU Child Care Committee
"Bargaining for Child Care"

The federal government's example to employers is unimpressive. More than 23 million children in the United States require day or after-school care. In 1982 there were federally-supported day care slots for only 500,000 children—a number insufficient to cover the needs of parents in New York City alone. Federal funding under the Social Security Act that provides primary support for state child care programs has been reduced in the Reagan administration, and the Dependent Care Tax Credit only helped those in the middle-income bracket.

The Pregnancy Disability Act of 1978, which gave pregnant workers the right to claim disability benefits offered by their employers, represented a significant gain for working mothers. But the act is limited to employers who already provide sick or disability leave benefits. Legislation requiring all employers to provide disability and parental leave for birth, sickness of a child, and adoption has been introduced in the House, but the proposed legislation falls far short of international standards.

Alternative work patterns such as flex-time and job sharing are being used by some working parents to ease child care problems. Other work arrangements include compressed and shortened workweeks, staggered hours, rotating shifts, work pauses, creative leave clauses, voucher plans, paid sabbatical and extended parental leaves.

The best way to achieve adequate, affordable and accessible child care for all Americans is through legislation, which organized labor continues to support. However, prospects for its enactment in the near future are dim. Therefore, it's up to unions to pursue innovative strategies within and beyond the collective bargaining process to attain needed child care services. The Ladies Garment Workers developed a jointly-funded child care center in New York with employers contributing $32 of the $82 weekly cost for each child and the Agency for Child Development subsidizing 50 percent of the operating cost.

WOMEN'S BILL OF RIGHTS

Women for Racial and Economic Equality (WREE), a national membership organization based in New York City, drafted this bill to rally people around the key issues that are basic to guarantee economic independence and social equality for women. WREE's "ultimate aim is to see all of these rights made the law and enforced."

1. The right to live in peace means nuclear disarmament, nonintervention by the U.S. in other countries, and an end to militarization of our economy and society.

2. The right to live in a peace-oriented society, redirecting the military budget to a budget for human needs and converting military production to civilian productions.

3. The right to employment at a living wage, including affirmative action to end discrimination, equal pay for equal or comparable work; paid parental leave and safe working conditions.

4. The right to organize without interference into trade

unions to enable the labor movement to represent the interest of all workers.

5. The right to a decent standard of living through Social Security benefits, pensions and a guaranteed income.

6. The right of every child to nurturing and full development including federally funded, nonracist, nonsexist childcare and public education from preschool through college.

7. The right to a federally funded national health care system, based on preventive medicine to include pre- and postnatal care, geriatrics, and industrial medicine.

8. The right to reproductive freedom including federally funded birth control and abortion upon demand, sex education, and an end to experimentation and sterilization abuse.

9. The right to live in decent affordable housing including government-funded construction and subsidies.

10. The right to a safe environment, free from toxic wastes and industrial pollution.

11. The right to a culture that reflects our multinational history and multilingual character and to a society free from racist and sexist violence and degrading images of women.

12. The right to participate fully in the democratic process guaranteed by the Constitution, especially the right to vote.

♦♦**Women for Racial and Economic Equality**
from the Nov/Dec 1986 issue of WREE-View

95 ⋄⋄ THE NEED FOR PEACE IS REVITALIZING U.S. LABOR

⋄⋄Benjamin Riskin⋄⋄

Benjamin Riskin is a veteran labor journalist and union activist who is, in his own words, proudest of "helping to win the 'portal to portal' decision establishing the 8-hour day for all underground miners in the U.S."

By early 1985, a majority of organized workers in the largest unions in our nation constituted a substantial part of an increasingly powerful movement. Linked through multiple coalitions, the movement has united people from labor, church, civil rights, women's, senior citizens, political action, and peace groups.

The possibilities that flow from these changes hold profound implications for our entire nation. They are based on two facts. One is the pervasive and well-grounded fear of nuclear annihilation arising from Reagan's policies of nuclear buildup and confrontation. The other is the disastrous impact of the military buildup on employment and wages, especially in the basic mass production industries. This military spending supports the expansionist policies of the transnational corporations and deepens the structural problems they have created for U.S. industry. These two factors have combined to produce a new and widening involvement in foreign affairs by the labor movement, the forging of greater links between organized labor here and labor movements abroad, and new independent participation in political action locally and nationally that hold exciting prospects for the future.

So widespread was labor support for eliminating the horrible threat of nuclear destruction that the top leadership of the AFL-CIO had to amend its hard-line resolution on "national defense" at its 15th Constitutional Convention, in Hollywood, California, in October, 1983 to read:

Among our membership, as in our society, a majority favor a verifiable bilateral nuclear freeze. Others are skeptical. But we are united in our conviction that the nuclear arms race must be halted and reversed, with radical reductions in the warhead stockpiles on both sides being the objective of arms control negotiations so that the nuclear balance, and thus deterrence, can be secured at much lower levels of potential destruction.

Though by no means a model peace resolution, it recognized that the majority of the members of the labor movement, as well as the majority of all people in the U.S., favor a nuclear freeze. More, it emboldened the newly-discovered majority to press for throwing the full weight of the labor movement on the side of peace.

At the Feb. 19, 1985 sessions of the AFL-CIO Executive Council, at Bal Harbour, Florida, this new majority sentiment was taken a step further. While the top leadership adopted a statement noting its past "longstanding support for a strong national defense," it blasted the Reagan Administration for insisting on "cutting taxes, especially for the wealthy, thereby shifting a greater burden for defense on working Americans." Charging the Reagan Administration with "boosting defense spending at the expense of social programs," the AFL-CIO Executive Council served notice: "We will therefore not support increased defense spending at the expense of programs that are vital to our domestic welfare."

This marked the first time the AFL-CIO withheld unqualified support for military budgets.

These changes in the AFL-CIO's official positions reflect the developing strength and activities of peace groups in the unions at both a national and community level. For example, 25 New York unions worked on the preparations for the June 12, 1982 Rally for a Nuclear Freeze and Disarmament in New York City. Many union officials were part of the steering committee to coordinate labor participation: Jacob Sheinkman, secretary-treasurer of the Amalgamated Clothing and Textile

♦♦LABOR MARCHES FOR PEACE♦♦

The ILWU contingent marches in the massive 1968 Mobilization against the Vietnam War in San Francisco.
♦♦Credit: Harvey Richards.

Workers; Victor Gottbaum, executive director of AFSCME District Council 37, the largest union in the Big Apple; and the top leaders of the Communications Workers, Machinists, District 65 UAW, Storeworkers, Teamsters, Food and Commercial Workers, Hospital Workers District 1199, Ironworkers, Nurses, the Coalition of Labor Union Women, and the Coalition of Black Trade Unionists.

They helped bring out one million demonstrators!

Out of this developed a New York Area Trade Union Committee on War, Nuclear Destruction and Military Spending, with leaders from Transport, Clothing, Fur, Public Workers, Storeworkers, and CLUW. In Baltimore, Maryland, leading trade unionists formed a Labor Task Force of the Maryland Campaign for a Nuclear Weapons Freeze consisting of the major labor organizations in that area—AFSCME, Steel, Teachers, Food & Commercial Workers, Hospital, Machinists, Furniture, and Garment. In Chicago, the Packinghouse Workers of UF & CW passed a resolution applauding their International Executive Board's endorsement of the call for an immediate U.S.-U.S.S.R. mutual freeze. Similar action was taken by United Steelworkers Local 1256, in Duquesne, Pennsylvania; by the Bucks County Council (AFL-CIO); the Ohio State Council of Machinists; by the International Brotherhood of Electrical Workers Local 1076 in Ohio. The Southern California Unions for Peace produced 77 local union endorsements and obtained 308,000 signatures calling for a pro-freeze proposition on the state ballot. By early 1985, 22 international unions and two national labor coalitions had endorsed the call for a U.S.-Soviet freeze, including most of the largest unions in our nation in the AFL-CIO and unaffiliated.

The Pennsylvania AFL-CIO 25th Constitutional Convention unanimously adopted four resolutions for Jobs With Peace, and launched a petition campaign to place a Jobs With Peace resolution on the November, 1984 ballot. In local elections, the Jobs With Peace resolution won in Los Angeles, Erie, Pennsylvania, and Racine, Wisconsin. It lost by a narrow margin in Mendicino, California.

Labor Joins National Mobilizations

For the April 20, 1985 Washington demonstration for Jobs, Peace and Justice, broad labor participation was developed in every section of the nation. It became necessary to plan companion demonstrations in San Francisco, Miami, Houston, Los Angeles and Seattle. Chicago's April Action coalition represented almost 200 groups. In Cleveland, more than 30 union locals worked with the Peace Action Coalition of North East Ohio, with the USWA and UAW playing leading roles in organizing the rally, while in Houston, the action was endorsed by the president of the Galveston County AFL-CIO, CLUW, and the Texas State Employees Union chapter, among others.

By 1987, labor sponsors of the annual Peace, Jobs and Justice Mobilization had expanded to include:

- Gerald W. McEntee, president of the American Federation of State County & Municipal Employees (AFSCME), AFL-CIO, with more than one million members;
- Mary Hatwood-Futrell, president of the National Education Association, unaffiliated, with 1,700,000 members;
- William Wynn, president of the United Food and Commercial Workers, AFL-CIO, with more than one million members;
- The largest union in war industry, the International Association of Machinists (IAM), whose president, William Winpisinger, co-chairs Committee for a Sane Future with Professor Seymour Melman;
- The 1987 list of sponsors continues with 18 national presidents: Kenneth T. Blaylock of the Government Workers; Frank D. Martino, Chemical Workers; Henry Nicholas, Hospital and Health Care Employees; Owen Bieber, Auto Workers; Bernard Butsavage, Molders; James J. Norton, Graphic Communications Workers; John J. Sweeney, Service Employees; Charles A. Perlik, Newspaper Guild; Cesar Chavez, Farm Workers; Morton Bahr, Communication Workers; Keith W. Johnson, Woodworkers; Joseph Misbrener, Oil, Chemical and Atomic Workers; James M. Kane, UE; William H. Bywater, IUE; James Herman, ILWU; David Livingston, District 65, UAW; as well as secretary-treasurers Cleveland Robinson, of District 65, and Jack Sheinkman of ACTWU, and the Coalition of Labor Union Women, and the Coalition of Black Trade Unionists. The April 25, 1987 march specifically opposed U.S. foreign policy in central America, apartheid in South Africa, and nuclear weapons.

Numerous unions are intertwined with broader coalitions of peace organizations on national and local levels. UFCW president William E. Wynn, is on the Board of Advisors of the Center for Defense Information, headed by Rear Admiral Gene R. La Roque, U.S. Navy (retired), an outstanding figure in the fight for peace. The independent Teamsters, and the AFL-CIO Building Trades are part of the myriad of area coalitions in New York, Philadelphia, Chicago, and California. The ILWU and UE work for peace side by side with IUE and other AFL-CIO unions whose predecessors voted to expel them from the CIO in the old McCarthy days of 1949. Gone are the days of labor blacklisting labor!

THE NEED TO BUILD COALITIONS

At the Convention of the Coalition of Black Trade Unionists in Cincinnati in 1984, Marc Stepp spoke as international vice-president of the UAW and Executive Board member of CBTU. Stepp began by describing the New Deal coalition that organized mass production industries and created the movement for progressive social legislation despite the depression of the '30s, and concluded:

> Now, as then, we are going to have to build coalitions with many different organizations, including other unions, community groups, socialists and Communists.... We need to unite on the ideas that are brought to the table.

International Solidarity

Many unions that started working on the central issue of the need for peace to guarantee survival are moving on to develop labor coalitions for solidarity with workers' struggles abroad. This movement arose from the growing consciousness that the structural breakdown of U.S. capitalism has left millions of workers with no hope for jobs, facing complete impoverishment, unless labor and its allies are able to change national priorities through a program of conversion from war production to production to meet the people's needs.

It has become clear also that the impoverished, unorganized, low-wage workers of Puerto Rico, the Caribbean basin, the Far East countries, and of all the underdeveloped countries of Asia, Africa and South America are equally victims of the transnationals, the most powerful being U.S. transnationals, architects of our own domestic economic crisis. Many U.S. workers come from these regions, and many are recent immigrants. Their international ties are strong and they are teaching the meaning of international solidarity to many native-born workers.

One result of this new awareness was the formation of the National Labor Committee in support of Human Rights and Democracy in El Salvador by the presidents of 24 national U.S. unions with local support. This committee issued "The Search for Peace in Central America"—a devastating expose of the terrorism and repression against the labor movement and people of El Salvador. Precisely when President Duarte of El Salvador was in Washington visting the AFL-CIO top leaders, and also meeting with Reagan, representatives of the National Labor Committee were testifying before Congress on the firsthand, eye-witness observations of their factfinding delegations in February 1985.

Labor Against Apartheid

When the picketing and arrests started in December, 1984 at the South African consulates throughout our nation demanding the freeing of jailed South African Black trade union leaders, among other issues, labor leaders from the national AFL-CIO office, heads of international unions, and local union officials—all rushed to the picket lines in solidarity. At the same time, in November 1984, members of ILWU Local 10 in San Francisco refused to unload ships with South African cargo, a dramatic example of international labor solidarity. Their job action sparked the grassroots movement.

Twenty-one major unions formed a Labor Committee against Apartheid, headquartered at the offices of the Amalgamated Clothing Workers in New York City. They welcomed unaffiliated unions—the Mine Workers, Teamsters, NEA, UE—which joined with AFSCME, CWA, IAM, ACTWU, UAW, ILGWU and others in planning a conference on "Labor and South Africa" with South African union leaders for March 1985.

At the AFL-CIO Executive Council meeting, Feb. 19, 1985, in Bal Harbour, Florida, the AFL-CIO top leaders sharply criticized leaders of affiliated international unions for dealing directly with trade union leaders of foreign countries without funneling labor contacts between US and other nations through the AFL-CIO, and particularly through its International Department. Under such a policy, no top leader of any foreign labor federation could be invited to any national union convention or conference, except through the AFL-CIO federation headquarters.

But the March 1985 conference took place! 400 trade unionists participated. While a top Black leader of the South African federation was prevented from attending, three heads of major South African unions—building trades, commercial, and textile—attended and spoke. Thus, it was established that individual unions are able to deal directly on a bi-union basis with their counterparts abroad, even if the national federation controls relations with other central federations. And a campaign was started to force U.S. employers to get out of South Africa, to divest their holdings there.

New Confidence—New Tactics

The U.S. labor movement emerged from the 1984 presidential election campaign with new confidence, fully aware of the shortcomings of the Democratic Party machinery, and emboldened by its exciting experiences in developing its own independent political action machinery. The excitement stemmed from the mass involvement of thousands of rank-and-file volunteer activists manning phone chairs, mailing, and developing registration drives that registered thousands of new labor voters. One union paper after another expressed the leadership's understanding that labor would never again be passive supporters, but that vigorous, better-informed and more experienced machinery would be developed to defend the interests of the common people in future political campaigns.

After helping defeat the Reagan Administration in the 1986 Congressional elections, the AFL-CIO Executive Council met with the new Democratic Senate and House majority leaders at their annual winter meeting in Bal Harbour. The federation urged them, and all Congress, to reject any further increases in military spending, pointing out that outlays for defense more than doubled between 1980 and 1986, while nonmilitary outlays, including social programs, rose less than half. A number of unions also announced the funding of economic research organizations to develop alternatives to the conservative economic agenda of recent years. Their goal: to develop economic policy issues that will shape the elections in 1988 and the after.

Challenging Reagan's Budget

Reagan's attack on PATCO taught some profound lessons. Top leaders of the fastest growing unions in our country—Wynn of the United Food and Commercial Workers, Sweeney of SEIU, McEntee of AFSCME, among others—know now that corporation union-busting campaigns and Reagan's undermining of the NLRB and other labor and social service agencies make new union tactics necessary. [*See AFL-CIO Report in sections 5 and 100.*] These tactics involve both domestic and international fronts. SEIU responded with a call to action in its Budget Bulletin, to defeat Reagan Administration's axing of social services while increasing the military budget.

Others responded by calling international labor conferences against the transnationals. The Labor Research Association (LRA) sponsored an outstanding session in New York City in 1983 and LRA and Canadian Research Association sponsored an even broader conference in Toronto in 1984. They brought together unionists from many fields and countries to review in depth the problems all workers and all unions in all countries face because of the transnationals. [*See Dick Barry's discussion in section 11.*] The conferees concluded that labor must develop the understanding and techniques for international coordination against the common enemy. At the same time, International Trade Secretariats—such as the Metalworkers Federation and the International Federation of Commercial, Clerical, Professional and Technical Employees (FIET)—have adopted policy resolutions resulting in international joint action.

Statement from Tokyo

The 20th World Conference of the International Federation of Commercial, Professional & Technical Employees (FIET), representing 8 million workers in 84 countries, resolved, in 1983:

> The billions spent on arms constitute a serious obstacle to the world's economic health.... Resources being wasted on the worldwide acceleration of the arms race is adding significantly to the loss of jobs ... [We need] to reduce military budgets and put resources into social programs leading to full employment....

In a world tied tightly together, labor's historic internationalism has become a practical need. Increasingly multinational companies dominate the world economy. *Their influence can only be matched by international workers' organizations of the same magnitude.* (My emphasis—BR)

Some U.S. unions are now affiliated with FIET, including SEIU.

In this spirit, the International Metalworkers Federation has taken on General Motors. The Federation convened an international conference of all unions representing GM workers in Vienna, Austria on March 27-28, 1985, with one item on the agenda: "A world union strategy for the auto giant." Union representatives from North and South America, West Europe, Asia and Africa were involved. Similar meetings are continuing to be held, in this and other fields.

UNIONISTS TOURING FOR PEACE

♦♦ The Editors ♦♦

Based on a report in Labor Today, *June, 1985, pp. 4-6.*

Increasing numbers of U.S. trade unionists have visited the Soviet Union as guests of the All Unions Central Council of Trade Unions since the State Department stopped denying passports to selected "unAmericans." In April, 1985, for example, a delegation organized by Trade Union Action for Democracy (TUAD) went to the Soviet Union as part of an international delegation of 400 trade unionists form around the world. This delegation was joined by one from the International Association of Machinists and Aerospace Workers that had come to discuss occupational safety and health, led by Eugene Glover, IAM International Secretary Treasurer.

During their two week stay, members of the delegation from ILGWU, Brotherhood of Carpenters & Joiners, and UE spoke to many trade union leaders and rank-and-file workers. Dan Kane, president of Teamsters Local 111 ACA/IBT in New York City, met with Lev Yakoulev, head of the 4 million member Soviet Teamsters Union, and attended a union meeting of 400 off-duty cab drivers. He and other delegates learned that:

♦ More than 130 million Soviet workers, representing 98+

percent of all wage and salary workers, belong to trade unions. Union membership is voluntary; workers apply and are admitted to membership.
- No worker can be discharged without the agreement of the regional trade union committee and then, only after the union finds another job for the worker. Single mothers are never discharged. Regional trade union committees, however, have the absolute right to remove the manager of any enterprise found guilty of violating the working agreement, safety provisions, etc.
- Dues are one percent of the salary or wage. The total trade union budget, including dues and government funds under direct control and administration of trade union organizations, amounts to more than twice the entire military budget of the Soviet Union. Unions run a network of hotels for their own members and for tourists, as well as classes and health spas.
- Officers of local unions are elected by secret ballot for terms of two and a half years. Only about 7 percent of trade union officials work full time or draw salaries from union organizations. No binding action can be taken by any trade union organization unless that action is agreed to by 75 percent of those affected by it. Unions act through monthly union meetings.

"Everywhere we went the air was permeated with hopes for peace," according to Johnnie Mae Jackson, ILGWU, Chicago. "Every toast we drank ended with the wish for 'Mir y druzhba'—peace and friendship."

On returning to the United States, the delegates said they accepted the challenge "to help break down the artificial barriers, be they imposed by the government agencies or some in our own ranks, that stand in the way of exchanges, formal or otherwise, between workers and unions in the United States and workers and unions in the Soviet Union."

Editors' note: The ability to break down these barriers has improved with the advent of the openness (glasnost) policy of Communist Party of the Soviet Union. In February 1987, representatives from many fields of work and many viewpoints in the United States joined 1,000 notables from 80 nations, meeting with 700 Soviet citizens in Moscow to discuss: "For a Nuclear-Free World, for the Survival of Humanity."

THIS IS JUST THE BEGINNING

We began by asserting that the U.S. labor movement is moving on the issue of peace, and that this opens up the possibilities for profound changes in our entire nation. We reaffirm that belief. Those who glibly predict the demise of the U.S. labor movement have misread our future. The will to live is strong. It fuels the struggle for peace, for justice, for a better life for all the people of the world.

◆◆Ben Riskin

96 ⋄⋄ PROPOSING A RATIONAL ECONOMIC PLAN TO THE LEGISLATURE

♦♦ Oregon AFL-CIO Employment & Economy Committee ♦♦

The following excerpts from this 1984 report are reprinted with permission of the Oregon AFL-CIO, Robert Baugh, Secretary-Treasurer. A fuller version of the report appears in the Summer 1984 issue of the Guild Practitioner (vol. 41, no. 3).

The issue most on the mind of Oregonians is the economy. For over three years this state has been in an economic crisis. The net result has been a series of special sessions in Salem to balance the budget and plenty of opinions on what the state should do. The most vocal opinions in the past few months concerning Oregon's economy and the state's "business climate" have come from various "blue chip panels" composed of representatives of the business community.

The following committee reports on Employment and the Economy, Taxation Policy and Safety, Health and Workers' Compensation, represent labor's "blue chip" response to our economic crisis. The reports represent an unprecedented effort on the part of the Oregon AFL-CIO to develop a comprehensive, fair and sound approach to planning Oregon's economy. It is apparent to our committee members the questions faced by legislators on economic development, taxation, and worker protection are crucial to the long range future of this state. The committee reports are designed to make the Oregon AFL-CIO an active voice in this legislative process....

Economic Development

Economic activities transcend geopolitical borders. Oregon is part of a regional and national economy and, because of this, the ability of the state to control economic development is limited. Federal preemption [exclusive regulation of] interstate commerce is one example of the limitations placed on state control. There are, however, three ways in which the state *can* control the internal economy.

1. Legislation can be used to control resource allocation and establish regulations governing land use, environment, safety and health, labor laws, workers' compensation, etc.
2. Taxation is used to raise revenues.
3. Revenues are then spent on the development of the infrastructure (roads, sewers, schools, housing, etc.), which is needed for economic development to take place.

Numerous studies and articles indicate that a business decision about where to locate a new facility hinges on such factors as: transportation, available workforce, workforce profile (skills, wages, absenteeism, unionization, fringe benefits, etc.), resources, energy, water and sewage availability, education and worker training. Tax and financial incentives are at the bottom of the list. Over the long haul these are relatively minor cost or savings items when compared to basic infrastructural needs. Ironically, many states, Oregon included, are increasingly promoting tax incentives, often at the expense of the infrastructure.

Capital and Labor: The Birth and Death of Jobs

It is necessary to create an economic development policy which equates what is happening in the capital market with what is happening in the labor market in the state. We need to look at the birth and death of jobs. The birth of jobs appears to be taking place in small businesses with 20 employees or less. However, these enterprises are extremely volatile and need access to equity capital to decrease the risk. Competition from bigger operations, poor management, and uneven regulatory requirements in areas such as workers' compensation and employment taxes, compound the problems of small business. The death of jobs is taking place in larger enterprises with several hundred employees. In some cases these enterprises are still operating at a profit when they close, but greater profits are available elsewhere.

Currently, Oregon's economic development policy looks only at the birth end of development and not at the death. An intervention policy to maintain existing industry makes good economic sense; otherwise we implement a policy that creates $5 an hour jobs, while $10 an hour jobs disappear.

Objectives for Oregon's Economic Development Agenda

A rational economic development agenda must be centered on replacing the declining private activities of the state—forest products, food and kindred products, and to a lesser degree, primary metals—with new activities that take maximum advantage of the existing industrial linkages. There are many activities that produce desirable goods and services for a national as well as a local market that fail to exploit these linkages. For example, a silicon chip factory may produce components for the Pacific computer market, but it does not salvage the plywood mills whose housing industry orders are drying up.

What process, then, can be followed to identify workable, cost effective production activities eligible for limited state economic development assistance? A rational response to this question begins with the identification of a set of key criteria [to use in comparing] potential economic development ventures. These include:

1. *Scale of Job Creation.* Would the ventures provide substantial employment to residents of Oregon?
2. *Conservation of Capital (and resources).* Would the firms producing the proposed outputs be able to reuse a significant portion of Oregon's existing stock of industrial facilities, idle or unused machinery and equipment, and resource base wisely?
3. *Local Economic Impact.* Would the new activities, at full scale, play a role in the local economy similar to that of the forest industry in the past? Would they constitute a set of

major "exports" for Oregon to international and national markets?
4. *Characteristics of Markets.* Are the demands for the proposed product lines sufficiently strong and enduring to justify large capital investments? Are the markets located properly for production to occur in Oregon?
5. *Use of Oregon's Comparative Advantage.* Would the contemplated ventures take full advantage of the state's existing displaced skilled labor force, industrial infrastructure, and of the key linkages among the industrial activities spawned by the region's legacy of housing market dependence?
6. *Market Countercyclicality.* Is demand for the venture's outputs stable or highly cyclical? If it is cyclical, does its cycle counteract or reinforce the shocks to the state economy that come from dependence on the housing market?
7. *Labor Cost Barriers.* Do the private sector firms producing similar or identical products pay wages as high as those to which Oregon workers are accustomed as a result of forest products' past high profitability?
8. *Transport Cost Barriers.* Is the cost of moving the proposed products from Oregon to market destinations prohibitively high? Or are there classes of products whose size, price and existing production sites allow Oregon to manufacture more readily than others?
9. *Advantages of Publicness.* Do some products make more sense than others as candidates for public or public/private production? Are there products whose cost of production could be especially reduced by state policies and are worth such special consideration?
10. *Profitability for Entry.* Are private firms now producing similar outputs characterized by above average, and less cyclical than average, profitability? Does selection of the product lines proposed move Oregon into a national sector growing sufficiently to allow for new entrants?

97 ♦♦ LEGISLATION PROMOTING FULL EMPLOYMENT

♦♦ **Charles Hayes** ♦♦

Charles Hayes is a former leader of the United Food and Commercial Workers, AFL-CIO. He is currently a member of the House of Representatives (D-Ill).
  See also sections 9, 16, and 100.
  Congressman Hayes introduced his first full employment bill in 1985 and made a strong speech in support that covers the basic arguments for such legislation, reported in the Congressional Record 99th Congress 1st Session H 1068-1078. *On March 4, 1987, he introduced a revised bill entitled the Quality of Life Action Act, including suggestions from many segments of society and sponsored by 39 Congressmembers. The bill was referred to committee, and hearings were scheduled in several cities on the need for its passage. Here we provide several verbatim extracts—in boxes—together with an adaptation of nearly the entire remaining text of the bill.*

♦♦♦♦♦♦♦♦♦♦♦♦♦♦♦♦♦♦♦♦♦♦♦♦♦♦♦♦♦

A BILL

To protect and improve the quality of life in the United States through a more vigorous, responsible and participatory capitalism supported by more business-like policy initiatives and budgetary practices by the President and the

Congress....

Sec. 2. Purposes

The purposes of this law are to establish a process whereby the Congress and the President of the United States shall cooperate in—

(1) protecting and expanding such basic elements in the quality of life as the right to earn a living at decent wages, and adequate income for those unable to work for pay;

(2) renewing and enlarging the productive capacity of private industries, investing in the infrastructure of public works and human services, and developing natural resources in a manner consistent with the maintenance of environmental quality;

(3) matching such enlarged productive capacity with such higher real wages and salaries as are needed by both middle and lower income people to buy goods and services and invest in the productive capacity of the country;

(4) providing thereby larger markets and better opportunities for enterprises with smaller unit profit margins to earn larger, more stable and less subsidized total profits on invested capital; and

(5) promoting opportunities for private initiatives and economic self-determination as a counterbalance to any undue concentration of Federal or corporate power by stimulating and unleashing the creative abilities of—(A) smaller and larger profit seeking enterprises and such other private sectors as labor, nonprofit enterprises, neighborhood organizations, cooperatives, and voluntary associations, and (B) town, city, county, and State governments in urban, suburban, and rural areas.

♦ ♦

Recognition of Fundamental Rights

In general, the Congress hereby recognizes that:

1. Every adult American able and willing to earn a living through paid work has the right to a free choice among opportunities for useful, productive and fulfilling paid employment (part- or full-time) at decent real wages or for self-employment; and
2. Every adult American unable to work for pay or find employment pursuant to 1. above has the right to an ade-

quate standard of living that rises with increases in the wealth and productivity of the society.

Each federal department, agency, and commission, including the Board of Governors of the Federal System, shall plan and carry out its policies, projects and budgets in a manner designed to help establish and maintain conditions under which all adult Americans may freely exercise the rights recognized above. No such department may directly or indirectly promote recession or unemployment as a means of reducing wages and salaries or inflation.

Overall National Policies

In the President's annual budget and economic report, the President shall transmit to the Congress a staged program to: 1) help establish and maintain conditions under which the rights recognized in section 2 may be exercised and, 2) implement the government's economic and social obligations under the Employment Act of 1946, the Full Employment and Balanced Growth Act of 1978, the Charter of the United Nations, and the Charter of the Organization of American States....

[This] program shall include general and specific policies and projects to:

1. Provide incentives for rules for quickly enlarging employment opportunities, while also reducing federal expenditures through staged reductions in real interest rates; reductions in the number of paid working hours without any corresponding loss in income; and increases in the number of private companies providing maternity leave with pay and childcare for preschool children of employees;
2. Vastly increase the opportunities for freely-chosen part-time employment, with fringe benefits, to meet the needs of older people, students, the disabled, and people with housekeeping and child care responsibilities;
3. Take such other steps to cope with increased joblessness caused by technologies that replace people with robots, including vastly improved opportunities for up-to-date and effective education, training or retraining;
4. Prevent or control inflationary tendencies through standby policies, including public controls over private price-fixing;

5. Provide improved federal incentives for increased employment by small, medium and large business enterprises, and by labor unions, professional associations and nonprofit, voluntary, and cooperative organizations, including neighborhood, tenant, homeowner, and self-help associations and organizations of family farmers, women, minorities, and the unemployed;
6. Promote conditions for more self-empowerment by people victimized by discrimination in hiring, training, wages, salaries, fringe benefits or promotion on the basis of prejudice concerning race, ethnic background, gender, age, religion, station in life, political or sexual orientation or personal disability;
7. Through these and other activities work towards reducing officially measured unemployment to the interim goal of 4 percent as set forth in the Full Employment and Balanced Growth Act of 1978 (15 USC sec 3101 note); and
8. Provide the Congress, business, labor, and state and local governments with more reliable and timely information on a) the total supply of people able and willing to work; b) the number of people in paid employment [and] the underground economy; c) the extent of underemployment, including employment at substandard wages; d) the extent of serious job insecurity among the employed; e) the estimated number of dependents of those who are jobless....

Reindustrialization programs and projects shall include policies aimed at achieving American leadership in goods production through such specific innovations as:

1. Agricultural systems geared to delivering kinds and quantities of food needed to abolish hunger and malnutrition in the world and the kinds and quantities of fiber needed for adequate clothing in all climates;
2. More efficient transportation and communication systems;
3. Passenger cars that are safer and more efficient than anything now produced in other countries;
4. Prefabricated (and exportable) housing modules that include communication, weatherization, lighting, plumbing, heating, cooking, and washing equipment etc.;
5. Mining urban regions for valuable materials that can be recovered through the integrated recycling of liquid, gaseous and solid wastes; and

6. The vastly improved software needed for supercomputers, artificial intelligence and all the above, [(1-6)].

Other programs shall include policies and projects to develop American leadership in services through:

1. Educational systems based on adding an "R" for Reasoning to the traditional Reading, 'Riting and 'Rithmetic;
2. Health services oriented toward better disease treatment and caring for the elderly;
3. Child care systems dedicated to excellence through staffs composed of several generations of both men and women; and
4. Systems for the repair of old and new types of equipment.

Public Works Private Employment

The goals and programs mandated above shall include provisions for federal grants and other incentives to encourage short- and long-term public works planning by town, city, county and state governments (and any of their agencies) in urban, suburban, and rural areas.

Local units of government shall be eligible for such grants to the extent that their strategic and tactical planning focuses on projects to improve the quality of life for all people in the area; renovate and enlarge the decaying infrastructure of public facilities and services required for productive, efficient, and profitable enterprise; utilize the wasted labor power of those suffering from joblessness and poverty; and be conducted under contracts awarded competitively to smaller as well as larger business enterprises or nonprofit enterprises, cooperatives, labor unions, [etc.] . . .

Jobs and International Economic Policy

To protect employment, wage levels, living standards and private industry, and peace in the United States and elsewhere, it shall be the policy of the federal government to cooperate with the governments of other countries and with the United Nations in helping develop an international community based on rising living standards, particularly for those people with the lowest levels of income, access to public facilities, free trade union organization, and political power.

The President and the Congress shall review whatever American laws, structures, procedures and regulations may interfere with carrying out this act and shall make or propose such short- and long-term changes and improvements as may best contribute to the successful carrying out of this act.

FOCUS OF REVIEW

In the conduct of such reviews, actions and proposals, special attention shall be given to whatever may be done—

(1) to protect employment in the United States by incentives and other actions to then prevent large corporations from moving all or part of their operations to other countries in order to escape labor unions, fair labor standards or environmental controls;

(2) to promote such higher levels of wages and salaries in such other countries as well as provide larger markets for their own industries and for imports of goods and services to the United States;

(3) to withdraw Federal incentives, guarantees, and tax concessions from any United States based transnational corporations whose operations in preindustrial or industrializing countries may directly undermine the standard of living in such countries, deny to employees the rights of free collective bargaining, or endanger peace; and

(4) reduce trade barriers without reducing general levels of employment in the United States.

The Federal Government shall make financial support for the International Monetary Fund and the International Bank for Reconstruction and Development conditional upon their development and implementation of such policies and procedures as will raise the standard of living in countries receiving any financial assistance from it, rather than impose austerity, and thereby contribute to economic viability, credit worthiness and the ability to import goods and services from the United States.

[T]he President shall propose to the United Nations a series of international and regional conferences on alternative methods of planning for the reduction of involuntary unemployment and underemployment....

[T]he Department of Labor shall provide financial and technical assistance to organized labor and cooperative, nonprofit and voluntary organizations, on how best to control facility closing and capital flight by large business; to facilitate transnational labor organization and collective bargaining; and to otherwise carry out the purpose of this section.

Conversion to Areas of Needed Civilian Expansion

In his or her annual messages, the President shall include specific proposals for a conversion planning fund to be administered by such agencies as the President may recommend. The purpose of this fund shall be to promote short- and long-term plans for coping with declines in civilian or military activities by developing specific projects for the expansion of economic activities in areas or sectors where needed. This fund should include no less than an amount equal to 1 percent of the amount appropriated for military purposes during each fiscal year....

Implementation

As part of the annual program developed by the President under this Act, the President shall transmit to the Congress a short- and long-term schedule for implementing the purposes of this Act.

The implementation schedule shall include recommendations for a restructuring of federal budget priorities to provide for: reductions in wasteful or unnecessary military expenditures; increased federal revenues through reducing or eliminating wasteful tax loopholes; reducing the interest on the federal debt by reductions in both federal deficits and real interest rates; the appropriate use of public and private pension funds to help attain the goals of this Act; and the creation of private and public development banks in urban and agricultural areas of high joblessness and poverty. [It shall also include recommendations for] the promotion of educational activities within each state on locally-based overall planning, with special attention to promoting the creative abilities of small, medium and large business enterprises, and of labor unions, professional associations, and nonprofit, voluntary and cooperative organizations, including neighborhood, tenant, homeowner and self-help organizations and organizations of the unemployed.

Pursuant to its responsibilities under the Employment Act of 1946, the Joint Economic Committee shall each year monitor actions proposed or taken under this Act and report its conclusions thereon to the Congress and the American people.

All budgetary data for specific programs shall include quantitative estimates of the direct and indirect impacts on: 1) reducing the number of people receiving unemployment compensation and public assistance; and 2) increasing tax revenues as a result of more people earning income subject to social security and income taxes and more business enterprises earning the larger, more stable and less subsidized total profits possible under conditions of full employment, ...

All over-all budget messages from the President to the Congress shall be full employment budgets based on policies and programs to reduce officially measured unemployment to the interim levels set forth in the Full Employment and Balanced Growth Act of 1978, and toward this end shall include:

1. A tax expenditure budget; ...
3. A wealth inventory providing information on changes in the type and estimated value of assets owned by local, state and national governments; personal wealth; and the country's net stock of both reproducible and nonreproducible tangible wealth;
4. A total impact analysis on the consequences flowing from each overall budget for levels of employment, output and prices, foreign trade and development, environmental quality, and the distribution of income and wealth;
5. Estimates of the direct and indirect flow of all federal outlays to each state and each district of the House of Representatives; and
6. The expression of debt and deficit data in constant as well as current dollars.

98 ♦♦ THE SPIRIT OF THE 1985 AFL-CIO CONVENTION

♦♦ The Editors ♦♦

The 15th biennial convention of the AFL-CIO in October 1985 debated the resolution on U.S. policy in Central America for an hour and a half. This was the first open debate on foreign policy since the CIO merged with the AFL in 1955 after expelling its left unions in 1949-50.

John T. Joyce, vice president of the Bricklayers, spoke first, opposing Reagan's foreign policy because it insists "on a military solution over a peaceful solution," and supporting the long official AFL-CIO resolution which condemned the Sandinista government of Nicaragua, applauded the election of "a proven democrat, Napoleon Duarte," in El Salvador, "the restoration of democracy in Grenada," and the work of AIFLD in the region [see section 86].

Then Kenneth T. Blaylock, president of the American Federation of Government Employees, rose "not to speak against the resolution, but to speak of its shortcomings." He reported what he was told in February, 1985, in El Salvador as he sat in the military commander's office. "He glibly told us that 'We will have this little war wrapped up in six months, because we have adopted a policy and a strategy of sanitization.'... [That] means with foot soldiers, with artillery and with aircraft you completely run all of the people out of an area."

Blaylock referred to the federal charges against him under a very restrictive reading of the Hatch Act [described in section 88], and concluded:

So every fiber in my body that triggers my reflexes and my basic instincts says to me, "If Ronald Reagan supports these efforts and if friends like the Coors family, who responded after Congress cut off the money to the Contras,... and others started raising private funds—if those two people are for it, we damn well better be against it."

Albert Shanker, president of the American Federation of Teachers, spoke in support of the resolution and this "healthy discussion. There is disagreement and there's no reason why it shouldn't be aired."

Jerry Brown, of the National Union of Hospital & Health Care Employees, rose in opposition to the resolution because it did not condemn aid to the contras:

For this labor movement to ... waffle on this issue seems to me that we haven't learned a thing from the history of the past 20 years, and the shame of this labor movement in not speaking out against American involvement in Vietnam.... [W]hen we say that we have to give a different image to the American people and to the American workers, we ought to look at how somehow or other we are always, always the shock troops of the cold war.

I don't buy into that. Our members don't buy into that and we ought to have a resolution that says no military aid to anybody in Central America, and let's do everything possible to end the poverty and exploitation, but no guns, no guns and no war in Central America.

After other pro and con speakers, Ed Asner spoke last, as outgoing president of the Screen Actors Guild:

Over the past four years I have had the honor of meeting many of you. We have shared struggles together, walked picket lines together, broken bread together. And our work in behalf of justice, dignity and employment for working people has made me proud.... But it does not make me proud to read in ... *Business Week* that the AFL-CIO is spending almost as much on what I am forced to conclude are misguided and ill-conceived foreign programs as we spend on domestic programs, thus making our federation, as *Business Week* says, global vigilantes.

... I don't want the labor movement used to do the dirty work of President Reagan or our large multinational corporations. And I don't want any of Orrin Hatch's National Endowment for Democracy money to do it either.

The debate led to inclusion of a compromise paragraph in the resolution:

Unfortunately the Reagan administration continues to place emphasis on a military, rather than a political solution to the conflicts in Nicaragua and El Salvador. But the AFL-CIO believes that a negotiated settlement, rather than a military victory, holds the best hope for the social, economic and political justice that the people of Nicaragua and El Salvador deserve.

This debate led Victor Reuther, the retired international affairs director for the UAW, to comment: "We haven't come as far as we should in democratic unionism.... They will still do what they want to do at the AFL-CIO headquarters, so long as the money is there." Nonetheless, "I left the hall feeling uplifted," said William Winpisinger, president of the International Association of Machinists. "We hit a new level of democracy in the AFL-CIO, and that augurs well."

99 ⋄⋄ NEW TACTICS FOR LABOR

ESOPS: THE WAY OUT OR THE WAY UNDER

⋄⋄ Norman Roth ⋄⋄

Norman Roth, a veteran of 51 years in the labor movement, helped found Labor Today *and was instrumental in setting up one of the first UAW training schools.*

This is excerpted from the June, 1985 issue of Labor Today, *reprinted with permission.*

Today, when record profits are accompanied by record business failures, a growing number of workers are being sold the idea that an employee stock ownership plan (ESOP) is the solution to their problems. According to the National Center for Employee Ownership (NECO), more than 6,000 companies set up ESOPs between 1973 and 1984, bringing the total in the country to approximately 7,000. The NECO also predicts that by the year 2000, "As many workers will be under ESOPs as will be members of unions." This poses serious questions for the labor movement and working people in general.

"There is no way workers on a meaningful basis can be managers and workers," says Lewie G. Anderson, a vice-president of the United Food and Commercial Workers (UFCW). "The interests of each group eventually clash. It just doesn't work." Anderson, who heads the UFCW's packinghouse division, says Rath Packing Co., for example, gave a "corpse to the workers." In 1979, Rath "sold" its 2,500 employees an eventual 60 percent control for the price of wage concessions. But last year, the company failed, closing its doors and leaving workers with worthless stock and a folded ESOP.

Until now the labor movement's attitude toward ESOPs has varied from hostility to indifference to near wholehearted support. However, labor cannot afford to remain ambivalent in its opinion or plan of action regarding ESOPs. For, in the main, ESOPs are nothing but a series of blind alleys and traps purposely designed to dismantle the labor movement.

The Truth of the Matter

The ESOP form of employee ownership is not a radical socialist idea. It grew out of a "theory of Capitalism" advanced more than 25 years ago by Louis O. Kelso, a San Francisco lawyer who founded the Kelso and Company Investment firm. The capitalist system, he argued, could be saved only by turning workers into capitalists through stock ownership. To acquire stock, he said, workers needed a credit mechanism to gain access to capital funds. Through banks (including Kelso and Company) that receive special tax breaks for loaning money to ESOPs, workers are able to get these funds. (Sixteen pieces of legislation that guarantee favorable tax breaks for support of ESOPs have been enacted by Congress since 1974.)

Even worse, workers are coerced by management teams to use their union pension funds to buy initial stock in a company. Says Lester C. Thurow, an economist at the Massachusetts Institute of Technology, "ESOPs that substitute for regular pension plans are riskier because the retirement benefits then depend on the fate of only one company." He argues that too much wealth is concentrated at the top in the U.S.—48 percent of all common stock is owned by only 1 percent of the population—but does not believe that ESOPs are the answer for redistributing that wealth.

Employee stock ownership plans date to the 1920s when rising security prices and increasing dividend payments encouraged employee stock ownership. In exchange for company loyalty, increased production, better quality work and greater profits, employers sold stock to their employees at lower than prevailing market prices. Then came the crash of 1929. The bottom dropped out of the securities market and with it the dreams and hopes of the workers who lost their jobs, their savings, and the value of the stock. All that remained was bitterness.

According to Barry Bluestone and Bennett Harrison, authors of "The Deindustrialization of America," control over everyday decisions in "worker-owned" companies tends to remain in the hands of the firm's original managers. They claim that hourly workers have a majority financial interest in less than one-tenth of all ESOP companies.

In all too many recent worker buyouts, managers have retained (or have been granted) far too much power, freezing out the shop floor worker-owners, giving themselves high salaries, devising ways to intimidate or eliminate opposition on the Board of Directors, and even serving on business committees that advocate right-to-work legislation or support union decertification campaigns. As Morton Klevan, a deputy administrator in the Department of Labor says, "A lot of ESOPs are really MESOPs—management enrichment stock ownership plans." "Management's rights" clauses giving the company (read "management") the "sole right" to manage the affairs of the business and to direct the working forces of the company are a part of nearly all ESOPs.

In reality, ESOPs are another way of shifting the economic burden onto the backs of workers. Instead of corporations accepting the responsibility of reinvesting in basic industry, ESOPs take the hard-earned money of workers to retool. Instead of guaranteeing workers a job, the corporations threaten them with a plant shutdown, a layoff, a move to a more profitable area of the country or of the world—or an ESOP. In short, ESOPs are a way for management to force workers to *buy* their jobs; to *pay money out of their own pockets*—to the tune of millions of dollars—*in order to work;* to force working people to rescue the very system that has taken the wealth produced by their labor and handed it over to the rich—again, and again. The conflicts inherent in worker ownership can never be reconciled as long as the main goal of company management is greater profits for those who own and control, at the expense of those who labor.

For example, the ESOP established at National Steel's Weirton Works in Weirton, West Virginia proved to be a gold mine for the company, but not for the shop worker-owners. Weirton, an 80-year-old complex, was sold to the ESOP for $386 million. Each of the 7,700 worker-owners gave up 20 percent of their wages and part of their fringe benefits in order to "buy" shares.

Mike Hravchek, a union steward with 26 years in the plant, [said] that the company had relied heavily on the workers' worst fears, telling them, "If you don't set up an ESOP you're going to be out of a job."

"The people at Weirton were taken in. We bought the place but we don't have a damn thing to say about it.... Although we agreed to a 6 year freeze on wages, ... the company chairman hired by the banks that designed the ESOP, gave substantial raises to 54 department heads. No one knew anything about it. All we can discuss, it seems, is the location of the toilets."

One year after the buy out, the *New York Times* featured an article about the ESOP: "While most steel companies lost money in 1984, Weirton Steel racked up $48 million in profits in the first 9 months. This was done with a 5 percent increase in staff, a 20 percent increase in steel shipped in 1984 over 1983 and far lower labor costs because of the 20 percent pay cut the workers accepted in order to finance the purchase of the plan." The workers gave up more than 49 million dollars in wages and benefits in the first nine months in order to show that 48 million dollar profit.

CHANGING TAX LAW TO ENCOURAGE REINDUSTRIALIZATION

♦♦ Ellen Green ♦♦

Ellen Green made this presentation at a workshop on Jobs, Unions and Full Employment at the Conference on Quality of Life Action: The Road to Full Employment, Oakland, California, Feb. 21-22, 1986

I'd like to share something I learned in the last couple of years as director of the California Project, which is a state-wide non-profit corporation that works on economic issues and tries proactive strategies to create jobs. In my previous work at the Plant Closures Project I had been missing an important part of strategy, which is tax policy and its relation to the creation of employment and unemployment.

I realize taxation is highly mystified for people, but it is not complicated. All three of these major causes of unemployment can be addressed through tax policy: mergers and acquisitions, plant closures, and capital flight to countries with cheaper wages.

First, mergers and takeovers: In 1983, 82 billion dollars was used in takeovers. If that money had been invested in new plants and equipment, it would have increased productivity by 25 percent. That would take care of a major chunk of unemployment right there. The tax policy connected to mergers is that the money borrowed for acquisitions, 40 cents of the dollar, is a tax write-off; these mergers are largely financed by us. *Business Week* theorized that taking away that write-off would stop 9 out of 10 acquisitions.

Second, plant closures: I've been in California since 1976 working on employment issues, first on affirmative action for women at Advocates for Women, and trying to help women get into skilled blue-collar work, especially women on Aid to Families with Dependent Children (AFDC), so that they could get enough money to support their families. But I found there weren't any good paying jobs left. Nobody had done much hiring in 10 years in San Francisco, so I followed the jobs to the East Bay. The Easy Bay said, "Sorry, those jobs are in Phoenix." So, through the initiative of the religious community, I was hired to begin the Plant Closures Project.

Working as an organizer on plant closures, I realized that tax policy was part of the cause. The name of the tax law that we must change is "accelerated depreciation on new plant and equipment." This is a wacky, false write-off scheme which says you can write-off new plant and equipment within a 5-10 year period when its life is 30-50 years. This is a motivation to close profitable operating plants rather than reinvest in them. You can make more money by buying new equipment and writing it off elsewhere in your conglomerate. Many plants built to take advantage of this tax law are constructed with the *intention* of closing them five years from the day they open. In a bill the House of Representatives passed and sent to the Senate in 1985, there was a realistic depreciation scale. That is a good reason to keep pushing for its passage.

Third, capital flight: Three points all add up to the same thing: tax policies that serve as incentives for multinational corporations to play shell games with their money. 1) A tax deferral that exempts profits earned in foreign countries from taxation by the United States. That should go. 2) A foreign tax credit under which you can shelter your profits. If you make the profits in a high tax country, you can claim these profits in a low tax country—the shell game theory. That should go. 3) A tax law allowing multinational corporations to treat all expenses as expenses in the United States, no matter where

♦♦ "SHARING" THE TAX BURDEN ♦♦

This cartoon first appeared in *Labor Today*.
♦♦ Credit: Peggy Lipschutz.

the money was actually spent. In other words, everything you spent to earn your profits is deductible on your domestic income tax, including anything you spent to make money in a foreign country.

As to the federal deficit: U.S. corporations have stopped paying taxes. They used to pay 25 percent of the federal revenues. Now they pay less than 6 percent. This, combined with the military buildup, is the reason for the deficit we're facing now. That's why we need to change tax law in addition to stopping the military spending, which is also not job-producing. We need to have corporations pay their fair share of taxes.

I am raising these tax questions so that people like you, who are organizers, will start thinking about them. Take time to read the tax articles in the papers and voice your opinions about the current tax bill. We may be able to have some influence on it.

On job creation: I encourage you to get in touch with your city councils. Find out, through them, what new developers are coming to town, what new businesses are moving in. See if you can't find a sympathetic council person to work on a strategy of negotiating jointly with that new developer for the privilege of doing business in your community. Sacramento is doing this. They have come to some alliance between the labor and city council people. The city is carefully obeying the law and negotiating that in recognition of some zoning changes for new development, the new construction will be union. This can turn Sacramento into a union town. Of course, the unions had to come to the point of expressing support for affirmative action and for local hiring, which are very important issues to confront in dealing with unemployment.

HOW TO DO IT

♦♦Plant Closures Project♦♦

The San Francisco-Bay Area Plant Closures Project had its act together by March 1987 in its Campaign to Save Blue Cross Jobs in Oakland. Excerpts from two of its mailing pieces provide basic information that can be adapted for almost any campaign.

TO: *Bay Area Community, Religious, Labor, and Consumer Organizations*

Office and Professional Employees Union Local 29 and the Plant Closures Project, along with concerned religious, community, and labor groups have launched a *Campaign to SAVE BLUE CROSS JOBS IN OAKLAND*, in the wake of the decision by Blue Cross to move corporate headquarters and hundreds of jobs out of Oakland. That decision has cost hundreds of workers their jobs—workers who are primarily black, Filipino, Asian, and Hispanic women; who are sole supporters of their families, and who are earning between $6.96 and $11.41 per hour at Blue Cross. The remaining Blue Cross jobs in Oakland are clearly in jeopardy as Blue Cross continues layoffs and relocation of work to Southern California. In addition, Blue Cross is currently offering severance benefits to non-union workers while union-represented workers are denied benefits.

The campaign seeks the support of the Oakland City Council, Alameda County Board of Supervisors, State Assembly and Senate members, and members of Congress to investigate Blue Cross' state tax-exempt status—an exemption worth millions of dollars to Blue Cross each year. Our community could have the say over how and when the issue of Blue Cross tax status is determined. While Blue Cross is holding our community hostage by bleeding our jobs and denying workers severance benefits, we in turn may hold the key to an issue that is worth millions annually to Blue Cross.

HERE IS HOW YOU CAN HELP:

Editors' note: The flyer urges people to send letters (samples enclosed) to the president of Blue Cross; to circulate petitions; to invite a speaker to address your group and to show a 17-minute video about the campaign.

BLUE CROSS TAX ISSUE FACT SHEET

This company enjoys a substantial public benefit that their competitors don't—state tax-exempt status.
* Historically Blue Cross and Blue Shield have enjoyed exemptions from federal income and California state premium taxes. These public benefits were extended when these companies incorporated in the 1930s because of the unique role they played in providing health care insurance to subscribers at a set community rate. In the 1940s other insurers entered the field and differences between companies lessened.
* In 1986 the federal Government Accounting Office (GAO)

found that the distinctions between BC/BS and commercial insurers were minimal, so *Congress passed a bill that stripped Blue Cross/Blue Shield of their tax-exempt status beginning in 1987.* [Now] the Secretary of the Treasury [can give] special treatment to the Blues to the degree that a portion of their business relates to high risk individuals and small groups.

* These companies still enjoy tax-free status in California. Commercial insurers in California are taxed under a gross premium tax. Blue Cross would pay $50 million in taxes for 1986 if taxed under gross premium tax.
* Much of the state's Tax Code is being rewritten to bring it into conformity with changes in the federal tax law. However, the change in BC/BS tax status is not included in current conformity bills.

QUESTIONS AND ANSWERS ABOUT TAXING BLUE CROSS

* Would health insurance costs go up if Blue Cross had to pay taxes? It might equalize competition between health care insurers, therefore tending to drive prices down.
* Wouldn't a tax change remove any incentive for the company to provide a public service to high risk/low income people? We are looking to tax reform proposals that would require all insurers in the state to share in the risk of insuring high risk individuals and small groups, a "risk pool" approach implemented in 15 states already.
* Are we just talking about getting revenge against a company? We hope that before we implement a plan about Blue Cross' tax status the company and the community will negotiate over tax status in exchange for a commitment of jobs for our community.

A NEW KIND OF WAR FOR THE UNITED MINE WORKERS

♦♦ Nicolaus Mills ♦♦

Nicolaus Mills is the author of The Crowd in American Literature *(Baton Rouge: Louisiana State University, 1986) and is working on a book about the Mississippi Freedom Summer of 1964.*

This article first appeared in The Nation, *November 8, 1986; it is reprinted with permission in a slightly shortened form. The word* "transnationals" has been used by the editors, rather than the author's "multinationals," in keeping with the definitions used by the United Nations. [See section 86.]

How does a union remain militant yet cope with the political realities of the 1980s? In recent years no union offers a better example than the United Mine Workers under Richard Trumka, a 36-year-old lawyer and former miner, who took over in 1982. The UMW's active membership has been reduced from 595,000 to 155,000, with 45,000 of those unemployed. They have little prospect of getting their jobs back so long as the decline of smokestack industries in the United States and the worldwide glut of cheap fuel continues. Even in West Virginia, where coal mining accounted for more than 22 percent of all employment in the industry's heyday before 1955, it is now 6 percent and falling.

Early in the 1980s, to get contract settlements, the union had given away vital health and safety protections, and it seemed likely the coal companies would be after more concessions when negotiations came around again. The international union each month was spending $500,000 more than it took in.

Trumka and newly-elected secretary-treasurer John Banovic immediately set about putting the international's house in order. They eliminated more than 100 staff positions, cut operating expenses by 28 percent, froze the wages of UMW officers and staff and sold union property to pay off loans that were costing $750,000 a year in interest on an overall debt of $4.6 million. In addition, they upgraded the UMW's investment portfolio so that its stocks would generate more income.

Internal changes were designed not only to improve efficiency but to make the union much more formidable when it came time to negotiate. Trumka made sure that miners, not outside consultants, would be responsible for decisions on day-to-day matters as well as long-term policy. Now, except for the legal staff, all department heads and their assistants are former miners.

No Takeaway Contracts

The key to Trumka's 1982 campaign, however, was the promise that under his leadership there would be "no backward steps, no takeaway contracts," a bold statement one year after President Reagan fired 11,400 air-traffic controllers, and at a time when union after union was agreeing to concessionary contracts. Fulfilling that campaign pledge meant coming to the 1984 Bituminous Coal Operators Association (BCOA) negotiations with a strike fund that would allow the UMW to hold out as long as needed. From then on, selective strikes against targeted companies rather than an industrywide general strike would be the UMW's principal weapon.

The strategy has paid handsome dividends to the union. The first came in 1984, when the BCOA, which has invariably gone into negotiations with huge coal stockpiles, found the UMW sitting on a $45 million strike fund, accumulated by assessing both its rank-and-file and its officers 2.5 percent of their salaries. The result was the first BCOA contract in 20 years negotiated without a strike. It raised wages by more than 10 percent, increased safety in the mines and placed stricter limits on subcontracting by BCOA producers.

The second dividend came last year, when the union concluded a successful 15-month strike (the final settlement is still being adjudicated in court) against A.T. Massey Coal Company, the nation's sixth largest coal producer. A $70 million strike fund enabled the UMW to give its members $200 a week in strike wages, pay for their medical insurance and weather a series of court injunctions. Above all, the strikers could hold out until the National Labor Relations Board affirmed their claim that Massey was guilty of unfair labor practices.

From the start, Trumka recognized that getting even a fraction of the UMW's unemployed miners back to work depends on forces beyond the coal fields. He maintains there is no need to accept as inevitable "the deliberate deindustrialization" of the economy, and is convinced that it is possible for unions such as the UMW to help change the way the public sees U.S. industrial policy. He argues that the country does not have to watch passively as unemployment grows and low-wage service jobs replace high-paying industrial work. His critique includes a blistering analysis of the behavoir of [trans]national corporations: ... "When it has been profitable for these corporations to invest overseas to take advantage of cheap wages or to spend billions on nonproductive mergers and acquisitions, then that has taken precedence over maintaining America's economic health and competitiveness here at home." Even worse, the transnationals have been allowed to avoid the consequences of their actions. They have not had to compensate the impoverished communities and unemployed workers they have left behind.

Regulation of the Transnationals

As an example of what's wrong, Trumka points to the massive Cerrejon Mine being built in Colombia with financing from the Export-Import Bank and a subsidiary of Exxon. The mine's output will compete with U.S. coal in both foreign and domestic markets. The remedy, Trumka insists, is regulation of the transnationals. Federal laws should not only require companies that are closing down to give adequate notification and severance pay; they should also provide for community and labor involvement in the company's decision. Most important, the U.S. government, like that of other countries, must help industries that are in trouble. Tariffs must be structured to insure that imported goods are not cheaper simply because they come from a country that allows slave wages or forbids unions. U.S. rail facilities and deep-water ports must be improved, and technology and resources must be used to benefit the economy.

Few union officials are so clear on what it will take politically to reverse America's industrial decline. Trumka is particularly compelling, however, because his argument for reindustrialization is not reducible to a replay of the philosophy behind an expanded welfare state. Rather, he wants to see an economy that functions so well that the state does not have to take on the responsibility of supporting unemployed citizens. Trumka focuses on what society owes to working people, not on what a charitable government might do for them.

Trumka calls for a "new patriotism" based on people rather than profiteering. Just as he sees the heads of the transnationals as a tiny, undemocratic elite, so he sees the changes that would protect American workers' wages as a benefit for the country as a whole. "We cannot expect to insure our freedom and promote peace throughout the world if our industrial heartland is allowed to wither and die," Trumka told the House Committee on Education and Labor. He reminded an AFL-CIO convention that unions had every reason to expect the government to help them during their time of need. "How many American coal miners and steelworkers have fought in Korea at our government's request, only to lose their jobs because of the importation of Korean steel? How many Americans fought in Vietnam at our government's request, only to find themselves now with no useful function in society? We think it is about time that the act of protection became a two-way street," said Trumka, who has opposed costly defense spending as a way of reviving the economy.

When the president of A.T. Massey declared, "Multinational corporations do not have a great deal of national loyalty and even less loyalty to southern West Virginia," and then announced that Massey engineers would be helping to design a coal mine in central China, the UMW immediately put the company on the defensive by reprinting its announcement in a full-page advertisement of its own that concluded, "It's time Massey owners showed some loyalty to the people who make their profits possible." In 1986, during Senate Judiciary Committee hearings in Cleveland on the bankruptcy of the LTV Corporation, Trumka called the company's attempt to cut off the health benefits of UMW workers who had retired from two LTV coal mines a "corporate mugging."

The UMW believes unions can change public opinion on key national issues. It is working closely with other trade unions on a series of problems that go beyond its constituency: supporting TransAfrica, the lobby that seeks to influence U.S. policy on South Africa; and, along with UAW president Owen Bieber, pushing the national boycott of Shell Oil Company to stop that company from doing business in South Africa. The UMW has also become a sponsor of Jeff Faux's progressive think tank, the Economic Policy Institute.

The union, which has traditionally supplied the shock troops of the American labor movement, is setting a crucial example for other unions, and for the American left. It is doing something the left hasn't managed to do since it lost power in the late 1960s—link progressive politics to the traditional values held by middle- and working-class Americans.

THE REAL THREAT: ENTERPRISE-BASED UNIONISM

♦♦ Lance Compa ♦♦

Lance Compa is Washington representative of the United Electrical, Radio and Machine Workers Union (UE).
He wrote this article for Economic Notes, *published by Labor*

Research Association (January-February 1987), reprinted with permission.

Many labor activists see the concessions wave of the 1980s as the biggest threat to the labor movement. But the larger threat is one of a new company unionism taking root in the labor movement, a unionism based in the single workplace of the single firm rather than among workers throughout an industry and in the working class generally. Some union leaders have adopted a strategy of enterprise-based unionism, where a single local union or group of locals in a single company seeks the best possible deal from the single firm's management.

In many cases the best deal possible means granting local-level concessions to save jobs. In other cases it means seeking wages and benefits higher than those of other workers in the firm or industry because of higher profitability or productivity in the favored facility. Often, enterprise unionists promote profit-sharing plans, or offer to link wages to productivity and profits, allowing concessions if profits fall.

Most "enlightened" employers and labor economists are today calling for a turn away from the supposedly old-fashioned, 1930's-style industrial unionism with its pattern-bargained, industry-wide agreements to a new era of "responsible," profit-and-loss-driven enterprise unionism. The push for enterprise unionism and the efforts of genuine trade unionists to preserve industrial unionism is the real crisis of the labor movement today. The fight against concessions is but one element in this deeper struggle.

Unions in every industry are faced with the crisis of industrial versus enterprise unionism.

- Auto workers saw their "Big Three" contract pattern fall apart after the Chrysler bankruptcy threat in the late 1970s. It took a tough strike by Chrysler workers to move back toward parity in the industry. Now the UAW is wrestling with company moves to play off one local against another through outsourcing threats. It is also struggling with the implications of a separate "Saturn" agreement at a new General Motors plant in Tennessee, and whether that contract's plan to tie wages to profits will spread into other basic auto plants.
- Steelworkers are now contending with separate, company-by-company bargaining after employers dissolved their industry bargaining council which reached industry-wide

contracts for nearly three decades.
- The United Mine Workers conducted a long strike to prevent the Massey Coal Company from establishing mine-by-mine bargaining apart from the national agreement.
- Teamster locals are plagued by company moves to break away from the Master Freight Agreement to bargain locally, and to change its biggest national contract, with United Parcel Service, into a series of city-by-city pacts.
- Communications workers are trying to maintain national bargaining with the regional telephone companies and other spinoffs of the former AT&T monopoly. Two of seven regionals want local bargaining.
- Electrical workers' unions are challenged by company efforts to turn national bargaining with a multi-union coordinated bargaining committee into union-by-union and local-by-local bargaining. Westinghouse workers had to strike in 1982 to block bargaining on a "business group" basis according to product line. GE uses joint ventures and plant sales to local managements to take shops out from under its national contracts.
- East and Gulf Coast shipping employers have announced their intention to bargain separately with the International Longshoremen's Association, in coastal talks and in separate, port-by-port negotiations aimed at putting longshore locals in competition with one another. [*And see section 10.*]

Backers of enterprise unionism portray the threat as coming from foreign producers in a world economy, appealing to workers' patriotism in "taking on the Japanese," for example. In practice the threat is the more immediate one of another local union, sometimes in the same national union, bidding wages and benefits downward to save jobs.

Destroying Solidarity

This breakdown of industrial unionism and advent of enterprise unionism pose a greater threat to the labor movement than concessions. Concessions can be won back in later bargaining, as many unions have shown. But a shift to enterprise unionism will destroy whatever class consciousness still exists in the labor movement.

From the point of view of the single plant or single firm, lower labor costs provide a competitive advantage. Union leaders are tempted to give special breaks to management in an attempt to save jobs. The same temptations exists on the upside: a firm or plant that is highly productive and highly profitable can bring demands for higher pay and benefits than those received by other workers in the same industry or other plants of the same company. This destroys solidarity in that industrial group.

It took decades of struggle for the labor movement to wrest industrial organizing and bargaining from employers. This allowed unions to take wages out of competition and to force owners to compete on the basis of better management, planning, equipment, materials flow, marketing, and other business techniques, instead of the historical solution of wage-cutting.

It is true that the industrial unionism built in the 1930s *has* reached its limits. A dozen unions represent the employees of GE, which now includes a swallowed-up RCA. Machine tool manufacturing sees machinists, auto workers, steelworkers, electrical workers, teamsters, molders and other unions negotiating different contracts with various branches of the same companies. Some unions waste millions of dollars competing for public employee bargaining units. Pilots, machinists, teamsters, transport workers and several flight attendant unions cross each other's picket lines in a scrambled airline bargaining mess. Electrical workers and communications workers' unions bargain separately with units of a giant like AT&T. Boilermakers, shipbuilders, metal trade councils, steelworkers and other unions deal with a struggling marine construction sector.

The labor movement needs more coordinated bargaining, progress toward union mergers, and legislative initiatives to permit broader bargaining units within companies and industries. Only strong, national unions with a single bargaining program for a company or an industry can confront the big employers that dominate the economy. And only strong national unions that prove they can stand up to a big company can attract unorganized workers to the labor movement.

Unionists are going to have to put aside their traditional differences if they are to see the twenty-first century from anyplace but the margins of U.S. economic and political life.

100 •• PROPOSALS FOR ACTION

GETTING TO THE GUTS OF WHERE WE WENT WRONG

♦♦ **William Winpisinger** ♦♦

William Winpisinger is president of the International Association of Machinists and Aerospace Workers (AFL-CIO). See also section 7.

This excerpt is from an address, "Proposals for Action," given to the Federation of Retired Union Members (FORUM) meeting on April 26, 1986 in Oakland, California.

We've gone through a lot of contortions over the recent past in the labor movement. Probably the most rewarding time I've had in my entire experience on the AFL-CIO Executive Council is the work we've done in connection with the Future of Work Committee appointed by President Kirkland in 1981. It caused us to do an enormous amount of study, a great deal of staff work, a good deal of professional polling all over the country to gather information on the scene in which we are operating in the 1980s, and to review the healthiest days of the '50s and '60s, the plateau of the '70s, the plunge in our fortune in the '80s.

Out of all that we rendered a report in 1983 on "The Situation of Workers and their Unions." It is a thorough-going analysis of what happened to us: the road up, the road flat, the road down, the erosion of jobs, the trade problem, and the activities of the right wing. It was done very candidly, I think probably for the first time in the history of the labor movement. And having set the scene, we went back to the drawing board in a series of meetings the likes of which I have never before been involved in. We all sat around a table, looked each other in the eye, confessed error, confessed indifference, analyzed our sins, second-guessed the Monday morning quarterbacks ourselves. We tried to get to the very guts of where we went wrong, and what we had to do to get right.

Out of that, two years later, came a report which embodied a series of recommendations that went to the Executive Council about the establishment of a new faith in the labor movement with a two-part goal. First, how to make ourselves more presentable to the American public at large, which still places us, in polls on "confidence in unions," somewhere between Richard Nixon and used car salesmen. Second, how do we begin to create a better feeling between the movement, the various international unions, and their memberships....

The Current Situation of the Labor Movement

We don't have any promise from American industry or entrepreneurs that the labor movement has a right to exist in the United States of America, let alone grow and prosper. Absent that kind of commitment, the labor movement has to come first. I submit to you that the movement is larger than any of us that are in it. Its survival must come first. That means that there are yet sacrifices to be made.

Of course, every time we assert that the institution must have first consideration, we render ourselves once again vulnerable to the charge that was popular when we were in that posture at an earlier time. There is only one other kind of politics in the world that puts an institution ahead of individuals. They are called Communists. They live in great abundance in some countries who run their governments as institutions in exactly that fashion. We always have kind of sheepishly pulled our necks in and tried to act like turtles when that charge is rendered against us.

And it is baseless, by the way. Just because an institution is worth protecting and takes care of its survival doesn't necessarily mean that you are practicing some kind of a foreign ideology. So we have got to dispel that notion as we move ahead in the United States of America.

THE THREAT FROM THE RIGHT

The current methodology is to use the right-wing pulpits proliferating all over the country, beginning with the bunch of kooks who declared Cold War in God's name on us, who preached incessantly in the name of Jesus Christ that he was a right winger. And I hope you know, as I do, that he wasn't, because I've read that book as I am sure you have, and we all know that he was a very benevolent and a very fair Jesus Christ.

I think it is an absolute, that if they don't enforce their doctrine officially using the right-wing pulpit in the name of God, then you will see in this country the first of a subtle but nonetheless real system of enforcement. You will see what comes with the transformation we have recently gone through as we have taken our half-hearted welfare state and converged it into a national security state. A national security state in every instance is accompanied by a national security police force. That's what we are ultimately heading for if we don't get it back on the track....

NEW METHODS OF ADVANCING THE INTERESTS OF WORKERS

◆◆ **AFL-CIO Committee on the Evolution of Work** ◆◆

In section 5, the Committee described the problems arising from the changing nature of work The excerpts in this section are also from the Committee's Report, issued February, 1935.

Our recommendations are based upon the fundamental premises stated at the start of the report: that the labor movement exists to advance the interests of workers as workers see their interests, and that to continue to perform their role, unions must come to grips with the current and changed realities workers face. Our aims—achieving decent wages and conditions, democracy in the workplace, a full voice for working people in the society, and the more equitable sharing of the wealth of the nation—remain unchanged. The means of securing those aims, while grounded in experience, must meet today's needs and anticipate tomorrow's aspirations.

There are, we believe, steps that can be taken to improve the efficacy of our traditional programs, and we will discuss those steps below. But from what has been said already, it is apparent that it is not enough merely to search for more effective ways of doing what we always have done; we must expand our notions of what it is workers can do through their unions. Accordingly, we begin with recommendations for new approaches that we believe worthy of examination.

Editors' note: All of the points made in the remainder of the Report are presented below, but the discussion of each point has been omitted.

1.1 Unions should experiment with new approaches to represent workers and should address new issues of concern to workers.
1.2 Consideration should be given to establishing new categories of membership for workers not employed in an organized bargaining unit.
1.3 The AFL-CIO should undertake a study of providing direct services and benefits to workers outside of a collective bargaining structure.
1.4 Unions should expand their use of the electronic media.
1.5 Coordinated-comprehensive corporate campaigns and the pressure of public opinion should be used to secure the neutrality of employers whose employees seek to organize a union and to assure good faith bargaining.
1.6 The AFL-CIO should establish a pilot project of experimental organizing committees.

While the new approaches described above are promising and worthy of trial, the heart and soul of the labor movement will continue to be the representation of workers through the medium of traditional collective bargaining and traditional organizing campaigns. The recommendations that follow are designed to enhance the efficacy of our efforts in these regards. They are divided into three categories: increasing membership participation in their unions; developing better communications with the public; and improving organizing techniques.

Increasing Members' Participation in their Union

Unions are their members. A union resurgence requires that the individual union member have the fullest possible opportunity to participate in his or her organization and receive the highest quality representation from the union.

2.1 Unions need to provide additional opportunities for members to participate in union affairs in ways quite different from traditional attendance at meetings.
2.2 Unions should increase the opportunities for members and national leaders to interact with each other.
2.3 Unions should make special efforts to provide an orientation program for new members.
2.4 Unions should devote greater resources to training officers, stewards and rank-and-file members.

Improving the Labor Movement's Communications

3.1 Efforts should be made to better publicize organized labor's accomplishments.
3.2 Union spokespersons need training in media techniques.
3.3 Efforts must be made at every level to better inform reporters about unions and trade unionism.
3.4 The AFL-CIO should develop a pilot project for a targeted area to test the usefulness of advertising to improve the public's understanding of labor.
3.5 Interferences with the right of workers to form a union should be forcefully brought to the attention of the general public to develop public support for labor law reform.

Improving Organizing Activity

There must be a renewed emphasis on organizing. The large increase in the workforce and in the extent of employer opposition requires an equal increase in the emphasis placed on, and the resources devoted to, organizing. All of the destabilizing changes we have detailed above have had the effect of decreasing the time and effort put into organizing. This trend must be reversed if any of the recommendations made below are to have any effect.

4.1 Organizers should be carefully chosen and trained.
4.2 Organizers should make greater use of modern technology.
4.3 Union leaders and rank-and-file members should be more

involved in organizing efforts.
4.4 Organizing targets should be carefully chosen to maximize the chance for success.
4.5 Small units should not be overlooked as organizing targets.
4.6 Unions should experiment with new organizing techniques.
4.7 When a unit is organized, unions representing other units of the same employer should coordinate assistance to the new unit to obtain a first contract.
4.8 Unions should make special efforts to attract those who belong to organized bargaining units but have not joined their union.

Structural Changes To Enhance the Labor Movement's Overall Effectiveness

There are a number of structural changes within the labor movement that would enhance our overall effectiveness.
5.1 The AFL-CIO Executive Council should adopt guidelines for use by affiliates contemplating mergers.
5.2 The AFL-CIO officers and staff should provide assistance to affiliates in effecting successful mergers.
5.3 The AFL-CIO should establish a mechanism for resolving organizing disputes among unions.
5.4 Unions must adapt modern budgeting, program analysis and planning techniques to union structure and finances.
5.5 A new method of funding state and local central bodies should be developed.

The preceding recommendations result from a searching self-examination and honest appraisal of our strengths and weaknesses and encompass a wide range of proposed actions to strengthen our unions and our movement and to enhance our ability to serve present and future members. This process of examination and appraisal must be continued within the Federation and within every affiliate as the basis for planning realistically for the future.

As the final note of this report, two quotes from our predecessors provide both a call to action and a reassurance. [The first came from then AFL-CIO President George Meany at the 1979 Convention]:

... the labor movement cannot be content with defending the status quo, or reliving past glories. We must constantly look to the future, develop new leadership, adapt policies to changing conditions and new technologies, but—always, always—with unswerving loyalty to the mission of the trade union movement as the instrument for improving and enhancing the working and living conditions of those who work for wages.

Editors' note: The final quote by Eugene V. Debs appears at the beginning of section 5.

POSSIBLE STRATEGIES FOR PENSION FUND INVESTMENTS

The National AFL-CIO has made four policy suggestions with respect to pension fund investments.

1. That pension fund money be invested in business enterprises which will increase the employment of [U.S.] workers.
2. That the social purposes of the investment be an important criterion, so that pension fund money goes into things which are vital to workers' lives, such as housing and health.
3. That the ability of workers to exercise their rights as shareholders be improved by pooling arrangements with investment advisors and coordinating pressure to affect investment decisions.
4. That investment not be allowed in anti-union projects.

The AFL-CIO has proposed the establishment of a "new independent institution," partially supported by pension funds and aimed at promotion of employment, as part of a broad program for the reindustrialization of the United States. This would include manufacturing, construction, transportation, maritime and other sectors necessary to revitalize the economy. It is suggested that this should be established by an act of Congress and directed by a board of directors equally representing the labor movement, employers, and the public.

They have urged increased pension fund participation in the AFL-CIO Mortgage Investment Trust. This currently encourages the construction of housing for workers by facilitating the investment of pension funds in mortgages and construction loans which are government guaranteed. It has also been recommended that an information system be established whereby AFL-CIO affiliates would be advised as to which companies should *not* receive investments.

♦♦Oregon AFL-CIO Employment and Economy Committee
[See also section 96]

DIVESTING INTERESTS IN SOUTH AFRICA AND NUCLEAR WEAPONS

♦♦The Editors♦♦

Since publication of the Oregon AFL-CIO Committee report in 1984, labor unions across the nation have taught employers that they better divest themselves of interest in the apartheid regime in South Africa. This campaign includes private employers with plants in South Africa, and government employers and pension funds with investments in corporations with plants in South Africa.

In November 1986, the voters in Berkeley, California, passed the Nuclear Free Berkeley Act, which requires the city to divest itself of all investments, including pension funds, "in businesses that knowingly engage in work for nuclear weapons or the components of nuclear weapons," and established the Berkeley Commission on Peace & Justice to carry out this goal. Similar weapons divestment legislation is being proposed to other cities and to pension funds in which unions participate.

ORGANIZING THE UNORGANIZED

♦♦The Editors♦♦

The material here is excerpted from Carolyn J. Jacobson's article, "Women at Work," in The AFL-CIO Federationist, *April 5, 1986. See also section 94.*

The 1986 convention of the Coalition of Labor Union Women (CLUW) approved a plan for a major CLUW conference in 1987 on the top priority issue of organizing the 36.5 million unorganized working women. Katerina Davis, a Chicana business representative for the Service Employees International Union (SEIU), and a member of the CLUW National Minority Task Force and the Labor Network on Central America, emphasized organizing as "a live or die situation." Morton Bahr, president of Communications Workers of America, told the CLUW delegates: "You are the future of the resurgence of the labor movement."

WHY WOMEN NEED UNIONS

"A union contract is the only sure way for working women to gain and maintain their economic freedom" at a time when "it takes two incomes to support a family."

"Women work for the same reasons men do—we need the money." What women don't need is the "tension, stress and guilt" that working women feel from trying to balance too many responsibilities with too few options.

CLUW will not be satisfied until the right to child care, care of elderly dependents, and family sick care is universally recognized.

♦♦Joyce, Miller, CLUW President
from remarks at 1986 CLUW Convention

President Shirley Carr of the Canadian Labor Congress urged CLUW convention delegates "to talk publicly" about the many concerns of working women because "we have suffered too long at the hands of those who would use us as women." She outlined the campaign for pay equity in several Canadian provinces and reviewed the CLC's program to overcome barriers to equality: affirmative action, pay equity, job training, educational leave, child care, parental leave, and an end to sexual harrassment. As union members, she said women must "not forget our sisters who are confronted by a whole host of other problems," including battering and prescription drug abuse. "Our share is half the world, half the politics and half the labor movement," she reminded the delegates.

FORWARD TO THE MILITANCE OF THE 1930s!

♦♦Leonard McNeil♦♦

For author note, see section 90.

The social and political triumphs of the CIO in the 1930s and '40s proved the value of the alliance between left and center forces in the trade union movement, and its ability to lead democratic mass movements. Rank-and-file groups like Ironworkers for Union Democracy [*described in section 90*] are part of the effort to rebuild the left-center coalition to provide an alternative to the labor leadership that still clings to the tattered flag of class collaboration. We believe that unions will continue their current decline unless they transform themselves into a "social movement with broad goals and a new concept of union membership that goes beyond dues-paying in a collective bargaining unit," as Herbert Hill has suggested. "And if it is transformed, the character of a new dynamic labor movement will be expressed most significantly in its active and special concern for the problems of racial minorities and women at the work place and in the community." (Herbert Hill, "The AFL-CIO and the Black Worker," 10 *Journal of Intergroup Relations* 5-78 (Spring 82)).

Yet the AFL-CIO accepted the findings of its Committee on the Evolution of Work in 1985, in a report that never mentions ending race and sex discrimination. "The Changing Situation of Workers and Their Unions" [*see excerpts in sections 5 and 100*] is also remiss in not calling for a program for jobs to provide full employment. It does not discuss the disproportionate unemployment of women and minorities, or everyone's right to a job.

The answer to complacency and conservatism in the trade union movement is not to be found in writing off labor, but rather in the struggle to make unions more powerful and consistent class instruments. If labor is to tone up its flaccid muscles and represent all its members, especially the lost constituency of women and minorities, it must acquire a sense of renewal and rededication to social progress.

The best and only hope for this sorely needed transformation lies in the mobilization and organization of the rank-and-file. The solution to sterility in the labor movement is much more than a question of replacing bad leaders with good leaders.

♦♦ RING IT IN THE MORNING ♦♦

Inspired by the song, "If I Had a Hammer," the artist portrays the role of women activists in the movement for peace, jobs, and justice.
♦♦ Credit: Irving Fromer.

Throughout its history, the U.S. labor movement has been split on how to deal with the concerns of its membership. There has been a dichotomy in the leadership between those who lead by following the popular prejudices of the times, and those who seek to mold a new consensus by offering new visions and new alternatives, including economic democracy and socialist perspectives.

One approach has been to try to keep workers apolitical, to keep us within the narrow confines of pure trade unionism, focusing solely on economic questions. This posture has caused workers to support a political party that does not represent workers, and to support a reactionary foreign policy. The assumption is that the employers and their class will never lose their economic or political power and we, as union members, must accept and work within the status quo.

The other approach has seen our interests as being diametrically opposed to capital. When organized labor represents its own interests, it can establish its own political party, speak out against imperialist aggression, oppose race and sex discrimination, support democratically-run unions, organize for peace, and serve the cause of justice in the workplace and in the community.

Workers have a right to hear these two ideological trends discussed and debated. Let class partnership versus class struggle trade unionism openly compete for the support of the membership. Let the rank-and-file evaluate the different analyses and policies. To do this, all restrictions left over from the Cold War must be eliminated from union constitutions so that Communists can belong to and be elected to union office. Workers have the right to choose for themselves between the basic currents of trade unionism.

Rank-and-file movements like IFUD have been effective in voicing discontent about labor's policies, leading to a new level of political debate. If the union movement is to revitalize and reaffirm its commitment to democracy and justice, increase its shrinking numbers, and defeat the corporate anti-union offensive, it has to return to basics. The rank-and-file must reassert their rightful control over unions, and push for an end to race and sex discrimination through affirmative action and other means.

UNITED LABOR MOVEMENT

Only a united labor movement can stop go-it-alone bargaining by single unions, or single locals with unions, that breaks down industry-wide standards. Only a united labor movement that is not preoccupied with old turf battles and Cold War ideologies can build firm ties to foreign labor movements to deal with transnational corporations. In the end, only a united labor movement that proves it can take on the companies and win will inspire unorganized workers to join.

We can keep on complaining about the labor law and the Labor Board and the union-busting consultants, and our complaints are fully justified. We need labor law reform and fairer law enforcement to protect workers' rights. But those unionists who built the labor movement did not have the benefit of labor laws or government agencies to help them. They went to the unorganized with a promise of strength in numbers, resolve in purpose, and unity in bargaining. That same strength and resolve and unity can organize millions of non-union workers and rebuild the U.S. labor movement in years to come.

♦♦Amy Newell, Secretary-Treasurer,
United Electrical Workers Union
from 11th Annual Labor Awards Luncheon,
Labor Research Association Journal

LET'S HIT 'EM FAST

♦♦Ron Teninty♦♦

For author note, see section 89.

We don't face the same kinds of problems in organizing that our predecessors faced back in the 1920s and '30s. They had a lot more problems, and we have a different class of people that we are trying to organize. There's a big difference now between sacrificing that mortgage on your home behind an organizing drive, and saying during the depression, "Yeah, I don't mind going out and breaking some heads. The worst that can happen is I can go to jail and get fed." Right?

So, let's concentrate on industries, and let's hit 'em, and hit 'em fast. Convince the people that the only way to win is to get out there in the streets, and we're going to win a higher percentage. Organizers in the Teamsters and other unions say, "If you just take those organizing drives where they convince the people to strike for recognition, the success rate has been above 80 percent." That's a far cry from the 43 percent we're winning now through Board elections. That should tell us something.

I say, let's head in that direction.

BASIC MORAL PRINCIPLES

♦♦ Charles Hayes ♦♦

For author note, see section 97; see also sections 9 and 16.

Extracted from the *Congressional Record*, Vol. 131, No. 26, March 6, 1985.

Some people think that moral vision should be left only to preachers in churches on Sunday and in synagogues on Saturday. We believe in moral values that are practiced every day of the week and every week and month of the year. We regard the present levels of unemployment, poverty, and distress as sinful. We think it is morally wrong to wait for the next recession before taking the kind of action required for true freedom, emancipation, dignity, and opportunity.

That is why our [Quality of Life Action Act] enunciates the basic moral principles of the right to earn a living and the rights of those unable to work for pay. That is why our bill embodies the vision of those many religious leaders who suggest that the great American experiment in political democracy should be extended by a new American experiment in economic democracy.

✦✦ **HONOR ROLL** ✦✦

These people helped us make this book possible by making pre-publication contributions.

Martha Acevedo
Irving Adler
Linda Akulian
Donna Allen
Mark Allen
Martha Leslie Allen
Karl & Ethel Amatneek
V. V. Arnautoff
Frank Arnold
Clifton Amsbury
Clyde Appleton
Shirley & Leo Auerbach
Helen Baker
Steven Barkan
Fran Barlow
Alan & Ruth Barnett
Mary Fagan Bates & Paul Bates
Eleanor Beach
Beth Behner
R.A. Berdish
Neil Berger
S. Berger
Gregory Bergman
Morris D. Bernstein
Berkshire Forum
Steven Birnbaum
Ruth Bishop
Doris K. Blank
The Boehm Foundation
G.E. Boehm
Max Bogner
Kay Boyle
Helen Brattin
Delmore & Hazel Brickman
Leona & Martin Brin
Charles D. Brown
Cleophas & Ursula Brown
Erik S. Brown
Esther & Archie Brown
Sarah & Edmund L. Bruno
John & Mary Burris
Joseph Byrnes
Humberto Camacho
Harold Cammer
Terrance M. Cannon
Marvin Caplan
Theresa K. Caplan
Meyer Case
Del Castle
Catholics for Peace & Justice
Isobel & Edwin Cerney
Louise Chazin
Mildred & Julian Chazin
Jean & Bill Cherevas
Anna Cherney
Paul & Miriam Chown
Andris Cirkelis
Lee Coe
Aaron Cohen
Robert Cohen
Zipporah Collins
Lance Compa
Sarah Cooper
Richard Correll
Joseph Costigan
Talmadge & Florence Creed
Margaret M. Cretser
John Cunningham
Benjamin & Julia Cunningham
Henry Danielowitz
Chandler Davis
Carl & Martha Davis
H.B. Davis
Larry R. Daves
Admiral & Dawn Dawson
Len DeCaux
Ernest DeMaio

Lloyd Dennis
Robert Dietrich
David Dillman
Louis Diskin
Dan & Laurie Zoloth Dorfman
Wolcott B. & Isabel Dunham
East Bay Women for Peace
Jane & Robert Edenbaum
Jim Eggleston
Frances Eisenberg
Jon B. Eisenberg
Monroe Eisenberg
Joseph & Joann Elder
Jacob O. Engelhardt
Claire Bradley Feder
Margo Anne Feinberg
Kathy Felch
Jerome & Cecelia Felcher
W.H. & Carol Bernstein Ferry
Jerry Fillingim
Celia & Joseph Fink
Charles P. Finn
Fred & Nina Firestone
May Fisher
Martin Fishgold
Marcia Fishman
Mel Fiske
Mildred & David Flacks
Mary Ann Flanagan
Henry Foner
Moe Foner

Leon Forer
Lucy & Jim Forest
James C. Forsyth
Vernon & Florence Fox
Susan Franklin Tanner
Tassia Freed
Frances Fritchman
Lucy Fried
Irving Fromer
Charles & Eileen Fujimoto
Mindy Thompson Fullilove, MD
Michael Funke
Mario T. Garcia
Charles Garry
Manuel Gelles
Glenn Goldstien
Ira Gollobin
Ernest Goodman
Walter Green
Marjorie H. Greenberger
Edith Greenstein
Vincent C. Gribben
Steve Gulick
Elizabeth Gunn
Estella Habal
Lucy Haessler
Vivian Hallinan
Samuel Handelman
Herbert Hardin
Earl Harju
Dennis Harley
Barbara Harvey
Arthur Heitzer
Bertha Ann Heller
Lee Heller
Philip Helms
Francis W. Herring
Richard Hershcopf
Rose B. Herskowitz

Fred Hirsch
Robert Hirsch
Ellenore & Joseph Hittelman
Jane Hodes
Gertrude & Rubin Hodess
Michael K. Honey
Myles Horton
Michael Howard
I.L.W.U. Local 142
I.A.M.
Eric Isbell-Sirotkin
Harold Jamison
Clinton Jencks
Christopher Jennings
Fiona St. John
Charlotte Johnson
Elmer E. Johnson
Harold Johnson
Karin Johnson
Lenna Jones
Joseph V. Kahn
Samuel Kamen
Daniel J. Kane
Marcia & Howard Katzman
Wells Keddie
Roger Keeran
Ron Kent
Sara Markham
Phyllis Kern
Martha Kentfield
Irving M. King
Mabel King
Ed Kinz
Lillian Kiskaddon
Richard Klein
Anna Koppel
Jacob A. Kramer
Henry Kraus
Sadie S. Krieger
Sarah & Maurice Kurzman

Ethel Lake
Corliss Lamont
Paul Landwehr
Harriet Whitman Lee
Jesse Lehman
Norman Leonard
Richard Lerner
Virginia Lerner
Kathie Lester
Anita Tuller Levine
Hank Levy
Deborah Lewis
Stephen Lewis
Gary Libby
A. J. Lima
Adele S. Lithauer
Robin Lloyd
Lee Lorch
Rosalind Lourie
Celia Luthy
Doug Magee
Maryann Mahaffey
Max Mandel
Robert & Irma Manewitz
Al Mangan
Gene Marchi
Ben Margolis
Sharon Mark
Kinsey Marshall
Rachel Marshall
Shauna Marshall
Bob & Ruth Martin
Carl Marzani
Natalie Masliyah
Catherine McCann
Shirley McDonald
Kathleen McElroy
Edward W. McGuckin
H & J McGuckin
Lawrence McGurty
Margaret McMurray
John McTernan
Tuz Mende
Thelma W. Meyers
E.J. Miller
Mark S. Mishler
Virginia Carrow Mitchell
Scott Molloy
Mary E. Moriarty
Toni Morozumi
Elizabeth Morrissett
Albert & Sarah Moyer
Celia Scott-von der Muhll
Ginnie Muir
N.E.C.L.C. Foundation
Sandy Nelson
Esther Newill
Tom Nicolopulos
Bruce Nissen
Helen Nocke
Rhoda Kellog Norman
David Oberweiser
William Obrinsky, MD
Otto H. Olsen
Paul Omelich
Ohio AFL-CIO
Oregon AFL-CIO
V. Padover
Joe Paff
Bernard Palmer
Yvonne Pappenheim
Will Parry
Joseph Peck
Al Perisho
Cecelia C. Pollack
Prof. William Preston, Jr.
Jim & Arline Prigoff
Patrick Quigley
Sally Rainer
John Randolph
Joseph Rapoport
Michael Ratner
Mrs. John Renarb
Frank Rentz
John Revitte
Alice & Harvey Richards
Thomas Richards
Rich Richardson
Irving & Jeanne Richter
Ross Rieder
James Robbin
Higdon Roberts, Jr.
Laura S. Robertson
Louis J. Rosenthal
Sam Rosenwein
Matthew D. Ross
Lynn Rossman
Mildred Sacks
Erwin A. Salk
Eleanor & Isadore Salkind
G. Samson
San Joaquin & Calaveras Central Labor Council
Ethel Sanjines
Joel Schaffer
Martha & Arthur Schaffer
Esther Schneider
Peter Schneider
Andrew Schoene
Mildred Schoenberger
Margaret Schumacher
Susan Scott
Julius Schwartz
Sylvia Schwartz
Peter Seeger
Edith Segal

Jeffrey Segal
Edward & Penelope Setchko
Oscar Shaftel
Claire Shallit
Alex Shames
Martee Shannon
Ralph Shapiro
Karim Sharif
Philip Sharnoff
George Shibley
Lee C. Sievan
Robert H. Silk
Eileen Silverstein
Christopher Simpson
Gertrude & Joseph Sindell
I. Philip Sipser
Rosalie S. Skovron
Florence Sloat
Sam & Dorothie Smith
Samuel Smith
Dr. Helen Sobell
Will Solomon
Laurence Sperber
Morris Stamm
Lisa Stearns
Mike Stein
Sylvia Steingart
Fred Steinmetz
Kenneth Stern
John Frith Stewart
Mark K. Stone
Donald Strasser
Jane Sure
George Sveum
Ethel & Edward Sweed
Jim Syfers
Myer & Beatrice Symonds
William K. Tabb
James & Janet Tam
Therese G. & Theodore Tanalski
Moe Tandler
Barbara Taylor
Pam Teller
Eugene TeSelle
Bertha Tenenbaum
Ida & Louis Terkel
John Thomas
Edith Tiger
The Tillow Fund
Eugene Tobin
Dale Treleven
Leo E. Turner
William Tuttle
Dorothy Tyrrel
Steven Unger
Walter & Patricia Urban
Matthew Ury
Van Bourg, Weinberg, Roger & Rosenfeld
D. B. Vance
James Varga
Veterans of the Abraham Lincoln Brigade
Charlotte F. & Leonard H. Wacker
Doris Brin Walker
Samuel Wallach
Esther Walter
Jonathan Walters
Al & Ann Wasserman
Linda Watkins
Fredrica W. Wechsler
Rose Weilerstein
Richard Weinmann
Edith & Bill Weintraub
Jack & LaMyra Weintraub
Marley S. Weiss
Fromma Wellman
Roy Wells
Fred Whitehead
Jay Wiener
William Wilkinsin
Henry M. & Deborah H. Willis
Beth Wilson
Dr. Leona Wolff
Women for Racial & Economic Equality
Kathy Yaksick

··INDEX··

ABBREVIATIONS USED

AAUP: American Association of University Professors
ACA: American Communications Association
ACLU: American Civil Liberties Union
ACTU: Association of Catholic Trade Unionists
ACTWU: Amalgamated Clothing and Textile Workers Union
ACWA: Amalgamated Clothing Workers of America
ADA: Americans for Democratic Action
AFDC: Aid for Families with Dependent Children
AFGE: American Federation of Government Employees
AFL: American Federation of Labor
AFL-CIO: American Federation of Labor-Congress of Industrial Organizations
AFM: American Federation of Musicians
AFSC: American Friends Service Committee
AFSCME: American Federation of State, County, and Municipal Employees
AFT: American Federation of Teachers
AID: Agency for International Development
AIFLD: American Institute for Free Labor Development
ALP: American Labor Party
AT & T: American Telephone & Telegraph Company
BCOA: Bituminous Coal Operators Association
Butchers Union: Amalgamated Butcher Workmen of America
CBTU: Coalition of Black Trade Unionists
CFR: Council on Foreign Relations
CGT: General Confederation of Labor
CIA: Central Intelligence Agency
CIO: Congress of Industrial Organizations
CIO-PAC: CIO Political Action Committee
CISTUR: Committee for International Support of Trade Union Rights
CLUW: Coalition of Labor Union Women
COMECON: Council of Mutual Economic Assistance
CORE: Congress of Racial Equality
CTAL: Latin American Confederation of Labor
CWA: Communications Workers of America
District 65: Distributive, Processing, and Office Workers of America
EEOC: Equal Employment Opportunity Commission
ESOP: Employee Stock Ownership Plan
FAECT: Federation of Architects, Engineers, Chemists & Technicians
FBI: Federal Bureau of Investigation
FE: Farm Equipment Workers
FEPC: Fair Employment Practices Commission
FIET: International Federation of Commercial, Clerical, Professional, and Technical Workers
Ford Local 600: UAW
FTA: Food, Tobacco & Agricultural Workers
GE: General Electric
GM: General Motors
HUAC: House of Representatives Committee on Un-American Activities
IAM: International Association of Machinists & Aerospace Workers
IBEW: International Brotherhood of Electrical Workers
ICFTU: International Confederation of Free Trade Unions
IFLWU: International Fur & Leather Workers Union
IFTU: International Federation of Trade Unions
IFUD: Ironworkers for Union Democracy
ILA: International Longshoremen's Association
ILGWU: International Ladies Garment Workers Union

ABBREVIATIONS USED

ILWU: International Longshoremen's & Warehousemen's Union
INS: Immigration and Naturalization Service
IT & T: International Telephone & Telegraph Company
IUE: International Union of Electrical Workers
IWO: International Workers Order
IWW: Industrial Workers of the World
Jim Crow: Segregation/discrimination against Blacks
Landrum-Griffin: 1959 Labor-Management Reform Act
McCarran Act: 1950 Internal Security Act (Subversive Activities Control Act)
MC & S: Marine Cooks & Stewards
MEBA-MMP: Marine Engineers Beneficial Association-Masters, Mates and Pilots
MFOWW: Marine, Firemen, Oilers, Watertenders and Wipers Association
Mine-Mill: International Union of Mine, Mill & Smelter Workers of America
NAACP: National Association for the Advancement of Colored People
NAM: National Association of Manufacturers
NATO: North Atlantic Treaty Organization
NCARL: National Committee Against Repressive Legislation
NEA: National Education Association
NIOSH: National Institute for Occupational Safety and Health
NLRA: National Labor Relations Act
NLRB: National Labor Relations Board
NMU: National Maritime Union
NNLC: National Negro Labor Council
NRA: National Recovery Administration
OAS: Organization of American States
OCAW: Oil, Chemical and Atomic Workers
OPA: Office of Price Administration
OPEIU: Office & Professional Employees International Union
OSHA: Occupational Safety & Health Administration
OSS: Office of Strategic Services
PATCO: Professional Air Traffic Controllers' Organization
RCA: Radio Corporation of America
SACB: Subversive Activities Control Board
SCEF: Southern Conference Educational Fund
SCLC: Southern Christian Leadership Conference
SCMWA: State, County & Municipal Workers Association
SEIU: Service Employees International Union
SISS: Senate Internal Security Subcommittee
SIU: Seafarer's International Union
Smith Act: Title 1 of 1940 Alien Registration Act
SNCC: Student Nonviolent Coordinating Committee
SUP: Seamen's Union of the Pacific
SWOC: Steelworkers Organizing Committee
Teamsters: International Brotherhood of Teamsters
T-H: Taft-Hartley Act (1947 amendments to Wagner National Labor Relations Act of 1935)
TNCs: Transnational Corporations
TUAD: Trade Union Action for Democracy
TUC: Trade Union Congress
TUEL: Trade Union Educational League
TUUL: Trade Union Unity League
UAW: United Auto Workers
UE: United Electrical, Radio & Machine Workers of America
UF & CWA: United Food & Commercial Workers of America
UFW: United Farm Workers Union
UFWA: United Federal Workers—CIO
UMW: United Mine Workers Union
UN: United Nations
UNRRA: United Nations Relief and Rehabilitation Administration
UOPWA: United Office & Professional Workers of America
UPWA: United Public Workers of America
USWA: United Steelworkers of America
Walter-McCarran Act: 1952 Immigration & Naturalization Act
WCL: World Confederation of Labor
WFTU: World Federation of Trade Unions
WPA: Works Progress Administration
WREE: Women for Racial & Economic Equality
YWCA: Young Women's Christian Association

♦ ♦

AAUP, 507; Red-baiting, 323
ACA, 264-265, 269, 304, 306-313, 380, 670
ACA v. Douds, 306-313, 410-411, 413, 708
ACLU, 476, 497, 507, 695
ACTU, 136, 210-211, 261-262, 273, 331-332, 343, 377
ACTWU, 813, 824, 826, 827, 829
ACWA, 269, 299, 396, 592, 630, 829
ADA, 336
AFDC, 817, 854
AFGE, 174-176, 398, 773, 813, 827; beyond pork chop issues, 777-778; 1968 Convention, 773-774; 1972 National Convention, 774; 1984 National Convention, 777-778; 1985 AFL-CIO Convention debate, 847
AFL, 328, 405, 432, 474, 629, 630, 640, 665, 727; and anti-Communism, 134, 164-168, 304; and black workers, 167; mergers, 667-670; organizing South after World War II, 164-168; raiding, 667
AFL Central Labor Council, 448
AFL-CIO, 731, 734-735; anti-Communism, 668; Bucks County, 826; Building Trades, 828; child labor testimony, 34; First Constitutional Convention, 668-669; foreign policy views, 669, 723-768; Galveston County, 827; leaders picket S. African consulate, 829; leadership influence peddling, 591; membership, 49; merger, 738; 1983 Convention resolution on nuclear arms race, 824; 1985 Convention, 847-849; 1985 foreign policy debate, 847-849; and NIOSH funding, 32; pension fund policy, 872-873; and spending for military, 65-67; women vice-presidents, 813
AFL-CIO Committee on the Evolution of Work, 39; new categories of members, 869 recommendations, 868-872;
AFL-CIO Executive Council, 738, 866; on national defense, 824, 830; 1985 meeting, 829
AFL-CIO Federationist, 813, 873
AFL-CIO Industrial Union Department, 110
AFL-CIO Mortgage Investment Trust, 872-873
AFL-CIO News, 818
AFM, 502, 503, 752

AFSC, 787
AFSCME, 827, 829; CIA funding, 732; District Council 37, 826; organizing women workers, 815; and pay equity, 81
AFT, 487, 752, 826, 848; Local 2, 814; Local 430, 492; Red-baiting of, 323; United Action Caucus, 787
AID, 729, 739, 741
AIFLD, 724-768; modus operandi, 743-745; resistance to, 761-762; rank-and-file bypassed in, 739-740; training programs, 743; *See also* specific countries
ALP, 269, 484, 685
AT & T spinoff companies, 864
Abortion, right to, 822
Abraham Lincoln Brigade, 130, 250, 473, 561, 707
Abraham Lincoln School, 250
Abt, John, 197
Academic freedom, 454-457, 472-490, 491-495, 504-508
Actors' Equity, 813
Addes, George, 327, 336, 338-340
Adelson, David, 380
Advocates for Women, 854
Aerospace industry, 56-58
Affirmative Action, 787-799, 818; arguments for, 792-796; attacks on, 793; goals, 799; like seniority, 795; statistics, 793,796; under Reagan, 775, 792; unions need, 796-797
African American Labor Center, 739
Afro-American, 551-552
Agricultural innovation, 842
Agricultural Labor Relations Act, 801
Agricultural Labor Relations Board, back pay awards, 802; budget slashed, 801-802; representation elections, 802; unfair labor practice charges, 802
Airlines, 639; deregulation, 87; and PATCO, 87
Airline unions, 86, 87
Alaska, Cannery Workers Union, 4
Albano, Debbie, 15
Albany, Georgia, 569
Albert Einstein College of Medicine, 490
Aldridge, Edward C., 57
Alexander, 280
Alexander, Harry, 445-446
Aliens, 553-560
Alinsky, Saul, 202-203
Allan, William, 328
Allende, Salvador, 744, 746, 751-753

Allen, Raymond B., 477
Alliance for Labor Action, 760
Allis-Chalmers, 326-341; strikes, 329, 337; wartime profits, 329; West Allis plant, 329; *See also* Christoffel, Harold
Alsop, Joseph and Stewart, 523
Alteman, Everett, 150
Amadis, Nello John, 673, 675
Amalgamated Meat Cutters v. NLRB, 417, 418
Ambrose, Otto, 742
America First Committee, 329
American Committee for Protection of Foreign Born, 201, 250, 594, 619
American Continental Congress for Peace, 287
American Council on Soviet Relations, 251
American Dream, 36-38
American Institute for Marxist Studies, 117
American Legion, 408, 458, 692-693
American Postal Workers Union, 776
American President Lines, 86
American Railway Union, 499
American Russian Institute of San Francisco, 251
American Smelting and Refin-ing, 595
American-Soviet Friendship Committee, 561
American Youth Congress, 350, 674
Ames, Robert, 598
Anaconda Copper, 740
Anderson, Jack, 776
Anderson, Lewie G., 850-851
Andres, Lloyd R., 50-52
Anti-Apartheid, 778, 818
Anti-Communism, 420, 453-471, 481, 682-710, 738; and AFL, 134; AFL-CIO raids, 211-212; and CIO, 134-136, 210-212, 237-242, 338; in early trade unions, 202-203; Philip Murray, 134-136; in South, 650-661
Anti-Semitism, 329, 424
Anti-Sovietism, 193-199, 317-321
Anti-Vietnam war movement, 788
April Action Coalition, 827
Aptheker, Herbert, 710
Arbenz, Jacobo, 732-733
Arbitration, 333, 700
Ariyoshi, Koji, 467
Armas, Carlos Castillo, 733
Armenta, Jess, 435
Armour & Co., 643
Arnautoff, Victor, 143, 150, 565

Arnold, Frank, 593
Aronson, Norma, 387
Asbestos exposure, 30-31
Asian American Free Labor Institute, 739
Asner, Edward, 102, 848
Associated Negro Press, 551
A.T. Massey Coal Company, 860, 862
Atlantic Pact, 388
Atomic Energy Commission, 347, 377, 530
Attorney General, 234-235, 564, 566, 641-642; list, 250-257, 443, 473, 482, 484
Auschwitz, 742
Austin, Richard, 490
AWARE, 710

BCOA, 860
Babcock & Wilcox, 378
Bacisin, John, 353-356
Baeza, Tony 714, 718, 721
Baggett v. Bullitt, 489
Bahr, Morton, 827, 874
Bail, 367, 368, 553, 554; denial of, 360, 365, 368, 410, 554-555
Bail fund, 555
Baker, Josephine, 550
Bakery, Confectionery & Tobacco Workers, 813
Bakke, Allen, case 791-792
Balasz, Walter, 365, 369, 370
Baldwin, Hanson, 317
Ballad for Americans, 129
Bancroft, Richard, 180
Bandinelli, Ranuccio, 478
Baptist Ministerial Alliance of San Francisco, 621; Baptist Ministerial Conference, 639
Bar admission, 710
Barbero, John, 682
Barnett, Ralph, 369
Barnett, Ross, 567
Barnes, Bianca, 149
de Barros, Adhemar, 748
Barry, Dick, 89
Bass, Charlotta, 554
Baugh, Robert, 835
Baxter, Halbert, 673
Bay Area Council Against Discrimination, 634-635
Bay of Pigs, 734, 746
Bazelon, David, 417
Beam, Paul, 453
Bechtel Corporation, 497-498
Beechert, Edward, 449, 453, 457, 463
Beeson, Duane, 721

Benson, Elmer, 558
Bergman, Lincoln, 151
Bergman, Miranda, 151
Berkeley Commission on Peace and Justice, 873
Berle, Adolph, 733, 746
Berman, Netta and Norman, 367, 368, 369, 372
Berne, Lou, 380
Bernstein, Al, 173, 174
Bertolini, F., 425
Bessie, Alvah, 509
Bethlehem Shipyards, 127
Bethlehem Steel, 50-52, 381, 681-706, 805
Bethune, Mary McLeod, 118
Beverly Enterprise, 816
Bias, in textbooks, 476, 508
Bieberman, Edward, 590
Biberman, Herbert, 599-601
Bieber, Owen, 827, 862
"Big Five," Hawaii, 447-471
Bigelman, Leo, 529
Biller, Moe, 777
Billings, Warren, 586
Bill of attainder, 309, 310, 413, 708
Bill of Rights, 374, 376, 499, 556, 569, 571, 695, 705
Bill of Rights Day, 695
John Birch Society, 572
Birmingham, 572
Birth control, 822
Bissell, Richard, 732-733, 751
Black, Hugo, 307, 309, 311, 313, 475, 562, 571, 611
Blacklist, 343, 499, 503, 509, 553, 710
Black market, 285
Blacks, business people, 345, 421; declaration of Negro voters, 1946, 118; discrimination by US government, 181-184, 389-398; employment, 228; hiring, 636-639; job discrimination, 117-118, 628, 792; jurors, 574; labor councils, 345; leadership, 660; musicians, 502; organizations, 563-564; organizers, 628-643; postwar political action, 117-118; press, 639; public workers, 389-398; representation, 629; seamen, 445; skilled trades, 118; students, 706; union leadership, 592, 662-666, 774; union membership, 6, 342, 434, 627-643; unity, 344-345; voter registration, 617; *See also* NNLC
Black women, 389-391, 638, 643-644; post-war discrimination, 118; super-exploitation, 644; women leaders, 774; Parks, Rosa, 648; Smith, Miranda, 617-618
Blankenhorn, Heber, 259
Blaylock, Kenneth T., 777, 827, 847
Blue-collar workers, federal, 773, 774
Blue Cross and Blue Shield, 856-858
Blue Eagle Codes, 379
Blue, Genevieve, 150
Bluestone, Barry, 852
Boanno, Danny, 153
Boatin, Paul, 343
Boeing Corporation, 57-58
Boggs, Michael, 728
Bogue, Virginia, 149
Boilermakers Union, 127
Bolz, Herman, 149
Book-burning, 530
Book Find Club, 513
Book of Common Prayer, 531
Boston School for Marxist Studies, 251
Boucher, Anthony, 143
Boudin, Leonard B., 383
Boulware, Lemuel, 375
Bouslog, Harriet, 467
Boycott, 550; bus, 649; Del Rey Tortilla, 770; grapes, 819; secondary, 383; Shell Oil, 862; United Farm Workers, 800-804
Boyd, Gerald, 641
Boyd, Leroy, 169-170
Braden, Anne, 648, 665
Bracho, Angel, 586
Bradley, Omar, 148
Branco, Castello, 750
Brandt, Joe, 672
Bratt, George, 535
Brazil, 750-751, 759; workers, 745-750
Brazilian Institute for Democratic Action, 747-748
Bread and Roses Bookstore, 151
Brennan, William, 607-608, 797
Bressler, Joseph, 490
Bricker, John W., 360, 373
Bricklayers Union, 847
Bridges, Harry, 127, 143, 270, 297, 298, 307, 430-433, 438-440, 448-470, 619-620
Bridges v. California, 307
Bridges-Robertson-Schmidt Defense Committee, 251
Bridges v. Wixon, 307
Brinkerhoff, Charles, 741
Brophy, John, 432

Brotherhood of Carpenters & Joiners, 832
Brotherhood of Railway and Airline Clerks, 751
Brotherhood of Railway and Airline Clerks, 751
Brotherhood of Railway Trainmen, 269
Brown, Archie, 245, 401, 418, 611, 707-708
Brown, Gus, 435, 436
Brown, Irving, 727, 728
Brown, Jerry, 848
Brown, John, 509, 633
Brown v. US, 708
Brownell, Herbert, 557-558, 560, 564, 679-680
Brownstone, F., 425
Bruce Church, Inc., 802-804
Bryant, Alden, 126
Bryson, Hugh, 402-403, 414, 417, 621-623
Bryson v. US, 417
Buckley, William F., 742
Buckmaster, L.S., 274
Budenz, Louis, 334, 335, 479
Buffalo Committee to Oppose HUAC, 703
Building trade unions, need for affirmative action, 787-797; Red-baiting, 629
Bundy, McGeorge, 505, 754
Burch, Dorothy, 645-646
Bureaucracy, charges of, 557
Burial of Old Beth, 50-52
Burns, Jack, 461-465, 532
Burt, Sam, 274, 405
Buse, Robert, 328, 330, 332-335, 340
Business Round Table, 79
Business unionism, 4, 97, 706
Butchers Union, 418, 537, 667; *See also* UF & CWA
Butler, John M., 377
Butler, Samuel, 732
Butsavage, Bernard, 827
Bywater, William, 827

CBTU, 212, 787, 826, 827, 828
CFR, 725-768
CGT, 193, 749
CIA, 530, 582, 728-760, 789; "Liberation Army," 733
CIO, 132, 297-305, 328, 380, 383, 406, 461-465, 474-475, 592, 593, 628, 629, 640, 730, 738; and anti-Communism, 134-136, 165-170; "blacklist" of communists, 1946, 236-242; Communist organizers, 202; Executive Board, 300, 303; expels unions, 233, 465, 619, 623; financial statements, 305; and ILWU, 86; international labor cooperation, 187-199, 726; merger 668-670; in 1930s and 1940s, 200-204; 1937 Convention, 261-263; 1946 Convention, 240-242; 1947 Convention, 618; 1948 Convention 387, 433; 1949 Convention, 298-299, 384, 675; 1950 black convention delegates, 305; 1950 Convention 615-616; no-discrimination policy, 154-155; Operation Dixie, 650; postwar philosophy, 198; postwar strike strategy, 207-211; and Progressive Party, 268-278; raiding Mine-Mill, 605, 667; and Red-baiting, 201; segregation in, 661-666; and Southern Conference for Human Welfare, 655; and Harry Truman, 274; in WFTU, 196
CIO Auto Workers Council, 360
CIO California Minorities Committee, 434, 435
CIO Cleveland Women's Auxiliary, 348
CIO Committee to Abolish Racial Discrimination, 165, 624
CIO Industrial Union Councils, 241
CIO-PAC, 109, 118, 201, 272, 273
CIO Tobacco Workers Organizing Committee, 173
CIO, Wayne County, 631
CISTUR, 762
CLUW, 212, 787, 813, 817-818, 826, 827; Center for Education and Work, 817-818; National Minority Task Force, 874; 1986 Convention, 818-821, 873-874
COMECON, 291
CORE, 563
CTAL, 730
CWA, 732, 751, 826, 827, 829, 874
Calderon, Celia, 586
Caen, Herb, 81
Cahn, Edmund, 587
California, Constitution, 493; Levering Act, 495
California Agricultural Labor Relations Act, 801
California Arts Council, 806
California CIO Council, 430-437
California Democratic Council, 713
California FEPC, 131
California Labor Federation, 98; 1980 Political Action Conference, 99-100
California Labor School, 137-151, 251,

California Labor School (*continued*) 452, 564-566; Children's Theatre 143; chorus and drama group, 143; and GI Bill, 138, 148; Labor Theatre, 141
California Medical Association, 528, 529
California Trucking Association, 714
Cal Trans, 797
Cambodia, 760
Cammer, Harold, 404
Cammer v. US, 416
Campbell, Mary Schmidt, 790
Canada, 407, 686; labor law, 49; Mine-Mill, 592; union movement, 89-97, 614, 682
Canadian Labor Congress, 90, 91, 874
Canadian Research Association, 831
Canadian Seamen's Union, 91
Cano, Bruno, 435
Cantor, Joseph, 681-706
Canwell Committee, 477
Capital flight, 845, 854-855
Capital Transit Company, 182, 391
Caplan, Marvin, 110-116, 544
Cappel, Walter, 332
Carawan, Guy and Candy, 571
Carey, James, 165, 191, 262, 375, 624, 640
Carillo, Elisio, 558
Carlisle, Harry, 554
Carlson, Frank, 554
Carr, Clarence, 211-212
Carr, Shirley, 874
Carroll, Terry, 289
Carson, Jules, 150
Cartwright, William P., 479
Carter Administration, 87
Casey, William, 742
Castle & Cooke, 448
Castro, Fidel, 734
Castro, Oscar, 434-436
Catholic, 406, 426, 445, 704; Catholic Church, 273; and Mine-Mill, 596, 599; *See also* ACTU
Catholic Lawyers Guild, 695
Cayton, Horace, R., 165
Cayton, Revels, 182, 622, 623, 627
Censored News of Your America, 709
Center for Defense Information, 827-828
Center for Trade Union Action & Democracy, 787
Central America, labor network on, 874
Central Unica de Trabajadores, 752

Cerney, Isobel, 137-151, 452, 564
Chacon, Juan, 586, 598
Chamber of Commerce, 81
Chambers, Virginia Derr, 595-601, 614
Chambers, Whittaker, 510
Chancey, Martin, 672
Chandler, Dorothy, 502
The Changing Situation of Workers & Their Unions, 39-49, 815; critique, 875
Chase National Bank, 285, 748
Chavez, Cesar, 800, 802, 827
Chemical exposure, 30, 32
Chemical Workers, 380, 827; *See also* OCAW
Chernin, Rose, 554, 556
Chester, William, 627
Chicago Federation of Labor, 18
Chicana union leader, 874
Chicanos, discrimination, 596-597, 599-601; in Mine-Mill, strike, 595-601; organizing, 6
Child care, 646, 819-821; collective bargaining on 819, 821; contract language, 820; legislation, 819-820; statistics 819; systems, 843
Child labor, 32-34
Chilean workers, 723-724, 744-745, 751-756, 761
China, Peoples Republic of, 315, 564, 566
Chown, Paul, 2-14
Christensen, Rudy, 634
Christians, Mady, 509
Christiansen, Leo, 143, 149, 150
Christoffel, Harold, 328-335, 340-341, 401
Christoffel v. US, 333-334, 341
Chrysler, 330, 642; bankruptcy threat, 863
Church, Frank, 750
Churches, 438-439, 476, 635, 638, 695, 710; *See also* Catholic, Jewish
Churchill, Winston, 132, 189-190, 199, 615; "Iron Curtain" speech, 209
Ciecorka, Frank, 149
Citizens Against Waste, 775-776
Citizens Committee for Harry Bridges, 252
Citizens Committee to Preserve American Freedoms, 503
Citrine, Sir Walters, 191, 195
Citron, Alice, 478
Civil liberties, 698, 701, 704
Civil rights, 418, 706

Index ♦ 891

Civil Rights Act of 1964, 70, 81, 559, 818; Title 7, 70, 798
Civil Rights Congress, 252, 436, 506, 640, 709
Civil rights movement, 650-661, 666, 788
Civil Service Commission, 180, 181, 183, 389-390
Civil War, 545
Clark, John, 593
Clark, Tom, 234-235, 242, 309, 402, 417; and *Jencks v. US*, 608
Class collaboration, 702, 706, 875
Class struggle unionism, 877
Clay, Cong. William, 22
Cleveland Building Trades Journal, 360
Cleveland CIO Council, 347-348, 361, 370, 674
Cleveland Federation of Labor, 361
Cleveland Police Subversive Squad, 672
Cline, Ray, 752, 754
Closed shop, 452
Coalition of Conscience, 659
Cobbs, Price, 529, 545
Cohn, Rabbi Franklin, 554
Cohn, Roy M., 411, 584, 588
Colby, William, 753
Cole, George, 805
Cole, Dr. Irwin, 529
Coleman, Thomas, 627
Collective bargaining, 28-29, 90, 328, 488, 670; area contract, 87; current problems, 58; and economic conversion planning, 61-63; in Federal sector, 397; General Electric, 90; Mine-Mill, 593
Colonial peoples, 632
"Colonizing," 683-704, 727
Committee Against False Economy, 175
Committee for Better Transportation, 635
Committee of European Economic Cooperation, 290
Committee on Government Operations, 21, 22
Committee for Maritime Unity, 438-444
Committee for a Sane Future, 827
Committee to Abolish HUAC, 503, 705
Communism, and Blacks, 165, 625, 629, 662-666; containment of, 404, 454; and fascism, 235; and racism, 204; and women, 674, 688

Communist Control Act, 611, 679-680, 707-710
Communist, domination, 307, 333, 454; front, 170, 492, 562, 642; indoctrination, 491; label, 298, 407, 652; menace, 407
Communist Manifesto, 148, 412
"The Communist Manifesto in Pictures," 519
Communist Party membership, charges of, 453, 455, 470, 498, 601-604, 640; denial of, 498; interrogation on, 420, 483, 495, 497; resignation from, 324; T-H charges of, 462, 473-474, 594, 671-678
Communist Party, Mexico, 594
Communist Party, USA, 250; accusations against, 299, 312, 339; and labor movement, 465; line of, 164, 386; SACB cases, 560, 680; sues, 475; sympathy for, 300, 334; victory of, 707-710
Communist Political Association, 250
Communists, 299, 348, 404, 440, 464; in auto industry, 335-336; benefits denied to, 710; in CIO, 164-168, 237-242, 303-304, 668; defined, 867; dismissal of, 477; influence in unions, 269, 310, 326-341, 603; organized CIO unions, 202; policies, 298; union officers, 877; in USWA, 681-706
Communist Worker, 641
Community Church, 575
Community medical center, 528-532
Compa, Lance, 862
Comparable worth, 69-81, 646, 817
Conant, James, 505
Condon-Wadlin Law, 487
Confederation of Mexican Workers, 192, 594
Conference on Negro Discrimination in Federal Service, 178
Congress of American Women, 513
Connecticut AFL-CIO, 814
Connell, James C., 360-373, 672
Connelly, Philip "Slim," 435, 516
Connor, "Bull," 568
Conspiracy, 454, 673, 676, 700
"Conspiracy of silence," 409
Consumer credit, 318
Contempt of Congress, 497, 499, 500
Contempt of court, 355, 371
Contract, winning after election, 785
Contracting out, 775
Contras, 756
Conversion from military production, 53-68, 821, 845

Conway, Jack, 759
Conyers, Rep. John, 83, 771
Cook's Union Local #44, 145
Cooper, Martin, 379
Coordinating Committee for the Enforcement of the D.C. Anti-Discrimination Law, 545-552
Coors, 848
Copeland, "Red," 170, 661, 663, 664
Cordiner, Ralph, 376
Cornell Institute for Women and Work, 815
Corona, Bert, 434
Corporate financing of elections, 99
Corporate profits, 204, 217-231, 296, 314-315, 318-321
Correll, Richard, 149, 248
Costello, Emil, 328
Council on Foreign Relations, 725-762
Council of Mutual Economic Assistance, 291
Cranefield, Harold A., 586
"Criminal Anarchy," 569
Crockett, George W., Jr., 627
Crouch, Paul, 470
Crowder, Earl, 664
Crozier, Clifford, 262
Crump, "Boss" Ed, 168, 652, 665-666
Cruz, Jose, 555
Cruz, Maria, 555
Crystal, Daniel, 545
Cuban workers, 84, 734
Culinary Workers Union, 4
Culture, a necessity, 805
Cummings, William G., 673, 675
Curran, Joe, 159-160, 198, 262, 274, 315, 438-440, 619-620, 622
Curtis, "Franco," 806-807

Daifullah, Nagi, 801
Daily People's World, 516
Daily Worker, 112, 253, 299, 316, 328, 334, 412, 413, 481, 491
Danbury Hatters, 383
Danly Machine Company, 15-19
Daugherty, Jim, 435
Daunic, Gilbert, 150
Davies, George, 356
Davila, Armando, 434, 436
Davis-Bacon Act, 35
Davis, D'Arnold, 355-356, 365, 369, 370
Davis, Henderson "Red," 661-664, 666
Davis, John P., 173
Davis, Katerina, 874

Davis, Leon J., 587
Davis, Nathaniel, 754
Davis, Nelson, 344
Day, Arthur H., 351-352, 356, 361
Day, Jack G., 677, 678
Deakin, Arthur, 191
Debs, Eugene V., 39, 201, 499, 504, 505
De Caux, Len, 132, 187-199, 216, 241, 249, 261, 271, 277
Decertification elections, 15-19
Deere, John, 337
Deindustrialization, 860; *The Deindustrialization of America*, 852
DeLacy, Hugh, 366
De La Cruz, Juan, 801
de la Cruz, Roberto, 803
de Lappe, Pele, 143, 149, 150, 637
De Maio, Ernest, 208, 262, 273
Democratic Party, 99-101, 453, 465, 581, 599, 691; 1944 convention, 269; 1984 election, 830-831; platform, 559
Denaturalization, 307, 555, 559
Denton, Jeremiah, 742
Dependent Care Tax Credit, 820
Deportation, 307, 433, 439, 443, 525, 559, 627
Deregulation, 87
Dermody, Joseph, 380, 585
de Sylva, 156
Deukmejian, George, 801-802
Dewey, Thomas, 120, 268, 272, 278, 475
Dewhurst, Colleen, 813
Diamond, Louis, 356
Diamond, Sigmund, 339
Dies Committee, 176, 302, 380; *See also* HUAC
Dillon Read and Co., 285
Disabled people's rights, 657
Disarmament, 95; *See also* Economic conversion
Discharge, 6, 696-697, 701; for political activity, 495, 497, 700-701; for union activity, 6, 16-19, 26-28, 44, 377
Discrimination, ethnic, racial, and sex, *See* Blacks, Chicanos, Japanese, Women, etc.
Distributive Workers of America, Local 65, 264-265, 271, 388, 623, 630
District 65, 264-265, 271, 388, 623, 630
Divestment, nuclear weapons companies, 873; South Africa, 873
Di Vittorio, Giuseppe, 192

Dixiecrats, 278
Dmytryk, Madelyn, 509
Doherty, John, 733, 745
Doherty, William, 725-758
Dombek, Joseph, 330, 332, 335
Domestic workers, 644; organizing, 815-816
Donahue, Tom, 728, 813
Donovan, John L., 175
Donovan, William, 742
Dotson, Donald, 22, 26
Douglas, William O., 307, 308, 313, 400, 409, 433, 475, 585, 611
Douglass, Frederick, 104-105
Douglass-Lincoln Society, 524
Doyle, Arthur W., 368
Driver, Melvin, 353-355
Dual unionism, 436, 641-642
Duarte, Napoleon, 829, 847
Dubinsky, David, 240, 336, 727-738, 759, 760
Du Bois, W.E.B., 413, 574-576, 627
Duffy, Adrian, 445
Duggan, Lawrence, 510
Duke, Patty, 813
Dulles, Allen, 729, 733
Dulles, John Foster, 733
Dungan, Ralph A., 754
du Pont, E.I., 325; and NLRB, 25
Durr, Clifford and Virginia, 648-649
Dyson, John Mack, 170, 662

EEOC, 22
ESOP, 850-853
Eastern Europe, 290-291, 295
Eastland, James O., 611, 653, 663-664
Ebasco Services, 378-384
"Economic Bill of Rights," 119
Economic concentration, 218-219, 224-225; federal ownership 226-227; private ownership, 227
Economic conversion, 53-68, 227-229; after World War II, 381; difficulties, 59-65; and Hayes Bill, 845-846
Economic Cooperation Administration, 290
Economic democracy, 877, 879
Economic Notes, 862-865
Economic planning, 835-838, 839-846
Economic Policy Institute, 862
Economic system, not working, 657-658
Edmunds, Pete, 622
Education, legislation to improve, 843; right to, 821
Education Amendments of 1972, 70

Edwards, Don, 705
Edwards, Ebby, 191
Ehrlich, Isaiah, 379
Einstein, Albert, 474
Eisenberg, Frances, 491-495
Eisenhower, Dwight D., 373, 530, 551, 557, 588, 639, 667, 733; CIO support, 272-273
Elber, Irwin, 150
Elections, presidential 1948, 278; union, 13, 14; *See also* CIO-PAC, NLRB
Ellis, Fred, 481
El Salvador, 83, 757-759, 761, 778, 847
El Taller de Grafica Popular, 287, 586
Emerson, Thomas I., 480, 705
Empire Zinc Company, 597-598
Employment Act of 1946, 120-121, 841, 846
Emspak, Julius, 496-497, 499
End of an Era, 806-807
Endicott-Johnson Company, 407, 408
Engels, Frederick, 412
Enterprise-based unionism, 862-865
Environmental, concerns, 837; movement, 656
Epicurus, 563
Equal Pay Act of 1963, 70, 818
Equitable Life Assurance Society, 815
Erikson, Adeline Cross, 149, 150
Escalator clause, 344
European Recovery Plan, *See* Marshall Plan
Evans, Robert, 369
Ex-Communist witnesses, 412-413
Export-Import Bank, 286-288, 861
Expulsion, union members, 712-722
Exxon, 861
Eyster, Rev. Fred, 800

FAECT, 378-384, 386
FBI, 468, 508; activities, 555, 568, 577-582, 584, 662; attacks, 592; and the Coast Guard, 443; and Curran, 438-440; files, 583; ILWU and Hawaii, 467; informers, 562, 603; investigation, 300, 414, 454, 675; and Jencks, 603, 609; and steelworkers, 686-687; 691
FE, 298, 303-304, 326, 337-339, 498-499
FEPC, 109, 177-185, 389-390, 497, 628, 633, 639; *See also* EEOC
FIET, 831-832

894 • Index

FSLN, *See* Sandinista Front for National Liberation
FTA, 166, 168, 169, 269, 304, 387, 430-434; Local 19, 661-666; Local 22, 616-618, 652; Memphis, 653
Fair Labor Standards Act, 32, 34
Fairchild Corporation, 350, 674
Falk, Adrien, 143
Farben, I.G., 729, 742
Farmer v. Fur & Leather Union, 411
Farmer Labor Party, 578, 581
Farmworker unions, 553; *See also* UFW
Farrington, Joseph, 453-454, 464
Fascism, 284, 434-435
Faulk, John Henry, 710
Faux, Jeff, 862
Fawick Airflex Company, 346, 348-372, 672
Federal deficit, 845, 856
Federal Employees Loyalty Program, 243-244; *See also* Loyalty oath
Federal Public Housing Authority, 520-522
Federal Radio, 381
Federal Renegotiation Board, 59
Federal Security Agency, 391
Federal Trade Commission, 183-184
Federal workers, organizing, 172-186, 389-398, 772-779; statistics, 772-773
Federation of Retired Union Members, 866
Feinberg Loyalty Law, 475, 489
Feldman, Sandra, 814
Feller, Abraham, 510
Feller, David, 693, 698
Fifth Amendment, due process guarantee, 265, 306, 309; employer hearings, 477, 485, 507, 700-701; judicial hearing, 603; self-incrimination privilege: congressional committee witnesses, 464, 496, 498-499, 692-699, 705; state committee witnesses, 493
Fightback, 788
Figueroa, Luis, 755
Filipino workers, 452
Finerty, John F., 586
First Amendment, congressional committee witnesses, 281, 464, 496, 498-500, 506, 695, 705-706; exercise of, 10; freedom of association, 563; T-H oath, 265, 306-313
Fisher, Avalo Allison, 402-403
Fisher, Earl, 169, 653, 660, 664-665

Fishermen and Allied Workers, 269, 304
Fitzgerald, Albert J., 269, 271, 273
Fitzmaurice, David, 360
Fitzpatrick, Thomas J., 496
Flattery, Hugh, 445-446
Flaxer, Abram, 237, 304-305, 392-393
Fleming, Robert, 695
Flex-time, 821
Flight attendants, 813; unions, 865
Flying squadrons, 328, 335
Flynn, Elizabeth Gurley, 710
Foner, Henry, 200
Foner, Philip, 164, 615, 790
Fontaine, Harold, 149, 622
Food & Allied Service Trades Department, 816
Forche, Carolyn, 105
Ford Foundation, 789
Ford, Gerald, 27
Ford Motor Company, 330, 381, 640, 641, 642; 1941 strike, 343; River Rouge, 630-631
Foreign agents registration law, 573-576, 710-711
Foreign born workers, 553-560
Foreign elections, influencing, 285-288
Foreign trade, 285-288
Forer, Joseph, 417, 545
Fortune 500, 775
Forty-hour week, 405
Frachon, Benoit, 193
France, 291-292; general strike, 292
Franco, Francisco, 615
Frankfurter, Felix, 308, 313, 475
Freedom of Information Act, 584-588
Freedom of speech, 576
Freedom of thought, 311
Freedom Train, 644
Freedman's Hospital, 391
Freeman, James, 467
Freeman, Richard B., 814
Free Trade Union Committee, 728, 732, 738; and CIA, 728
Free Trade Union Institute, 739
French Revolution, 291
Frick Group, 742
Friedman, David, 479-480
Friedman, Robert, 621, 625
Friele, Berent, 740, 748
Fritchman, Stephen H., 528-532, 554
Fromer, Irving, 149, 622, 876
Fuchik, Julius, 580
Fujimoto, Charles, 451-470
Fujimoto, Eileen, 467-470

Full employment, 778, 792; legislation promoting, 839-846; right to, 821
Full Employment and Balanced Growth Act of 1978, 841, 842, 846
Fullilove, Mindy Thompson, 117, 627, 633, 643, 660
Fur and Leather Workers, *See* IFLWU
Future of Work Committee, 866

GE, 67, 347, 359, 381, 635, 642, 645, 864; Canadian subsidiary, 90; collective bargaining, 90; Knolls nuclear laboratory, 377; Local 707, 646; Lynn plant, 376; North Carolina plant, 13
GE Electric Bond and Share Co., *See* Ebasco Services
GM, 326, 330, 351, 381, 642, 747; plant in Tennessee, 863; workers, 832
Galbraith, John Kenneth, 103-104, 505
Galvan, Eppy, 435-436
Gangsterism, 261-263
Garcia, Manuel, 434
Gardner, Fred L., 673, 675
Gardner v. Broderick, 489
Garfield, David, 675
Garfield, John, 509
Garvin, Victoria, 630
Gatewood, Ernestine, 150
Gay people's rights, 657
Geer, Will, 598-601
Gellert, Hugo, 316
Geneen, Harold, 753
General Services Administration, 372
Geneva protocol, 483
Ghetto, 476
GI Bill, 138, 139
Gilbert, Louise, 149, 654
Ginger, Ann Fagan, 504-508
Ginger, Jim, 809-812
Ginger, Ray, 203, 504-508
Gitlow, Benjamin, 413
Gladstein, Richard, 498
Glass Bottle Blowers, 752
Glover, Eugene, 832
Gloversville, New York, 409
Godson, Roy, 740
Gold, Ben, 270-271, 419-429; in CIO, 210, 236-241, 246-247, 263, 297-303; in Communist Party, 404-405, 407, 427-428; fur worker, 429; IFLWU president, 405-417
Gold v. US, 402, 411-418

Goldberg, Arthur, 693, 698, 737-738, 740, 741, 748, 757
Goldblatt, Lou, 451-461, 586
Goodlett, Carleton, 627
Goodman, Ethel, 636
Goons, 445-446
Gordon, Lincoln, 746, 748, 749
Gorman, Patrick E., 418, 537-538, 586
Gottbaum, Victor, 826
Goulart, Joao, 747-749
Government Operations Subcommittee on Manpower and Housing, 23
Government workers, 172-186, 389-398, 413-414, 525, 772-779, 827
Grace, J. Peter, 740, 741-742, 754, 756; Commission, 775-776; Company, 741, 742
Grant, W.G., 343
Graphic Arts Workshop, 149, 565, 622, 654
Graphic Communications Union, 827; Local 388, 809-812
Great Britain, health care, 531; labour party, 292; nationalization,, 292; post World War II, 187-188, 189-191, 195-199; TUC, 190; unemployment, 292
Great Depression, 4, 111, 119, 217-218
Green, Ellen, 853-856
Green, John, 210, 262
Green, William, 132-133, 164, 202, 269, 272
Greenfield, Samuel, 486
Grenada, 83, 847
Grievance procedure, 330, 458, 466, 697-701
Griffin, Herman, 150
Griswold, Erwin, 697
Gromyko, Andrei, 190
Gropper, William, 501
Grossman, Hazel, 150
Guaranteed income, right to, 821
Guatemala, 530, 733; Guatemalan workers, 430, 733-734, 761
Guinier, Ewart, 391, 627
Gustafson, Elton and Sarah Reidman, 490
Gutride, Minnie, 472-473

HUAC, 336, 501, 519, 640-641, 740; and Allis-Chalmers, 333; "The American Negro and The Communist Party," 642; Buffalo hearings, 691-692, 695, 703-705; charges, 692-693; and Civil Rights, 571-572;

HUAC (*continued*)
  Dies Committee, 176, 302, 380; in Hawaii, 447, 460, 462-467, 470; in International Harvester strike, 376; Los Angeles hearings, 502-503; and Mine-Mill, 602; movement to abolish, 656; and NLRB elections, 279-282; and NNLC, 627, 640-641; "100 Things You Should Know," 347; San Francisco hearings, 497, 708, 712; in Twin Cities, 579; and UE, 496-499; and victim's letter, 510-511; in Winston-Salem, 617, 653; and *Yellin v. US,* 500
Haessler, Carl, 339
Haig, Alexander, 742
Hall, Gus, 672, 682
Hall, Jack, 451-469
John Hancock Insurance Co., 387
Handelman, Samuel, 356
Hanna, Harry, 371-372
Hanna Mining, 747, 748, 749
Hanson, Rhonda, 172, 389, 397
Harlem, 628
Harlem Committee for Better Schools, 478
Harlem Trade Union Council, 253, 629
Harriman, Averell, 197, 198, 669
Harris, Marie Richardson, 391
Harris, Tom, 309
Harrison, Bennett, 852
Hartford, Ken, 528
Hartley, Fred, 333, 337; Labor Committee, 473
Harvard University, 504-508, 697; business school, 505-506
Hashmall, Frank, 672
Hastie, William H., 118
Hatch Act, 181, 773, 777-778; charges, 847
Hatch, Orrin, 848
Hatwood-Futrell, Mary, 69-80
Haug, Fred, 324, 350, 361, 364, 372, 402-403, 607, 671-678; Marie, *See* Marie Reed
Haug v. US, 402-403, 607, 671-678
Hawaii, Communist Party, 447, 453-457, 463, 465-470; ILWU, 447-471; longshore strike, 1949, 459-462; statehood, 454-463
Hawaii Civil Liberties Committee, 253, 456-457
Hawaii Employment Relations Act, 452
Hawkins, Octavia, 627, 643
Hayden, Bits, 149, 519

Hayden, Sterling, 705
Hayes, Charles, 82-85, 119, 879; full employment, 839-846; Quality of Life Action Act, 839-846
Haywood, Allan, 270, 620
Haywood, Margaret A., 545
Health care benefits, 524, 531; terminated on plant closure, 805
Health insurance companies, 856-858
Health and safety issues, 815; legislation, 778, 818, 843
Hearst newspapers, Red-baiting, 330-331
Heath, Edith, 143
Hecht Company, 549-551
Helms, Richard, 733, 753
Henderson, Leon, 336
Henning, John, 98
Henry, Lyndon, 421
Heritage Foundation, 57
Herman, James, 827
Hernandez, Lee, 435
Hickey, William, 741
Higgins, Marguerite, 317
Highlander Folk School, 138, 649, 655
Hill, Charles, 627
Hill, Herbert, 875
Hill, Luther, 638
Hill, Rick, 33
Hillman, Sidney, 135, 189-190, 196, 197, 269, 272
Hines, Lewis, 640
Hinton, Deane R., 754
Hiring hall, 448-449
Hiroshima and Nagasaki, 115, 726
Hirsch, Fred, 723-768
Hispanic Labor Council, 771
Hiss, Alger, 510
Histadrut, 748
Hitchcock, George, 150
Hitler-Stalin non-aggression pact, 334
Hobbing, Enno, 745
Hoch, Myron, 490
Hogan, Austin, 380
Hollywood, 102-107, 447, 509-512; Ten, 281, 464, 509
Home Relief Bureau Workers, 379
Honey, Michael, 168, 660, 661
The Honolulu Record, 467
Hood, William, 344, 627, 632, 639, 640, 641
Hook, Sidney, 477
Hoover, J. Edgar, 414, 584
Hospital & Health Care Employees, 815-816, 827

Hotel & Restaurant Employees, 2, 4; Yale University strike, 815
House Committee on Education and Labor, 861
House Select Committee on Children, Youth & Families, 819
Housing, low-cost, 524; prefabricated, 842
Housing Authority, 515
Houston, Charles H., 182, 545
Howe, Mark De Wolf, 507
Hravchek, Mike, 852-853
Huberman, Leo, 148, 386
Hudson, Kent, 614
Hughes, Charles W., 486
Hughes, Langston, 107, 533
Human right, to a job, 594
Human Rights Cantata, The, 125
Humphrey, Hubert, 374-376, 581, 759
Hunsicker, Oscar, 368
Hupman, Everest, 402-403
Hurd, Joy Seth, 368
Hutchinson, Barbara, 813
Huxtable, Richard S., 351-361, 366, 371
Hydrogen bomb, 530
Hyun, David, 554

IAM, 55, 593, 672, 826, 827, 832, 849, 866; Lodge 2155, 672
IBEW, 12, 375, 826
ICFTU, 726, 730, 731
IFLWU, 128, 826; Gloverville strike, 211-212; and Progressive Party, 269-271; Red-baiting, 210, 239, 323-324; and Rosenberg-Sobell Case, 587; and T-H Act, 263, 324, 399-400, 402, 404-429; and wage increases, 297-298; and withdrawal from CIO, 303-304
IFTU, 190, 191, 195
IFUD, 787-791, 877; *The Loadline,* 789; Red-baited, 789
ILA, corruption in, 620; hiring discrimination, 154-155; and ILWU, 86; and Minimum Standards Agreement, 87-88; and NMU, 445; and National Negro Labor Council, 629; 1934 San Francisco Strike, 448-449; separate port-by-port negotiations, 864
ILGWU, 127, 555, 730, 770-771, 826, 829, 832-833; child care center, 821
ILO, *See* International Labor Organization
ILWU, 140, 142, 307, 315, 353, 468, 670, 827, 828; Annc Rand Research Library, 142; anti-Nazi strike and picket, 245; Black and white workers, 154-155; CIO expulsion of, 304, 619; Communist Control Act, 707-708; Democratic Party politics, 453-455; FBI investigations, 584; Hawaiin statehood, 454; history, 86; HUAC in Hawaii, 463-466; joint organizing with Teamsters, 780; Local 10, 829; Local 23, Tacoma, Washington, 86; Local 26, 434, 435; and Progressive Party, 269-270; Red-baiting, 323, 347, 453-471, 619-620; Smith Act, 467-471; solidarity actions, 353, 630, 713; 1934 strike, 448-449; 1949 strike, 447-471; T-H oath, 266, 461-463, 611; wage increases, 297
ILWU Dispatcher, 468, 620
INS, 307, 410, 433-434, 436, 553-560, 599-601, 770; employees in AFGE, 773; Council, INS-AFGE Councils, 779; "Operation Terror," 558
IT & T, 381, 734, 748, 751, 753
ITU, *See* International Typographical Union
IUE, 93, 375-377, 624, 827, 828
IWO, 523-527, 561, 684-685
IWW, 201, 613
Ickes, Harold, 501
Ignacio, Amos, 457, 458, 466
Imbrie, James, 705
Immigrants, Black, 796; British, 682; European, 795
Income and Jobs Action Act of 1985, 83, 119
Independent Progressive Party, 137, 432
Industrial concentration, 683-703
Industrial homework, 818
Industrial unionism vs. enterprise unionism, 865
Inflation, World War II, 222
Informers, 413, 453, 457-458, 470, 562-563, 581, 584, 673, 675-676
Infrastructure, development of, 836, 840
Injunctions, 351, 355, 356, 361, 365, 372, 383, 411, 569
Inland Steel, 265, 270
Institute for Global Education, 595
Institute for Industrial Relations, UC-Berkeley, 2, 800
Insurance, 523-527
Integration, shipboard, 439

Intellectuals, 580, 581, 692
Inter-American Regional Organization of Workers, 730-743
Internal Revenue Service, 181, 525
International Bank for Reconstruction and Development, 844
International Book Store, 519
International Brigade, for Loyalist Spain, 348
International Brotherhood of Teamsters, Chauffeurs & Warehousemen, *See* Teamsters
International Federation of Christian Trade Unions, 94
International Federation of Petroleum and Chemical Workers, 732, 747
International Federation of Professional and Technical Engineers, 384
International Harvester, 168, 337, 376, 381, 593; Louisville plant, 651-652
International Labor Day, 594
International Labor Organization, 20
International labor solidarity, 726, 761-762, 828-830, 834
International Metalworkers Federation, 832
International Monetary Fund, 844
International solidarity, 594
International Trade Secretariats, 731-732, 742, 743, 831
International Typographical Union, 24, 260, 713
International Woodworkers, 402, 680
"Iron curtain speech," 209
Iron Range, 577-582
Ironworkers, women and minority applicants, 791-792
Ironworkers Local 378, 787, 791
Isabel, George, 662
Isthmian Steamship Company, 153-154
Italy, under Marshall Plan, 284-288
Izuka, Ichiro, 450-470

Jack Reed Labor Studies, 138
Jackson, Don, 599
Jackson, Robert, 307, 312-313
Jackson, Jesse, 83, 659
Jacobson, Carolyn J., 813, 873
Janowitz, John Edward, 673
Jansen, William, 472, 478, 480, 484
Japan, competition, 864; postwar industry, 319
Japanese, discrimination against US citizens in World War II, 310, 449-452
Jarrico, Paul and Sylvia, 596-598
Jefferson School, 138, 149, 254, 562-563, 685
Jefferson, Thomas, 312
Jehovah's Witnesses, 308, 312
Jencks Act, 608
Jencks, Clinton, 402-403, 595, 597, 601-610; T-H charges dismissed, 607
Jencks v. US, 602-610
Jenkins, David, 139, 145, 148, 150
Jenner Investigating Committee, 490
Jesus Christ, 868
Jewish, 434, 684, 685, 695
Jewish Labor Committee, 728
Jewish Labor Council, 18
Jewish People's Fraternal Order, 254, 523, 524
Jim Crow, 540, 637; in AFL, 167; in CIO, 168, 305; and Civil Rights' Movement, 658; and government policy, 389-398; and HUAC, 502-503; in military, 116; opposed by FTA, 169; Negro Labor Council, 629, 632-634, 636; Progressive Party, 275; and UFWA, 177-180; in Washington, DC, 544-552
Job Action Conference, 634
Job creation, 837-838, 856
Job discrimination, 787-799
Job sharing, 821
Jobs, Peace and Justice Demonstration, 1985, 826-827
Jobs with Peace resolutions, 826
Johnson, Hugh, 202
Johnson, Joe, 627
Johnson, Keith, 827
Johnson, Lyndon, 416, 738
Johnson, Dr. Mordecai, 615-616
Johnson v. Transportation Agency, Santa Clara County, California, 797-799
Johnston, Eric, 133, 550, 740-741
Joint Anti-Fascist Refugee Committee v. McGrath, 254, 561
Joint Apprenticeship Training Committee, 788-789
Jordan's Studio, 442
Jouhaux, Leon, 191
Joyce, Diane, 798
Joyce, John T., 847
J.P. Morgan and Co., 285, 325
Jun, John, 555
Jurisdictional battles, 337, 668
Jurors, 413-415; Blacks, 574; Jews, 575; jury trial, 708

Kagan, Mimi, 150
Kahn, Albert E., 523
Kaiser Aluminum, 792
Kaiser Industry Archives, 114
Kane, James, 827
Kane, Dan, 832
Kaplan, Raymond, 510
Kaufman, Irving, 526
Kawano, Jack, 464-470
Keeran, Roger, 326, 342
Kefauver, Estes, 666
Keller, Fred, 369, 370
Kelso, Louis O., 851
Kemp, Bessie, 585
Kennecott Copper, 595, 605
Kennedy, John F., 376, 397, 559, 738, 747
Kennedy, Robert, 568, 747, 759, 760
Kenny, Robert, 143, 554
Kent, Morton E., 510
Kent, Rockwell, 710
Kent State, 761
Kenyatta, Jomo, 568
Key System Transit Lines, 634-635
Keyishian v. Board of Regents, 489
Keynesian economics, 318
Kiendl, Theodore F., 479-480
Killen, Lili Ann, 150
Killiam, John, 402-403
Kim, Diamond, 555
Kim, Fanya, 555
Kimoto, Jack, 467
King, Martin Luther, 559, 572, 658-659, 760
Kirkland, Lane, 728, 740, 757, 758, 761, 813
Kissinger, Henry, 505, 729, 753
Kiviat, Charlie, 153
Klausner, Rachel, 585
Kleps, Albert, 356, 358, 366
Klevan, Morton, 852
Knight, O.A., 732
Knights of Columbus, 373
Knights of Malta, 742
Knights of White Camelia, 254
Kochert, Rieta, 645
Koestler, Arthur, 317
Kolko, Gabriel, 290
Kolko, Joyce, 290
Koppel, Stanley, 149
Koppelman, Harold, 529
Korchien, Jules, 379, 380
Koreans, 555
Korean steel, 861-862
Korean War, 319, 410, 470, 562, 588, 603-604, 667, 738
Kornfeder, Joseph, 479

Korry, Edward, 753
Korstad, Karl, 170
Kottra, Jim, 808
Kraus, Henry, 514
Krause, Joseph, 368, 369
Krchmarek, Anthony, 672-673
Kreitner, Frieda, 369
Kremer, I.S., 294
Kres, Joe, 349-357, 364-365, 369-372, 675
Kresge, 548-550
Krug, J.H., 545
Kubisch, Jack, 754
Ku Klux Klan, 57, 254, 275, 361, 638, 657, 707
Kuntz, Rose, 555
Kuznetsov, Vasili, 189-191
Kyle, D.V., 666

LTV Corporation bankruptcy, 862
Labor Center Reporter, 800
Labor Committee against Apartheid, 829
Labor party, need for, 98-101
Labor Research Association, 201, 254, 831, 862-863
Labor spies, 526
Labor Today, 15, 36, 82, 89, 770, 832, 850-853, 855
Labor unity, 89-97; and transnationals, 95-96
Labor Youth League, 683
Lackawanna, 683-706
La Follette, Robert M., 277
LaGuardia, Fiorello, 288
Laird, Melvin, 740, 754
Landrum-Griffin Act, 2, 21, 718, 721
Lanham Act, 515
Lannon, Al, 315
Lansdale, Edward, 735
La Raza Silk-Screen Project, 151
La Roque, Gene R., 828
Lausche, Frank J., 364, 366
Lawrence, Josh, 155, 163, 315
Lara, Alejandro Molina, 758
Lawson, John Howard, 492, 544
Lazo, Torres, 757
Leadership Conference on Civil Rights, 110
Leather Workers Union, 298, 406-407; AFL, 406; New England, 416; *See also* IFLWU
Lebrun, Lolita, 678
Lederman, Abraham, 477
Lee, Canada, 118
Lee, Ernest, 728, 732
Legislative work, AFGE, 776

Lelli, Philip, 86
Lenin, V.I., 412
Lenin Institute, 413, 415
Leonard, Andy, 719-722
Leonard, Jonathan S., 814
Leonard, Richard, 336
Lepke, 405
Lerner, James, 374
LeSueur, Meridel, 577-582
Levering Act, 492, 495
Levitt, Martin Jay, 2-14
Lewis, John L., 175, 191, 202, 612; attacked by big business, 325; autocratic methods, 342, 612; and CIO in South, 655; and FAECT, 380; left-center CIO unity, 134, 201; No-Strike Pledge, 221; on T-H, 246, 260, 302-303, 338
Lilburn, John, 507
Lilienthal, David, 347, 377
Lincoln, Abraham, 415
Lincoln School, 138
Lindberg, Charles, 329
Lindsay, Bob, 151
Lipschutz, Peggy, 855
Litton Industries, 93
Livingston, David, 827
Lockheed Corporation, 67
Locomotive Engineers, 667
Lodge, George Cabot, 737, 740
Loeb, Philip, 509-510
Lohman, Walter, 402-403
London, Milton, 529
Long, Edward, 447, 451, 456, 460, 469
Lopez, Frank, 434, 435
Los Angeles, Board of Education, 491-492
Los Angeles Committee for Defense of the Bill of Rights, 553
Los Angeles Committee for Protection of Foreign Born, 553-560
Los Angeles Community Medical Center, 528-532
Los Angeles County Federation of Labor, 805
Los Angeles Educational Association, 255, 492, 494
Los Angeles, Greater, CIO Council, 432-436
Los Angeles Philharmonic Orchestra, 502
Lovestone, Jay 727-728, 732, 738, 760, 761
Louis, Joe, 204
Louisiana Un-American Activities Committee, 710
Louisville Negro Labor Council, 635
The Louisville Story, 651
Loyalty investigations, 177
Loyalty oath, employer, 391, 506; government, 243-244, 516; teachers, 372, 475-476, 489; union, 698-699; *See also* Taft-Hartley non-Communist oath
Loyalty oath trials, teachers, 479-482, 485, 489-493, 495
Loyalty order, 523
Loyalty screening, by Coast Guard, 620; and opposition to Jim Crow, 621
Lozano, Rudy, 770; Commission for Justice for, 771
Luboviski, Barry, 788
Lucchi, Pietro, 299
Luce, Henry, 215
Lucky Store, 803
Lucio, Tony, 163
Lumber industry, 642
Lumer, Hyman, 672
Lundberg, Harry, 622
Lusk loyalty oath, 475
Lynn, William, 662

MC & S, 155, 269, 304, 315, 402, 414, 417; black members, 622; expelled from CIO, 621
MEBA-MMP, 154
MFOWW, 154
MacArthur, Douglas, 194, 540
MacDougall, Curtis D., 268
Macklis, Sam, 380
Magnuson Bill, 179
Mallory, Brenda, 789
Management, consultant, 2, 4, 7-13
Mandel, Fred, 673
Mandel, Max, 382
Mann, Thomas, 749, 754
Marcantonio, Vito, 209, 247, 264, 283, 303, 325, 344, 414-416, 484, 575
March of Labor, 620
March on Washington, 1983, 659
Marine Draftsmen's Association, 381
Marine and Shipbuilding Union, 262
Markland, Lem, 357
Marquart, Frank, 335
Marrufo, Ray, 614
Marsh, Ernest, 434
Marshall, Dorothy, 554
Marshall, F. Ray, 165
Marshall, George C., 289-290
Marshall Plan, 229, 260, 283, 287, 297, 299, 300, 303, 388, 432, 435;

Marshall Plan (*continued*)
  Soviet view, 294-296
Martial law, 449-451
Martin, Bob, 152-163, 275-277, 314-315, 438-446
Martin, Homer, 326
Martinez, Richard, 748
Martino, Frank D., 827
Martinsville Seven, 629
Marty, Joe, 435
Marx, Karl, 412, 505; Marxist, 508
Masses & Mainstream, 287, 533, 535, 539
Matson Lines, 86
Matthews, J.B., 509
Matthews, Ralph, 624
Matthieson, Francis O., 510
Matusow, Harvey, 601-605; *False Witness,* 609
May Day, 156, 414, 566
Mazey, Emil, 194
McCarran Internal Security Act, 315, 553, 554, 555, 567-572
McCarran, Sen. Pat, 602
McCarthy, Bill, 440
McCarthy, Joseph, 209, 280, 301, 319, 376, 409-410, 508, 530, 584, 588, 642
McCloy, John J., 748
McCone, John, 748, 753
McCormack, Peter, 588
McCortney, Margaret, 646
McCrea, Ed, 661-664
McCurdy, Foster, 369
McDonald, David, 261, 682, 700, 702
McDonald's, 803
McEntee, Gerald W., 827, 831
McGee, Willie, 410, 629
McGowan, Father, 461
McGrath, J. Howard, 250-257
McGrath, Thomas, 24
McGurty, Lawrence, 661, 664
McKenna, Paul, 772, 779
McKenzie, Howard, 159, 315
McKie, Bill, 343
McLaughlin, Judge, 412, 415
McMurray, Lloyd, 720-722
McNeil, Leonard, 787, 875
McSmear, Dick, 565
McWilliams, Carey, 492
Meany, George, 418, 667, 732-733, 737, 740, 741, 755, 759, 760, 872-873
Media, union use of, 870
Meehan, Suzanne, 800
Meiklejohn, Alexander, 477, 704, 705
Meiklejohn Civil Liberties Institute, 301, 385, 504

Melish, William H., 558
Mellon, Andrew, 217
Melman, Seymour, 58, 827
Memphis, 661-666; FTA, 653; Greater CIO Council, 168-170; garbage workers, 659
Mende, Tuz, 385-388, 439
Mergers, of corporations, 670; and takeovers, tax consequences, 853-854
Mergers of unions, 418, 607, 613-614, 667; CIO-AFL, 667-670
Merriam, Eve, 539-543
Merrill, Louis, 386
Merritt, Walter Gordon, 383
Mesarosh, Stephen, *See* Nelson, Steve
Metal Trades Association, 329
Mexican-American, union leaders, 435; workers, 557, 595, 597, 614; *See also* Chicanos
Mexican union leaders, 192, 434
Mexico, Mine-Mill, 592
Meyer, Charles, 753
Meyer, Cord, 738
Meyer, Cord, Jr., 732
Meyers, Blackie, 315, 439
Meyers, George, 176, 397
Mezey, Phiz, 149
Michigan Fund, 740
Michigan School of Social Sciences, 254
Military, and unions, 56-58, 60
Military Bases, civilian employees, 773
Military-industrial complex, 56
Military spending, 62, 824, 830
Miller, George, 32
Miller, Joyce, 813, 814, 874
Mills, Nicolaus, 858
Mills, Saul, 274
Milwaukee County Industrial Union Council, 328
Mindszenty, Cardinal, 377
Mine-Mill, 239, 266, 304, 324, 353, 399-403, 586, 670, 679-680; Denver conspiracy trial, 605-606, 611; International Executive Board, 606; Local 890, 596-602, 613-614; The Long Strike, 597-598; nationwide strike, 610; New Mexico, 595-610; and racism, 595; *The Salt of the Earth,* 592-614; in South, 653; and Teamsters, 611
A Miner's Life, 772, 779
Minimum Wage Study Commission, 1981, 34

Minority jobs protection, 178-179
Minton, Sherman, 309, 313
Misbrener, Joseph, 827
Mississippi Sovereignty Commission, 571
Mitchell, Clarence, 182
Mitchell, George S., 165
Mitchell, Walter, 554
Moffatt, Stanley, 554
Mondale, Walter, 101
Monopolies, 218-219, 224; monopoly capitalism, 283-285; *See also* Economic concentration
Montgomery, Alabama, 648-650, 656-657; Movement, 656-657
Mooney-Billings case, 586
Moore, David, 343
Moreno, Luisa, 430-434
Moreno, Wenecslao, 753
Morado, J. Chavez, 287
Morgan City, Louisana, 442
Morgen, Carl, 430
Morison, Samuel Eliot, 410
Moritt, Fred G. 475
Moss, Maximilian, 479
Mosteller, Gordon, 149, 150
Motion Picture Association, 740
Moulder, Morgan M., 496-497
Muir, Virginia, 723
Mujal, Edsebio, 734
Mullen, Clara, 585
Multinational corporations, 730-731, 859; *See also* TNCs
Mulzac, Hugh, 639
Munich, 371
Murder, Inc., 405-406, 770
Murphy, Frank, 307
Murphy, Robert, 197
Murray, Sen. James, 120
Murray, Philip, 166, 347; anti-Communist policy, 134-136, 210, 236-242, 387, 430-434; Catholic, 135, 461; CIO president, 166, 261-262, 297, 387, 616, 738; and John L. Lewis, 302-303; no strike practice, 208, 449; and Progressive Party, 268-274; and T-H oath, 246-247, 249, 265, 308, 338; USWA president, 236, 261, 303, 682; after World War II, 132-136, 190-193
Murrow, Edward R., 317
Mussolini, Benito, 284, 285, 288
Mutual home ownership program, 515-522

NAACP, attacks on, 563-564, 569, 656, 710; campaigns, 634; Florida, 570; and HUAC, 640; Montgomery, 648; and NNLC, 635, 638, 641
NAM, 81, 133, 201, 243, 669
NATO, 297, 299, 300
NCARL, 503, 705
NEA, 69, 488, 827, 829; and pay equity, 79-80; report, 474
NIOSH, 32
NLRA, 7, 23, 26, 121, 221, 243, 265
NLRB, avoid going, 782-784, 786; case backlog, 3, 13, 20, 21, 24-26; collective bargaining orders, 28-29; crises in, 24; decertification orders, 15, 17, 259, 310, 399-400, 605-606, 621; employees in AFGE, 773; employees union, 776; Massey Coal Co., 860; organizing campaign rules, 7, 28; and privacy of membership records, 392; Reagan board, 22-30; representation elections, 7-13, 29-30, 266, 279, 352, 375, 376, 387, 408, 441, 463, 488, 617, 770, 782, 814; and SACB, 679-680; and T-H, 258-260; 383, 675; unfair labor practice charges, 10,11 27-28, 383; and Wagner Act, 451; *See also* Taft-Hartley non-Communist oath
NMU, 148, 442, 516-517, 627, 685; anti-discrimination policy, 154; Black leadership, 155, 163, 619-620, 629, 661; CIO, 442; Coast Guard screening, 443-444; Committee for Maritime Unity, 438-440; Communists in, 154, 160-163; democratic practices, 152-153, 441-446; educational programs, 152-153; expulsion charges, 441, 445, 446; and Filipino workers, 452; improvement of working conditions, 314-315; 1947 convention, 440; organizing, 153-163; raiding, 622; Red-baiting, 262, 323, 619-620; segregation, 661, 666; and T-H, 259; and UOPWA, 385-386; Women's Auxiliary, 152
NNLC, 212, 255, 627, 644; destroyed, 642; Maritime Commission, 639; *Struggle*, 641
NRA, 175
NY/CLU Child Care Committee, 820
Nachmanoff, Arnold, 754
Nakano, Bert, 464-465
Nathan Hale Bookstore, 350
The Nation, 565, 571, 858-862
National Alliance Against Racist & Political Repression, 771

Index ♦ 903

National Association of Letter Carriers, 776
National Catholic Welfare Conference, 461
National Child Labor Committee, 34
National Civic Federation, 727
National Committee To Abolish the Poll Tax, 656
National Committee on Segregation in the Nation's Capital, 544
National Conference on the Problems of Women Workers, 645-647
National Congress of Unemployed Organizations, 771
National Council of American-Soviet Friendship, 255
National Council of the Arts, Sciences, and Professions (ASP), 201
National Endowment for the Arts, 806
National Endowment for Democracy, 848
National Federation of Federal Employees, 174-176, 776
National Guard, 448, 601
National Labor Committee in Support of Human Rights and Democracy in El Salvador, 829
National Lawyers Guild, 545, 561, 564, 757
National Lawyers Guild Practitioner, 2, 835
National Master Freight Agreement of 1964, 87
National Negro Congress, 164, 391, 628; attacked, 170, 173
National Right-to-Work Committee, 22; Legal Defense Foundation, 22
National Security Council, 735, 751
National Treasury Employees Union, 776
National Union of Hospital & Health Care Employees, 848
National Women's Trade Union League, 547
Native American ironworker, 33
Navarette, Natalia, 558
Navy Department, 181, 515
Nazi, financing, 742; rewarding, 292-293; sympathizers, 329
Needle trades, 406
Negro, 514, 520, 524; *See also* Blacks, NNLC
Negro Labor Committee, 632-640; Yearbook, 635
Negro Labor Victory Committee, 179, 628

Negro musicians, 533-534
Negro National Anthem, 630
Negro Woman's Day, 642
Nelson, Andrew, 155
Nelson, Anne, 815
Nelson, Edward L., 524
Nelson, Eleanor, 176
Nelson, Ralph, 680
Nelson, Steve, 672
Neruda, Pablo, 542
New Deal, 1, 21, 218, 290, 379, 628, 648; Coalition, 828
Newell, Amy, 878
Newman, Winn, 81
New Masses, 248
New methods of advancing workers' interests, 868-872
Newspaper Guild, 346, 732, 827
Newspaper and Mail Deliverers' Union of New York and Vicinity, 24
New York Area Trade Union Committee on War, Nuclear Destruction & Military Spending, 826
New York City, Board of Education, 475-479
New York City Teachers Union, 124, 472-490; *Teacher News*, 482
New York, Greater, CIO Council, 274
New York Post, 482
New York School of Social Work, 350
New York State, Board of Regents, 475, 476
Nicaragua, 778; National Guard, 756; workers, 83, 756-757, 761
Nicholas, Henry, 827
Niebuhr, Reinhold, 336, 587
Nitzberg, Leo, 150
Nixon, Richard, 60, 404, 532, 565, 648, 751, 753, 760-761, 867; wage freeze, 774
Nixon, Russell, 271, 586
Non-Communist oath, *See* Loyalty oath, Taft-Hartley non-Communist oath
Noncomplying union, 409
Norman, E. Herbert, 510
Norton, James, 827
No-strike clause, AFGE constitution, 774
No-strike pledge, 203, 220-221, 395, 449, 702; North American Aviation Company, 221; UMW, 221
Novikoff, Alex, 490
Nuclear disarmament, 821
Nuclear freeze, 778, 824
Nuclear Freeze & Disarmament Rally, 1982, 824, 826

Nuclear power plants, 64
Nuclear Weapons Freeze, 826
Nuremburg trials, 742
Nyden, Philip Williams, 682, 690, 702

OAS Charter, 841
OCAW, 259, 387, 677, 732, 752, 827; and NMU in Port Arthur, 155-163
OPA, 220, 674
OPEIU, 388; Local 29, 723
OSHA, 11, 20, 22, 33; Reagan record, 31-32; and Supreme Court, 32
OSS, 729, 730, 737
Oakes, Grant, 337
Obermeyer, Charles, 386
O'Brien, Harvey, 359
Office of Personnel Management, 22
Office workers, 379; *See also* UOPWA, OPEIU
Ogden Corporation, 16
O'Hara, James, 34
Ohio CIO Civil Rights Committee, 674
Ohio School of Social Science, 255
Ohio State Council of Machinists, 826
O'Keefe, Richard B., 416
Old age pensions, 524
Olszanski, Mike "Oz," 36-38
O'Neill, Robert, 751
O'Neill, Tip, 101
Operating engineers, 797
Operation Dixie, 109; AFL, 167-168; CIO, 166-168, 650, 655; UPWA, 185
Operation Terror, INS, 558
Oppenheimer, J. Robert, 530
Oregon AFL-CIO, Employment and Economy Committee, 835, 873
Organizing, AFGE, 776; AFL-CIO, Committee proposals, 870-873; Black workers, 627-642; company-wide, 780; experimental committees, 870-871; federal workers, 776; full-time, 781; industry-wide, 784-786; move fast to contract, 783-786; sign cards, 783; strike for recognition, 783-784; Teamsters, 780-786; women, 873-874
Orr, Harold, 494-495, 714, 718, 721
Osman v. Douds, 313
Other America Project, 33, 114, 128, 206
O'Toole, Donald L., 243
Oxman, G. Bromley, 246

PATCO, 20, 87, 93, 107, 831
Pacific Maritime Association, 621
Pacific Northwest Labor School, 255
Packard, Emmy Lou, 62, 149
Packinghouse Workers-CIO, 269, 667
Paine, Thomas, 507
Painters Union-AFL, 680
Paisley, William A., 566
Palmer, Bernard, 378
Panama Canal Zone workers, 390-395, 773
Panzino, Frank, 496
Paper Workers, 387
Parental leave, 818
Park, Chung Hee, 555
Parks, Rosa, 648-649
Parks, Sam, 627
Parun, Steve, 149
Passport, denial, 394, 832
Patman, Wright, 732
Patri, Giacomo, 143, 149
Patton, George S., 125
Pauling, Linus, 554, 558
Paull, Irene, 581-582
Pay equity, 69-81, 646, 817
Peace, 645; labor's need for, 823-832; movement, 823-832; right to live in, 821; unions' participation in peace demonstrations, 825-828; workers' right to, 68
Peace Action Coalition, 827
Peace and Freedom Party, 713
Peace Information Center, 573-576
Peace and Reconstruction Act of 1948, 288
Pearl Harbor, 524
Peck, Robert, 530
Peekskill, 410, 629
Pension fund investments, 872-873
Pension rights for women, 818
Pentagon, 56, 58, 60, 94, 146, 148, 747
People's Education Center, 255, 492, 494
Peoples, Frank, 673, 675
People's Institute of Applied Religion, 255
People's Republic of China, 532
People's Songs, 367
People's World, 603
Pepper, Claude, 190, 386
Perjury charges, House Education and Labor Committee investigation, 335, 341; Taft-Hartley, 324, 401-403, 463, 606-607, 621; union hearing, 698-699

Perlik, Charles, 827
Perlin, Marshall, 583
Perry, Thomas, 530
Pershing, John "Blackjack", 557
Persily, Joseph, 496
Peru, 741
Pezzati, Albert, 587
Phelps Dodge, 595
Philadelphia Bulletin, 280
Philadelphia School of Social Science and Art, 255
Phoenix pacification program, 758
Picketing, 307, 331, 352, 549, 550, 555, 638; mass, 335
Pickett, Clarence, 705
Pickman, Isador, 298
The Pilot, 386
Pinkerton Detective Agency, 329
Pinochet, Augusto, 753, 754, 755
Pinsky, Paul, 380
Pittsburgh Courier, 551, 624
Plantations, 449-454
Plant Closures Project, 853-854, 856
Plant closures in US industries, 854; garment, 724; light electrical, 724; shoe, 724; steel, 724;
Plumbers and Fitters Local 393, 723
Poland, 107
Police Subversive Activities Squad, 368
Political Affairs, 412
Political deportations, 553, 560
Political strikes, 310
Poor People's Campaign, 659
Pope Pius XII, 373
Populists, 268
Portal to portal pay, 823
Porter, John, 554, 556
Postal Telephone and Telegraph International, 747-748
Postwar corporate objectives, toward labor, 205-207; toward USSR, 205
Postwar strikes, 205-207
Potash, Irving, 405
Potofsky, Jacob, 263, 299, 592
Poverty, elderly, 817; women, 817
Precision Scientific Co., 399-400, 605, 607
Pregnancy Disability Act of 1978, 818
President's Annual Budget, 841
Pressman, Lee, 197, 270
Preventive medicine, right to, 822
Priestly, J.B., 317
Productivity, 702
Profiteering, military contractors, 59
Profit rate, on foreign investments, 725

Profit-sharing plans, 863
Progressive Citizens of America, 269
Progressive Labor Party, 702
Progressive Party, 107, 268-278, 303, 328, 366, 368, 371, 439, 497, 631, 662, 666; Southern campaign, 275-277
Project Engineering Company, 381-382
Proletarian literature, 578
Prudential Insurance Company, 387
Public Education Association, 476
Public Health Service, 181
Public housing, 710
Public Workers Stand Together, 772, 773, 779
Public works programs, 843
Puchala, Linda, 813
Puerto Rican Nationalists, 678
Puerto Rican workers, 623, 828

"Quality Control Circles," 60
Quality of Life Action Act, 839-846, 879; CLUW supports, 818
"Quality of Working Life" programs, 61
A Quarter Century of Un-Americana, 501
Queens College, 478
Quilici, Bob, 714
Quill, Michael, 274
Quinn, James C., 360
Quinn, Thomas, 496-497, 499
Quotas, 793, 798

RCA, 381, 865; Communications, 264
RKO, 139
Rabinowitz, Victor, 258, 264-265, 306-313, 701
Racism, within SIU, 154; used to break strike, 18; in World War II, 204; *See also* Jim Crow, Blacks, Chicanos, etc.
Raiding, 408-409, 436, 667-668
Railroad unions, 86, 87, 240, 669
Railroads, 639, 642
Rainbow Coalition, 659
Raine, George, 682
Raineri, Vivian McGuickin, 346, 364, 645, 671, 772
Ramirez, Natalia, 558
Randall, Byron, 149
Randolph, A. Philip, 624
Rapp-Coudert Committee, 475, 490
Rath Packing Co., 850-851
Ray, Reuben, 345

Reagan administration, against affirmative action, 792; and Central American policy, 756-759, 847-848; and deregulation, 87

Reagan foreign policy, AFL-CIO resolution on, 824

Reagan, Ronald, 742, 750, 829; child labor policy, 34; and Cold War, 658; contra policy, 756-757, 847-848; economic doctrine, 20; and Grace Commission, 775; international labor practices, 20; labor policies, 35, 103-104, 106; PATCO strike, 20, 831

Red-baiting, *See* individual entries, *See also* anti-Communism

Red Scare, 203; *See also* anti-Communism

Reed, Beatrice, 173

Reed, John, 202

Reed, Marie, 324; conspiracy case, 402-403, 607, 671-678; Fawick strike, 349-373; women workers, 645-647

Reid, Harry, 462

Rein, David, 414

Reindustrialization, 861, 872; programs, 842

Reinecke, Aiko, 455-467; school hearing, 456-457

Reinecke, John, 454-467; school hearing, 456-457

Reinthaler, Eric, 672, 673

Remes, Andrew, 672

Republican Party, 98, 414, 469, 552

Retail clerks, 418, 732; *See also* UF & CWA

Reuther, Victor, 734, 740, 741, 759-761, 849

Reuther, Walter, 191, 237, 727, 738; and Black workers, 624; changing policies, 759-761; *Colliers* article, 317-318, 337; and FAECT, 381, 384; and Progressive Party, 269; and Red-baiting, 136, 210, 238-240, 298, 327, 331-333, 336-337, 342; and T-H Act, 262-263, 327, 337-342; and union solidarity, 203, 207, 273, 327, 344, 667-669

Revenue Act, 1946, 329

"Reverse discrimination," 794-795

Revolts, anti-war, 511; Black, 511; student, 511

Revueltas, Rosaura, 599-601

Reynolds, Bertha, 386

Reynolds, Hobson, 627

Reynolds, Mosetta, 789

Rhee, Syngman, 557

Rice, Father Charles, 211, 377

Rice, Pat, 344

Richards, Harvey, 825

Richardson, Marie, 176; *See also* Harris, Marie

Richardson, Thomas, 173-174, 179, 182, 627

Richardson, Tim, 713-722

Richter, Irving, 339, 340

Riesel, Victor, 599

Riess, Bernard, 490

Rieve, Emil, 210, 237, 263, 269, 298, 299, 396

Rifkind, Simon, 383

Right to earn a living, 839-840; Symposium, 780

Rights of Man, 507

Right to strike, 176-177; under Reagan NLRB, 27

"Right-to-work" laws, 168, 669

Rightwing pulpits, 868

Rinaldo, Fred, 553

Riskin, Alexander, 529

Riskin, Benjamin, 823, 834

Rivera, Rosendo, 435

R.J. Reynolds Tobacco Company, 616-618, 652

Roberts, Holland, 137-151, 566

Robeson, Paul, 118, 131, 173, 344-345, 410, 617, 627, 639, 662, 666

Robinson, Cleveland, 623, 827

Robinson, Earl, 129

Robinson, Teresa L., 627

Robinson, Tony, 143

Rockefeller, David, 725, 736-737, 747

Rockefeller, Nelson, 733

Rodriguez, Arturo, 802

Rolfe, Edwin, 509

Romano, Joe, 15

Romig, Florence, 646

Romualdi, Serafino, 728-748

Roosevelt, Franklin D., and Blacks, 100, 628; New Deal and Labor, 218, 272; 1937 economy drive, 175; 1940 election campaign, 272; 1941 Fair Employment Practices Commission, 177, 628; 1944 election campaign, 120-121, 201; and 1945 World Trade Union Conference, 189-190; and post-World War II policies, 119-121, 132; and Progressive Party, 275; strike-breaking, 221; and Unemployment Councils, 202; Wagner Act, 202; and Works Progress Administration, 111; World War II and Labor, 380

Rosenberg Committee, 582
Rosenberg Era Art Project, 586
Rosenberg, Ethel and Julius, 410, 526, 583-588
Rosenberg Foundation, 139
Rosenberg-Sobell Case, 583-588
Rosenberg-Sobell Committee, 497, 584
Ross, Malcolm, 179
Rostow, Walt, 416
Roth, Norman, 850
Rowe, Frank, 149, 151, 301
Rubber Workers, 274
Rubenstein, Avrum, 149
Rubenstein, Bill, 150
Rukeyser, Muriel, 143
Runaway industries, 724-725
Runyan, 354
Rural Electrification Administration, 776
Russell, Rose, 474, 480
Russian War Relief Committees, 583
Rutledge, Wiley, 307, 308
Ryan, John, 713, 717, 721
Ryan, Joseph, 620

SACB, 564, 566; hearings, 562; Mine-Mill hearings, 605, 607, 611-612; and NNLC, 642; and Subversive Activities Control Act, 679-680
SCEF, 564, 655
SCLC, 563
SCMWA, 172, 173; *See also* AFSCME
SEIU, 100, 816, 832, 874; *Budget Bulletin,* 831; District 925, 72, 815
SISS, 510, 602, 627, 663, 703; and Mine-Mill, 605, 611; in South, 653
SIU, discrimination, 154; Red-baiting, 154, 160-163; tactics, 160-162
SNCC, 563
SUP, 86
SUP/SIU, 154
SWOC, 682
Sabath, Adolph J. 209
Sacco-Venzetti case, 586
Safeway Stores, 634
Saillant, Louis, 193
Salazar, Antonio de Oliveira, 615
Salem witch trials, 480
Salt of the Earth, 598-601
Salvadoran Committee of Trade Union Unity, 758
Salvadoran workers, 757-759
Sam Adams School, 138, 256
Sandinista, 847
Sandinista Front for National Liberation, 756

San Francisco-Bay Area Plant Closures Project, 856-858
San Francisco Council of Jewish Women, 137
San Francisco, general strike, 127, 448
San Francisco Sun-Reporter, 620
Sanjines, Carl, 153
Santa Clara Central Labor Council, 593, 723, 745
Sarasohn, Peggy, 150
Sarvis, Dave, 143, 150
Sarvis, Winifred, 150
Sawyer, Harold, 147
Scabs, 17, 27, 88, 355, 452, 460; and affirmative action, 796
Scheinkman, Jack, 827
Scherer, Marcel, 379
Scherer, Paul, 379
Schie, Eileen, 361-372
Schneiderman v. US, 307
Schlochower, Harry, 480, 485-486
Schoenberger, Mildred, 472, 485
School of Jewish Studies, 256
Schultz, Reinhard, 33, 114, 128, 206, 790
Schwartz, Murray E., 24
Schweiker, Richard, 32
Schwellenbach, Lewis B., 330
Schyten, John, 380
Scottsboro case, 648
Screen Actors Guild, 102, 813, 848
Scribner, David, 676
Sears, Roebuck and Co., 636-639, 643
Seattle Labor School, 256
Second-class citizenship, 559
Secondary boycott, 384
Security checks, 710; *See also* Loyalty oath
Security Index, 584
Segregation, racial, in CIO, 624, 661-666; in Hawaii, 466; in the South, 572; US government, 389-398; in the workplace, 684; *See also* Racism, Jim Crow, Blacks, etc.
Self-incrimination privilege, *See* Fifth Amendment
Selly, Joseph, 237, 380
Seniority plans, 6, 16
Seniors, organizing, 6
Severeid, Eric, 143
Sex equality, 69-81, 619
Sexism, *See* Women
Sexual harrassment, 579-582, 818
Shaftel, Oscar, 490
Shanker, Albert, 848
Sharnoff, Philip, 214, 317

Shaye, Max, 641
Sheil, Bernard J., 246
Sheinkman, Jacob, 824, 826
Shell Oil Co., 381, 862
Shepro, Cyril, 530
Sherwood, Barbara, 511
Sherwood, Robert, 317
Sherwood, William K., 510
Shevchenko, Taras, 686
Shiloh Baptist Church, 390
Shipbuilding workers, 387; foreign flags, 314
Shipyards, 514
Shlakman, Vera, 490
Shop steward, 8
Shulemowitz, Ruth, 150
Shuttlesworth, Fred, 572
Sigal, Clancy, 327
Sigler, Kim, 336-337
Silex, Humberto, 593-595
Silex, Maria de Jesus, 594
Silva, Frank, 464-465
"Silver-gold workers," 390-395
Simon, Sid, 380
Simon, William, 742
Simpson-Mazzoli Bill, 779
Sinarquista Union, 434-435
Sinatra, Frank, 143
"The Situation of Workers & their Unions," 866
Slappy, Thelma, 585
Sleeping Car Porters Union, 648
Smith Act, 443, 457-470, 556, 571, 684, 685, 710; CP leaders' convictions reversed, 609; trials, 553, 564, 579
Smith, Ferdinand, 155, 315, 439, 619, 627, 629
Smith, Margaret Chase, 317
Smith, Miranda, 166, 617-618
Smith, Walter Marvin, 510
Snow, Edgar, 130
Sobell, Helen L., 583; Marco and Sidney, 587
Sobell, Morton, 526, 583-588
Social Security, 121, 524, 530, 710; funding child care programs 820
Social Security Act, 218
Social Security Administration, 773, 775
Socialism, 576, 595
Socialist, 328, 350, 418, 537, 687; groups, 14; perspectives, 877
Socialist Party, 136, 334
Socialist Workers Party, 683
Society of Design Engineers, 381
Solidarity, 448-471, 684-699, 878;
Danly Machine Co., 18; international labor, 726
Sombrotto, Vince, 777
Somers, Jane, 585
Somoza, Anastasia, 756, 757
Sorro, Bill, 789
South, 567-572; 648-666; *See also* Civil Rights Movement; Operation Dixie
South Africa, divestment, 778; labor leaders, meeting with US labor, 829-830
South African Union, 559
Southeast Asia, 616
Southern California Unions for Peace, 826
Southern Conference for Human Welfare, 655
Southern Negro Youth Congress, 173, 256, 656
Southern Patriot, 665
Southwest Labor Studies Association, 593
Soviet-American relations, 331
Soviet trade unions, 381, 382
Soviet Union, 126, 290-291, 315, 531, 575, 615; foreign policy, 338
Spain, 386
Spanish Civil war, 511
Spanish-speakers, *See* Chicanos
Speedup, 339, 646
Spock, Benjamin, 677
Springsteen, Bruce, 808
Stainback, Ingram, 452-465
Stalin, Joseph, 132, 189
Stamler-Hall-Cohen hearing, 706
Stamm, Eleanor, 358, 373
Stamm, Morris, 349, 354, 365-373
Standard of living, right to adequate, 840-841
Standard Oil, 734, 747
Stark, Joe, 315
"Star Wars," 818
State Department, 181, 283-286, 510, 530, 584
States' Rights Democratic Party, 707
Stawicki, John, 363, 365
Steadman, Charles, 356, 361
Steelman, John, 204, 208
Steidl, John, 356, 372
Stein, Annie, 547
Stein, Sidney, 672
Steingart, Harry, 379, 380
Stellato, Frank, 343, 344
Stephenson, Faye, 348
Stepinac, Archbishop, 377
Stepp, Marc, 828

Stern, Barbara, 151
Sternbach, Jack, 382
Stettinius, Edward R., 139
Stevenson, Adlai, 746
Stevenson, Miriam, 554
Stewart-Warner Corp., 375
Stilwell-Lansdale Report, 735-736, 743-744, 750
Stilwell, Richard, 735
Stockholm Peace Appeal, 566, 573-574, 663
Stokes, Allison, 662
Stoltzfus, Emilie, 813
Stoolpigeon, 395, 555; *See also* Informers
Strack, Celeste, 150
Strauss, Dudley, 490
Strauss, Leon, 586
Strikes, 27, 47, 127, 206-208, 245; Allis-Chalmers, 1941, 245; American Zinc Oxide, 351; Bethlehem Steel, 1919, 689; Bruce Church, 803-804; Buckeye Cellulose Company, 662; Chrysler, 863; Copper, 610; Danley, 16-19; Ebasco, 378, 381-384; Empire Zinc Co., 597-598; Fawick, 346-372; general, 448-449; Gloversville, 211; Hawaii, 452-453, 459-462; IFLWU, 1926, 405, 409, 413; ILWU, 1938, 245; Locomotive Engineers and Railway Conductors, 667; Massey Coal Co., 862, 864; members' right to decide, 47; Memphis, 662; Mine-Mill, 597-598; 1945-1946, 205; 1946-1947, 326-335, 337, 652; 1952, 667; 1955-1956, 669; no right, federal employees, 773; North American Aviation Co., 221, 396; NMU, 438; NYC teachers, 486-487; oil refinery workers, 667; PATCO, 20; political, 245-246, 310; Pullman, 499; for recognition, 879; Reynolds, 617-618; right to, 27; San Francisco, 1934, 448-449; selective, 859; Teamsters, 667, 714-716; telephone operators, 667; timing of, 13; TWA stewardesses, 819; UE, 376; united CIO strategy, 207-208; United Federation of Teachers, 487-488; United Furniture Workers Union, 663; Univis Lens, 351; USWA, 1952, 667; violence, 599; Westinghouse, 1982, 864; wildcats, 690, 714-715; Yale University, 815
Strike-breaking, 221, 452
Strike fund, UMW, 1983, 859-860

Strike wages, 860
Strikers, Mexican-American, 597-598; women, 597-598
Struik, Dirk, 505
Strunk, Arthur F., 673, 675
Student movement, 788; in San Francisco, 706; Talladega, 569
Sugar, Maurice, 340
Suzuki, Lewis, 149
Sweatshop, 405-406
Sweeney, John, 100-101, 365, 366, 827, 831
Sweeney, Vincent, 682
Swing, Joseph M., 557, 558
Systems modernization, 775

T-H, *See* Taft-Hartley
TNCs, 724-730, 731, 737-768; joint action against, 93; limitations on, 844; regulation of, 860-861; victims of, 829; *See also* Multinational corporations
TUAD, 832; Northern California Committee, 715
TUC, Britain, 190
TUEL, 201, 405-406
TUUL, 201, 406
Taft-Hartley Act, 519; ACA and Local 65, 264-265; and AFL compliance, 260; "belief and support" clause, 411-412; and Blacks, 167-168; and CIO compliance, 260, 262-263, 302, 305, 436, 592; citizenship requirement, 594; compliance, 440; conspiracy convictions, 402; cooling-off period, 324; and FE-CIO compliance, 499; and First Constitutional Convention of AFL-CIO, 669; First and Fifth Amendment, 265; and Ben Gold, 300; in Hawaii, 461-469; history, 2, 21, 243-249, 315, 320, 392, 395, 583-584; injunction, 324; Vito Marcantonio, 247-248; NMU compliance, 440-441; no-strike provision, 177; non-complying unions, 313, 463; restrictions on unions, 11; section 8(b)(4)(A), 381-383; and Ferdinand Smith, 439; and Ray Talavera, 721; and Truman, 258, 308, 325, 461-462; and UAW 1946-1947 strikes, 326-327; and UE compliance, 675; and UMW 1949 strike, 324-325
Taft-Hartley non-Communist oath, 244-245, 249, 259-260, 264-267, 306, 308-313, 327, 337-338, 342, 343, 349, 387, 408, 411-418, 427,

Taft-Hartley (*continued*)
440-441, 443, 458, 592, 671-673, 675, 707-710; ILWU non-Communist affidavit, 463; and Clinton Jencks, 601-609; and Mine-Mill, 601-606; and perjury cases, 324, 401-403, 606-607, 621; repealed, 611
Taft, Robert A., 243
Takahashi v. Fish & Game Commissioner, 307
Takeaway contracts, 859
Talavera, Ray, 713-722
Talladega movement, 569
Tanner, Susan Franklin, 805-806, 808
Tariffs, 861
Tavenner, Frank, 462, 496
Tax law, to encourage reindustrialization, 853-856
Taxation, policy, 836; incentives, 836; in World War II, 225-226
Taylor, Glenn, 271-272
Teachers' Guild, 487
Teachers Union, and FAECT, 380; of Philadelphia, 484; *See also* New York City Teachers Union
Teamsters, 8, 9, 12, 86, 87, 155, 454, 667, 760, 826, 828, 829, 878; area contract, 87; contracts with grape growers, 801; Joint Council 7, 712-720; joint organizing with ILWU, 780; Local 85, 712-722; Local 111, 832; Local 208, 714; and Mine-Mill, 611; National Master Freight Agreement of 1964, 87, 864; organizing, 780-786
Teamsters Defense Fund, 719
Telegraph and telephone workers, 667
Teninty, Ron, 780-786, 878
Tenney Committee, 491-495
Tenney, Jack, 139, 433
Terminal Island Four, 554
Termination, *See* Discharge
Terrell, Mary Church, 544-552
Terror, climate of, 539-543
Texas, 155-163, Attorney General, 416
Texas Oil Company, and NMU organizing, 155-163
Texas Rangers, 162
Texas State Employees Union, 827
Textile industry, 642
Textile Workers Union, 271, 298, 299, 409, 436; *See also* ACTWU
Thatcher, Herbert S., 545

TheatreWorker's Project, 50-52, 805-806, 808
Thomas v. Collins, 307
Thomas, Julius, 182
Thomas, Lowell, 317
Thomas, Norman, 730
Thomas, R.J., 332, 333, 336, 338-339
Thomas, J. Parnell, 333; *See also* HUAC
Thompson, David, 467-468
Thompson, Ernest, 630, 631
Thompson's, Essie, 546
Thompson's Cafeteria, 546-547, 552
Thornhill v. Alabama, 307
Thought control, 310, 312-313
Thurow, Lester C., 851
Tianti, Betty, 814
Title VII, *See* Civil Rights Act of 1964
Tilman, Ray, 155
Timone, George A., 476, 482, 487-489
Tobacco industry, 642; *See also* R. J. Reynolds, FTA
Tobin, Maurice, 461-462
Tokiss, Joe, 384
Toledano, Vicente Lombardo, 143, 192, 594
Tom Paine School of Social Science, 256
Torrez, Anita, 598, 602
Torrez, Lorenzo, 598, 602, 614
Townsend, Willard, 165, 617, 624
Toy & Novelty Workers, 387
TransAfrica, 862
Transnational corporations, *See* TNCs
Transportation systems, 842
Transportation unions, 86
Travis, Maurice, 633, 639; T-H oath charges, 605-606, 610; violence against, 606
Travis v. US, 400, 402, 403
Treasury Department, 564, 566
Trials, by unions, Greater New York CIO Council, 274; NMU, 441-443, 445, 446; Teamsters, 713-721; UAW, 342-343
Trieste, 286
Trippe, Juan, 740, 754
Truman Administration, 289, 404; Executive Order on FEPC, 182, 184, 212; screening program, 620
Truman Doctrine, 260, 275, 290, 317
Truman, Harry, and Blacks, 180, 551, 649; Cold War, 208-209, 615; and Executive Order on Fair Employment Practices, 389; and full

Index ♦ 911

Truman and Blacks (*continued*)
employment bill, 120; and Loyalty Order, 523, 649; and post-war economy, 133-134; and post-war industrial disputes, 133, 233, 393, 460-461; price controls, 204; and Progressive Party, 268-278; and Taft-Hartley Act, 258, 308, 325, 461; and Walter-McCarran Act, 556
Trumbo, Dalton, 282
Trumka, Richard, 859-862
"Trumpet Player," 533-534
Truth, Sojourner, 541
Turncoats, 691-692
Tuskegee Institute, 630
"Two Gun" Smith, 157-163
Two-tiered wage structure, 16
Tyler, Francine, 149

UAW, 194, 364, 829; Canadian, 95-96; and CBTU, 829; constitution, 336, 343; Convention, 1947, 339-340; Convention, 1949, 624; and Danly Machine strike, 18; District 65, 826, 827; Executive Board, 331, 332, 336, 38, 340, 342; and FAECT, 381; Ford Local 600, 331, 342-345, 629, 630, 640; international affairs 759-762, 849, 862; in International Harvester Memphis plant, 168; Local 45, 368; Local 248, 326-341; outsourcing threats, 863; and Peace, Jobs & Justice Mobilization, 827; and Progressive Party, 271-272; raiding, UOPWA, 387, Mine-Mill, 593; Red-baiting, 136, 323; and Rosenberg-Sobell case, 587
UAW-AFL, 356, 359, 360, 361, 371; Local 797, 365, 366
UAW Training Schools, 850
UE, 2, 93, 364, 380, 674, 827-829, 832, 862, 878; of Canada, 89-91, 93; CIO expulsion, 298, 303-304; "Communist domination," 347; constitution, 346, 347; corporate attack, 374-377; FBI surveillance, 584-585; HUAC hearings, 376-377, 496-498; Local 707, 359-360; Local 735, 346-373, 671-672, 674; Local 1421, 434, 435; NLRB decertification, 399; and NNLC, 630, 631, 635, 642; and Progressive Party, 269-271, 273; Red-baiting, 323; SACB hearings, 679-680; survival, 670; T-H oath cases, 259, 402, 671-678; Westinghouse local, 347; *See also* FE
UF & CWA, 18, 26, 82, 418, 816, 826, 827, 850; Department Store Clerks, 713; Legal Department, 26-30; *See also* Butchers Union, IFLWU
UFW, 93, 712, 713, 827; boycott, grapes, 800-804; Direct Marketing Department, 803
UFWA, 172-186
UMW, 829; new kind of war, 858-864
UN, 139, 288, 483, 843; founding 109, 121-122, 190-199; General Assembly, 559; Human Rights Commission, 559; petition to, 558
UN Charter, 121-124, 841; Article 2, 123; Articles 55 and 56, 123-124; US treaty, 124
UN Covenant on Economic, Social, and Cultural Rights, 20
UNRRA, 285
UOPWA, 304, 346, 384, 385-388, 439; Red-baiting, 323
UPWA, 172-186, 304, 387, 389-398, 627, 630-631, 773, 826; campaign for FEPC, 184-185; Local 713, 394; New York Teachers Local 555, 475; Operation Dixie, 185; Red-baiting, 323
USWA, 96, 135-136, 204, 261-262, 269, 593, 629, 630, 664, 682-706, 737, 792, 798, 827; Birmingham, 657; "colonizers," 681-703; constitution on Communists, 693-694; Convention of 1946, 303; Convention of 1954, 702; Dues Protest Committee, 690-691, 702; HUAC witnesses, 500; industry-wide contracts, 863; Local 1256, 826; Local 15271, 15-19; Oldtimers Foundation, 92; organizing committee, 165; and Peace, Jobs and Justice Mobilization, 827; raids, 409, 605-606; rank-and-file, 690-691, 702; strikes in 1952, 667; T-H case, 306, 308, 309; wives, 688-689
USWA Local 1845, Steelworkers Welfare Action Unemployed Council, 805
Underground Railroad, 628
Undocumented workers, 770
Unemployed Councils, 202
Unemployment, 83; black, 794; effects on workers, 50-52; major labor problem, 782, 786; in other

912 • Index

Unemployment (*continued*)
countries, 58, 83, 120-123, 293;
technologically-caused, 58; West
Germany, 293; *See also* Full employment
Unemployment compensation, 524,
696-697, 710
Unfair labor practices charges, 366
Ungvary, John, 366
Unifying Hispanics and Blacks, 771
Union buster, 3-14, 351; appeal to
women, 816
Union coalitions, 816
Unions competing for units, 865
Union contracts, collective bargaining
strategy, 61-63, 155-163, 459, 670;
demands, 5-6, 462; *See also* specific
issues
Union delegations to Soviet Union,
CIO, 197-198
Union of Hawaiian Workers, 458
Union membership participation, 870
Union mergers, 871
Union organizing, 141, 152-163, 175-
176, 305, 307, 387, 406-407, 451,
651-652; campaigns, 4-12; *See also*
Operation Dixie
Union raiding, AFL, 612; AFL-CIO,
613-614; Black & Latino members,
613; CIO, 612-614, 617; of FTA Local 22, 617; of Mine-Mill, 612-614;
and racism, 613; resistance in Canada, 614; by USWA, 613; by United
Transport Service Employees, 617
Union of Technical Men, 379
Union trials, 298-299
Unitarian, 528-532
United Community Construction
Workers, 788
United Construction Workers Association, 788
United Federal Workers, 773; CIO,
172, 391; National Anti-Discrimination Committee, 179-180; *See
also* UPWA
United Federation of Teachers, 487
United Fruit Company, 438-439, 445,
732-734
United Furniture Workers, 172-173,
175, 178-179, 658, 663; Local 576,
434-436
United Labor Planning Committee,
738
United May Day Committee, 257
United Parcel Service, 864
United Public Workers v. Mitchell,
181

United Rubber Workers, 630
United States, citizenship, 431; foreign policy, 105-106, 198-199, 628,
724-762
US Air Force, 56-58, 604; Strategic
Air Command, 125
US Army, 111-116, and anti-Sovietism, 129; "Army Talks" program,
129-130; black troops, 116; Office of
Secretary, 181
United States v. Brown, 708
US Chamber of Commerce, 273, 740
US Coast Guard, 314-315; screening
program, 438, 443-446
US Commission on Civil Rights, 81
US Constitution, 349, 368, 369, 493,
568, 695; Fifteenth Amendment,
795; Fourteenth Amendment, 795;
Thirteenth Amendment, 795; *See
also* Fifth Amendment, First
Amendment
US Customs employees, 773
US economy, 318-320; armament industry, 53-68, 319; post World War
II, 214; production, 319; "Small
wars" economy, 319; statistics, 294
US Employment Service, discrimination policies, 180
US Government, 389, 445-446; Bureau of Engraving & Printing, 390-
391; Census Bureau, 389; Department of Agriculture, 773; Department of Commerce, 390;
Department of Justice, 286, 390,
416, 510, 551; Department of Labor, 8, 22, 773; Union of Compliance Officers, 776; Information
Service, 747; as open shop employer, 396; Post Office, 631; Reconstruction Finance Corporation,
390; State Department, 729-759,
832, employees, 773; Treasury Department, 390; Veterans Administration, 117-118, 389, 710; War
Labor Board, 329-330; *See also*
INS
US House of Representatives, Committee on Education and Labor,
333, 335, 341, 347; HUAC, *See*
HUAC; Investigating committees,
496-503
US interference in Central America,
CLUW opposes, 818
US military bases, AFGE, policy, 778
US Navy, 348
US Senate, SISS, *See* SISS
US Steel, 325, 747; council, 270

US Supreme Court decisions, Attorney General's list, 561; bar admissions, 710-711; CP leadership v. SACB, 560, 680; contempt of Congress, 499-500, 704; contempt of court, 416; denaturalization,, 307; deportation, 307, 555; discharge for political beliefs, 475, 485-486; discharge for union activity 6, and back pay, 596; government workers' political rights, 181; Landrum-Griffin anti-Communist rule, 708; military political discharges, 710-711; NLRB decertification, 399, 400, 417, 607; organizing rights of unions, 307, and Blacks, 710-711; passports, 710-711; perjury, 333-334, 341; pregnancy discrimination case, 818; racial discrimination, 307, 552; religious freedom, 307-308; Rosenberg-Sobell case, 585; SACB registration order, 560; Smith Act, 470, 526, 609, 710-711; State "un-American" laws, 710-711; T-H oath, 306-313, 402-403, 417-418, 607-611

United Steelworkers v. Weber, 798
United Textile Workers, 396
United Transport Service Employees, 617
Unity, Black and white workers, 629, 633, 661-666; men and women workers, 646
University of Buffalo, 703
University of California, Academic Assembly, 479; Berkeley students, 708; Labor Center for Educational Research, 2, 12
University of Vermont, 490
University of Washington, 477, 489
Un-Louisiana Activities Committee, 571
Un-Mississippi Activities Committee, 571
Urban League, 635, 638, 663-664
Utility Workers, 435

Van Bittner, Alfred, 166, 262
V-J Day, 515
Veterans of the Abraham Lincoln Brigade, 257, 560
Veterans' Administration, 117-118; employees, 773
Victims, 483, 509-511
Vietnam War, 418, 656, 759-760; AFL-CIO and, 848; black draftees, 794

Vigilantes, 582, 596-601
Vincent, Craig and Jenny, 596
Vinson, Frederick M., 310, 585
Vinson-Trammel Profit Limitation Law, 59
Visa denial, 394
Vivian, C. Tyndell, 567-572
The Voice (MC & S), 623
Voice of America, 510
Vote, federal employees' right to, 773
Voting for Blacks, 650, 652, 665-666

WCL, 94
WFTU, 94 190 193, 338, 388, 438, 444, 726, 730; communist participation, 196-197; denied UN advisory status, 191; draft constitution, 193; founding convention, 194
WPA, 380, 790
WREE, *Women's Bill of Rights,* 821-822; WREE-View, 818-821
Wage Earner, 331-332
Wage freeze, 344
Wage Grade Bill, 774
Wagner Act, 2, 11, 244, 333, 451; history, 43-45; provisions, 21; *See also* NLRA, NLRB, Taft-Hartley Act
Wallace, George, 572
Wallace, Henry A., 246, 260, 268-278, 297, 371, 388, 432, 435, 439, 497, 662, 666, 705; *See also* Progressive Party
Wallace for President Labor Committee, 271
Wallach, Samuel, 473-474
Walt Whitman School of Social Science, 257
Walter-McCarran Act, 555, 557, 562, 564; *See also* INS
Walters, Vernon, 747, 749, 750
Ward, Harry F., 558
Warren, Earl, 499, 697, 708
Washington Afro-American, 624
Washington, Bert, 636
Washington, DC, home rule, 391
Washington, Harold, 770-771
Washington Pension Union, 257
Watkins, John T., 498-500
Watkins v. US, 499-500
Watts, 528
Wayne, John, 447
Weaver, George L.P., 165
Weaver, Robert C., 118
Weber, Brian, 791-792
Weick, Paul C., 676
Weinberger, Caspar, 57
Weinfeld, Edward, 411

Weinstock, Louis, 680
Weintraub, Jack, 712-722
Weirton Steel, 852-853
Wellman, Saul, 336
Welles, Orson, 143
Welsh, Joseph, 507
West Germany, 291-293; Marshall Plan helped, 295-296
West Indians, 394
West, James, 672
Western Electric, 264
Western Federation of Miners, 592, 610
Westinghouse, 377; Atomic Turbine Plant, 13
West Virginia Board of Education v. Barnette, 307-308
Weygandt, Carl V., 37, 365, 368, 369
White, Charles, 790
White Citizens Councils, 572, 707
White-collar Commission, 386
White-collar unionists, 814
White-collar workers, 772
White, Harry Dexter, 509
White, Walter, 336
Whitney, A.F., 269
Wilkinson, Frank, 493, 503, 705
Wilkinson, Jean, 493
Williams, Aubrey, 705
Williams, Gordon, 141, 150
Williams, Harry, 150
Williams, Kenneth, 617
Williamson, John B., 672
Willis, Edwin E., 705
Wilson, Charles E., 210
Wilson, Dagmar, 572
Wilson Meatpacking Co., 643
Wilson, Michael, 598-601
Winant, John, 510
Winpisinger, William, 53, 202, 827, 849, 866
Winter, Alexander, 240
Winter, Carl, 379
Wiretaps, 584
Wisconsin Employment Relations Board, 331, 332
Wisconsin Industrial Union Council, 328
Wise, Stephen S., 246
Wisner, Frank, 733
Witch-hunt, statistics on victims, 401-403, 500, 509-510, 670, 710-711; *See also* Red-baiting
Witt, Nathan, 603-604
Wobblies, *See* IWW
Wollenberg, Albert C., 720-721

Women, discrimination against, 596, 597, 643-647, 792, 797-799, 818; heads of households, 816-817; rights of, 643-647; *See also* Comparable worth, Sexual equality, Sexual harassment
Women for Peace, 385
Women Workers, blue collar, 391, 773-774, 787-797, 814; Hawaiian strike opponents, 459; ironworker apprentices, 90, 789; job access, 817; organizing tactics, 6, 815-822; in public sector, 389-398, 772-779; statistics, 813, 816-817, 819; and unemployment, 514; union delegates, 630; union leadership, 646, 774, 813, 814; and UOPWA, 385-388; wage differentials, 69-81, 645-646, 815; white-collar, 385-388, 773, 798-799, 814-815
Women's Bill of Rights, 821-822
Wood, James F., 125-131, 497-498, 504
Woodworkers Union, 4, 827
Woolworths, 636, 706
Worker safety and health, 30-32; *See also* OSHA
Workers' Schools, 561
Workforce, changes, 42-43; self-perceptions, 45-47
Workmen's Circle, 523
World Bank, 748
World Congress of the Defenders of Peace, 573
World Magazine, 618
World Peace Council, 573
World Trade Union Conference, 95, 189-198
World War II, 145, 385, 431, 434; and Black workers, 650; economy, 222-227; GIs return from, 109; Japanese-Americans in, 113
Wright, Charles H., 117, 627, 633
Wright, Frank Lloyd, 144
Wright, Fred, 85, 586
Wright, Morris, 612
Wynn, William E., 827, 831

YWCA, 350, 674
Yakoulev, Lev, 832
Yale Law School, 480, 523
Yamamoto, Lawrence, 149, 622
Yates v. United States, 470, 609
Yellin v. United States, 500, 704
Young, Coleman, 176, 627, 630-631, 634, 641

Young Communist League, 250, 511
Young, Frances, 509
Young, Howard, 380
Young, Murray, 490
Young Progressives of America, 685
Young, Stephen, 674
Youth, organizing, 6; subminimum wage, 34-35
Yugoslavia, 286

Zellner, Bob, 571
Zimmerman, Don, 28
Zionist "colonizers," 683
Zirpoli, Andrew, 150
Zitron, Celia, 477-478

ABOUT THE EDITORS

Ann Fagan Ginger has been a linotype operator, union organizer, labor lawyer, and constitutional law professor. In 1965 she founded Meiklejohn Civil Liberties Institute and continues to serve as its president. Her books include: *The National Lawyers Guild: From Roosevelt through Reagan, A Documentary History* (with Eugene M. Tobin) (Temple University Press, 1987), *Jury Selection in Civil and Criminal Trials* (2 vols.) (Lawpress, 1984–85), *The Relevant Lawyers* (Simon and Schuster 1972), *The Law, The Supreme Court, and the People's Rights* (Barron's 1977), *The New Draft Law* (NLG 1966–1970), and *Issues for the Eighties* (Just Books 1981). She is the first chairperson of the Berkeley City Commission on Peace and Justice.

David Christiano, with master degrees in U.S. History and Library Science, has worked at Meiklejohn Institute since 1973 as archivist, editor, and reference librarian. He is active in Oakland civic affairs and as a teacher. His books include four editions of *Human Rights Organizations & Periodicals Directory* (Meiklejohn Institute 1975–1983).

About Meiklejohn Civil Liberties Institute

The Institute, now in its 23rd year, is a unique public interest resource center that helps people use law and history in working for peace, jobs, and justice. Since 1984, MCLI has been concentrating on developing Peace Law. The Institute's publications include: *The Angela Davis Case Collection* (1974), *The Pentagon Papers Case Collection* (1975), *The Human Rights Docket* (1979), and *Peace Law Packets* (1985-current). Its extensive archives include collections on Peace Law and the right to earn a living. Its annual October Symposium explores basic social issues and constitutional law questions.

About the Series

The Cold War Against Labor is the third title in Meiklejohn Institute's Studies in Law and Social Change. *The Ford Hunger March* by Maurice Sugar (1980) is the first; *Alexander Meiklejohn: Teacher of Freedom* by Cynthia Stokes Brown (1981) is the second.